THE 'FEMALE' DANCER

The 'Female' Dancer aims to question dancers' relationships with 'female' through the examination and understandings of biological, anatomical, scientific, and self-social identity. The volume gathers voices of dance scientists, dance scholars, somatic practitioners, and dance artist-educators, to discuss some of the complexities of identities, assumptions and perceptions of a female dancing body in an intersectional and practically focused manner.

The book weaves a journey between scientific and somatic approaches to dance and to dancing. Part I: 'Bodily Knowledge' explores body image, hormones and puberty, and discussions around somatic responses to the concept of the gaze. Part II: 'Moving through Change', continues to look at strength, musculature, and female fragility, with chapters interrogating practice around strength training, the dancer as an athlete, the role of fascia, the pelvic floor, pregnancy and post-partum experiences and eco-somatic perceptions of feminine. In 'Taking up Space', Part III, chapters focus on social-cultural and political experiences of females dancing, leadership, and longevity in dance. Part IV: 'Embodied Wisdom' looks at reflections of the Self, physiological, social and cultural perspectives of dancing through life, with life's seasons from an embodied approach.

Drawing together lived experiences of dancers in relationship with scientific research, this book is ideal for undergraduate students of dance, dance artists, and researchers, as well as providing dancers, dance teachers, healthcare practitioners, company managers and those in dance leadership roles with valuable information on how to support female identifying dancers through training and beyond.

Claire Farmer is a senior lecturer in Dance Science at Middlesex University, UK.

Helen Kindred is a senior lecturer in Dance at Middlesex University, UK.

THE 'FEMALE' DANCER

a soma-scientific approach

Edited by
Claire Farmer and Helen Kindred

Routledge
Taylor & Francis Group

LONDON AND NEW YORK

Designed cover image: © Heidi Seetzen: 'Female Torso'

First published 2024
by Routledge
4 Park Square, Milton Park, Abingdon, Oxon OX14 4RN

and by Routledge
605 Third Avenue, New York, NY 10158

Routledge is an imprint of the Taylor & Francis Group, an informa business

British Library Cataloguing-in-Publication Data
A catalogue record for this book is available from the British Library

Library of Congress Cataloging-in-Publication Data
Names: Farmer, Claire, editor. | Kindred, Helen, editor.
Title: The 'female' dancer : a soma-scientific approach / edited by Claire Farmer and Helen Kindred.
Description: New York : Routledge, 2024. | Includes bibliographical references and index.
Identifiers: LCCN 2023055538 (print) | LCCN 2023055539 (ebook) | ISBN 9781032466903 (hbk) | ISBN 9781032466897 (pbk) | ISBN 9781003382874 (ebk)
Subjects: LCSH: Ballet—Study and teaching. | Ballerinas. | Gender identity. | Somesthesia. | Human ecology. | Dance—Psychological aspects. | Dance—Physiological aspects. | Dance—Research—Methodology.
Classification: LCC GV1788.5 .F46 2024 (print) | LCC GV1788.5 (ebook) | DDC 792.801/9—dc23/eng/20240325
LC record available at https://lccn.loc.gov/2023055538
LC ebook record available at https://lccn.loc.gov/2023055539

ISBN: 9781032466903 (hbk)
ISBN: 9781032466897 (pbk)
ISBN: 9781003382874 (ebk)

DOI: 10.4324/9781003382874

Typeset in Sabon
by codeMantra

CONTENTS

NOTES ON CONTRIBUTORS

Cover artist bio

Heidi Seetzen

Heidi Seetzen is an artist and sociologist. After working as a lecturer at Kingston University for many years, she trained at the London Art Academy in order to explore sculptural techniques and develop her artistic practice. Her work is predominantly sculptural and figurative. She uses everyday materials, such as fencing wire, bricks, reclaimed wood, stones or cement to explore the fragility of human existence and embodied experiences of becoming. Her intricate wire sculptures are intended to convey the sense of movement and emotion embedded in human gestures. Through the use of negative space - the 'empty' spaces circumscribed through wire - her sculptures invite viewers to contemplate the relationship between inner and outer selves, and between embodied and situated experience.

Editor bios

Claire Farmer

https://orcid.org/0000-0001-9379-5719

Claire is a senior lecturer in Dance Science at Middlesex University and an Early Career researcher, currently undertaking a PhD investigating upper body strength in dance. Claire's academic research lies in dance physiology and biomechanics, alongside research into the impact of dance on the aesthetics and health of mature dancers. She is also particularly interested in the gender balance of medical and sports/dance science research and how this informs training practices.

Claire holds a BA (Hons) Dance Studies with Drama, theatre and performance studies from Roehampton University and an MSc Dance Science from Trinity Laban Conservatoire of Music and Dance and is also a qualified strength and conditioning coach. Claire has worked extensively with UK dance and circus companies including All or Nothing Aerial Dance Theatre, Gravity and Levity, Pagrav Dance Company and Dance East CAT programme.

Dr Helen Kindred

https://orcid.org/0000-0001-5747-3333

Helen is a dance artist-scholar whose work is underpinned by the practice and philosophy of Bartenieff Fundamentals. Helen has toured internationally as a performer, working with Daghdha Dance Company, Janet Kaylo, Doug Varone, taught within and beyond formal education and presented choreographic work at venues, festivals and conferences over the past 28 years. Helen is Co-Artistic Director of DancingStrong Movement Lab with Dr Adesola Akinleye, and Director of Dance and Professional Practice programmes at Middlesex University London. Helen earned her BA (Hons) Dance Studies degree and later MFA Choreography from Roehampton University. She holds a PhD from Middlesex University—*dancing the in-between-ness: (re)articulating Bartenieff Fundamentals through improvised dance performance-making* (2021). Her work engages with people and places, creating opportunities for learning through improvised play and performance using touch, text, sound and image.

Author bios

Avatâra Ayuso

https://orcid.org/0009-0000-0380-5603

Avatâra Ayuso is a choreographer, Artistic Director of AVA DANCE COMPANY, a cultural leader and activist in the dance world. She is the founder and director of the charity AWA DANCE (Advancing Women's Aspirations with Dance). Her artistic practice aims to overcome eurocentrism, by promoting cultural exchanges among artists. In her most recent projects, she has collaborated with artists from Burkina Faso, Japan, Senegal, Chile, Taiwan, Morocco and Nunavut (Canadian Arctic). In 2021, Avatâra undertook a Clore fellowship placement with the United Nations Foundation Global affiliate Girl UP ALC (America Latina y el Caribe).

Dr Carolina Bergonzoni

https://orcid.org/0000-0001-8244-1579

Carolina Bergonzoni (she/her) is a dance artist, a somatic educator and practitioner, and an emergent scholar. Carolina holds a PhD in Arts Education, a BA and MA in Philosophy, and an MA in Comparative Media Arts. She is the 2023 recipient of the Outstanding Dissertation Award for the Arts and Inquiry in the Visual and Performing Arts in Education SIG of AERA. Her practices span between dancing, writing and teaching from the body. Carolina is the Artistic Associate of All Bodies Dance Project, an inclusive dance company that brings together dancers with and without disabilities. She has directed two audio-described movies and has been part of Translations, a dance created for the non-visual senses.

Dr James Brouner

https://orcid.org/0000-0001-7938-2803

James Brouner is the course leader for Sport and Exercise Science programmes at Kingston University, London. James also delivers biomechanical curriculum on the MSc Dance Science at Trinity Laban Conservatoire of Music and Dance. James' research interests are across both Sport and Dance with a focus on fundamental mechanical mechanisms and how they affect movement quality and how fatigue can have an impact on movement efficiency. James also researches performance analysis to explore the global understanding of in-event metrics and locomotive actions taken by performers, with the aim to enhance training and overall performance.

Janine Cappello

https://orcid.org/0000-0002-2949-3094

Janine Cappello, BFA, MA, SFHEA, lives in Pennsylvania, USA and is a former senior lecturer at the University of Wolverhampton, UK, and former Chair of Dance and Theatre at Eastern University, PA, USA. Janine continues her research on aging and range of motion and incorporates this into her master teaching, while blending this with a focus on nutrition as a vehicle toward optimal health and career longevity for dancers.

Jasmine Challis

https://orcid.org/0009-0002-3754-5197

Jasmine is an accredited nutritionist and dietitian on the UK Sport and Exercise Nutrition Register (SENR) focusing on dance. She has worked across dance genres for over 30 years, giving talks and running workshops for dance students, dancers and dance teachers, and providing 1:1 sessions for dancers and dance students. She completed a MRes in Sport and Exercise Science (with distinction) in 2018; her research project was with Irish dancers. She also works with circus performers and acting/technical students, and continues working clinically, mainly with those suffering from eating disorders. Her book, *Nutrition for Dance and Performance* was published in 2023.

Anna Dako

https://orcid.org/0000-0003-0136-2268

Anna Dako is an interdisciplinary artist and a somatic movement educator and therapist with nearly 20 years of international experience working with dance, movement and creative arts. Anna's experience stretches from practice-based research, dance dramaturgy and site-specific productions. She is the author of many scholarly articles on dance research and wellbeing and her latest book, based on eco-somatic practice, is titled: *Dances with Sheep— On Re-Pairing the Human–Nature Condition with Felt Thinking and Moving towards Wellbeing* (Intellect Books, 2023).

Anna is the founder and director of Dunami—Movement, Arts, Wellbeing, a platform for ecologically mindful growth, psycho-somatic health and creative development through arts and intercultural dialogue. As a writer, she focuses on arts-based research, eco-psychology and environmental philosophy perspectives. In her private practice she specialises in supporting and working through versatile psycho-somatic imbalances. She also loves guiding experiential walks and working with children and young people, both in therapy and creative education.

Shilpa Darivemula

https://orcid.org/0000-0003-4229-8274

Shilpa Darivemula is an obstetrician-gynecologist currently pursuing a Generalist Reproductive Health Fellowship, with a focus on clinical research and epidemiology, at University of North Carolina with the Department of Obstetrics and Gynecology and the Gillings School of Public Health. She is the director of the Aseemkala Initiative (www.aseemkala.org) and Race.Culture.OBGYN (www.racecultureOBGYN.org) with a dedication to improving reproductive medicine disparities' research and cultural Health Humanities.

Kars Dodds

https://orcid.org/0009-0008-3078-7277

Kars Dodds (they/them) is an expatriate American genderfluid multimedia and performance artist whose work aims to situate playfulness, joy and memory within a queer narrative. They are beginning their MRes at Middlesex University, where they will be conducting research on Trans and Gender Non-Conforming AFAB performance phenomenology and sexual embodiment.

Stella Eldon

https://orcid.org/0000-0001-6748-3287

Stella trained at Laban, working as a dancer before retraining as a visual artist with a site-specific and socially engaged practice. Recent self-reflection led back to dance. Stella is a dancer with EncoreEast and an ethnographic researcher. She gained a master's in dance (Community Practice) at Middlesex University. Stella's research explores Age and Dance; how it expands the experience of dance, not limits it. She is interested in what is possible for older dancers and what is missing from dance because of the bias towards youth. Her practice research focuses on improvisation and site responsive choreography.

Dr Gemma Harman

https://orcid.org/0009-0005-7016-5729

Gemma Harman is a senior lecturer in Dance and Dance Science at the University of Chichester. She has extensive experience as a teacher, lecturer and researcher working across a number of conservatoires and Higher Education institutions across the sector. She has a BA (Hons) in Performing Arts (Dance) from Middlesex University and both an MSc Dance Science (with Distinction) and PhD Dance and Music Science from Trinity Laban Conservatoire of Music and Dance (Emerton Christie Charity funded). Gemma is the creator of ResDance, a podcast dedicated to research methodologies and methods in dance practice: anchor.fm/gemma-harman

Chloe Hillyar

https://orcid.org/0000-0003-2118-4040

Chloe Hillyar is a doctoral candidate at Queen's University Belfast. Her PhD explores the physiological and psychosocial implications of pregnancy within the context of an elite dance career in the UK and Ireland dance sectors. After achieving First-Class Honours at the UK's leading dance conservatoire, Chloe began her career as a professional dancer performing at high profile establishments such as the Royal Opera House, Channel 4 and The Place. Chloe is the recipient of numerous scholarships and awards and has published for academic journals and industry leading organisations.

Dr Nicky Keay

https://orcid.org/0000-0001-6663-7010

Nicky is the author of *Health Hormones and Human Potential: A guide to understanding your hormones to optimise your health and performance.*

Nicky is an honorary clinical lecturer, Division of Medicine, University College London. She researches in areas of exercise endocrinology, with publications in this field. Nicky's clinical endocrine work is mainly with exercisers, dancers and athletes. Nicky works to provide a more personalised approach for female hormone health. She authored the British Association of Sports and Exercise Medicine Health4performance.co.uk online resource. Nicky is medical adviser to Scottish Ballet and a keen dancer herself taking four ballet classes per week.

May Kesler

https://orcid.org/0009-0003-0881-9061

May Kesler has been dancing since childhood. She became a physical therapist, specialising in dance medicine and manual therapy, after graduating from Columbia University in 1982. Her passion for anatomy in motion was enhanced by learning about fascia and biotensegrity for the last 20 years. She continues to choreograph and perform dances based on anatomy, including producing several award-winning dance videos. May has taught internationally on Fascia through the Lens of Dance. She is the director of both Keslerdances and Kesler Physical and Massage Therapy, LLC, in Chevy Chase, MD, where she lives with her husband, daughter and several very sweet companion animals.

Kate March

https://orcid.org/0009-0007-5866-591X

Kate March is an internationally acclaimed performer, choreographer, painter and poet, based in Charleston, South Carolina. She received her BA in Dance from Connecticut College (Summa Cum Laude) and her MA in Choreography from Middlesex University in London (Highest Distinction). She is currently a PhD candidate at the University of the Arts London—Central Saint Martins, exploring women's lived body experiences of pain and endometriosis in and through an embodied creative practice. Ms March carefully weaves together performance art, dance, visual art, poetry, fashion, film and creative technology to produce distinctive conceptual experiences that draw audiences into her outré world.

Lucy McCrudden

https://orcid.org/0009-0009-7566-9976

Lucy McCrudden is Founder/CEO of Dance Mama™, a non-profit organisation advocating and celebrating professional dancing parents, highlighting the issues that they face and providing inspiration, information and support. Lucy's 20-year career has dove-tailed her own work with key positions in learning and participation with world-class organisations, including The Place and The Royal Opera House. She has taught over 19,000 people and has engaged with a wide variety of cultural organisations in consulting, management, choreography and presenting/public speaking roles. She is an ambassador for PiPA Campaign, Secretariat, Scientific Advisory Board—Active Pregnancy Foundation. She received an Honourable Mention for the inaugural AWA Woman in Dance Award and was a nominee for the One Dance UK Awards 2021, a nominee for AWA Woman In Dance Leadership award and was given 'Change Maker' One Dance UK Award 2022, the same year she delivered her TEDx talk as she embarked on her PhD at Christ Church Canterbury University.

Jayne McKee

https://orcid.org/0009-0003-2720-0475

Jayne is a senior lecturer in Dance in Higher Education at the University of Chichester where she is Programme Leader for BA (Hons) Dance Education and Teaching, and MA Dance: Advanced Practice. She has a BA (Hons) in Dance Theatre and Diploma in Advanced Performance from The Laban Centre for Movement and Dance, and an MA: Dance Performance from University of Chichester. She has extensive experience as a dancer, teacher and lecturer. Her specialisms and research interests include dance education and training and the exploration of fascial architecture in relation to dance theory and practice.

Amelia Millward

https://orcid.org/0009-0006-9489-9150

Amelia is an independent Dance Science Researcher and Dance Educator currently working as a Clinical Research Program Coordinator in Salt Lake City, Utah. She has been a member of the dance community in a multitude of ways for over 20 years; including as a student, teacher, performer and choreographer. She holds a bachelor's degree in dance: Body Science and a minor in Neuroscience from Marymount Manhattan College, and a master's degree in dance science from Trinity Laban Conservatoire of Music and Dance. Amelia's objective is to create a more empathetic dance community through education, research, advocacy and inclusion.

Dr Siobhan B. Mitchell

https://orcid.org/0000-0002-4085-3898

Siobhan trained vocationally as a dancer before completing a BA Hons in Dance Studies, an MSc in Dance Science, and an MRes in Health and

Wellbeing. Siobhan completed her doctorate in 2018 and currently works as a Research Fellow in Child and Adolescent Health. Siobhan's doctoral research explored the psychological and social implications of pubertal timing in adolescent ballet dancers. More recently, Siobhan founded the GuiDANCE Network, a collaboration which aims to enhance practices in the dance sector around growth and development. Siobhan is passionate about education on adolescent development and delivers workshops for dance teachers, students and parents.

Celeste Nazeli Snowber

https://orcid.org/0000-0003-1316-9377

Celeste Nazeli Snowber PhD is a dancer, poet/writer and award-winning educator who is a Professor in the Faculty of Education at Simon Fraser University. Celeste has written extensively and her books include, *Embodied Inquiry: Writing living and being through the body*, three collections of poetry and her most recent book is *Dance, Poetics and Place: Site-specific performance as a portal to knowing*. Celeste creates site-specific performances in the natural world, including botanical gardens and sites between land and sea. Celeste lives outside Vancouver, BC and is a mother of three amazing adult sons. She can be found at www.celestesnowber.com.

Professor Angela Pickard

https://orcid.org/000-0003-0292-3194

Angela Pickard has performed, created, taught, presented and researched dance in her roles as dancer, choreographer, teacher, adviser, consultant and academic. She is the first professor of Dance Education in the UK. She is Editor in Chief for the leading international journal *Research in Dance Education* and member of the Research committee and Dance to Health Champion with International Association for Dance, Medicine and Science.

Angela is currently the Director at the Sidney De Haan Research Centre for Arts and Health, is leading the MA Arts, Health and Performance courses at Canterbury Christ Church University and also supervises PhD students (including co-author Lucy McCrudden). She works with a range of participatory and elite dance organisations developing dance pedagogy and practices. Angela has researched and published work in dance and embodied identity, dance and education, widening access and opportunities, and dance science, health and wellbeing. She is currently engaged in research related to dance and pregnancy and post-partum, critical dance pedagogy, dance with adolescent dancers and dance with early years.

Celia Shaw Morris

https://orcid.org/0009-0008-9233-5698

Celia Shaw Morris (they/she) is a movement artist based in Berlin, originally from New England, USA. They earned a BA in Dance and Comparative American Studies from Oberlin College (2019), studies that embedded a commitment to questioning the world through the body. In Berlin, as a member of dajci* collective, they researched failure and desire from a queer perspective. Their creation work has been supported by the Projektfonds Kulturförderung Friedrichshain-Kreuzberg and performed in Berlin, Vienna and London. In tandem, they co-facilitate movement improvisation classes, are a certified Lagree Method trainer, and fight with their housing community against imminent eviction.

Sandra Sok

https://orchid.org/0000-0001-6690-4131

Sandra is a dance-scholar, philosopher, artist-researcher, political scientist, somatic practitioner, yoga teacher and performer with more than 20 years' experience of dancing, performing and teaching in Croatia and abroad. She always trys to combine a set of movement principles and elements into one synergy and give participants a new and holistic healthy approach to body and mind involving LBMS in her work in body connectivity with the breath. 'All is between peace and conflict, gravity and verticality, relationship with the air and the ground, yet the strong awareness of dynamic alignment, neck-pelvis-toe connection, self-perception and breath in the conscious movement.' Sandra holds a BA in Philosophy and Religion Science, at the Faculty of Philosophy and Religious Studies in Zagreb and a master's degree obtained at the Faculty of Political Science in Zagreb. She also holds an MA in Somatic Studies at the Middlesex University and completed one-year Women Studies Programs in Zagreb and the Programme for International Yoga Practitioners at Swami Vivekananda Yoga Anusandhana Samsthana University in Bangalore, India. Sandra is also very active in dancing, researching and attending international dance and movement conferences as a lecturer.

Shreya Srivastava

https://orcid.org/0000-0002-6979-4625

Shreya Srivastava is a fourth-year medical student at Albany Medical College in Albany, NY. She received her BS in the interdisciplinary studies of biology and music from Union College. She is interested in internal medicine and humanistic methods of understanding and treating human health. Shreya conducts research on the intersection between the performing arts, medicine and culture.

Erica Stanton

https://orcid.org/0000-0002-5402-2569

Erica is a dance teacher, choreographer and teaching mentor. She is a graduate of Bedford College and of Sarah Lawrence College, where she was the recipient of the Bessie Schönberg Scholarship. She has supported the professional development of dance teachers for over three decades and works closely with Sonia Rafferty and David Waring as Simply for the Doing, a project which supports dance teachers and their practice.

Erica specialises in Limón technique which she has taught in the UK, the USA and New Zealand. Her work in curriculum development includes the first MFA Choreography programme in the UK, which is based at the University of Roehampton.

Rebekah Wall

https://orcid.org/0009-0002-1998-9552

Rebekah graduated from Edge Hill University in July 2023, after studying a BA (Hons) Dance and achieving a first-class degree. At Edge Hill, she trained in contemporary, jazz, ballet, flamenco and capoeira, as well as teaching and choreographing ballet for the dance society and competition team. As part of her degree, Rebekah researched topics including the benefits of movement sessions for students at Pupil Referral Units, the importance of body conditioning for female contemporary dancers, and body image in recreational ballet.

Brooke Winder

https://orcid.org/0000-0003-1370-4149

Brooke Winder is an associate professor and coordinator of the Dance Science degree program at California State University Long Beach, and also serves patients through her clinical practice, Renew Motion Physical Therapy Inc. Dr Winder researches pelvic floor dysfunction in dancers and other performers, and her work has been presented at many national and international conferences. She is a Board-Certified Specialist in Orthopedic physical therapy and a BASI-Certified Pilates Instructor. Dr Winder has a Doctorate in Physical Therapy from the University of Southern California, a BFA in Dance from Chapman University, and formerly danced professionally with Southern California-based Backhausdance.

ACKNOWLEDGEMENTS

This book has been a long time in the dreaming, thinking, talking and writing; from a tiny seed of curiosity to wondering why this resource didn't exist and how it could possibly be dreamed into existence. As female dancers working in dance science and somatic practices, we were aware that the information female dancers needed was out there through the shared expertise of wonderful colleagues and peers, but we wondered if that information was making its way to those who needed it.

You can't know what you don't know you need to know.

The final publication is the product of the many moments in dancing of the editors and all the contributing authors, to whom we are so grateful for their generous sharing of experience and research.

We want to extend our heartfelt thanks also to the dancers that we've moved with, learnt from and been inspired by, throughout the lifetime of this publication and beyond, to our dear colleagues at Middlesex Dance for their endless support and encouragement. To our families for the encouragement, inspiration, words of support and motivation, even when the ideas and tasks seemed huge and challenging; particularly in those moments! To friends and colleagues who have offered a critical eye and valuable sounding board throughout this process. To each other for bringing forth the richness of different perspectives, being able to engage in open and honest debate around the subjects of this book, tackle the difficult questions together, supporting not only the development of this project through to publication but also challenging ourselves further in our own learning through shared experiences.

Most of all, thank you to the dancers who came before, who paved the way with their wisdom and experience, and to those who will follow and continue to bring forth their knowledge.

To Steph and the team at Routledge, for their support, advice and patience along the way and for having faith in our shared vision.

During the development of this book, we have been overwhelmed by the response to the themes, demonstrating the need for, and interest in, this topic. It is our hope that this book is just the first stepping stone to more accessible information, for female dancers to feel empowered in their own training and life journey within the dance sector and beyond.

PREFACE

Celeste Nazeli Snowber
Professor, Simon Fraser University
Canada

There is an anatomy of having a body and then there is an anatomy of being a body. *The 'Female' Dancer: a soma-scientific approach* incorporates both—the fullness of what it means to be a dancer and what it takes to be sustained as a dancer throughout a lifetime. Too often, within artistic disciplines, there is emphasis on skill, technique and execution and not an emphasis on the rigour and vigour necessary for a healthy relationship with one's art and body. I keep wondering what it would have been like to have a book like this early in my own career as a young woman dancer. I would not have felt so alone, and would know to trust my own voice more, knowing all growth is important for my dance, and all is possible. Now, as an older dancer, who dances full-out in my sixties, these are the voices I longed to hear then and need now.

Here is a book that can be a companion, that brings a multidisciplinary perspective to the journey of the dancer; one to return to through each stage of life. Central to this collection are connections to science and somatics, nutrition and intuition, longevity and lived experience, inspiration and intersectionality. This is a feast for the soma, a handbook imbued with wisdom and a guide to what it means to be a human being in dance.

Just as there is the need in our bodies to have all our systems working—the cardiovascular, nervous, lymphatic, circulatory, endocrine and respiratory, the dancer requires an integration of all parts of themselves. This book, *The Female Dancer*, is like the interstitial fluid carrying oxygen to our cells as it addresses the circle of needs through various curated authors. The uniqueness of this book is the inclusion of multiple paradigms, methodologies and approaches considering the female dancer. As a way into moving through this exceptional collection, I invite you as a reader to allow for the poetic to speak to its fullness. It is impossible to adequately honour the breadth and depth of contributions from diverse perspectives. The words in the following poem are inspired by, and taken from, the profound array of writers in the book and speak to the worlds they travel. May you, in turn, be nourished as you read this book and may their knowledge and wisdom accompany you through a dancer's life.

A life of dance/dancing a life

How does one dance their way through time,
place, injuries, challenges
across the span of a lifetime—
between hormones and hindrances
strength and fragility
life cycles and fluctuations

where the wisdom of the body
considers the demands of the dancer's
body, mind, pelvis and heart?

Here the female voice is present
in articulating dance practice
in each stage of life
through the imperfect and fruitful torso
deconstructing gendered perspectives
queering the concept
and embodiment of gender

Where we feel the relation to the earth
and multiple identities are central
to navigating the worlds
we belong and long in
so the dancer and person
can viscerally honour

an embodied feminist approach
the porousness of the body—
dancer as teacher
dancer as mother

dancer as one in transition
dancer as life-giver and leader
dancer as one in grief or pain
dancer as more
than body image

where they can audience themselves
where wellbeing is crucial to growth
and balance is possible between
training, nutrition, growth
inwardly and outwardly

Dance can be known as—

Creativity, corporeal, ceremony
interiority, improvisation, illumination
somatic, sensuous, supportive
fascia, freedom, flexibility
paradoxical, passionate, powerful

Vulnerability can be an ingredient
for artistic creation
as much as pliés, contractions, and research
for dance is so much more

What we know to be true
a way of being and thinking
in the world
where hope and discomfort are partners
and we celebrate
the limitation and fullness of who we are

All are ingredients
for a life of dance
and for dancing a life.

INTRODUCTION

Claire Farmer and Helen Kindred

The book

The chapters of this book share generously the lived experiences of the authors through personal experiences and professional practice. Through this publication we have opened space for shared embodied memories, moments from practice, expanded research and case studies, and reflections on self and the dance industry. We share this book with respect for the authors' honesty and generosity in bringing, at times, very personal experiences, and encourage the reader to exercise care toward their own life experience at the time of reading this book. We recognise the wounds that dance has created for some, and healed for others, and invite the reader to meet the book with curiosity and wonder while seeking the support they may need in processing their own relationships with dance. At the end of the book, we have offered a list of resources to help direct dancers to further advice and care in relation to some of the themes surfaced through the chapters of the book.

Untangling Her-stories

As female dancers whose lives and work are entangled in the dance sector, we (the editors) are viscerally aware of the beauty and integrity of the art form, while being fully cognisant of the lack of knowledge, support and understanding of the needs of the female dancer in training, throughout and beyond their career. While strides have been made by individuals and some organisations to expose and address iniquities in the dance industry, there is currently no academic resource compiled specifically for female dancers. Our intention with this edited publication is to offer a resource which aims

DOI: 10.4324/9781003382874-1

to open conversation, shared experiences, and provide valuable information that is often muted in a patriarchal societal structure. This book is for those identifying as female dancers, and those working alongside them, to dive into for guidance, nurturing, and support. Reflecting on the learning through our own lived experiences as females in the dance industry, we recognise some of the challenges faced by female dancers today and note how difficult it can be for younger dancers to navigate an unknown field, to feel prepared for, and response-able to, their experiences.

> The study of the human body involves both mystery and fact: there is much that is known and equally as much that is left unknown. This paradox suggests that we need to value both the information and the questions about what it means to be human (Olsen, 2004, p.11).

It is this thinking about the rich complexities of the human body in motion that underpins the framework for this book. An exploration of the scientific and the somatic in conversation with each other, meeting and diverging, pulsating, and blurring boundaries as we (editors and contributors) tussle with the diverse experiences of what it might mean in the twenty-first century to identify as a 'female' dancer. The dialogue between inner and outer; our bodily self-awareness of the biological, psychological and physiological processes working furiously throughout our lives, adapting, changing, in and out of balance, with our outwardly-facing sense of self in-the-world – socially, culturally, and politically – is addressed through the journey of a soma-scientific approach to understanding holistically the wants, needs, demands and desires of the 'female' dancer.

In coming to the title of this book, we began digging into some of the exchanges of the relationships of this book; questioning what it means to identify a dancing body as 'female', for whom, to whom, and in what contexts? What 'body' are we talking about as we peel back layers in order to build an informed picture for dancers? What body is invisible within the scope of research and education in dance? We are using the term 'female' with recognition of the fluidity of the many complexities, layers, nuances and intelligences of the word. At times, within the chapters, there is an identification of female through a biological lens, relating to biological sex-specific structures and related systems; at other times, female is used in relation to a gendered experience of the world, the structures, and systemic patterns as experienced by a female identifying body. We recognise that these uses of female are themselves part of a spectrum of lived experience. We use the term 'body' to speak to the whole person, mind–body–spirit–self and we have invited authors to speak to 'female' in ways that enable them to identify personally and professionally.

A theme throughout this book is inequality, the lower status, opportunity, visibility, and celebration of the female dancer. This is revealed through the chapters dealing with evidence-based data, which, at times, simply lacks any representation of females, and so renders them invisible within the research that is informing future training trends, as much as it emerges through the experiential data from the perspectives of females dancing in a (heteropatriarchal) world. There are many perspectives shared in this book, feminist, eco-feminist, physiological, biological, psychological, philosophical, psychosomatic, and we arrive, therefore, as editors, at a soma-scientific approach not as a distilling of perspectives but, rather, an expanded opening of knowledge shared through the interplay of multiple perspectives.

In the dreaming of, and preparations for, this book, we have welcomed different voices, modes of sharing and articulating experiences, practice, and research. To this end you will encounter chapters written in a variety of styles; some utilising scientific and anatomical language, some sharing through more poetic and creative expression, others, reflections as first-person experiences. Dance is an embodied experience, and, thus, it is important to us that the book captures the evidence-based knowledge on topics that have an impact on our experiences as female dancers, in relationship with the lived experiences of female identifying dancers at different stages of their journey, across a range of circumstance and context. It is our hope that these voices speak to the varied, nuanced, and multi-faceted experiences of the female dancer, and encourage you, the reader, to connect in ways that feel meaningful to you in your own journey.

Experiences of 'female' in the dance sector

'Gate after gate seemed to close with gentle finality behind me. Innumerable beadles were fitting innumerable keys into well-oiled locks; the treasure-house was being made secure for another night' (Woolf, 2015, p. 12). In *A Room of One's Own* (originally published in 1929), Virginia Woolf reflects on her experiences as a female writer of being denied access to education on the grounds of her perceived gender. Daphne Spain discusses this oppression through a lens of 'spatial segregation' (1992, p. 143) highlighting the segregation of men and women in places of learning in the USA of this era and beyond, echoing the separate spheres for women and men in society and noting the double disadvantage experienced by Black women through the additional layer of racial segregation. One of the mechanisms through which a group of people can maintain power over a group with less power, spatial segregation depicts the gender dynamics at play within western society.

The 'Female' Dancer is born out of an aim to reduce barriers to education in the context of knowledge of female experiences within dance. Herein you will find 'female' voices spanning more than 50 years, bringing a wealth of lived experience and knowledge to the fore. We hope that female dancers will feel empowered through knowledge gained from shared experiences and supported in making informed choices about their training, healthcare, roles, work practices and experiences. By opening this dialogue, we hope to lay the stepping stones to further, wider and open conversations around what it means to train, live and work as a female dancer, and to address the systemic barriers and inequities found throughout the sector.

Aims and scope of this book

With no current publication addressing the multitude of experiences of female dancers, and recognising that it is not possible to cover all of this information within this book, we hope that the information it contains will provide a starting point to unpack this complex journey, to nurture conversations, and foster change.

Female healthcare, performance optimisation, injury management and life cycle is a complex phenomenon. Historically, women have been excluded from medical trials due to concerns over the impact on their health, particularly fertility concerns, and complex methodological considerations relating to the menstrual cycle (Elliott-Sale et al., 2021). In addition, participation in physical activity by females was previously heavily discouraged, with only 2.2% of total participants in the 1900 Olympics being women, increasing to 38.2% in 2000 (ibid.) and 44.2% in 2023 (Costello et al., 2014).

The vast majority of high-quality sports and exercise medicine data, and medical data that is drawn upon for exercise testing and prescription is based upon studies that utilised male at birth participants (Costello et al., 2014; Elliott-Sale et al., 2021; Mujika & Taipale, 2019). With many gaps in dance medicine and science, we often also draw upon research from sports science when considering dancers in training and performance. While research in dance medicine and science appears to focus more predominantly on female participants, the known physiological and morphological differences (Costello et al., 2014) between sexes, specifically in relation to endocrinology and its impact on body systems and performance (Elliott-Sale et al., 2021), require sex-specific exercise testing and prescription. These disparities appear as restrictions in the application of training parameters through biological adaptations, as well as through hierarchical, social constructs that affect those who identify as female, and their experiences in these spaces. These disparities need addressing and this can only be done through open dialogue around the needs of females training and working in these spaces.

Dance is a predominantly female populated sector (Van Dyke, 1996), although positions of leadership are often held by men (Hanna, 1988; Van Dyke, 1996). The US based Dance Data Project has found that of 73 venues studied in the US, only 36% of executive leadership (CEO, Executive Director, Programming Director) and 35% of those on a board of directors were women (Dance Data Project, 2022). Similar research in the UK, though, has shown a higher proportion of women in executive leadership roles, with 67.4% of women holding these positions, and 56% of women in Artistic Director roles (AWA Dance, 2023). Despite the higher levels of female leadership in the UK dance sector, 79.8% of women perceive an imbalance in leadership (ibid.), raising questions about the visibility of the women in these positions.

The female experience is not a singular pre-defined path, and we recognise that it may encompass some, or all, of the topics covered in this book, as well as many others. We embrace these nuances in a holistic consideration of the experiential 'female' dancer, providing a breadth of embodied, empirical and lived experience. We place value on embodied experience and, in doing so, interweave biological, physiological and psychological information with the lived experiences of female identifying dancers.

Structure of the book

'Bodily Knowledge' (Part I), begins by embracing the work of Siobhan Mitchell (Chapter 1), Rebekah Wall (Chapter 4), Carolina Bergonzoni (Chapter 5), Amelia Millward and James Brouner (Chapter 6) as we follow the experiences of growing up in dance, the challenges faced with changing body shapes, and pressures of dance training. Jasmine Challis (Chapter 3) and Nicky Keay (Chapter 2) guide readers through the biological reasons for these changes, analysing the choreography of female hormones throughout the life cycle, making cases for fuelling your body and addressing the associated risks of eating disorders that may arise in a sector with a focus on a particular physical aesthetic.

Adolescent years allow us an opportunity to learn about our individual and unique body, our passions and preferences as we begin exploring ourselves and the world around us. Building on this knowledge, we begin to experience and challenge the systems and structures around us and embrace change within.

'Moving through change', Part II of this book, explores bodily adaptations through strength training and experiences of gendered spaces (Claire Farmer, Chapter 7), pregnancy and the professional dancer (Chloe Hilyar, Chapter 10), the importance of the pelvic floor (Brooke Winder, Chapter 8), a dancer's relationship with pain and specifically endometriosis (Kate March, Chapter 9), the role of fascia (May Kesler, Chapter 11), and our relationships as females dancing with, within, and becoming nature's flow (Helen Kindred and Sandra Sok, Chapter 12).

Part III, 'Taking up space' highlights the complex and intertwined roles of females dancing. Lucy McCrudden and Angela Pickard offer guidance on how to understand your rights as a parent and the support that is available to those working in the performing arts (Chapter 13). Erica Stanton (Chapter 14) draws on memories and reflections on experiences of dancing with women as she shares the richness of dancing together. Addressing visibility, expectation and positionality of gendered roles in dance, Avatâra Ayuso (Chapter 15), Kars Dodds (Chapter 16) and Shreya Srivastava (Chapter 17) bring experiences that span leadership in the contemporary dance sector, queerness and coming out, and aesthetics of Bharatanatyam dance.

Finally, Part IV of the book brings together the 'Embodied Wisdom' of practitioners and scholars with reflections on the 'self' in dance practice from Gemma Harman and Jayne McKee (Chapter 18), dancing poetically through life's seasons with Celeste Nazeli Snowber (Chapter 20), and moving within a somatic dialogue of change (Anna Dako in collaboration with Martina Polleros, Chapter 22). Janine Capello looks at the (perceived) life span of the dancer (Chapter 19) and Stella Eldon shares her embodied ethnographic research with Encore East, reflecting on dancing as a community of older women (Chapter 21).

The chapters in this book, while exploring shared knowledge and experience, collectively highlight the significant lack of research relating to female training and experiences within dance. We hope that this book acts as a point of departure for building robust data and arguments for sex and gender-specific choices, and to recognise the differences in dancers' life cycles.

We hope that this resource serves as a trusted guide for understanding better the physiological, biological and psychological changes and challenges that occur throughout the human life cycle. By sharing stories and knowledge, we hope you may find resonance in your own life experiences and comfort in collective knowing. We trust that in this knowledge you may feel empowered to make informed choices, to challenge embedded, problematic structures and find kindship with your fellow female dancers. We hope this book inspires learning through open and honest dialogue, creating safer, more supportive and tailored training, education, and working environments for female dancers.

References

AWA Dance (2023). *Leadership gender balance in UK dance sector report.*

Costello, J. T., Bieuzen, F. & Bleakley, C. M. (2014). Where are all the female participants in Sports and Exercise Medicine research? *European Journal of Sport Science*, 14(8), 847–851. https://doi.org/10.1080/17461391.2014.911354

Dance Data Project (2022a). *2022 Dance venue leadership & programming report.* Retrieved January 19, 2024 from https://www.dancedataproject.com/dance-data-project-examines-equity-in-leadership-and-programming-at-u-s-dance-venues/

Elliott-Sale, K. J., Minahan, C. L., de Jonge, X. A. K. J. et al. (2021). Methodological considerations for studies in Sport and Exercise Science with women as participants: A working guide for standards of practice for research on women. *Sports Medicine (Auckland, NZ)*, *51*(5), 843–861. https://doi.org/10.1007/S40279-021-01435-8

Hanna, J. L. (1988). *Dance, sex, and gender: Signs of identity, dominance, defiance, and desire*. University of Chicago Press.

Mujika, I., & Taipale, R. S. (2019). Sport Science on women, women in Sport Science. *International Journal of Sports Physiology and Performance*, *14*(8), 1013–1014. https://doi.org/10.1123/IJSPP.2019-0514

Olsen, A. (2004). *Bodystories: A guide to experiential anatomy*. UPNE

Spain, D. (1992). *Gendered spaces*. University of North Carolina Press.

Van Dyke, J. (1996). Gender and success in the American dance world. *Women's Studies International Forum*, *19*(5), 535–543. https://doi.org/10.1016/0277-5395(96)00048-9

Woolf, V. (2015). *A room of one's own and three guineas*. Oxford University Press.

PART I
Bodily knowledge

1

GROWING UP IN DANCE

Experiencing the pubertal transition in leotard and tights

Siobhan Mitchell

Introduction

Growth and maturation is a developing area of interest in dance research and practice. In the past 5–10 years there has been a significant increase in research and application in sport (Cumming, 2022; Hill et al., 2023; Patel et al., 2021) and increasing interest in the topic within dance (Bowerman et al., 2014; Kolokythas et al., 2023; Mitchell, 2018). Contemporary research in this area advances findings from the 1980s (Brooks-Gunn & Warren, 1985, 1989) that highlight the importance of social context regarding psychosocial outcomes in adolescence; the social context of dance found to amplify detriment to psychological wellbeing during puberty (Brooks-Gunn & Warren 1985; Brooks-Gunn et al. 1989; Mendle et al., 2007). Evidence of contemporary experiences of maturation in a vocational ballet training context suggest that puberty has implications for the physical and psychosocial adjustment of dancers and that these implications appear to differ relative to the timing of puberty (early, 'on-time', or late) (Mitchell et al., 2020, 2021, 2022). Studies have also started to explore associations between injury and maturation in dance, with further research needed (Bowerman et al., 2014; Kolokythas et al., 2023). Findings raise several areas for further investigation: education and training across the sector; the need for contemporary datasets; and understanding current practices in the dance sector around growth and development.

Throughout this chapter you will be provided with excerpts from the lived experiences of early maturing dancers. These excerpts are from semi-structured interviews conducted with ten early maturing female ballet

DOI: 10.4324/9781003382874-3

dancers aged 11–17 (mean age 14.1 years) from three vocational bal-let schools in the UK as part of the author's doctoral research (Mitchell, 2018). Age of menarche for these dancers ranged from 10 to12 years. These excerpts will provide insight into the experiences of these dancers and offers a perspective on early maturation in this context.

What is adolescence?

The period of adolescence encompasses physical, social, emotional and cognitive development, considered to begin aged ten years and span into the early twenties (Worthman & Trang, 2018). As social and cultural concepts of adult milestones such as finishing education, marriage and becoming financially independent now occur later, the adolescent period continues to extend (Dahl, 2004; Worthman & Trang, 2018). This is because adolescence is defined by social and cultural notions of what it means to be an 'adult'. While physical development puberty) is based within the teenage years, other aspects of development (cognitive skills), are partially experientially led, and therefore continue developing long after sexual and physical maturation are achieved (Dahl, 2004). In most societies, entry into adolescence coincides with the recognition of puberty, and this transition from childhood to adulthood instigates a social transformation encompassing aspects of social life including work, greater levels of responsibility, and partner choice (ibid.; Worthman & Trang, 2018). This concept of social adolescence applies widely and differs by gender and level of importance within specific cultural environments (ibid., 2018).

In dance subculture, highly stylised dance forms, such as ballet, hold their own notions of social adolescence. For example, in pre-professional ballet training contexts, adolescents are arguably required to display greater levels of discipline, responsibility and maturity than one might expect from early adolescents outside of this context. In line with wider western culture, expectations for boys and girls in ballet differ distinctly. In ballet, pubertal changes may be welcomed for boys, bringing benefits of strength and power, yet seen as detrimental for girls, shifting them away from the prescribed ideal of a more pre-pubescent physique (Pickard, 2012).

The term puberty encompasses the process of physical changes which indicate the beginning of adolescence. Puberty presents a significant challenge for adolescents involved in physical endeavours, dance in particular. During this developmental phase, young dancers contend with physical, psychological and social changes; many of which directly affect performance, technique, selection and retention, psychological wellbeing, and injury risk. Concurrently, the expectation for continued improvement remains and intensity of training increases.

Puberty describes not a single event, but a complex set of interrelated changes (Dorn et al., 2006). It can be defined as the period of rapid change leading to physical and reproductive maturation (Petersen & Taylor, 1980).

These changes include increased body mass and height, the attainment of mature reproductive capacity, changes in the distribution of body fat, the development of a variety of secondary sexual characteristics, and shifts in body proportions (Tanner, 1962). Puberty is also associated with significant changes in drives, motivations, rapid changes in hormone levels, psychology and social life (Blakemore et al., 2010; Tanner, 1962). For females, the most pertinent, and typically most overt, pubertal changes include increasing body mass, rapid changes in limb length, body size and distribution of body fat, breast development and the onset of menarche (Summers-Effler, 2004). While the growth spurt in stature receives most attention, the weight spurt can be more challenging for many young dancers. The weight spurt happens for girls around nine months after the most rapid period of growth in stature (i.e., peak height velocity) (Malina et al., 2004). Then, roughly between six months to one year after the most rapid period of growth (in conjunction with the weight spurt), menstruation should begin (ibid.).

Menarche describes the first menstrual cycle. Menarche is one of the last events to take place in puberty, with breast development and the growth spurt in stature commonly occurring before menarche (Dorn et al., 2006). Consequently, menarche is not a good indicator of the onset of puberty. Most studies of menarche in dance are focused on the timing of its onset and associated implications (Brooks-Gunn & Warren, 1985; Steinberg et al., 2022). Few studies have explored experiences of menarche in the dance environment, but those that do describe menstruation as an inconvenience and, particularly for young dancers, something that is shameful or embarrassing. The experiences of dancers describe how menstruation in this specific context can be especially challenging to negotiate and manage.

Menstruation as a taboo and a challenge

... one girl has just started her period, in my class but no one knows...Yes. She wouldn't tell anyone ... We've been able to talk to each other about it.
(Mitchell, 2018, p. 381).

Yeah, because everyone can see everything but at school you've got your uniform on and no one knows what's going on underneath it, but then, at dancing you're stripped back, just in your leotard and tights, and everyone can see everything, so it's quite, like, 'judgy' in that way ... At dancing, your period, I think that's the hardest thing, because if it's bad and it goes in your tights, everyone can see and at school you've got your black tights on and you're completely fine. And that's, kind of, hard. I would say that was definitely the hardest thing for me.
(Mitchell, 2018, p. 189)

A reoccurring theme for young dancers, which is prevalent in existing literature, is breast development. Breast development can be perceived as a particularly negative aspect of physical development for young ballet dancers, with greater breast development associated with drop out from vocational ballet training and as unconducive to a career in ballet (Hamilton et al., 1997; Mitchell et al., 2016).

The challenge of visible physical change

In a study of adult professional ballet dancers those who had a smaller growth spurt in height and minimal breast development described experiencing less difficultly adapting to puberty during their training:

> *I was fairly lucky in a lot of ways … my boobs didn't get that much bigger. I didn't have breasts too big for ballet and I didn't … I didn't gain a ton of weight or have a massive growth spurt that completely limited my flexibility.*
> *(Mitchell et al., 2021, p. 4)*

Early maturing girls in pre-professional ballet training raised visible physical changes such as breast development as a particular challenge:

> *… I hated it. I hated it. As soon as, like, boobs started to grow and stuff I really didn't like it and, no, it was horrible … I still thought that the body of a twelve-year-old was how it was supposed to be forever and I was like, "What the hell is this?" but then, I don't know, I just really didn't like it and started to put on weight other places as well and it just wasn't nice. (Mitchell, 2018, p. 167)*

Existing research supports the notion that social interactions which form a response to physical changes, such as breast development, can have an impact upon the subsequent meaning individuals attach to those changes (Summers-Effler, 2004). In this context, negative social interactions and responses to breast development may contribute to stigmatising normal pubertal changes, particularly those which are made more visible by the constraints of the ballet environment.

Pubertal timing

In girls, the onset of puberty typically occurs between 10 and 11 years of age; however, individual variation in the age at which puberty occurs is considerable, with some girls experiencing puberty well in advance or delay of same age peers (Mendle, 2014). The timing of puberty can vary by up to five years, thus chronological age is not a good indicator of physical development at puberty (Malina et al., 2004). The average sequence of pubertal change for females begins with breast development (as early as 7–8 years old), development of pubic hair (from age 11), peak height velocity, i.e., the point of most rapid growth (average age 12) and onset of menarche. The latest data on age of menarche in the UK suggests 12.9 years as the average (Rubin et al., 2009; Whincup et al., 2001).

The timing of maturation is largely genetically determined (Kaprio et al., 1995; Rowe, 2002); however, it can be influenced by environmental stressors (acute and chronic) which can delay or accelerate the maturation process (Gluckman & Hanson, 2006). For example, in response to chronic stressors such as famine, puberty may be delayed and in response to acute stressors such as the absence of a father, puberty can be accelerated (ibid.; Westendorp & Kirkwood, 1998). Involvement in intensive sport or dance training may also constitute an environmental stressor. However, our understanding of the effect that sports training has on the growing child is limited due to difficulty in distinguishing the independent effects of training from those of normal growth (Baxter-Jones & Maffulli, 2002). Research in gymnastics suggests that intensive training does not appear to attenuate pubertal growth and maturation rate, timing or tempo (Malina et al., 2013). Similar findings have been reported in novice dancers across a range of dance styles, though there is not yet longitudinal data that addresses young dancers in vocational ballet training (Matthews et al., 2006).

The biological timing of pubertal events can be pivotal in determining the trajectory of physical developments; late maturation leading to a lean physique and earlier maturation presenting greater aesthetic challenges for young dancers (Gay et al., 2014). Early maturing girls experience greater pubertal gains in size, absolute/relative fat mass and absolute lean mass. This more intensive growth spurt results in comparatively greater torso growth, relative to shorter leg length (ibid.; Malina et al., 2004). Late maturing girls experience smaller pubertal gains in height, weight and fat mass, greater gains in relative lean mass and subsequently possess a more linear physique; limbs grow during childhood and thus a greater period of time growing in childhood results in these individuals developing longer limbs relative to a shorter torso (Gay et al., 2014).

Whether or not particular timing is favourable may depend on the type of activity in which a young person is involved. For example, early maturation can be seen to be advantageous in many physical activities and sports which involve power and strength, whereas late maturation, which results in a smaller and more lean physique, may be more favourable for endurance, aesthetic sports or performing arts, such as ballet (Ackland, Elliott, & Richards, 2003; Monsma, 2008; Myburgh et al., 2016).

Late maturing girls in pre-professional ballet training emphasised that the extent of physical development is key: 'For ballet, it's good to look older but you don't want bits, you know what I mean' (Mitchell et al., 2020, p. 236). They observed their peers who were already undergoing pubertal changes and felt pleased that they did not have to deal with these challenges yet: 'I'm quite happy that I've not really grown up yet' (ibid., 2020, p. 236), and 'I like it because everybody moans about it. I just feel so happy because mine's not started yet' (ibid., 2020, p. 236). Dancers related this inconvenience to pubertal events such as menarche—being on your period when attending a ballet class—and experiencing visible changes such as breast development.

The preference for slim bodies in ballet is well established. This requirement places great pressure upon changes at puberty, which has been described as a 'make or break' event for young dancers in terms of their suitability for a career in ballet (Mitchell et al., 2016; Pickard, 2013). In ballet, earlier age of menarche and greater breast development have been highlighted as characteristics of those who did not complete professional training, suggesting that certain physical developments are not considered to be as conducive to a career in ballet (Hamilton et al., 1997).

Literature is largely in agreement that early maturation is not socially advantageous for females, particularly within social contexts such as ballet, where there are clear preferences and benefits associated with later maturation (Burckhardt et al., 2011; Hamilton et al., 1988). Ballet teachers have been shown to perceive early maturing girls less positively (Mitchell et al., 2016). Physical changes associated with earlier maturation such as widening of the hips, breast development and an increase in fat stores, were viewed as not 'conducive' to a career in ballet. In contrast, ballet teachers perceived late maturing girls more positively in terms of their physical characteristics and potential for a career in ballet (ibid.). Mixed opinions as to the benefits associated with early, average and late maturation have been reported by ballet teachers (Brooks-Gunn & Warren, 1985; Mitchell et al., 2016). Opinions ranged from views in agreement with previous findings, that later maturation gives a nicer 'look', to perceiving earlier maturation to be a potential advantage in terms of getting a lot of the 'growing done' before serious training or auditions begin, to viewing the timing of maturation as irrelevant (Mitchell et al., 2016). These findings diverge from the general consensus presented in existing literature that up to 70% of professional ballet dancers are late maturing (Hamilton et al., 1985, 1988; Bradshaw & Karin, 2016). While there are, in many ways, advantages associated with later maturation in the ballet world, there are also potential merits to earlier maturation. This is supported by contemporary data with adolescent girls in pre-professional ballet training (Mitchell, 2018).

Early maturation ... getting it over and done with

The experience of some early maturing girls tells us there may be some benefits of going through puberty at an earlier age. For example, going through puberty during earlier training years can provide dancers with time to adjust and regain flexibility and coordination and to negotiate growth related injuries.

> In year 9 we have our big appraisal and that's quite an important appraisal. It's where we either get assessed out or we can stay for the next few years. So the reason I think it's quite good at the moment that I'm growing now is because I'm getting it over and done with. I'm having all my injuries now because of my growth and so hopefully I won't have them in year 9 because I've started so early.
>
> *(Mitchell, 2018, p. 166)*

Research on maturity timing is very limited in dance; existing studies focus predominantly on ballet dancers (Brooks-Gunn & Warren, 1985, Brooks-Gunn et al.,1989; Mitchell, 2018; Mitchell et al., 2016, 2017, 2020, 2021, 2022) with some data available for contemporary dancers. It should be noted that these studies do not address ethnicity within these genres. Reported outcomes in relation to maturity timing differ across these two genres in relation to dropout and selection. For example, while maturation timing is reported to be associated with dropout in studies of ballet dancers, a study with pre-professional contemporary dancers reported no effect of maturation in terms of distinguishing those who dropped out from those who continued training, suggesting that dance style plays an important role (Aujla et al., 2015). For contemporary dancers, there is no existing research to suggest whether there may be a selection bias toward dancers of particular maturity timing at the professional level. However, data relating to average age of menarche in adolescent contemporary dancers, suggests no strong maturity bias (Aujla et al., 2015). Average age of menarche in this sample was 12.6 years, suggesting on-time maturation to be normative for dancers specialising in contemporary styles (Aujla et al., 2015). While ballet and contemporary dancers frequently practise other dance styles as part of their training, the differing aesthetic demands and training regimes of different dance styles necessitate differences in body composition and body type (Liiv et al., 2013); this, in turn, may impact upon the relative importance of maturity timing for factors such as selection and dropout. Further research is needed across a wider range of dance genres along with consideration of the effects of ethnicity and cultural heritage of the dancers to substantiate these differences.

Shaping growing minds

Physical development at puberty is only one piece of the puzzle. The timing of physical change and how an individual adapts to biological changes may be crucial in terms of their experience, with maladaptive responses increasing risk to psychological health and wellbeing (Brooks-Gunn & Warren, 1985;

Summers-Effler, 2004; Yuan, 2012). Girls who enter puberty at an earlier age are, from a cognitive and socio-emotional perspective, less prepared to deal with the increased pressures and expectations that adulthood brings (Mendle et al., 2007; Sherar et al., 2010). This disparity in timing between physical and cognitive development can lead to vulnerability in young dancers; while a dancer may be physically and sexually mature with regard to the brain and the body, they may be relatively immature in terms of self-control and the ability to regulate feelings (Dahl, 2004).

Greater gains in fat mass make early maturing individuals, both dance and non-dance, more susceptible to a range of negative psychosocial outcomes, such as negative body image and disordered eating, within environments that accentuate peer comparison and thinness (Brooks-Gunn & Warren, 1985; Brooks-Gunn et al., 1989; Sherar et al., 2010). Consequently, early maturing girls are, as a group, more likely to engage in maladaptive coping behaviours and/or health risk behaviours, such as smoking and drinking (Mendle et al., 2007). While research specific to dance populations has not been conducted in all these areas, existing evidence holds that earlier maturing ballet dancers are at greater risk of disordered eating, psychopathology and poor body image compared to their later maturing peers (Brooks-Gunn & Warren, 1985).

While developmentally, adolescence represents a period of strength and resilience, there is a health paradox associated with this period; despite maturational improvements across several domains, overall morbidity and mortality rates increase by 200% during adolescence (Dahl, 2004). How an individual adapts to biological, psychological and physical changes at adolescence can be significant in determining the direction of these outcomes. For young dancers, positive and relatively rapid adaptation to changes is important, with key decisions made about retention and progression throughout the vocational training years. Research highlights the importance of key figures for adaptive responses at puberty (Raja et al., 1992), particularly in terms of their impact upon the social environment or learning climate (Cumming et al., 2005). In the context of ballet, key figures may include teachers, peers and parents. Their influence upon the environment in which a young dancer develops may have significant implications for psychosocial outcomes at puberty (Mitchell et al, 2016; Stark & Newton, 2014).

Perceptions of biological timing and the social context which shapes these perceptions appear to be particularly significant within a ballet context. While there are clear physical and psychological implications relating to objective measures of maturity timing, there is a growing body of research which stresses the importance of perceptions of maturity timing alongside more objective measures of biological timing, particularly with reference to psychological and social outcomes (Graber et al., 2004; Moore et al., 2014). That is, how we perceive puberty may be as, if not more, important than puberty itself.

Research suggests that puberty and associated pubertal changes are perceived as negative within the dance world (Mitchell et al., 2016). Young dancers are attuned to the expectations and values of their social world and so valued conditions, such as late maturation, and less valued conditions, such as earlier maturation, may have significance for young dancers (Pickard, 2013). Research into recollections of puberty and disordered eating holds that disliking physical changes of puberty, alongside feeling unprepared, predicted eating disorder symptoms; suggesting that how young women experience the pubertal transition can influence aspects of wellbeing in adulthood (Moore et al., 2016). In addition, how girls perceive pubertal experiences relating to physical changes, such as negative views relating to normative physical changes and feelings of preparedness, helps to explain disordered eating (Moore et al., 2016).

Being the 'odd one out'

Early maturing dancers report perceiving conflict between the ideals of the ballet subculture and the physical changes of puberty; responses from their environment, from teachers and/or peers, signal this conflict.

> ...sometimes I get bullied for being more mature than everybody and everything...Sometimes people have cringed...And laughed.
> *(Mitchell, 2018, p.169)*

Lack of cultural and social acceptance of early maturing bodies can extend to experiences of bullying and social exclusion. A lack of social acceptance has been reported by adolescent dancers, with early maturation, in particular the more visible aspects such as breast development, being considered as taboo (Mitchell, 2018; Mitchell et al., 2021). In this sense, dancers experience a response from their social world that visible changes related to early maturation hold negative value.

Research has shown that long term effects of maturation hinge more on subjective interpretations than objective indicators (Moore et al., 2016). In contexts such as vocational dance training, self-perception of maturation may be of amplified importance. Where later maturation is the norm, on-time maturation may be perceived, relative to one's peers, as early and thus that individual may experience more similar psychosocial issues to that of an early maturing individual (Brooks-Gunn & Warren, 1985). Moreover, there is evidence to suggest that perception of development remains comparatively stable throughout the period of puberty and adolescence (Cance et al., 2012).

Social stimulus value describes the interactions among adolescent bodily changes, personality and sociocultural variables; the social stimulus value of physical changes depends on the social context in which they occur (Mitchell et al., 2017; Petersen & Taylor, 1980). For instance, the body size and shape of a female dancer may influence a dance teacher's evaluation of current ability and future potential (Mitchell et al., 2016). The social stimulus value of pubertal change within the context of vocational dance training is also an important consideration. Research from sport supports the importance of this within student perceptions of training. For female artistic gymnasts, greater body size was associated with negative interactions with coaches; taller and heavier girls reported less encouragement, reinforcement and instruction, and more punishment and ignoring of mistakes (Cumming et al., 2005).

Consistent with existing literature, dancers describe significant individuals, such as the dance teacher, as playing an important role in terms of how dancers perceived pubertal changes and their responses to those changes;

> ...I was a little bit shocked, definitely taken aback when they pulled me into their office...from the end of the last year to over the summer and then to the beginning of that year, that the relationship between us, was not the same so I said, 'I want to talk to you, I want to see what's going on' and their answer was literally, 'your body has changed' and I'm like, 'this is what this is all about, are you kidding me?' And they were like, 'you don't see this?' ...It's also just to see someone that you thought you knew and I loved these teachers and they really liked me too and then to come back and be treated like that, made me feel really bad about myself. So, I had to work much harder, because they weren't going to look at me for my body, maybe they would look at me for my work ethic.
>
> *(Mitchell et al., 2021, p. 6)*

Growing up in dance—what can we learn from the experiences of dancers?

While there is limited research on maturation timing in dance, studies of the experiences of early, on-time and late maturation in pre-professional and professional dancers provide some evidence (Mitchell, 2018; Mitchell et al., 2020, 2021, 2022). Research with girls in vocational ballet training suggests there are three key areas affected by differing maturity timing: Social support, time to adjust, and training experiences (injury, selection and evaluation). Moreover, the advantages and disadvantages associated with pubertal timing may vary relative to dancer's phase of training and the demands and challenges they experience during these unique phases.

Social support

A qualitative study with adult professional ballet dancers found that lived experiences of puberty in the dance context were characterised by conflict and struggle, coming to terms with physical changes and possessing grit and grace in order to successfully negotiate puberty, succeed and survive in professional ballet (Mitchell et al., 2021). Factors such as social support, the timing and extent of pubertal changes, dance teacher behaviours, and the ballet training context, influenced the extent to which dancers experienced conflict and struggle and how easily they were able to come to terms with their adult physique.

In terms of supporting adolescent dancers to cope with and adjust to pubertal change, there may be additional benefits for earlier maturing girls. Early maturing ballet dancers complete this period of their development within the vocational training environment, which has the potential to offer support and to facilitate healthy adaptation. This could be important as social support is suggested to be a key factor associated with the development of coping strategies (Fergus & Zimmerman 2005; White & Bennie 2015). Later maturing ballet dancers may not have the same opportunities to develop coping strategies, having comparatively more amenable physical characteristics for the majority of their training, thereby less opportunity to overcome challenges in the same way as their early maturing counterparts (Mitchell et al., 2020). Moreover, late maturing ballet dancers experience growth and maturation in their later training years and have to adapt during their transition to further training or a professional career, potentially offering less social support and opportunity for the development of coping strategies. Social context has been found to be a critical determinant of resilience versus vulnerability (Mendle et al. 2007). Accordingly, schools and teachers should look to facilitate greater resilience through providing an adaptive social context for the adolescent ballet dancer.

Time to prepare and adjust

The experiences of early maturing adolescent dancers are distinct from those of late and on-time adolescent dancers. The key contrast between the experiences of early, on-time and late maturing adolescent dancers is preparedness. Firstly, preparedness for the changes of puberty: while early maturing girls described feeling inadequately prepared and supported as they entered puberty (Mitchell, 2018), on-time girls have reported greater peer support (Mitchell et al., 2022) and late maturing girls have reported benefitting from the experiences of others (Mitchell et al., 2020). Wider literature evidences early maturing individuals as a minority in dance training with Brooks-Gunn & Warren (1985) reporting that only 6% of the girls in dance company schools they studied were early maturing.

The second aspect of preparedness, which contrasts with studies of late and on-time maturing adolescent dancers, is readiness for evaluation and auditions at the end of training (Mitchell et al., 2020, 2022). Consistent with emerging qualitative evidence with both dancers and dance teachers (Mitchell et al., 2016, 2022) yet contrary to the cultural norms of the ballet world, dancers perceive a number of physical and developmental benefits to advanced physical maturation within the context of vocational ballet training. These benefits relate directly to the timing of physical growth and maturation relative to the training and evaluation systems of vocational ballet schooling in the UK. Early maturing dancers experience physical changes early on in their training, at a point that is arguably less crucial in terms of evaluation and assessment. The timing of pubertal change, relative to training and evaluation, provides these individuals with time to adjust to the changing body, both physically and psychologically, in readiness for end of training evaluation and auditions.

Training experiences

In contrast to the experience of early maturing dancers, later maturing dancers reported feeling left behind; experiencing physical change and ongoing physical injury during the crucial later training years and needing time to 'catch up' before final evaluations and testing (Mitchell et al., 2020). Late maturing dancers described aesthetic advantages, congruent with the well-established bias toward a later maturing physique for ballet; being 'small' and not having 'bits' were highlighted as advantageous for these dancers in terms of maintaining a more pre-pubescent look and thereby conforming more easily to the expectations of the ballet world (Mitchell et al., 2020). However, this tentative evidence also suggests that late maturation is not a panacea. Despite aesthetic advantages, later maturing dancers were disadvantaged by the current training system which sees them undertaking the most crucial training period during their most rapid period of growth (Mitchell et al., 2020).

Moving forward in the sector

There is a paucity of research on the topic of growth and development specific to young people in dance. In the last five years there has been some progress in this area with previous papers on the topic dating back to the 1980s (Brooks-Gunn & Warren, 1985, 1989). A survey of UK dance teachers conducted in collaboration with One Dance UK in 2016 found that over half (59.5%) of dance teachers had not received any education or training on growth and maturation. Since this survey, provision of education for teachers around the topic of growth and maturation has increased. This is now being offered as part of continuing professional development courses and in places is integrated into teaching course content. However, as yet, it is not a 'core pillar' of dance teacher training.

Contemporary experiences of maturation in a vocational dance training context support the contention that puberty has implications for the physical and psychosocial adjustment of dancers and that these implications appear to differ for early, 'on-time' and late maturing dancers (Mitchell et al., 2020, 2021, 2022). The research raised three areas for further investigation: education across the sector, developing datasets, and practices in the dance sector. These areas have been explored further as part of the GuiDANCE project—Growing up in dance: Enhancing education and creating sustainable practices in growth and maturation. The GuiDANCE project was a collaboration between multiple partners in the UK dance sector. The collaboration aimed to address challenges associated with the pubertal transition in dance and to better equip the sector to support healthy development. A review of current practices and data was employed alongside survey and interview methods, to develop understanding of education, training, and practice around growth and development in the UK dance sector. Co-creation workshops were employed using this learning as a starting point to generate best practice guidelines for managing growth and development in dance. The GuiDANCE Network was established in 2022 to continue this work and has begun to action these guidelines, creating a network, a repository with resources, and establishing best practice in training and education.

Conclusion

While the relationship between the social context of ballet and late maturation is well-supported (Brooks-Gunn & Warren 1985; Hamilton et al. 1997; Johnson 2018), recent research calls into question long-standing assumptions about early maturation as a solely disadvantageous condition for young ballet dancers (Mitchell et al., 2016, 2021). Qualitative research with ballet teachers, pre-professional ballet dancers and adult professional ballet dancers reports potential benefits to earlier maturation as it gets the growing out of the way before more serious training begins (Mitchell, 2018; Mitchell et al., 2016, 2021). This evidence suggests that while there are many advantages associated with later maturation in the ballet world, there are also potential merits to earlier maturation which warrant further investigation.

The timing of pubertal changes appears to have an effect, not only in terms of the ability to meet the social expectations of the ballet world, but on the subsequent psychological wellbeing of individuals relating to how changes are perceived within their social context. The social context of ballet has been found to amplify the effects of maturation timing and the resulting detriment to psychosocial wellbeing (Brooks-Gunn & Warren, 1985). Early and on-time maturation within a ballet training context was associated with higher incidences of eating pathologies than in early and on-time non-dancers (Brooks-Gunn & Warren, 1985). Actions taken by those who support adolescents in dance, such as prioritising context-specific education on growth and maturation and enhancing opportunities for social support could equip those in the dance sector to better support healthy adolescent development.

Action points for the dance sector

The findings from studies to date elucidate the complex interplay between maturity timing, the dance environment and perceptions of pubertal change. While there is much room for further research in this area, from existing research we can draw a few broad recommendations for applied practice to facilitate healthy adaptation at puberty within the context of ballet.

Enhancing opportunities for social support

While we cannot provide early maturing dancers with more time in order to feel more prepared for changes at puberty, we can address education and social support.

- Bio-banding is one approach which groups young people by biological rather than chronological age. Adopting these principles within the context of ballet may enhance opportunities to build social support, particularly for early maturing girls.
- Research is beginning to document the benefits of this approach for young athletes in contributing towards their physical, psychological, and social development (Cumming et al., 2017).

Prioritising education for dancers and dance teachers

- Education for young dancers beyond the basics, and in a capacity which is applied to their context, could be of particular benefit to early maturing dancers, to help them to prepare for and manage changes at puberty. Additionally, an understanding of what is 'normal' and changes that are temporary, may help dancers to better support each other.
- Generating greater understanding among dance teachers and professionals, in terms of normal pubertal development and differences in timing, among a group of female dancers could help in many ways. For example, puberty in ballet is heavily stigmatised as a negative event; if teachers had greater knowledge surrounding growth and maturation, they could adapt their teaching practices to take advantage of those aspects which are strengthened by puberty, and the expectations of young dancers regarding normal pubertal development may also be better informed.

References

Ackland, T., Elliott, B. & Richards, J. (2003). Gymnastics: Growth in body size affects rotational performance in women's gymnastics. *Sports Biomechanics*, 2(2), 163–176. http://dx.doi.org/10.1080/14763140308522815

Aujla, I. J., Nordin-Bates, S. M. & Redding, E. (2015). Multidisciplinary predictors of adherence to contemporary dance training: Findings from the UK Centres for

Advanced Training. *Journal of Sports Sciences*, *33*(15). 1–10. http://dx.doi.org/10.1080/02640414.2014.996183

Baxter-Jones, A. D. G. & Maffulli, N. (2002). Intensive training in elite young female athletes. *British Journal of Sports Medicine, 36*(1), 13–15. http://dx.doi.org/10.1136/bjsm.36.1.13

Blakemore, S. J., Burnett, S. & Dahl, R. (2010). The role of puberty in the developing adolescent brain. *Human Brain Mapping, 31*(6), 926–933. http://dx.doi.org/10.1002/hbm.21052

Bowerman, E., Whatman, C., Harris, N., Bradshaw, E. & Karin, J. (2014). Are maturation, growth and lower extremity alignment associated with overuse injury in elite adolescent ballet dancers? *Physical Therapy in Sport, 15*(4), 234–241. http://dx.doi.org/10.1016/j.ptsp.2013.12.014

Bradshaw, E., & Karin, J. (2016). Growth, maturation and injury patterns of Australian elite adolescent ballet dancers. Paper presented at the Dance Health Seminar, Australian Catholic University, Melbourne.

Brooks-Gunn, J., Attie, I., Burrow, C., Rosso, J. T. & Warren, M. P. (1989). The impact of puberty on body and eating concerns in athletic and nonathletic contexts. *Journal of Early Adolescence, 9*(3), 269–290. http://dx.doi.org/10.1177/0272431689093006

Brooks-Gunn, J., & Warren, M. (1985). The effects of delayed menarche in different contexts: Dance and non-dance students. *Journal of Youth and Adolescence, 14*(4), 285–300. http://dx.doi.org/10.1007/bf02089235

Burckhardt, P., Wynn, E., Krieg, M.-A., Bagutti, C., & Faouzi, M. (2011). The effects of nutrition, puberty and dancing on bone density in adolescent ballet dancers. *Journal of Dance Medicine & Science, 15*(2), 51–61.

Cance, J. D., Ennett, S. T., Morgan-Lopez, A. A. & Foshee, V. A. (2012). The stability of perceived pubertal timing across adolescence. *Journal of Youth and Adolescence, 41*(6), 764–775. http://dx.doi.org/10.1007/s10964-011-9720-0

Cumming, S. (2022). The impact of growth and maturation upon children's participation in sport and physical activity. In M. Toms and R. Jeanes (Eds.), *Routledge Handbook of Coaching Children in Sport* (pp. 238–249). Routledge.

Cumming, S. P., Brown, D. J., Mitchell, S., Bunce, J., Hunt, D., Hedges, C., et al. (2017). Premier league academy soccer players' experiences of competing in a tournament bio-banded for biological maturation. *Journal of Sports Sciences, 36*(7), 757–765. http://dx.doi.org/10.1080/02640414.2017.1340656

Cumming, S. P., Eisenmann, J. C., Smoll, F. L., Smith, R. E. & Malina, R. M. (2005). Body size and perceptions of coaching behaviors by adolescent female athletes. *Psychology of Sport and Exercise, 6*(6), 693–705. http://dx.doi.org/10.1016/j.psychsport.2005.01.002

Dahl, R. (2004). Adolescent brain development: A period of vulnerabilities and opportunities—keynote address. *Adolescent Brain Development: Vulnerabilities And Opportunities, 1021,* 1–22. http://dx.doi.org/10.1196/annals.1308.001

Dorn, L. D., Dahl, R. E., Woodward, H. R. & Biro, F. (2006). Defining the boundaries of early adolescence: A users guide to assessing pubertal status and pubertal timing in research with adolescents. *Applied Developmental Science, 10*(1), 30–57. http://dx.doi.org/10.1207/s1532480xads1001_3

Fergus, S., & Zimmerman, M. A. (2005). Adolescent resilience: A framework for understanding healthy development in the face of risk. *Annual Review of Public Health, 26,* 399. http://dx.doi.org/10.1146/annurev.publhealth.26.021304.144357

Gay, J. L., Monsma, E. V., Smith, A. L., DeFreese, J. & Torres-McGehee, T. (2014). Assessment of growth and maturation in female athletes at a single point in time. *Women in Sport and Physical Activity Journal, 22*(2), 76–82. http://dx.doi.org/10.1123/wspaj.2014-0018

Gluckman, P. D., & Hanson, M. A. (2006). Evolution, development and timing of puberty. *Trends in Endocrinology & Metabolism, 17*(1), 7–12. http://dx.doi.org/10.1016/j.tem.2005.11.006

Graber, J. A., Seeley, J. R., Brooks-Gunn, J. & Lewinsohn, P. M. (2004). Is pubertal timing associated with psychopathology in young adulthood? *Journal of the American Academy of Child & Adolescent Psychiatry, 43*(6), 718–726. http://dx.doi.org/10.1097/01.chi.0000120022.14101.11

Hamilton, L. H., Brooks-Gunn, J. & Warren, M. P. (1985). Sociocultural influences on eating disorders in professional female ballet dancers. *International Journal of Eating Disorders, 4*(4), 465–477. http://dx.doi.org/10.1002/1098-108x(198511)4:4<465::aid-eat2260040407>3.0.co;2-0

Hamilton, L. H., Brooks-Gunn, J., Warren, M. P. & Hamilton, W. G. (1988). The role of selectivity in the pathogenesis of eating problems in ballet dancers. *Medicine and Science in Sports and Exercise, 20*(6), 560. http://dx.doi.org/10.1249/00005768-198812000-00007

Hamilton, L. H., Hamilton, W. G., Warren, M. P., Keller, K. & Molnar, M. (1997). Factors contributing to the attrition rate in elite ballet students. *Journal of Dance Medicine & Science, 1*(4), 131–139. http://dx.doi.org/10.1177/1089313x9700100402

Hill, M., John, T., McGee, D. & Cumming, S. P. (2023). 'He's got growth': Coaches' understanding and management of the growth spurt in male academy football. *International Journal of Sports Science & Coaching, 18*(1), 24–37. https://doi.org/10.1177/17479541221122415

Johnson, H. A. (2018). Dancing to death: Why are eating concerns endemic among female ballet dancers? A textual analysis of published memoirs. Available From ProQuest Dissertations & Theses Global; ProQuest One Literature. Retrieved January 14, 2024 from https://www.proquest.com/openview/ac2694871eece95e87d16376fff9e9cb/1?pq-origsite=gscholar&cbl=18750

Kaprio, J., Rimpelä, A., Winter, T., Viken, R. J., Rimpelä, M. & Rose, R. J. (1995). Common genetic influences on BMI and age at menarche. *Human Biology, 67*(5), 739–753.

Kolokythas, N., Metsios, G. S., Dinas, P. C., Galloway, S. M., Allen, N. & Wyon, M. A. (2023). Growth, maturation, and overuse injuries in dance and aesthetic sports: a systematic review. *Research in Dance Education, 24*(2), 115–137. http://dx.doi.org/10.1080/14647893.2021.1874902

Liiv, H., Wyon, M. A., Jürimäe, T., Saar, M., Mäestu, J. et al. (2013). Anthropometry, somatotypes, and aerobic power in ballet, contemporary dance, and dancesport. *Medical Problems of Performing Artists, 28*(4), 207–211. http://dx.doi.org/10.21091/mppa.2013.4041

Malina, R. M., Baxter-Jones, A., Armstrong, N., Beunen, G., Caine, D. et al. (2013). Role of intensive training in the growth and maturation of artistic gymnasts. *Sports Medicine, 43*(9), 783–802. http://dx.doi.org/10.1007/s40279-013-0058-5

Malina, R. M., Bouchard, C. & Bar-Or, O. (2004). *Growth, Maturation and Physical Activity* (2nd ed.). Human Kinetics.

Matthews, B. L., Bennell, K. L., Mckay, H. A., Khan, K. M., Baxter-Jones, A. D. et al. (2006). The influence of dance training on growth and maturation of young females: A mixed longitudinal study. *Annals of Human Biology, 33*(3), 342–356. http://dx.doi.org/10.1080/03014460600635951

Mendle, J. (2014). Beyond pubertal timing. *Current Directions in Psychological Science, 23*(3), 215–219. http://dx.doi.org/10.1177/0963721414530144

Mendle, J., Turkheimer, E. & Emery, R. E. (2007). Detrimental psychological outcomes associated with early pubertal timing in adolescent girls. *Developmental Review, 27*(2), 151–171. http://dx.doi.org/10.1016/j.dr.2006.11.001

Mitchell, S. (2018). Health and Wellbeing in Elite Female Ballet Dancers: Implications of Maturity Timing [Unpublished doctoral thesis]. University of Bath]. Retrieved January 14, 2024 from https://researchportal.bath.ac.uk/en/studentTheses/health-and-wellbeing-in-elite-female-ballet-dancers-implications-

Mitchell, S. B., Haase, A. M. & Cumming, S. P. (2020). Experiences of delayed maturation in female vocational ballet students: An interpretative phenomenological analysis. *Journal of Adolescence, 80,* 233–241. http://dx.doi.org/10.1016/j.adolescence.2020.03.005

Mitchell, S. B., Haase, A. M. & Cumming, S. P. (2021). Of grit and grace: Negotiating puberty, surviving, and succeeding in professional ballet. *Women in Sport and Physical Activity Journal, 29*(2), 127–138. Retrieved January 12, 2023 from https://journals.humankinetics.com/view/journals/wspaj/29/2/article-p127.xml

Mitchell, S. B., Haase, A. M. & Cumming, S. P. (2022). On-time maturation in female adolescent ballet dancers: Learning from lived experiences. *Journal of Early Adolescence, 42*(2), 262–290. https://doi.org/10.1177/02724316211036752

Mitchell, S., Haase, A., Cumming, S. & Malina, R. M. (2017). Understanding growth and maturation in the context of ballet: A biocultural approach. *Research in Dance Education, 18*(3), 291–300. http://dx.doi.org/10.1080/14647893.2017.1387525

Mitchell, S. B., Haase, A. M., Malina, R. M. & Cumming, S. P. (2016). The role of puberty in the making and breaking of young ballet dancers: Perspectives of dance teachers. *Journal of Adolescence, 47,* 81–89. ttp://dx.doi.org/10.1016/j.adolescence.2015.12.007

Monsma, E. V. (2008). Puberty and physical self-perceptions of competitive female figure skaters II: Maturational timing, skating context, and ability status. *Research Quarterly for Exercise and Sport, 79*(3), 411–416. http://dx.doi.org/10.1080/02701367.2008.10599506

Moore, S. R., Harden, K. P. & Mendle, J. (2014). Pubertal timing and adolescent sexual behavior in girls. *Developmental Psychology, 50*(6), 1734–1745. http://dx.doi.org/10.1037/a0036027

Moore, S. R., McKone, K. M. & Mendle, J. (2016). Recollections of puberty and disordered eating in young women. *Journal of Adolescence, 53,* 180–188. http://dx.doi.org/10.1016/j.adolescence.2016.10.011

Myburgh, G. K., Cumming, S. P., Coelho-e-Silva, M., Cooke, K. & Malina, R. M. (2016). Growth and maturity status of elite British junior tennis players. *Journal of Sports Sciences, 34*(20), 1957–1964. http://dx.doi.org/10.1080/02640414.2016.1149213

Patel, T. S., McGregor, A., Fawcett, L., Bekker, S., Williams, S., Williams, K. & Cumming, S. P. (2021). Coach awareness, knowledge and practice in relation to growth and maturation and training load in competitive, young gymnasts. *International Journal of Sports Science & Coaching, 16*(3), 528–543. http://dx.doi.org/10.1177/1747954120978486

Petersen, A., & Taylor, B. (1980). The biological approach to adolescence: Biological change and psychosocial adaptation. In J. Adelson (Ed.), *Handbook of Adolescent Psychology*. New York: Wiley.

Pickard, A. (2012). Schooling the dancer: the evolution of an identity as a ballet dancer. *Research in Dance Education, 13*(1), 25–46. http://dx.doi.org/10.1080/14647893.2011.651119

Pickard, A. (2013). Ballet body belief: Perceptions of an ideal ballet body from young ballet dancers. *Research in Dance Education, 14*(1), 3–19. http://dx.doi.org/10.10 80/14647893.2012.712106

Raja, S., McGee, R. & Stanton, W. (1992). Perceived attachments to parents and peers and psychological well-being in adolescence. *Journal of Youth and Adolescence, 21*(4), 471–485. http://dx.doi.org/10.1007/bf01537898

Rowe, D. C. (2002). On genetic variation in menarche and age at first sexual intercourse: A critique of the Belsky–Draper hypothesis. *Evolution and Human Behavior, 23*(5), 365–372. http://dx.doi.org/10.1016/s1090-5138(02)00102-2

Rubin, C., Maisonet, M., Kieszak, S., Monteilh, C., Holmes, A. et al. (2009). Timing of maturation and predictors of menarche in girls enrolled in a contemporary British cohort. *Paediatric and Perinatal Epidemiology, 23*(5), 492–504. http://dx.doi.org/10.1111/j.1365-3016.2009.01055.x

Sherar, L. B., Cumming, S. P., Eisenmann, J. C., Baxter-Jones, A. D. G. & Malina, R. M. (2010). Adolescent biological maturity and physical activity: Biology meets behavior. *Pediatric Exercise Science, 22*(3), 332–349. http://dx.doi.org/10.1123/pes.22.3.332

Stark, A., & Newton, M. (2014). A dancer's well-being: The influence of the social psychological climate during adolescence. *Psychology of Sport and Exercise, 15,* 356–363. http://dx.doi.org/10.1016/j.psychsport.2014.03.003

Steinberg, N., Siev-Ner, I., Zeev, A. & Tenenbaum, S. (2022). Is there an association between joint range of motion and muscle strength in young female dancers? And, does it depend on the effects of age and menarche? *Research in Sports Medicine,* 1–16. http://dx.doi.org/10.1080/15438627.2022.2031199

Summers-Effler, E. (2004). Little girls in women's bodies: Social interaction and the strategizing of early breast development. *Sex Roles, 51*(1–2), 29–44. http://dx.doi.org/10.1023/b:sers.0000032307.16204.ec

Tanner, J. M. (1962). *Growth at Adolescence* (2nd ed.). Blackwell Scientific.

Westendorp, R. G., & Kirkwood, T. B. (1998). Human longevity at the cost of reproductive success. *Nature, 396*(6713), 743. http://dx.doi.org/10.1038/25519

Whincup, P. H., Gilg, J. A., Odoki, K., Taylor, S. J. & Cook, D. G. (2001). Age of menarche in contemporary British teenagers: Survey of girls born between 1982 and 1986. *British Medical Journal, 322*(7294), 1095–1096. http://dx.doi.org/10.1136/bmj.322.7294.1095

White, R. L., & Bennie, A. (2015). Resilience in Youth Sport: A Qualitative Investigation of Gymnastics Coach and Athlete Perceptions. *International Journal of Sports Science &; Coaching, 10*(2–3), 379–393. http://dx.doi.org/10.1260/1747-9541.1 0.2-3.379

Worthman, C. M., & Trang, K. (2018). Dynamics of body time, social time and life history at adolescence. *Nature, 554*(7693), 451. http://dx.doi.org/10.1038/nature25750

Yuan, A. S. V. (2012). Perceived breast development and adolescent girls' psychological well-being. *Sex Roles, 66*(11–12), 790–806. http://dx.doi.org/10.1007/s11199-012-0138-2

2

FEMALE DANCER HORMONE HEALTH

Nicky Keay

Introduction

Female hormones are crucial to the health and performance of dancers. An understanding of female hormones for a dancer can help her navigate the path to optimal health and performance, throughout her career.

This chapter will provide the background of why female hormones are so important for dancers for their health and performance. I will outline the ways hormones change over a dancer's career with practical advice and suggestions of how to manage these changes to ensure a healthy, fulfilling and sustainable dance career. I will make reference to symbolism and mythology at times to illuminate female energies and historical significance.

Act 1 menstrual cycle hormone choreography

Hormones are internal chemical messengers that are transported in the blood stream throughout the body. The word hormone derives from ancient Greek meaning 'setting in motion'. Hormones literally bring DNA, the blueprint of life, to life, by directing how and when our genes are expressed. Hormones unlock our personal potential in terms of health and performance. As dancers we go to class in the hope and expectation that we will improve our dancing. Have you ever wondered how doing dance classes translates to dancing better? The answer lies in our hormones as these set in motion positive adaptations so we can be *citius, altius, potius*: a dancer with fast, nimble footwork, jumping higher and a dancer with strength.

Horme is the goddess of energy, effort and action and this reflects what female hormones bring to dancers to enable them to perform to their best. The

DOI: 10.4324/9781003382874-4

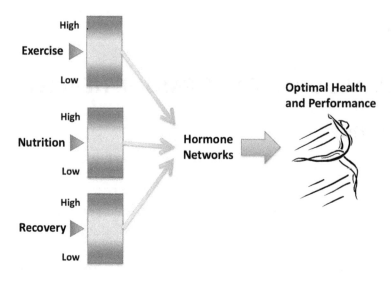

FIGURE 2.1   Harnessing hormones with permission *Hormones, Health and Human Potential*, 2022, Keay

good news is that dancers can harness their hormones through their choices around training, nutrition and recovery. This is illustrated in Figure 2.1 (Keay, 2022). Achieving the optimal balance and timing of exercise, nutrition and recovery will support healthy hormone networks. This in turn enables achievement of good mental and physical health and dance performance. Every dancer knows that it is important to put together all the steps in harmony to achieve a good *enchaînement*, for example. The same applies to supporting good hormone performance by ensuring the elements of exercise, nutrition and rest are combined in the most effective way. Although Hippocrates from ancient Greek times was not a dancer, or a dance teacher, he did indicate that the surest way to health was through giving each individual just the right amount of nourishment and exercise. Not too little and not too much.

The extra challenge that female dancers face, personifying the goddess of energy, effort and action, is that out of all the hormone networks, those of the menstrual cycle display the most beautiful and complex choreography. This is shown in Figure 2.2 (Keay, 2022).

The menstrual cycle can be divided into two acts. The first act is called the follicular phase describing the selection and development of a follicle containing an egg that will be ovulated. After ovulation has occurred, the next act of the menstrual cycle is the luteal phase. This is when the body and in particular the endometrium (lining of the uterus) is being prepared to welcome a fertilised egg. If this does not occur, then the endometrial lining is shed producing a menstrual period.

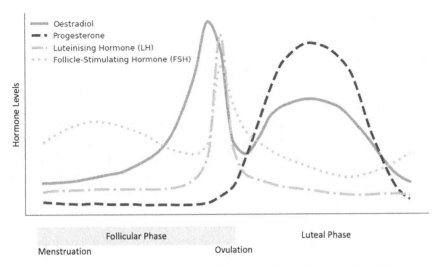

FIGURE 2.2   Menstrual cycle hormone choreography with permission *Hormones, Health and Human Potential*, 2022, Keay

The start of a menstrual cycle is heralded by the start of the menstrual period. During this time the female hormones are relatively quiescent. Progressing into the follicular phase, oestradiol (the most active form of oestrogen) produced by the ovaries starts to ramp up. This causes a surge in the control hormones follicle-stimulating hormone (FSH) and luteinising hormone (LH) produced by the pituitary gland in the brain. The pituitary gland is appropriately described as the conductor of the endocrine orchestra as the control hormones released by the pituitary gland direct the members of the endocrine orchestra, the various endocrine gland dispersed throughout the body. In the case of FSH and LH, the surge in these pituitary hormones towards the end of the follicular phase of the cycle, triggers ovulation when the dominant ovarian follicle releases an egg.

That is not the end of proceedings for the dominant follicle that released an egg. The remnants of this follicle left behind in the ovary form the corpus luteum. This is why the second act of the menstrual cycle is called the luteal phase, as the corpus luteum takes centre stage by producing progesterone. Progesterone is so named as this hormone is 'pro' (in favour of), 'gestation' (pregnancy) and thickens the lining of the endometrium and generally prepares the body for a potential pregnancy.

The time for this menstrual cycle choreography to play out can be anything from 22 to 35 days. This is the time from the start of one period, to the beginning of the next. There can be slight variation from one cycle to the next, but as advised by the Royal College of Obstetrics and Gynaecology, provided your periods are occurring within this time frame, this suggests your hormones are fluctuating in a healthy way.

Dancing in time with the menstrual cycle

What does this menstrual cycle hormone choreography mean in practical terms for a dancer? The best piece of advice is to get in tune with how you personally feel during your menstrual cycle. Just as with any dance performance, there will be subtle differences in the performance of each dancer's hormone choreography; in terms of timing of hormone changes, levels of hormones and most crucial of all: personal biological response to these hormones.

Making a personal diary of how you feel over your cycle to pick up any patterns is a great starting point. There are variety of menstrual tracking mobile applications (apps), but there is nothing wrong with the old-fashioned pen and paper approach (the only option for older dancers like me as a youngster!). If you do use an app, just be aware that the recommendations often are generic and may not necessarily be applicable for you as a dancer. For example, theoretically women should feel at their best in late follicular phase, before ovulation when oestradiol is at its highest. On the other hand many women find this is challenging time, including a professional cyclist who reported that she found training seemed harder at this time in the cycle in contrast to her teammates (Lebrun et al., 2020).

The ideal way of tracking your menstrual cycle is having the possibility to share and discuss with a medical person with experience of working in female hormones and with individual dancers. As medical advisor to Scottish Ballet I work regularly in this way with dancers. I set up a menstrual tracking system that dancers could share with me. That way I could work with each dancer to help her work out ways to perform to her best throughout her cycle. It is not possible to change the date for the opening night of a performance, but it is possible to predict where you might be in your cycle and have practised any particular strategies beforehand. For example, if you tend to feel lacking in energy during the luteal phase of your cycle, then we would work out ways to help you continue dancing to a high level. In a similar way, you will rehearse steps and make sure your costume and shoes are all ready for opening night. It is really important to do the same practice and dress rehearsals when it comes to the menstrual cycle (Keay et al., 2021).

The other reason for tracking menstrual cycles is that a menstrual period is a barometer of healthy internal female hormones, essentially a free monthly medical check. Monitoring when periods occur is effectively a valuable training metric. If periods become irregular or stop, this could be an early warning sign that there may not be the optimal balance of exercise, nutrition and recovery.

Flash points in the menstrual cycle

Menstruation

Although menstruation is a valuable barometer of internal healthy hormones, this can still be a challenging time for some dancers. Keeping well hydrated and ensuring a good iron intake (to compensate for loss of iron from the menstrual bleed) is a very good starting point. Studies show that for those who experience cramps, doing gentle movement like Pilates is helpful (Kim, 2019). Anti-inflammatory medication can also help with cramps. If these simple measures don't work and pain is so severe that you repeatedly have to miss class, then it is advisable to seek medical input.

Ovulation

There are conflicting studies which report that just before ovulation, with the ramp up in oestradiol there may be an increased risk of anterior cruciate ligament (ACL) injury (Lebrun et al., 2020). This is a ligament that stabilises the knee joint and is very important for dancing. From experience of having ruptured my ACL, I advocate that dancers should be aware that there are many contributing factors to sustaining this injury and this type of injury is more prevalent in contact sports (Lebrun et al., 2020).

Luteal phase

If ovulation has occurred, this phase is associated with progesterone levels which are much higher than during the follicular phase. Progesterone is a hormone that increases metabolic rate. In other words, the rate at which you use food energy is increased. This is why you may feel hungrier during this phase of the menstrual cycle, so it is a good idea to pre-empt this by being on top of carbohydrate based fuelling snacks like bananas. Another effect of progesterone increasing metabolic rate during the luteal phase is to increase body temperature which can leave you feeling hot and bothered.

Dancer hormone story

Manon was a 22-year-old professional dancer. She noticed that there were times when she couldn't sleep so well and felt hungrier and grumpier than usual. This wasn't necessarily linked to training load, so Manon wasn't sure what was going on. After I recommended tracking her menstrual cycles, she noticed that these symptoms were recurring in the week or two before her next period was due. We discussed that this indicated that Manon was suffering from some premenstrual issues. We discussed some strategies to deal with this including taking a few more snacks like bananas and cereal bars between classes. Making sure that sleeping was in a well-ventilated room and where possible making sure that rest and recovery time really was that, and not doing extra practice. Understanding the causes of these cyclical symptoms and what to do, really helped Manon to dance to her best throughout her menstrual cycle.

Hormonal contraception

It is every woman's personal choice what, if any, form of contraception she wishes to use. It is important to make an informed choice that is best for the individual. When it comes to hormonal contraception, there are broadly two types: progestogen only (synthetic form of progesterone) and combined hormonal contraception containing synthetic versions of both progesterone and oestradiol. Depending on the exact type and way of taking these, generally speaking you may not experience any bleeding with progestogen only, whereas it is usual to get a withdrawal bleed with combined versions.

Probably the most important point to emphasise is that all combined hormonal contraception and some versions of progestogen only (like depot injections) supress the production of pituitary hormones FSH and LH and therefore the production of ovarian hormones and ovulation. This is shown in Figure 2.3 (Keay, 2022). This can be very helpful in the treatment of some medical conditions like endometriosis which are 'driven' by fluctuations of female hormones. On the other hand, if your hormones are already supressed, due to an imbalance in training and/or nutrition, then it is not helpful to take hormonal contraception that reinforces this. This is outlined in Endocrine Society guidelines (Gordon et al., 2017) and in the National Institute of Clinical Excellence (NICE) information for the UK.

Low energy availability

With the increased demands of dance comes the challenge of balancing training, nutrition and recovery. Imbalances in dancer behaviours can result in low energy availability. This can cause disruption of female hormone function.

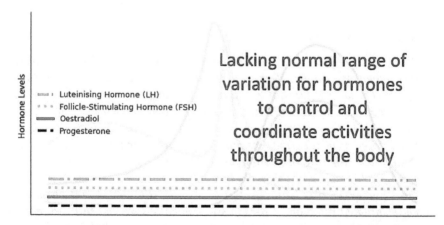

FIGURE 2.3 Suppressed female hormones with permission *Hormones, Health and Human Potential*, 2022, Keay

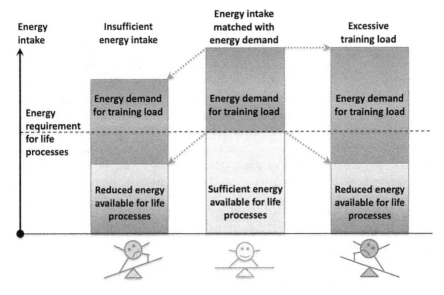

FIGURE 2.4   Low energy availability with permission *Hormones, Health and Human Potential*, 2022, Keay

What is low energy availability? It is essentially a mismatch between energy intake and energy demand. We derive energy from the food we eat. This energy is prioritised to cover movement, like dance training. The residual energy left over is known as energy availability, which is the energy required to keep us alive in a rested sedentary state. Even lying in bed all day takes a lot of energy! Energy is required to keep all the fundamental physiological processes ticking over: breathing, the heart pumping, the brain working and maintaining body temperature. For women this includes keeping menstrual cycles occurring. In Figure 2.4 the central bar shows a happy dancer where energy intake is sufficient to cover the energy demand from dance training and the demand for staying healthy.

In contrast the dancers on either side are in a situation of low energy availability, where the residual energy is not sufficient to maintain full healthy function of all the body processes. This could arise unintentionally as shown on the right bar (Figure 2.4), where the dancer has increased training load, forgetting to match with increased energy intake. The dancer on the right is in intentional low energy availability as she has consciously restricted food intake in the belief that this this will improve her dance performance.

Relative energy deficiency

Sustained low energy availability can lead to adverse outcomes in both health and performance outlined in Relative Energy Deficiency in Sport

(REDs) (Mountjoy et al., 2023). Don't be confused by the name. Although REDs includes the word 'sport', really it would be more accurate if 's' represented syndrome (Keay et al., 2019). Syndrome is the word used to describe a collection of symptoms caused by a particular condition. Relative energy deficiency, occurring in athletes and dancers does indeed cause a range of problems impacting both health and performance (Keay and Francis, 2019).

For female dancers experiencing REDs this often includes loss of periods (amenorrhoea). This type of amenorrhoea is called functional hypothalamic amenorrhoea (FHA). The word 'functional' is to distinguish from medical or physiological conditions causing amenorrhoea. Examples of physiological amenorrhoea include pregnancy and menopause. In contrast FHA is an adaptive response by the body to low energy availability, switching off periods to 'save energy' at the hypothalamic 'control' centre.

The ensuing low levels of oestradiol and progesterone is not a good situation for many systems in the body. For example, oestradiol is the queen hormone when it comes to bone health. This is associated with an increased risk of soft tissue and bone injury. Where there is concern about bone health, then as described above, taking the combined oral contraceptive pill will not help. Rather temporising hormone replacement therapy (HRT) is advised.

Ovarian hormones are also important for neurological function. Low levels can be associated with low mood and difficulty picking up new choreography. This is because the brain is not efficient at processing new information and implementing this in movement where there are low levels of oestradiol and progesterone. For female athletes and dancers experiencing low energy availability digestive issues can often be a problem. Just like all the systems in the body, the digestive system needs energy to function effectively. I often see dancers in low energy availability reporting bloating and constipation. On the surface this seems strange as the dancer will often report eating lots of fibrous foods. However, these foods are voluminous with low energy density and displace more nutritious foods as you feel 'full'.

Is low energy availability really a problem for dancers?

The high risk of REDs amongst dancers was demonstrated in our recent published study assessing dancers internationally across dance genres (Keay et al., 2021). A concerning high proportion of female dancers reported indicators of low energy availability and risk of REDs from their responses to a dance specific energy availability questionnaire. This included up to a third of respondents experiencing amenorrhoea. A particularly striking finding was the link between psychological factors and physical and physiology status. Dancers reporting anxiety over body weight/shape, eating and missing training, corresponded to those with lowest body weight and menstrual disruption. Low energy availability is a very important area of dancer hormone health, especially for those in training, aspiring to be professional dancers, or independent dancers who may not have access to the support afforded at large professional dance companies (Keay, 1998). Identifying those dancers particularly at risk is a priority as a preventative measure (Keay, 2000; Women's Health Concern, 2017).

How to identify and support dancers at risk?

The challenge of identifying dancers at risk of low energy availability is that on the surface the dancer may appear healthy. The dancer may not look underweight and may not have sustained a bone stress injury. Yet. However, such a dancer is unlikely to reach her personal full potential and jeopardises a sustainable dance career.

Raising awareness of REDs in the dance community is very important to prevent these adverse outcomes for a dancer's hormone health. Early detection of the warning signs of low energy availability enables supportive measures to be offered. Where low energy availability has caused cessation of menstruation, appropriate medical management needs to be provided to help in restoration of female hormone network function. The good news is that this is a reversible situation, although that is not to underestimate the psychological challenge of changing behaviours in the case of intentional energy restriction.

The aim is for the dancer to clear the energy deficit, which will enable rebooting of the hormone networks, including restoration of regular menstrual cycles. This will mean redressing the balance between dancer behaviours around training and nutrition (Keay and Francis, 2019). The key is to fuel in a consistent way over the day. This means starting with the foundation of three regular meals a day with a portion of complex carbohydrates and protein. Examples of foods rich in protein are meat, fish, dairy products, along with vegetable-based sources. Examples of complex carbohydrate are bread, cereals, oats, rice, pasta and potatoes. I often find that dancers are hesitant about carbohydrates but remember that female hormones have a predilection to a consistent intake of complex carbohydrate.

For dancers it is really important to fuel around training. For example, always dance with some fuel on board; this may mean topping up with a banana or cereal bar between classes or rehearsals. Also make sure you are refuelling within 20 minutes of stopping dancing with a combination of carbohydrate and protein (a banana milk shake is ideal).

Dancer hormone story

Oriele was a dancer in her final year of pre-professional training and was hoping to win a contract with a company during audition season. She thought that by losing a bit of weight that this would improve her chances. The problem was that Oriele was already slim, so by restricting energy intake, this tipped her into low energy availability. She started to feel fatigued and her periods stopped. When I explained that restricting food intake was counterproductive to her dance performance, she started to relax her restrictive eating to align with what she was consuming beforehand. The first indication that Oriele had been successful in clearing her energy deficit was that she had a smile on her face. She also reported that she found it easier to pick up new choreography and apply corrections. Her periods also restored. I am pleased to report that Oriele went on to secure a contract with a professional dance company.

Act 2 Female hormones over your dance career

The choreography of menstrual cycle hormones does not stay the same over your life. These hormones will be quiescent during childhood. Things start ramping up moving into puberty, with physical changes occurring. This culminates in the start of menstrual cycles at the age of menarche. The average age of menarche is 12 years, although it can be a little later for dancers. Nevertheless, periods should have started by the age of 15 years. If not, this is called primary amenorrhoea and will need investigating to exclude any medical issues. If none are found, then the next step is to explore the balance of training and nutrition as the cause and to make any necessary adjustments.

   Why is it so important for periods to start by 15 years of age? Periods indicate that ovarian hormones are being produced. As discussed above, these hormones are essential for many aspects of health and performance. In particular, the attainment of strong, heathy bones is a prerequisite for dancers. As you can see from Figure 2.5, focusing on the upper curve, bone mineral density closely follows how oestradiol varies over our life. With menarche and the rapid increase in oestradiol, this is reflected by a big increase in bone

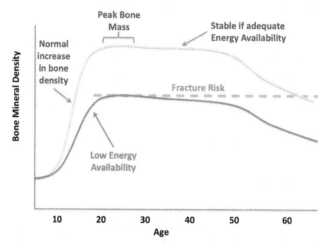

FIGURE 2.5   Impact of hormones on bone health with permission *Hormones, Health and Human Potential*, 2022, Keay

mineral density to reach peak bone mass (PBM) around about early twenties. Bone density then remains relatively stable, provided periods remain regular, until menopause around age 50, when the ovaries retire, and oestradiol levels drop. Bone mineral density declines in step with this fall in oestradiol.

The lower line (Figure 2.5) shows what happens to bone mineral density accrual if nutrition is insufficient to support the start of periods and associated increase in oestradiol. Attainment of PBM is stalled. This is the finding from a study of 87 dancers and non-dancer counterparts over three years (Keay et al., 2020). Those dancers in training who had delayed onset of menarche and/or disrupted periods maintained lower bone mineral density, particularly at the lumbar spine, compared to those who did not experience delayed menarche. In other words, although dancing is good for bone health, if this is not backed up with sufficient nutrition to support the start of regular periods, then this has a negative effect on bone health. This is of concern as it increases the risk of bone injury.

Pregnancy

Pregnancy is a time when female hormones change dramatically from the fluctuations of the menstrual cycle, to maintained steady high levels of both oestradiol and progesterone produced by the placenta. This temporarily turns off the production of pituitary hormones FSH and LH, as ovulation is not required. Relaxin is a hormone produced during pregnancy and post-partum and as the name suggests makes ligaments more pliable. For dancers this is important to remember as stretching should be limited to maintenance stretching. Don't be tempted to 'over-stretch' as this could result in injury. In general terms, in line with current guidance, you can keep dancing as long as you feel comfortable. Breast feeding is made possible by high levels of prolactin. High prolactin tends to turn off periods, which is why your periods may not resume while breast feeding. It is also important to remember that breast feeding is high energy and calcium demand. If you do go back to participating in class during this time, you need to be especially vigilant that you are eating sufficiently to cover all your energy demands.

Menopause

There are other hormone changes for the female dancer during her career. Although menopause is a natural physiological event that occurs during a woman's life, this can be challenging for dancers. Providing information about these hormone changes and giving dance specific advice on how to manage these is very important. All female dancers will experience menopause, which is when the ovaries retire from producing the main female hormones oestradiol and progesterone. Rather than the intricate choreography of the menstrual cycle hormones ovarian hormones remain at the monotone low levels and pituitary hormones FSH and LH at high levels.

Menopause is a point in time when the ovaries retire and after which the dancer will experience no further periods. The average age is 51 years of age, although menopause can occur anytime between 45 and 55 years of age. However, the menopause is not an on/off switch. There is a transition time called the perimenopause which typically starts from 40 years of age onwards. This is probably even more challenging than the menopause itself as during this time the menstrual cycle hormones start mistiming, effectively sometimes ahead or behind the 'music'. The tell-tale sign is shortening of cycle lengths. The period can also be variable in flow: sometimes heavy, sometimes light. Other potential symptoms are hot flushes, 'brain fog', new onset of headaches, digestive issues and aches and pains not related to injury.

Although a dancer may have retired from performing in many contexts of classical/theatrical dance, she may well have transitioned into the next phase of her dance career, which may be as a teacher. This is an important part of a dancer's career having built up experience and knowledge that she can impart to young dancers. However, the challenges of changes in hormones around menopause, whether this is physically, mentally, or a combination of all these factors, can mean that many women feel they cannot continue in their job. Fortunately, there are strategies to get the most from this phase of your life. As a dancer you will have weight bearing exercise covered. However, it is important to try and add in some specific strength work. The other important factors are nutrition and sleep. Making sure you are hitting protein requirements is particularly important to resist the tendency to lose muscle mass as hormones decline. Sleep is important as suboptimal sleep interferes with appetite regulation.

What about HRT? Unfortunately, there has in the past been a lot of misinformation about the risk of breast cancer, disseminated through the media. Although there is a slight increase in risk of breast cancer when taking HRT, this is the same as taking the combined contraceptive pill. It is a much lower risk compared to not following a healthy lifestyle in terms of exercise and nutrition. In fact, doing regular exercise reduces your risk of breast cancer (WHS, 2024. The main reason for taking HRT is to improve quality of life and mitigate the symptoms associated with menopause. There is also evidence that HRT reduces the risk of developing poor bone health and osteoporosis (British Menopause Society, 2022). This is an important consideration for many dancers, especially if you have previously experienced amenorrhoea. In a study of retired, premenopausal dancers I found for those dancers who had delayed menarche and/or amenorrhoea. This had a negative effect on bone mineral density (Keay et al., 1997).

As with hormonal contraception, it is every woman's personal choice whether to try HRT, or not. The most important thing is to make an informed choice, being aware of the pros and cons. I think it is also important to be realistic. HRT is not the elixir of youth. Nevertheless, it can make a big difference to your quality of life and long-term health to help you keep dancing. I often get asked when is best time to start HRT and what is the optimal form? The British Menopause Society advise that starting HRT as close as possible to the menopause is most effective. You can start taking HRT in perimenopause to synchronise with your cycle and help you ease into menopause and beyond. In terms of the top shelf type of HRT, this is comprised of oestradiol taken through the skin (patch or gel) combined with 'mild' micronised progesterone (soft capsule or can be taken vaginally). Unless you have had a hysterectomy, it is important to take both oestradiol and progesterone as the latter acts as endometrial protection. The other important practical point is to start at a low dose of oestradiol and gradually increase, if required. It is possible to have too much of a good thing!

Conclusions

A female dancer's hormones are a complete performance during her life. There can be challenges along the way to overcome. This is why continuing support for hormone health throughout a dancer's career is vital. Building networks and information hubs for dancers will contribute to improving and optimising female dancer hormone health throughout her life.

References

British Menopause Society (2022). Prevention and treatment of osteoporosis in post menopausal women. Retrieved February 11, 2024 from https://thebms.org.uk/publications/consensus-statements/prevention-and-treatment-of-osteoporosis-in-women/

Gordon, C. M., Ackerman, K. E., Berga, S. L., Kaplan, J. R., Mastorakos, G., Misra, M., Murad, M. H., Santoro, N. F. & Warren, M. P. (2017). Functional hypothalamic amenorrhea: An Endocrine Society clinical practice guideline. *The Journal of Clinical Endocrinology and Metabolism, 102*(5), 1413–1439. https://doi.org/10.1210/jc.2017-00131

Keay, N. (1998). Dancing through adolescence. *British Journal of Sports Medicine, 32*(3), 196–197. https://doi.org/10.1136/bjsm.32.3.196

Keay, N. (2000). The modifiable factors affecting bone mineral accumulation in girls: the paradoxical effect of exercise on bone. *Nutrition Bulletin,* 219–222. http://dx.doi.org/10.1046/j.1467-3010.2000.00051.x

Keay, N. (2022). *Hormone, health and human potential.* Sequoia Books.

Keay, N., Fogelman, I., & Blake, G. (1997). Bone mineral density in professional female dancers. *British Journal of Sports Medicine, 31*(2), 143–147. https://doi.org/10.1136/bjsm.31.2.143

Keay, N., & Francis, G. (2019). Infographic. Energy availability: Concept, control and consequences in relative energy deficiency in sport (RED-S). *British Journal of Sports and Exercise Medicine, 53,*1310–1311.

Keay, N., Lanfear, M. & Francis, G (2021). Clinical application of interactive monitoring of indicators of health in professional dancers. *J Forensic Biomech.* 12(5). http://dx.doi.org/10.1101/2021.09.25.21263895

Keay, N., Overseas, A. & Francis, G. (2020). Indicators and correlates of low energy availability in male and female dancers. *BMJ open sport & exercise medicine*, 6(1), e000906. https://doi.org/10.1136/bmjsem-2020-000906

Keay, N., & Rankin, A. (2019). Infographic. Relative energy deficiency in sport: an infographic guide. *British Journal of Sports Medicine*, 53(20), 1307–1309. https://doi.org/10.1136/bjsports-2018-100354

Kim, S. D. (2019). Yoga for menstrual pain in primary dysmenorrhea: A meta-analysis of randomized controlled trials. *Complementary therapies in clinical practice*, 36, 94–99. https://doi.org/10.1016/j.ctcp.2019.06.006

Lebrun, C. M., Joyce, S. M. & Constantini, N. W. (2020). Effects of female reproductive hormones on sports performance. In A. Hackney & N. Constantini (Eds.), *Endocrinology of physical activity and sport. Contemporary endocrinology* (pp. 286–289). Humana. https://doi.org/10.1007/978-3-030-33376-8_16

Mountjoy, M., Ackerman, K. E., Bailey, D. M., Burke, L. M., Constantini, N., Hackney, A. C., Heikura, I. A., Melin, A., Pensgaard, A. M., Stellingwerff, T., Sundgot-Borgen, J. K., Torstveit, M. K., Jacobsen, A. U., Verhagen, E., Budgett, R., Engebretsen, L. & Erdener, U. (2023). 2023 International Olympic Committee's (IOC) consensus statement on Relative Energy Deficiency in Sport (REDs). *British journal of sports medicine*, 57(17), 1073–1097. https://doi.org/10.1136/bjsports-2023-106994

Womens' Health Concern. (2017). Understanding the risks of breast cancer. Retrieved February 11, 2024 from https://www.womens-health-concern.org/wp-content/uploads/2019/10/WHC-UnderstandingRisksofBreastCancer-MARCH2017.pdf

3

FEMALE DANCERS

Food, nutrients and body composition

Jasmine Challis

Female dancers and food

Sharing nutritious food, that tastes great, with friends/supportive family is one of the experiences which many humans, globally, enjoy and gain so much more from the experience than just the nutrients the food supplies. Food is core to human existence: it is as essential as the air we breathe and the water we drink. Along with its role as fuel, there are additional, sometimes complicated, aspects of the human relationship with food: the social and, more particularly, the psychological aspects. Socially food can be used to bring people together, as well as to celebrate. Neither of these is necessarily different across the sexes. There are team meals after matches for footballers, whether male or female, and dance companies, particularly on tour, may eat together, as may groups of students in training. But even in one meal and one day we can see differences between the sexes starting to emerge: males on average undertaking similar levels of activity will have higher energy (from carbohydrate and fat) requirements than females (Redman et al., 2014). Here, and throughout this chapter female and male are used in a biological sense. The estimated average requirement for energy (kcal) for active men ranges from 2800–3000kcal per day, depending on age, whereas for active females the equivalent value is 2300–2400kcal per day (Scientific Advisory Committee on Nutrition, 2012). As an average some will need more and some less, but the sex difference is notable. Protein intakes are currently based on body weight, so are individual but comparable for males and females. For micronutrients it is a little more complex. While for some micronutrients the guideline amount is proportional to energy intake such as with some B vitamins, for many other micronutrients the recommendations for females are no

DOI: 10.4324/9781003382874-5

different from males. There are a smaller number, for example iron, where the requirement for females is higher than for males, yet in a lower energy intake, meaning the diet for a female dancer needs to be more nutrient dense. This is discussed in more detail shortly.

Females are at higher risk of experiencing eating disorders and disordered eating (Sweeting et al., 2015). The relationship of female dancers to food and nutrition is very individual; some dancers have a great relationship with food, while others experience disordered eating or eating disorders. Males are not exempt, but the risk is lower, though exact statistics for any country are hard to come by, particularly for disordered eating, as this condition covers a wide spectrum of distress related to food, and all sufferers may struggle to get recognition and support.

The attitudes to male and female nutrition 'fuelling' are historically and sadly still not consistently identical. This is not to say that female and male nutritional requirements are identical; as mentioned above they are not, and there will also be a range of requirements within each biological group. For males there are fewer parameters that will alter requirements within an age group. If body composition and activity are known in males, there are currently no other considerations unless there is any physical disability that could increase or decrease metabolic requirements.

Male hormone levels do not fluctuate significantly on a regular basis unlike those in many females. The consequences of hormonal fluctuations in females can impact on nutritional requirements, such as the need to replace iron lost in menstruation. There can also be impacts on appetite from fluctuating hormone levels in females, with changes in food preferences and appetite in the pre-menstrual days being well-recognised for many females. Others notice differences in appetite at other points in the cycle, such as ovulation. There is a lack of robust data looking at energy use and appetite over the menstrual cycle, and a review paper by Hackney (2021) concludes that more research is required. Hackney (2021) raises the challenges of making sure menstrual cycle data is accurate, as even within females with regular cycles there can be shifts in the phase length of cycles, linked with hormone levels, and these hormones may impact on appetite and energy levels. Assumptions on where a female dancer may be in her cycle without verifying will not allow accurate conclusions regarding energy needs/appetite to be drawn. Hunger fluctuations may be more linked to the physiology of what is happening within the uterus, while hormone levels may drive appetite in a different rhythm. These nutritional and appetite variations are separate to the complex relationships dancers, particularly females, can have with food, nutrition and body image. As mentioned above males will also experience different relationships with food and food intake, also with body image, but the risk of negative consequences from this are recognised as lower.

Nutrient requirements

Requirements for female athletes and dancers are currently under-researched as most sport nutrition research has been carried out in male athletes. There is a recognition now in discussions in conferences and media of the need to address this, despite the additional methodological challenges of working with females due to hormonal variations. These challenges include consideration of the impact of the use of hormonal contraception during fertile years and hormone replacement therapy (HRT) when natural hormone levels drop due to menopause (or other situations where female hormones are not at levels to support wellbeing) as well as the changes seen in pregnancy and lactation, and pre-post-menopausal differences. For some nutrients the recommended intakes will be very similar, if not identical, for all female dancers regardless of their hormonal status. For other nutrients there will be ranges that may overlap for females (across all phases of the lifecycle) and males. Pregnancy brings a number of changes to food and nutrition: before pregnancy and into early pregnancy females are advised by national bodies such as the National Health Service (NHS) in the UK, the Centers for Disease Control and Prevention (CDC) in the USA and Healthdirect in Australia to take additional folic acid (to reduce the risk of neural tube defects—spina bifida). In pregnancy there are also a number of foods that are not advisable, such as unpasteurised milk and products made from it, liver, raw fish and raw shellfish sometimes made more complicated by nausea (particularly in early pregnancy) and heartburn (later in pregnancy).

Nutrients of concern to the female dancer

Energy, derived from carbohydrates and fats, together with that contributed by protein, is needed on a daily basis, to allow the body to function optimally. Energy requirements are influenced by body muscle content, so females, with a need for higher body fat content, typically require less energy than a male at the same height and weight. The challenge for female dancers is to achieve a more nutrient dense diet than that required by men, as most countries recommend an iron intake for women of at least 150% of that needed by men. Iron is a nutrient that is hard to absorb; the Australian nutrition guidelines include the following statement about iron absorption: 'Absorption is about 18% from a mixed western diet including animal foods and about 10% from a vegetarian diet' (Australian Government, 2013). The recommendations for calcium, phosphorous, iodine and copper (and selenium in the USA and Canada) are mostly the same for adult males and females. In Australia, the USA and Canada a higher intake of calcium is advised for women from the age of 51 years, while recommendations for zinc intake (and selenium in the UK) are proportionately lower than for the male population. As dairy foods, such as milk, cheese and yoghurt are major suppliers of calcium, phosphorus and iodine in the average diet, those who don't include these foods, using plant-based alternatives, need to consider how well their alternative has been fortified, and whether supplements may be needed.

As well as having an adequate energy intake per 24 hours, the timing of this over the day is now thought to be potentially important in sustaining normal hormone levels (Mountjoy et al., 2023). This applies to both males and females, but as mentioned above females are identified as being at higher risk of disordered eating and eating disorders (Culbert et al., 2021), and along with this can go a fear of gaining body fat, resulting in restricted energy intake. Distributing the energy from an adequate total intake in meals and snacks over the waking hours is being increasingly recognised as being helpful to signal to the body that all is well and normal hormonal levels can be maintained. This adequate intake will itself not be an identical amount every day. Energy needs in particular, together with protein and some B vitamins and minerals (for example those lost in sweat) will vary primarily with dance and other exercise/activity levels, and consideration needs to be added for female hormonal/physical status, such as pregnancy, and goals of training such as strength gain.

Despite the variations in nutrient requirements across the female dancer's life, common sense, and science, would suggest that, as highly active people/athletes, there should be equal focus on the 'need for fuel' for both sexes. When one hears reports of a paper left after a nutrition class in an elite dance school saying 'girls—eating is cheating' this is disturbing at many levels. Food is fuel, enjoyable fuel yes, but remains so much more complicated for many in the dance world.

It is not acceptable to convey messages to any dancer that they should not be fuelling their body appropriately. The body has complex systems to ensure it remains in energy balance, neither too much nor too little energy, over time, and restricting intake disrupts this in the short term, and brings risks of not meeting requirements for micronutrients such as iron, calcium and B vitamins. Any deficiency can impact on health, wellbeing and performance. There are no foods which are absolutely 'good' or 'bad', and any messages conveying this are ignoring the complexity of human food and nutrition. No one can live on only vegetables or fruit, for example, without soon becoming unwell, just as living exclusively on cake or biscuits will result in nutritional deficiencies. Female dancers will do well to focus on nutrient dense foods as energy requirements are lower, but this does not entail restricting intake. A balanced diet for female dancers will include all food groups, with no food being banned, more a need to consider the amounts and frequency foods are eaten over days/weeks when considering what makes up an appropriate diet for a female dancer. The human body, when given the range of nutrients it needs will signal to the brain when nutrient needs are met. Satiety and satiation are complex mechanisms which respectively allow us to know when we have eaten enough at a meal, and when the time to eat/re-fuel has arrived. Unfortunately, the intense nature of most dancer training schedules mean that food is fitted into often short, and possibly not regular, time slots, which make responding to appetite more of a challenge.

Food groups are often referred to as 'protein' 'carbohydrates' and 'fats' and separately 'fruits and vegetables' but this is an over-simplification. Foods rich in protein will also supply micronutrients while foods designated as 'carbohydrates' contain a variety of other nutrients: grains, for example the wheat or rye found in bread or pasta supply some protein, as do oats and barley, and each of these will also supply some B group vitamins and minerals. The wholegrain varieties will provide the greatest range of additional nutrients, though some more refined (white) varieties have micronutrients added. Potatoes are a good source of vitamin C and potassium while sweet potatoes are rich in vitamin A and potassium. While we do not need fats in the quantities we do for carbohydrates and protein rich foods, fats are essential, and small amounts in every meal will help fat soluble vitamin absorption, as well as also being important for satiety and satiation, so hunger doesn't kick in too quickly between meals. Fruit, salad and vegetables are great sources of many micronutrients and fibre (needed for healthy bowels) and a good portion of one or more of these at meals will contribute to the sense of satiety experienced after meals which contain a good balance of nutrients—and also taste good. While we can survive perfectly well on meals which 'tick the boxes' for nutrients but perhaps are prepared in a way that means taste isn't great, which is necessary when there is no alternative, it is unhelpful for wellbeing to deliberately choose foods which aren't enjoyable, as this can increase the risk of cravings and over-eating on the normally 'forbidden' foods at times.

Body composition

Let us think now about body characteristics in dance, and whether there are limitations for female dancers with particular body characteristics. If we look at sport, we see that some sports such as rowing, boxing and powerlifting have weight categories: the aim is to provide more of a level playing field, as athletes with more muscle and those who are taller will potentially have an advantage of either range of movement and/or strength/power. Interestingly fencing, although a combat sport, has no weight categories as experience has shown that any body type has the potential to be successful with the right training. Although dance may involve partner work, there are no weight categories, and anecdotally when one partner has to lift another, the weight of the lifted dancer is not a reliable indicator of how challenging a specific lift may be. Height may be relevant; research to date suggests that injuries from lifts mainly occur due to poor biomechanics (LaFortune, 2008) rather than weight but there is a lack of specific research on different types and demands of lifts in dance to substantiate this.

In many other sports there are advantages to having specific characteristics; for example in basketball height is recognised as an advantage. In general, height offers advantages in many sports, though not in those linked to horse riding: in horseracing the weight categories and handicap system require jockeys to be at lower than average weights, and the consequences are that unhealthy weight management strategies are used by many jockeys. In dance, as with fencing while being taller or shorter than average will bring advantages in performing specific steps, there will also be challenges. Some choreography will be more challenging for the taller dancer—where long limbs can be a disadvantage especially when movements need to fit into fast music—other choreography will be harder for the shorter dancer to perform with the same extension as a tall dancer will. There is no perfect body, and everybody has challenges to their physique, which can include flexibility in one or more areas of the body, strength, stamina and proprioception.

Breaking was included for the first time for both men and women at the 2024 Olympic Games, providing a further link between sport and dance, at an extremely high level. Human bodies are amazing, and dance can be enjoyed by different body types, and abilities. Ask yourself whether the dancer(s) you most enjoy watching are those with a specific body type, or whether there is more to a dance performance. Certainly, there is scope for a dancer to perform well whether they have a smaller or bigger body. It is not healthy to be below natural body size, and while many dancers have restricted their food intake to sustain a smaller physique, there are significant health consequences with reduced food intake on the mind and body. At high body weights there may be challenges to undertaking some choreography—there may be a point where partner work involves a lift that is above the available partners' strength/power, even if they are well trained. This is very different to the issues which have been in the media, of dancers being given feedback that they are 'too big' either in absolute terms, or, very specifically, for costumes.

Dancers need costumes that fit them: for this, measurements are needed, and it would seem most appropriate to have a working dialogue between those who will be making costumes and those wearing them. Ideally costumes will be made from fabrics with some 'give' in. Where costumes need to be made from materials which have limited ability to adapt to slight changes in body shape then it is advisable to have liaison between the costumes team and the dancers to discuss, and where necessary find the best solutions. Bodies can and do change shape over time, for many reasons, including changing training regimes, pregnancy, after childbirth, and the fluctuations in body water and bloating that can occur over a female menstrual cycle. Anecdotally it can happen that, rather than clothing which is objectively too small being perceived in this way, instead a dancer may feel that they themselves are 'too big'. This can contribute to disordered eating behaviour and mental distress. If a dancer is experiencing this then the support to examine these views and find ways to manage this situation would be beneficial.

While measurements are necessary to create costumes, the need to weigh any adult dancer must be questioned. Weight is not a marker of strength or technique, nor an indicator of body shape. Two dancers of the same height and weight can be very different in appearance and ability. Weight monitoring can be necessary is some medical situations, but it should be undertaken by medical staff rather than dance staff. Different dance genres have variable amounts of focus on weight/shape. In urban styles, contemporary and most national dances there is less focus and/or criticism around body shape that is more seen in ballet, and sometimes in ballroom, Latin and musical theatre, but there is work to be done across the dance world to ensure that feedback to dancers is constructive and appropriate—looking at skills and technique rather than criticising body composition.

Both male and female dancers are subjected to scrutiny of their bodies, typically in clothing designed to make assessment of dance technique as easy as possible as well as to allow effective movement. In some areas of sport there has been a recent move away from some clothing that females have felt uncomfortable wearing when it has been noticeably skimpier than that of males. In dance this varies, with ballet dancewear being revealing for both sexes but the lack of choice, notable more in some dance genres than others, contributes to the lack of control which is recognised to exist in dance. Where leotards are the norm, those females with large breasts may find that while they can access leotards with inbuilt bras, or wear a sports bra under some styles of leotard, if they are required to wear a costume not of their own design this support may be lacking, which is uncomfortable and undesirable for breast tissue at times. Anecdotally dancers have undergone breast reductions to minimise this issue, which is a drastic solution to a situation where the body is healthy but perceived as inappropriately shaped.

There are many areas within dance where dancers have less control over their lives than many of their peers and this includes rigid training programmes and then often uncertainty in career pathways. These impact on both males and females of course, but females are at increased risk of disordered eating. The adolescent period, where growth spurts can vary both in age of initiation and duration, and the changes that occur in females in particular with increases in body fat levels brings challenges to accepting body image, particularly for early and late maturers with regard to looking different from many of their peer group (Mitchell et al., 2020). Where lower weight dancers are given more prestigious roles in performances there is a risk of their peers feeling that losing weight is necessary to further their career. Research problematising weight loss diets in relation to increased risks of eating disorders is available (Polivy, 1996; Memon et al., 2020) and I suggest that dancers seeking to lose weight do so only through consultation with a health care professional, if possible one specialising in eating disorders. In contrast for male dancers, with a focus on strength and athletic ability, there is more of a perception that being 'strong and powerful, as well as flexible'—having a bigger frame, bigger muscles—is more of the physical attribute that will accelerate their career. The predominant shape for male dancers does change, from slimmer/leaner to more musculature, but in general there is much less pressure that might result in a restricted dietary intake.

Power, control and the impact on the dancer

Dancers spend their lives being scrutinised and criticised—though in more supportive environments this 'criticism' is provided in very constructive and collaborative ways. However, abuse can happen, and has happened. With regard to the impact on dancers' wellbeing, abuse is recognised as a trigger for disordered eating and eating disorders. Cordes et al. (2021) noted that homosexual men prefer a more muscular body image, and research investigating whether this impacts on their judgement of female bodies is needed, as well as what this means for the treatment of male dancers. There is potential that a homosexual male in the position of choreographer, director, while having the ability to professionally evaluate technique and dance interpretation may inadvertently look for and reward a more boy-like/less adult woman body. Disordered eating and eating disorders usually result from a genetic predisposition, combined with a perfectionistic hard-working personality, potentially also impacted by trauma, that finds control or use of food allows management of negative emotions, including those around lack of control (Barakat et al., 2023). Paying attention to supporting dancers in training to find constructive ways to manage what is a challenging training and career will minimise the risk to both males and females of developing disordered eating and eating disorders. As the risk is higher in females, and experientially and anecdotally numbers of females are greater than males other than in elite vocational ballet schools where equal numbers are selected, then the impact will be more significant in the female population.

With Relative Energy Deficiency in sport (REDs) being a concern for the female dance population, what can dancers and dance teachers do to support fuelling the female dancer body adequately? Identification of situations where dancers will be at increased risk of under-fuelling is a useful start. Ensuring staff and/or management have training and support in identification of REDs and disordered eating issues, and there is a clear pathway to signpost those dancers needing support will provide a clear framework where there can be avoidance of shame, and a focus on minimising the risk to health and the return to full dance as smoothly as possible, reducing the cost at both personal and financial level.

Red flags for dancers and teachers—it's not always about being underweight

What are signs for dancers to look out for which suggest that getting support at an early stage would be helpful to avoid the development of an eating disorder?

1. An over-focus on weight and shape: for example, weighing themselves daily or more often and experiencing unhelpful thoughts about self-worth, skills and abilities based on the number on the scales.
2. An over-focus on food, feeling the need to restrict food intake, rather than being able to meet requirements with a wide variety of foods.
3. No longer being able to join in social situations that involve food and experience the food on offer.
4. Over-exercising, either within dance, or undertaking amounts of exercise outside dance that is done to increase the sense of control rather than to benefit wellbeing. This could include rigidity with steps to walk daily, or timing/distances run.

Teachers are likely to pick up on some of these situations, and in addition, they may well be able to see fluctuating or unexpectedly low energy levels, rapid, temporary, changes in body shape (due to shifts in fluid), lower mood and lower concentration. More frequent illness or injury can have many different causes other than under-fuelling or eating issues. These causes would include the impact of stress on the body which could be the consequence of challenges in life, such as family situation or financial constraints, poor diet due to unintentional poor choices (possibly linked to reduced appetite) or tiredness (which itself can have many causes).

While a clear route to support for those who are experiencing disordered eating/eating disorders/REDs is necessary, there are further areas to consider. One important aspect is that unhealthy eating, where dancers are deliberately making choices not to fuel their body adequately, is neither encouraged, nor normalised. Creating time for refuelling in the schedule for dancers—whether students or teachers in the case of those in training—is one constructive way to give a clear message that nutrition is valued. Along with this, supporting adequate rest and recovery will give the message these are also valued. Ensuring education is provided that reminds female dancers that, where expected, regular periods are the goal, rather than irregular or no periods, is another positive message that supports female dancer health.

What can dancers themselves do to support a healthy relationship with food?

1. Be mindful of psychological wellbeing. If mental health is less good seek professional support for this.
2. Notice any changes in their relationship with food, and seek professional support if food starts to be restricted or used to try and manage emotions.
3. Eat enough of a variety of foods and eat with others regularly if possible. Remember no one food is either good or bad.
4. Seek professional advice before trying to change weight, as weight loss diets can precipitate disordered eating in some individuals.
5. Be aware of their relationship with exercise. If exercise starts to have a compulsive element to it, seek professional support to manage this.

Case study

This composite case study from my professional experience within clinical practice is an amalgamation of dancers; all identifying features have been removed, so while it reflects lived experience it does not pertain to one person. It reflects a situation which can easily be dismissed as not being a serious problem, which does disservice to the suffering disordered eating and eating disorders can bring, and the outcomes that can be possible.

A dance student we will refer to as Sophia is halfway through the first year of her dance degree, aged 18. Teachers have raised concerns to the counselling section of student services, as Sophia is looking tired, and her concentration appears to be variable in classes. Her attendance has become more erratic. She seems less happy than she had been at the beginning of the academic year. In dance classes she has been noted to be 'body checking'—pinching areas of her body such as thighs and abdomen, and looking in the mirror more than other students. Teachers feel she may have gained some weight, but so have a few other students in the year, and weight gain moving away from home is not unusual.

The dance faculty has formulated a support system where students of concern are referred to student services. Sophia is invited to a meeting, where welfare staff explain that teaching staff are concerned for her wellbeing. Sophia becomes very upset, and after initially claiming that she is 'fine', does open up that she feels she is not in control of her food. She is trying to control her weight by dieting, and eats little during the day, but in the evenings in her room she often binges on snack food. She feels unwell after this and her sleep is poor. In class all she can think about is how big she is, and about food, as she is very hungry most of the day. Her mum, who is very slim, tells Sophia she needs to use more self-control when they talk about this. Sophia asks if she can get appetite suppressants to help her lose weight. The welfare team advise her to see her GP, who will be able to assess whether there is a need for psychiatric support and/or medication. They arrange, with Sophia's agreement, for her to start counselling with a therapist qualified and experienced in eating disorders treatment. They also arrange, again with Sophia's agreement, for her to see a specialist dietitian who works both with dancers and those with eating disorders, after Sophia has had a few counselling sessions. The dietitian explains to Sophia that binges are a very normal consequence of extreme dieting while being very active, explores with her what her body needs and why, and formulates a meal plan that will allow Sophia to meet her nutritional needs—any attempt to lose weight will almost certainly either perpetuate the binges or possibly precipitate a slide into a restrictive eating disorder.

A review with the dietitian four weeks after the initial meeting, with ongoing weekly therapy/counselling, finds Sophia much more confident in her eating plan, enjoying dance and academic classes and time with her friends again. There have been challenges and she has not kept to the plan 100%, but she is able to see that when she does her energy, mood and wellbeing benefit. Counselling will continue as needed for more weeks. Sophia was advised to keep to the stabilising meal plan for at least the next year and seek further advice before any potential attempts at weight loss, to review in the first instance the necessity for this. The cessation of binges will stop weight gain, and greater energy from regular nutrition will allow her to benefit optimally from her training. Once her relationship with food is healthier, Sophia can, in time, move to intuitive eating, neither restricting nor binging which is likely to allow her body to find its own natural body composition.

Conclusion

Food intake and body composition in female dancers can be impacted by many factors. Some of these can, at first glance, appear to be unrelated to these areas of health and can potentially be overlooked. Consideration of these varied factors in a compassionate way is useful to wellbeing. The nutritional needs of the female dancer are different from those of the male dancer, and can vary over the dancer's training and performing years. Meeting physiological nutritional needs without these being compromised by using food in response to psychological pressures is the goal for the healthy dancer. If the female dancer struggles with a healthy relationship with food and their body, support to establish better patterns is available and access is encouraged.

References

Australian Government (2013) Australian dietary guidelines: Providing the scientific evidence for healthier Australian diets, Eat For Health, National Health and Medical Research Council: Australian Government, https://www.eatforhealth.gov.au/guidelines

Barakat, S., McLean, S. A., Bryant, E., Le, A., Marks, P., Touyz, S. & Maguire, S. (2023). Risk factors for eating disorders: Findings from a rapid review. *Journal of Eating Disorders, 11*(1), 8. http://dx.doi.org/10.1186/s40337-022-00671-1

Cordes, M., Vicks, S. & Hartmann, A. S. (2021). Appearance-related partner preferences and body image in a German sample of homosexual and heterosexual women and Men. *Archives of Sexual Behavior, 50*(8), 3575–3586. https://doi.org/10.1007/s10508-021-02087-5

Culbert, K. M., Sisk, C. L. & Klump, K. L. (2021). A narrative review of sex differences in eating disorders: Is there a biological basis? *Clinical Gherapeutics, 43*(1), 95–111. https://doi.org/10.1016/j.clinthera.2020.12.003

Hackney, A. C. (2021). Menstrual cycle hormonal changes and energy substrate metabolism in exercising women: A perspective. *International Journal of Environmental Research and Public Health, 18*(19), 10024. https://doi.org/10.3390/ijerph181910024

LaFortune, S. (2008). A classification of lifts in dance: Terminology and biomechanical principles. *Journal of Dance Education, 8*(1), 13–22. https://doi.org/10.1080/15290824.2008.10387354

Memon, A. N., Gowda, A. S., Rallabhandi, B., Bidika, E., Fayyaz, H., Salib, M. & Cancarevic, I. (2020). Have our attempts to curb obesity done more harm than good? *Cureus, 12*(9), e10275. https://doi.org/10.7759/cureus.10275

Mitchell, S. B., Haase, A. M. & Cumming, S. P. (2020). Experiences of delayed maturation in female vocational ballet students: An interpretative phenomenological analysis. *Journal of Adolescence, 80*, 233–241. http://dx.doi.org/10.1016/j.adolescence.2020.03.005

Mountjoy, M., Ackerman, K. E., Bailey, D. M., Burke, L. M., Constantini, N., Hackney, A. C., Heikura, I. A., Melin, A., Pensgaard, A. M., Stellingwerff, T., Sundgot-Borgen, J. K., Torstveit, M. K., Jacobsen, A. U., Verhagen, E., Budgett, R., Engebretsen, L. & Erdener, U. (2023). 2023 International Olympic Committee's (IOC) consensus statement on relative energy deficiency in Sport (REDs). *British Journal of Sports Medicine, 57*(17), 1073–1097. https://doi.org/10.1136/bjsports-2023-106994

Polivy, J. (1996). Psychological consequences of food restriction. *Journal of the American dietetic association, 96*(6), 589–592. http://dx.doi.org/10.1016/s0002-8223(96)00161-7

Redman, L. M., Kraus, W. E., Bhapkar, M., Das, S. K., Racette, S. B., Martin, C. K., Fontana, L., Wong, W. W., Roberts, S. B., Ravussin, E. & CALERIE Study Group (2014). Energy requirements in nonobese men and women: Results from CALERIE. *The American Journal of Clinical Nutrition, 99*(1), 71–78. https://doi.org/10.3945/ajcn.113.065631

Scientific Advisory Committee on Nutrition. (2012). *Dietary reference values for energy*. The Stationery Office.

Sweeting, H., Walker, L., MacLean, A., Patterson, C., Räisänen, U. & Hunt, K. (2015). Prevalence of eating disorders in males: A review of rates reported in academic research and UK mass media. *International Journal of Men's Health, 14*(2), 10. 3149/jmh.1402.86. https://doi.org/10.3149/jmh.1402.86

4

BALLET CULTURE AND BODY IMAGE IN RECREATIONAL DANCE TRAINING

Rebekah Wall

Introduction

This chapter will explore and question how young female-identifying dancers' body image is affected by taking ballet class in recreational settings. The chapter is presented in two halves: section 1 will focus on giving a contextual overview of the professional ballet world, exploring the origins of the 'ballet body' culture and how it has developed. Section 2 will focus on my personal experiences of body image perception as a female recreational ballet dancer. In this section, some of the research presented will be taken from memories of my own experiences in class. Through an autoethnographic approach, this chapter will share my insight on this culture within ballet, from a young age. In addition, the chapter will discuss how this culture seen in top ballet companies and schools (Schultz, 2020), has become present within extra-curricular ballet classes. It will also explore ways young dancers can access information on the 'ballet body' (Klapper, 2020).

To date, there is little research that explores the recreational ballet dancer (Clark & Markula, 2017). A recreational dancer is someone who chooses to take dance classes as an extra-curricular activity. While some have the intention of continuing their training professionally, many students attend these classes as a hobby (Klapper, 2020). I have been taking recreational ballet classes since the age of two and chose to continue my dance training further at university. Although I was not training to become a professional in ballet, I continued to take ballet classes both as a part of my degree, and the student led society ballet classes. It is from these experiences that I have collected qualitative data for this research, referencing personal journal entries and reflecting on memories of my experiences of body image.

DOI: 10.4324/9781003382874-6

To research this topic, it is important to form a clear understanding of what the term 'body image' means. An explanation by Alexias and Dimitripoulou states, 'The term 'body image' describes the visual idea-view of a person concerning his/her body' (2011, p. 98). This suggests that body image is the term used to describe how one thinks about their body and therefore, is an internalised experience. This could also imply that it may be difficult to research this topic, as it could encounter ethical concerns, as well as relying on potential participants being very open and honest with the researcher. This is another reason that the personal reflections in section 2 of this chapter are from my own experiences.

What is a 'ballet body' in the professional ballet world?

The 'ballet body' has been recognised by dancers and researchers alike (Aalten, 2007). However, what the ballet body is and what it looks like does not have a straightforward answer. Peter Boal, Artistic Director of Pacific Northwest Ballet stated in an interview with *Pointe* magazine, 'body types do change in ballet' (Boal, 2011, p. 4). This suggests there is not one 'ballet body', but an ever-changing cycle of varying 'ballet bodies'. Aalten (2007) explains the 'ballet body' is 'presented to a dancer by her teachers, ballet masters and choreographers. This ideal body has a specific form and the ability to perform specific movements endlessly and with ease' (Aalten, 2007, p. 113). The perspective of Aalten (2007) puts blame on the leaders of ballet within the professional world implying the requirement for a specific body type comes from the top of the hierarchy. Therefore, the dancers are not in control of their own appearance. In a research paper studying young ballet dancers' ideas of their bodies, Pickard adds; 'the field of ballet and schools then produce and reproduce a particular bodily aesthetic according to demand' (2013, p. 7). This 'demand' (2013) could refer to an appearance desired by top ballet companies at a given time. Consequently, this suggests there is not a specific body type that defines 'ballet body' but it is a trend set by leading choreographers and company directors. This could influence the way students view their body, and each generation has slight differences in the body goal. So, to revert to the question, 'what is a ballet body?', it is whatever those with the most power in the ballet world want it to be.

At the beginning of the 20th century, many famous dancers, such as A. Mathilde Kschessinska, were visibly muscular, with wider hips and typical 'womanly' figures (Schultz, 2020). This opposed what choreographer, and founder of the New York City Ballet School, George Balanchine was seeking in his dancers during the mid-20th century (Schultz, 2020). Balanchine created a specific aesthetic requirement for his dancers, a key element being extreme thinness (Seibert, 2005). Balanchine normalised protruding bones and ribs, as well as going to extreme lengths to achieve such looks (Kiem,

2014). The Balanchine body ideal may be continuing to influence modern ideals. When in conversation about the impact height and weight has on the casting of dancers with *Pointe* magazine Boal (2011) shares:

> We were looking for pinheads. Which I suppose accentuates what Balanchine was looking for: length—length of leg, length of arm, length of neck, which goes right through to smaller heads.
>
> *(Boal, 2011, p. 4)*

To further this point, the Balanchine 'ballet body' aesthetic has become a key association with ballet. Rocher Barnes (2022) explains in their work entitled 'The Unconventional Ballet Body in the 21st Century';

> By the traditional ballet body, I refer to the white, thin, long-legged, narrow hips and able body of the female dancer, a description drawn from ethereal images of fairies and sylphs and later idealised in Balanchine's aesthetic.
>
> *(Rocher Barnes, 2022, p. 2)*

The latest 'ballet body' aesthetic can be easily accessed by students and teachers through means such as publications and social media (Ritenburg, 2010). Ritenburg concluded that a specific body type became recognisable of principal dancers in the New York City Ballet and 'continues to be normalised through references in a range of popular magazines and through images and written text of children's books about ballet' (2010, p. 71). A specific example of media encouraging a certain body type for ballet dancers is Warren's (1989) 'Classical Ballet Technique'. This publication contains a chapter entitled 'The ideal body structure and proportions for classical ballet dancers' which appears to set out some clear rules regarding what a ballet body can and cannot be. Warren states, 'It is never acceptable to be overweight,' and 'plastic surgery can make oversized bosoms smaller' (Warren, 1989, p. 64).

Quotes such as these being in the same publication that focuses on the technique of ballet could be seen to draw parallels between the two; it is implied that without the ideal ballet body you cannot participate in the technique. To enhance this, the publication features a labelled diagram of a young female who the author believes has all the attributes of a perfect ballet dancer (Warren, 1989, p. 66). With this visual evidence available for anyone to view, recreational dancers can see what is deemed 'ideal' and compare their own body to the image. This could lead to the development of a negative perception of their body. It is important to recognise the age of this publication, however it is still accessible to this day, and the body type specified in this book is the most common body type seen in media being released in this age (Rocher Barnes, 2022). Overall, this could suggest that dancers are being shown a specific body type, and skin colour, from an early age, and it is reinforced as they are exposed to new media. By seeing one body type consistently being referred to as right for ballet, dancers may begin questioning their own body image (Ritenburg, 2010).

Qualitative studies that explore a dancer's experience with body image give insight into how the Balanchine body aesthetic has resulted in negative attitudes towards oneself. When interviewing female college dancers, Reel et al. (2005) reported that many students had increased anxiety about their appearance and felt they should lose weight to be a dancer.

There has been conversation in recent years addressing the issues of body image in professional ballet dancers, and what can be done to shift this dynamic. In an article written by Henderson (2021) for *Dance Magazine* entitled 'What would it take to change Ballet's aesthetic of extreme thinness?', each point made appears to have a common theme, lack of scientific research. Many of the 'rules' of ballet are myths that have been passed down through company directors and choreographers (Henderson, 2021). Dance science research disproves many of the reasons given for female dancers to be extremely thin (Henderson, 2021). A dancer's body must not be seen as a prop to hold a desired aesthetic. It should be seen as an athlete's body, with strong muscles which allow them to perform safely (Henderson, 2021).

Personal experiences

When analysing my own experiences, I suddenly became aware of several consistent habits I have which impact my performance when taking ballet classes; caused by my perception of my body. I must note my position in this research; the period I am reflecting on took place during my teenage years. This is important to add as this may have an impact on why I had been perceiving my body in such ways. According to Huebscher (2010) hormonal differences, family issues during development and media exposure can all have negative effects on teenage girls' self-esteem, thus causing a negative perception of the body. Though relevant, my autoethnographic research suggests influences of ballet have caused my perception of my body to change so while these external factors may have had an impact, taking ballet classes has had a significant and noticeable effect.

> *I am standing in front of a wall of mirrors. The teacher is speaking but I am not listening. The speech is simply white noise which often I cannot identify. There are others in the room, but in this moment, I cannot see them. All I see is a body in the mirror. A body that belongs to me but suddenly does not look or feel like mine. I can feel the whole silhouette of my being. It looks all out of proportion; not how I recall it appearing before I entered this room. I see short stubby legs, a strangely long torso which is wide and unflattering.*

I see a face which holds chubby cheeks and tired puffy eyes. Immediately I adjust my stance to a more relaxed and slouchy position with an arm placed across the front of my protruding abdomen which is made more obvious by the cutting line of my pink ballet tights. I pull my tights up in the hope that they suck in my waist, and it does work, until they inevitably shift as I move again. I try pulling my leotard up in the hope my legs will look longer and more elegant, but then all I see is the flesh that protects my hip bones, so I use my two index fingers to draw it back down. Subtly turning to the side, I hope this profile will appear how I believe it should: slender, lean, and long. This is not the case; I see arms which carry too much flesh and boobs which are too big to be a ballerina. I suck in my stomach thinking this will fix all my insecurities, alas it is unsustainable. I give up. I look at the floor and pride myself on my petite and narrow feet, the only part of my body which I see fit to be classed as a ballet dancer. All in this time I have missed the instructions and vital feedback to help me improve my technique. The teacher has finished speaking, and we must perform again.

April 2022.

There is a culture in the ballet world of being 'feminine', yet not having typical feminine features. This is partially evidenced by Desmond as they state, 'the strict limits on body size and shape for girls and women dancers reinforce a denial of the female body in favour of an ideal boyish petiteness' (1997, p. 95). The idea of a 'boyish petiteness' (1997, p. 95) could imply there is a desire to have a flat chest and straight narrow hips. Furthermore, there is an implication of female dancers believing that by having a lack of typical feminine features (breasts and wide hips), dancers will look even smaller and therefore be more suitable to perform the art. Many ballet dancers have reflected and recognised this culture in ballet. In a study conducted by Gray and Kunkel exploring the different themes female ballet dancers encounter in practice, dancers reported that there was pressure to 'look like little boys' and be a 'breastless, hipless, long-limbed shape' (2001, p. 14). This is also something I, the recreational dancer, had on my mind when I danced as evidenced by my journal entry. I felt that with less obvious feminine structures I would appear more like a ballet dancer, perform better and therefore I would be more worthy to be in the room. In a study concerning female ballet dancers in training, 'one dancer perceived having breasts as a disadvantage when trying to wear dance costumes' (Reel et al., 2005, p. 47). This not only links to my previous point but could also infer that dance costumes are another way dancers feel pressure to have a specific body type to perform in ballet.

My teacher asked me to try on a costume for the show which would be performed later that year (2015). She said to me 'you are the smallest one so you should fit in this' as I was handed a red satin leotard which had lengths of red chiffon sewn around the waist, neatly finished with a thin piece of shiny green ribbon to hide the seams. I had seen this costume before, when some of the older girls wore these dresses in a previous show. I have become the older girl that I once looked up to. I stepped into the leg holes and pulled the costume up straight past my ankles, shins, knees, thighs. Then it stopped. I couldn't pull it past my hips. I tugged at this delicate handmade dress which looked so beautiful on the hanger as I so desperately wanted to wear it. Not for its beauty, simply because I knew it was the smallest dress. I wanted the knowledge and confirmation that I was the smallest out of my class. I felt my skin turn hot and my mind filled with dread at the thought of having to admit out loud 'it's too small for me'. My teacher tuned to me and saw me struggle. I took the dress off and handed it back, then walked home knowing I didn't fit the costume.

April 11, 2022

This memory suggests that my insecurities were reinforced by not fitting a costume as I felt I had to fit the costume rather than the costume had to fit me. In my experience of recreational dance training, costumes were reused year after year and altered to fit each dancer. I recall feeling embarrassed if the costume needed to be made bigger, and proud if it was too big for me. If it was too big, my ballet teacher would comment on it, again unintentionally reinforcing this competition I had in my own head. This could suggest that recreational ballet teachers may have a part to play in influencing how the dancers view their bodies, potentially without knowing it. In my experience, my teachers never made direct statements telling students that they needed to look a certain way. However, I do recall comments about our bodies being made. In my case, I was always one of the tall ones, who was at the back of our show pieces simply for this reason. I also have memories of being told by my teacher how thin I was, which I always took as a huge compliment.

To assure myself I deserve to be in the dance studio, I scan the other bodies in the room. I take note of how everyone is standing, what everyone is wearing, and how the shape of my body compares to theirs. I watch their reflections in the mirror as they move to a new position to ensure I have a clear picture of their body. All the things I have just scrutinised about myself, I check on each person in the room. How do they compare to me? Do I believe I look smaller than other people in the class? If so, how many? Am I the smallest? These questions occur in my head frequently and depending on the move or exercise we complete, I ask them again. If the way someone is standing changes, I glance to see how I place compared to them now. It feels like a competition, except no one knows they are partaking, because in reality the only participants are myself and the negative thoughts that circle my mind as I dance. If someone appears smaller than me, I begin to come up with reasons as to why this is. Did I have a big lunch, am I due on my period, have they got tighter clothing on than me? I feel good about myself if I am the smallest in the room and perform with more confidence if this is the case. If I am not the smallest in the room, I believe my technique is not as good. I try to reassure myself with my love for the art, telling myself 'Who cares what you look like?' Alas it is not enough. The bad thoughts outweigh the positive ones and I feel helpless, once again checking where I place in this imaginary game. I glance across the room again and see one of my peers laughing. I envy her.

March 7, 2022

The competition previously spoken about would go further than it being me against me, as shown by this excerpt from my journal, I involve others in my quest to be the 'perfect ballerina'. It appears I only desire to be the most 'ideal' out of those who surround me, and if it is only myself in the room, I want to be noticeably small.

In two of these excerpts, mirrors have been suggested as being used as a tool, not to check my dancing, but to assess my body. In my experience in recreational dance training, classes would take place in the local village community halls which were not designed for dance classes; therefore there were no dance mirrors. One of the halls I danced in had one mirror in the corner of the room, which usually had a curtain covering it. This was not always the case, as there were times, for example when we worked at the barre, that we were in line with the mirror and encouraged to look at our alignment, or we were sent over by the teacher to check our technique during centre practice. It was not until I was much later into my teenage years that four portable mirrors were purchased by my dance school. Prior to this point, I had always done body checks by touch. Placing my hand at the top of my ribs and guiding it down across my stomach to see if it was flat. As well as this, I would use the reflections in the windows to assess my appearance. I recall doing this while I was in a navy-blue leotard, the uniform for grades three and four which I completed around the ages of 9 to 11. When the mirrors arrived, I was able to be more subtle about how I was assessing my 'place' in this competition. Suddenly I was able to see everyone's body without having to look directly at them.

There has been much conversation regarding the use of mirrors in dance training, and their positive uses as a learning tool but also the negative side-effects of young people seeing their body so regularly (Radell, 2019). In some cases, dancers would observe their body in the mirror so often that they became an object open to constant criticism from themselves, psychological competition between others and regulated behaviour patterns which could cause a dissociation between the body they see in the mirror, and them as a person (Radell, 2019). Some of these elements discussed by Radell (2019) resonate with my own experiences.

Pickard suggests that a dancer's body is 'a core part of a ballet dancer's habitus' (2012, p. 27). Referring to Pierre Bourdieu's work, habitus can be defined as the internal beliefs which become familiar to all people of the same collective (Bourdieu, 1993). Using Bourdieu's theory in relation to the 'ballet body', it can be inferred that although details may differ between students, the idea and pressure ballet students feel to have a specific aesthetic and question how they see their own bodies may be a widespread issue, including those who are taking ballet classes for the joy of dance.

I made observations of my peers during my research, as I wanted to see if there were any cues of common body image issues that were similar to my own. This research was not conducted as an experiment, but these observations are things that have stood out to me in class, as someone who also questions their body image when in a dance class. Several peers have commented that they see themselves as 'fat' and 'insecure' due to taking ballet class. I also observed classmates looking at their side profile in the mirror, sucking in their stomachs and then relaxing, on different occasions. There have been many conversations between peers about their bodies and what they see as 'wrong' with them. The conclusion often drawn from these conversations is that their insecurities stem from being a dancer from a young age, as it has put a constant spotlight on their appearance. While this cannot be validated as evidence for my argument, it certainly leads me to ask questions regarding the thought process behind these actions.

This chapter has explored several elements of recreational ballet training that has affected my perception of my body and could be affecting other dancers in the same category. It is evident how personal experiences of body image are in ballet, which can be understood through my journal entries. It is difficult to draw a simple conclusion for such a complex internal issue. Having said this, this research has demonstrated that ballet classes have affected the way I perceive my body in a negative way and caused unhealthy thoughts, which can lead to unhealthy actions. The culture of the professional world has been the biggest cause of the issue; however, this has had consequential effects on other areas of recreational training. The expectation and association of being a ballet dancer with the 'ballet body' puts pressure on the dancer to look that way to feel valid as a ballet dancer. The competitive aspect of any sport has manifested in ballet to be the 'perfect' ballet dancer, not only with the best technique, but with the best body too. Mirrors have allowed this competition to become easily monitored by dancers in the class, as they can constantly see their own reflection. Without analysing factors that are not revolved around ballet, I cannot say this is completely due to ballet; however I can conclude ballet, and the culture that follows it, is a large factor of the issue.

References

Aalten, A. (2007). Listening to the dancer's body. *The Sociological Review, 55(1)*, 109–125. https://doi.org/10.1111/j.1467-954X.2007.00696.x

Alexias, G., & Dimitropoulou, E. (2011). The body as a tool: Professional classical ballet dancers' embodiment. *Research in Dance Education, 12*(2), 87–104. https://doi.org/10.1080/14647893.2011.575221

Boal, Peter. (2011). Too fat? Too thin? Too tall? Too Short? Retrieved April 19, 2022. https://pointemagazine.com/ballet-body-issues/.

Bourdieu, P. (1993). *Sociology in question* (Vol. 18). Sage.

Clark, M. I., & Markula, P. (2017). Foucault at the barre and other surprises: A case study of discipline and docility in the ballet studio. *Qualitative Research in Sport, Exercise and Health, 9*(4), 435–452. https://doi.org/10.1080/21596 76X.2017.1309451

Desmond, J. (1997). *Meaning in motion: New cultural studies of dance.* Duke University Press.

Henderson, Garnet (2021). What would it take to change ballet's aesthetic of extreme thinness? Retrieved July 15, 2023 from https://www.dancemagazine.com/ballet-body/

Gray, K. M., & Kunkel, M. A. (2001). The experience of female ballet dancers: A grounded theory. *High Ability Studies, 12*(1), 7–25. http://dx.doi.org/10.1080/13598130120058662

Huebscher, B. C. (2010). Relationship between body image and self-esteem among adolescent girls. *The Journal of Social Psychology, 146*, 15–30.

Kiem, Elizabeth (2014). George Balanchine: The human cost of an artistic legacy. Retrieved April 21, 2022 from https://www.huffpost.com/entry/post_6717_b_4640946

Klapper, M. R. (2020). *Ballet class: An American history.* Oxford University Press.

Pickard, A. (2012). Schooling the dancer: The evolution of an identity as a ballet dancer. *Research in Dance Education, 13*(1), 25–46. https://doi.org/10.1080/146 47893.2011.651119

Pickard, A. (2013). Ballet body belief: Perceptions of an ideal ballet body from young ballet dancers. *Research in Dance Education, 14*(1), 3–19. https://doi.org/10.108 0/14647893.2012.712106

Radell, S. A. (2019). Mirrors in dance class: Help or hindrance. *International Association for Dance Medicine and Science.* Retrieved May 22, 2023 from https://iadms.org/media/3586/iadms-resource-paper-mirrors-in-the-dance-class.pdf

Reel, J. J., SooHoo, S., Jamieson, K. M. & Gill, D. L. (2005). Femininity to the extreme: Body image concerns among college female dancers. *Women in Sport & Physical Activity Journal, 14*(1), 39–51. http://dx.doi.org/10.1123/wspaj.14.1.39

Ritenburg, H. M. (2010). Frozen landscapes: A Foucauldian genealogy of the ideal ballet dancer's body. *Research in Dance Education, 11*(1), 71–85. http://dx.doi.org/10.1080/14647891003671775

Rocher Barnes, C. (2022). *The unconventional ballet body in the 21st century,* [Unpublished Doctoral dissertation], University of Maryland, College Park. https://doi.org/10.13016/n8rq-bitm

Schultz. I (2020). What is a 'ballet body'? Retrieved April 18, 2022 from https://medium.com/@IreneSchultz/what-is-a-ballet-body-37055c167550

Seibert, B. (2005). *George Balanchine.* The Rosen Publishing Group, Inc. Buffalo, NY.

Warren, G. W. (1989). Classical ballet technique. University Press of Florida, Colombia.

5

A SOMATIC APPROACH TO AUDIENCING

Carolina Bergonzoni

Introduction

Looking back at my dance training journey, I realise that for years I trained to be witnessed and judged by others and by my own reflection in the mirror. The act of performing became so precious, precarious, indeed 'an act', that I temporarily lost the joy of dancing and the pure pleasure of moving my body. It took me years to find the excitement and the joy of moving again. From a phenomenological perspective, I write, dance, live and breathe with an understanding that I *am* this body. I don't just *have* a body (Snowber, 2016, 2018, 2022). I am the physicality, presence, messiness, sweat and breath that is me. Yet, during my dance training in techniques and practices such as ballet, contemporary and somatics, I often felt that *my* body was reduced to *a* body.

In this chapter, I will discuss the politics and the comparison between *the gaze* and *the stare* in relation to Eurocentric ballet and contemporary dance practices. It is important to note that when I refer to dance, I am referring to the systems, practices and values that I have experienced during my dance training; these are forms of dance such as ballet and contemporary that uphold specific aesthetics that are not necessarily shared across other dance forms.

Phenomenology, through the lineage of Edmund Husserl and Maurice Merleau-Ponty, has articulated the difference between the body as a subject (*Leib*) often referred to as the lived body, and the body as an object (*Körper*) to indicate that we *are* bodies and challenge the Cartesian dualism of body and mind. In describing the ways in which we perceive our bodies, Merleau-Ponty talks about 'a mode of unity' that is unique to 'one's own body' (2012, p. 151). With the best of intentions to account for the idea of both *having* and *being* a body, his definition of the body remains outward, and I challenge

DOI: 10.4324/9781003382874-7

the notion of the lived body (in the past tense) and argue for the idea of the living body (in the gerund tense), which has been moved forward by somatic scholars. A dancer's body is full of living experiences that resonate and arise in the dancing (Fraleigh, 1987).

I will begin this discussion by touching on the development of the concept of the gaze in Western philosophy. The gaze is conceptualised as the act of looking at what we desire, whereas the stare is defined as a gaze of an ableist nature: a prolonged, intense, penetrating and scrutinising look. I will draw on scholarship from scholars and activists who identify as disabled (Davies, 2008; Garland-Thomson, 2006, 2009, 2017) to develop a framework for analysing the effects of both the gaze and the stare on the dancing body across the disciplines of ballet and contemporary dance. Disability and feminist scholarship serve in this chapter to analyse the intersectional sociopolitical systems of ableism and sexualisation of the female body, providing insights that develop a critical framework for discussing the female dancing body.

Finally, I will offer a somatic approach that takes into consideration the *what* and the *how* of 'audiencing' one's dance, and offer three ways of theorising somatic ways of audiencing the female dancing body. Both inside and outside of the discipline of dance, our bodies are inscribed by culture. Dance centres the body, forcing us to question the ways in which we look, gaze or stare at bodies (Garland-Thomson, 2006, 2009, 2017). Somatic practices help us to become more aware of our habits, including social and cultural practices, to discover new pathways, and to understand how unique each body is (Batson, 2009; Eddy, 2009, 2017; Green, 2001, 2002; Johnson, 2018). Our bodies are always embedded in the environment; therefore, we cannot escape the political implications of the social conditions in which the body lives. Ideals of the dancer body are spread throughout dance practices and cultures (Albright, 1997; Bergonzoni 2021, 2022; Davies, 2008). My body, as a dancer and as a woman, has often been and continues to be consumed as an object on display; as Anne Burnidge suggests:

> Often in the dance field there is a preference for regarding dancers and bodies as third-person objects to be externally viewed and judged by others, discounting the first-person subjective view that takes into account the thoughts, feelings, and sensations of the individual as a somatic, holistic entity.
>
> *(2012, p. 45).*

When I dance, my body becomes 'a body' that needs to fit certain aesthetic parameters based on the genre. Each body is unique in its articulation. Bodies are not neutral, yet when talking about bodies, especially in the field of dance studies and somatic scholarship, there is a tendency to refer to a standardised, normalised and often idealised body. In 1995, Lennard J. Davis introduced the term 'normalcy' to shift the focus from the construction of disability to the construction of normalcy (Davis, 1995; 2013). Davis critiques the gene-alogy of the words 'normal', 'normality' and 'norm' as synonymous with 'ideal'. In the English language the word 'normal' started being equated with 'constituting, conforming to, not deviating or different from, the com-mon type or standard, regular, usual' (Davis, 2013, p. 2) around 1840. In 1997, a few years after the introduction of Davis's notion of 'normalcy', Garland-Thomson proposed the notion of 'normate' to indicate:

> the social figure with which people can represent themselves as definitive human beings. Normate, then, is the constructed identity of those who, by way of the bodily configurations and cultural capital they assume, can step into a position of authority and wield the power it grants them.
>
> *(1997, p. 8)*

Garland-Thomson uses feminist disability theory to make way for 'unseat-ing the dominant assumption that disability is something that is wrong with someone' (Garland-Thomson, 2013, p. 336). The idea of a *neutral* and com-pletely adaptable body was still prominent in dance training in the late 20th century. In describing their training in somatics, Doran George writes about how the field kept promoting 'the idea of a natural body as an invisible yet essential category of nature' (George, 2020, p. 2) and highlights how this aim for inclusion actually enacted exclusion and reinforced differences (George, 2020). George critiques the field of somatics for not addressing systemic forms of oppression and how this lack of awareness, masked with spiritual-ity, naturalism and the idea of a 'natural body' has generated the conditions for more exclusion.

The gaze and the stare

I approach the notion of the gaze theoretically, as a concept from West-ern philosophy elaborated by Simone de Beauvoir (2010), Jean-Paul Sartre (2021) and Michel Foucault (2003). Although an in-depth analysis of the gaze is beyond the scope of this chapter, an overview of the history, and its politics, in Western philosophy will help us in understanding the focus of this chapter in relation to how systems of power, aesthetics and epistemologies are upheld. Considering Sartre's theorisation of the look [*le regard*] (often translated as the gaze) in *Being and Nothingness* (2021). Sartre defines the Other's gaze as what forces us to see ourselves. The Other's look is what makes us vulnerable, reminding us that we 'have a body that can be hurt' and that we are 'occupying a place' (p. 355). When we are seen, our body comes into existence as an object that can and will be judged. Sartre describes the anxiety, tension and 'alienation' (p. 360) that comes with the awareness of being looked at. The structure of dance, particularly dance training, strongly reinforces these feelings, as the presentation of dance is heavily reliant on the visibility of bodies being seen. It is undeniable that 'dance, unlike other forms of cultural production such as books or paintings, makes the body visible within the representation itself' (Albright 1997, p. 63).

According to Sartre, we are not instinctually objects of our awareness. However, the gaze of the Other transforms us into one. It is through the gaze that we become aware of being gazed at; through this process, we see ourselves through the eyes of the other as objects. When we consider dance practices this theorisation is crucial. I argue that when fully embodied, dancers experience their action in the act of dancing: they are 'living experiences' (Lloyd & Smith, 2021, p. 3). The moment that the gaze, whether of themselves or others, objectifies their dance, dancers are no longer *in* the dancing. To me, the feeling of being myself, in the dancing, is one of attuning to my somatic sensations: I sense my movement and I feel moved while moving from within.

Foucault's (2003) notion of the 'clinical' or 'medical gaze', elaborates on Sartre's notion in a pivotal mode. For both philosophers, the external gaze—for Foucault this is explicitly an external power—transforms us by changing and defining our identity. As an example, we choose to wear different clothes culturally, or depending on the task we are about to do. I have worn 'formal clothes' when I needed to be *the academic*, and pink tights and a unitard to be *the dancer*. As a dancer, as I describe in more details later, I have lost weight and changed shape, in order to try to hide my form. As a kid, I wanted to have prescription glasses because they would make me into the image of 'the smart kid'. The body is always charged with political, social and economic values precisely because of an external gaze. The choices we make, and the desires we have to fit in, uphold dominant political, patriarchal systemic views and underpin the way we navigate these issues.

The clinical gaze described by Foucault (2003) constitutes the roots of pathologisation in the medical field and in the formation of the medical model of disability. The medical model considers disability as a health problem or an impairment that can and should be treated to return to what is considered *normal* or *healthy*. Activists have argued that the medical model doesn't reduce impairments, but rather proliferates them (Sandahl & Auslander, 2005, p. 129). Garland-Thomson critiques the clinical gaze by writing:

> [the clinical gaze seeks to] outlaw aspects of human variation into constricting categories and to diagnose differences as pathology. [...] Not only does it survey our exteriors to establish boundaries, but clinical observation invades our interiors to reckon the true relationship between inside and outside, between visible and invisible.
>
> *(2009, p. 49)*

The other side of the aesthetic objectification of the gaze is that bodies carry political and artistic messages. Each body on the dance stage has the potential to challenge the hegemony of the ideal of dancers' bodies. But is this enough to reconceptualize dance aesthetics and the ways in which we look, stare and gaze at bodies in and outside of dance? As highlighted by disabled activists and scholars, disability demands a rediscovering and reconsidering of looking, gazing and staring. Particularly when we consider disabled dancers, this becomes an opportunity to 'redefine the aesthetic process of the gaze itself' (Davies, 2008, p. 61). Garland-Thomson defines the disabled body as the one that we stare at, one 'to-be-looked-at and not-to-be-looked-at' (Garland-Thomson, 2002, p. 57), which creates a binary separation between disabled and non-disabled bodies, rather than considering different bodies as human variations (Garland-Thomson, 2002, 2005).

In *The Second Sex* (2010) Simone de Beauvoir highlights how women don't encounter their bodies as a site of freedom and self-expression, but rather learn that their role is to be watched, judged and chosen by men. While de Beauvoir was sharing this feminist perspective in 1949, this is a behaviour that is reinforced heavily within dance today; dancers are constantly scrutinised and assessed based on their appearance. De Beauvoir, like Sartre, talks about the conflict a girl/woman experiences when she no longer exists as an autonomous person. During puberty, she realises that she only exists as an object. She writes:

> Her breasts show through her sweater or blouse, and this body that the little girl identified with self appears to her as flesh; it is an object that others look at and see. "For two years I wore capes to hide my chest, I was so ashamed of it," a woman told me.
>
> *(2010, p. 369)*

This statement is central to the argument I am proposing. Puberty deeply impacts the way in which females in dance perceive their changing bodies, changes such as breasts buds, gain in mass and different body proportions. In the context of ballet and contemporary dance—the dance forms in which I grew up—self-judgment, comparison and constant comments about the body continue to be part of the culture. I went through puberty at a very young age and would be considered an early maturing girl (Brooks-Gunn & Warren, 1985; Mitchell et al., 2017; Mitchell et al., 2020; Mitchell et al., 2022). As an eight-year-old, I was not prepared to sprout into an adult overnight. Like most female dancers I know, I tried to fight against what was happening in my body: hips and breasts growing was associated with becoming a less valuable dancer. I developed postural habits and used multiple bras in an attempt to hide my newly discovered breasts and resemble what I thought was the ideal dance body: a body that wasn't supposed to grow, the body of a child. I spent many years adapting and successfully changing my body to fit certain ideals and standards. My body folded, shrank and narrowed as much as it possibly could, to take up as little space as it possibly could.

See and be seen in dance training

Dancers are constantly seen, judged and corrected based on the way they look by teachers, competition judges, choreographers and the public. However, for the female dancer 'neither of these gazes is usually quite as debilitating or oppressive as the gaze which meets its own image in the mirror' (Albright, 1998). The female dancers' gaze is one of the strongest critics of their own body image. A dancer's relationship with the mirror is complicated. On the one hand, mirrors can be useful tools for checking one's posture, form and lines. On the other hand, the use of mirrors trains dancers to become an expert at objectifying their own body and movement (Doria & Numer, 2022; Zoletić & Duraković-Belko, 2009). Dancers can learn from a young age to analyse their shapes and forms in the mirror constantly, which may lead to them negatively scrutinising every inch of their bodies. If nothing ever looks good enough, then nothing ever feels good enough. De Beauvoir's analysis of becoming woman unpacks how the gaze affects us.

> The little girl feels that her body is escaping her, that it is no longer the clear expression of her individuality; it becomes foreign to her; and at the same moment, she is grasped by others as a thing: on the street, eyes follow her, her body is subject to comments; she would like to become invisible; she is afraid of becoming flesh and afraid to show her flesh.
>
> *(2010, p. 369)*

Throughout most of my dance training, but particularly in the formative years from pre-puberty until around the time I was 16, I was never taught how to feel my body and, more than once, I wanted to escape my body. This, unsurprisingly, turned into an eating disorder, something that is not uncommon in ballet (Arcelus et al., 2014; Doria & Numer, 2022), particularly in studios and environments in which teachers, choreographers and adjudicators celebrate thinness. The self-objectification of the female dancer's body is in constant relationship with the 'ideal body', which manifests in Western aesthetics as a sexualisation of a pre-pubescent body. The focus on the image reflected in the mirror didn't allow me to feel in my body.

My body didn't feel like it was mine and, I believe, this is a shared statement among many dancers (see Croft, 2017). There was an implicit assumption that I could feel my body, but I am most certain that for almost ten years, I had relied on the mirror and its image of me to feel my body in space. Somatic and phenomenological approaches reimagine our bodies as places for knowledge to be uncovered, created and re-created (Fraleigh, 2015, 2018; Snowber, 2022; Whatley et al., 2015; Williamson et al., 2014). They reframe our bodies as porous, spaces for knowledge, memories, learning, breathing, dancing to pass through.

I clearly remember, as if it were yesterday, the first time I fully felt my body moving. It was a Saturday afternoon in 2006, during a class taught by Italian dance artist Simona Bertozzi. At that time, when I first encountered somatic dance techniques, I didn't have a name for it. All I knew was that the approach of the teacher was different from what I had previously experienced and that I was struggling to follow instructions without having mirrors, nor a form or shape to copy. Simona asked us to let go of our knees and to feel the weight dropping, as if someone was cutting a string from above. I had done that exact movement over and over again for years; dropping my weight was second nature. But I had never felt it. Before that day, I had been imitating the gesture of dropping my weight. I was so accustomed and used to copying movements that I simply always performed the movement. With Simona's guidance to tune into the sensation of dropping, for the first time, I could feel gravity. That experience revealed to me that I had spent most of my dance training never fully connected to my body: I was using my body to perform for a gaze and external validation. I was working on strength, flexibility, fluidity and technique that could be identified as fitting the ballet/contemporary imposed aesthetic.

Until then, I was never *in* my body. It was only at this time, when I first discovered somatic practices such as Feldenkrais, Body-Mind Centering®, and the Laban/Bartenieff Movement System that dance shifted: from teaching me how to self-objectify and care a lot about how people saw me, to teaching me how to feel and be in my body. That day, I truly felt my body. I didn't only experience anatomical or physical sensations as suggested by a teacher, I really met my own body. From that point forward, I have been on a path of trusting that the body knows, and that dance and my body are teachers.

To be an audience of my own dance

The theoretical implication of the gaze and the stare in dance are strongly connected with judgment and critique, both of self and others. As a strategy for working away from the gaze and the stare, I offer three somatic approaches to 'audiencing' one's dance.

I offer the term 'audience' as an active verb, one that encompasses the bodily motions and corporeal perceptions comprising an active and interactive 'audiencing' of my own dance. For theatre scholar P. A. Skantze, 'at the heart of the practice of being a spectator' is a 'methodology of care' (2017, p. 176). I propose that we can be the audience, physically present and invested in a methodology of care, of our own dances. The concept of *audiencing* our own dances becomes an act of healing and generosity towards the body, and dance.

The etymology dictionary defines audience as:

> the act or state of hearing, action or condition of listening, from Old French *audience*, from Latin *audentia* "a hearing, listening," from

audientum (nominative *audiens*), present participle of *audire* "to hear," from PIE compound *au-dh- "to perceive physically, grasp," from root *au- "to perceive"'.

(Online etymology dictionary, n.d.)

This definition supports the idea of using the word audience as an active verb, rather than just as a noun. I conceptualise *audiencing*, as a verb that carries the active connotations of leaning into the performance, perceiving what's going on through our skin and senses, and encompassing the bodily motions and corporeal perception of an active and interactive audiencing. The standard idea, which is inherent in the definition of perceiving physically—as if grasping objects and Others—appears to be directed outwards, taking little account of the inner senses that afford perceptual access to the body as inherently motile.

If we accept perception as the reciprocity between the body and its surroundings (Merleau-Ponty, 2012), I define audiencing as bodily perceiving. The idea of bodily perceiving considers the embodied experience that is the act of audiencing, one which positions the body as an embodied relationship of its surroundings rather than Merleau-Ponty's relationship between the body and its surroundings. When I audience my own dance, I bring dance into life through shifts in attention; simultaneously, I am dancing and I am audiencing by doing 'the work of the spectator' (Reason et al., 2016). Audiencing one's own dance is a difficult task because it is a constantly changing process: it is an improvised dance within a dance.

One of the biggest challenges that I have found is audiencing my whole body while I am in the dancing. My body is not simply a unity of parts; my body is the sweat, the droplets of saliva, the hair, the heat left in the space after I dance. My body is the sensations of pain, pleasure, flow and staccato that I experience while I dance. My body is the changes in breathing patterns, in my thought process, in the ability to feel and sense the space and the others in it with me. The task becomes: how can I be *with* my body and *in* my body, while also maintaining a relationship with the space I am dancing within?

A somatic approach to audiencing

The definition of audiencing that I offer considers the perspective of the dancer. In dialogue, I identify 'gradations of audiencing', a term inspired by Enrico Pitozzi 'gradations of presence' (2012) and by Sarah Whatley's five viewing strategies (2007).[1] Although Whatley theorises five viewing strategies based on the 'presumption of difference'—whether conscious or not—that audience members bring with them when witnessing disabled dancers on stage, these strategies have informed my understanding of audiencing any dance, as they bring into question the gaze, the stare and notions of perception.

These gradations of audiencing show that there isn't a binary between audiencing and not-audiencing the dancing body, but rather a spectrum of possibilities. I theorise three variations of audiencing myself and my dancing, and within each of them, different gradations of somatic awareness. I offer these strategies as ways for female dancers to connect with their bodies without objectifying them. For clarity, I will consider the three variations of audiencing as separate modes of somatic awareness; however, I also recognise that we are constantly weaving in and out of them. Audiencing always begins by attuning to the body, after which the three variations of *shapeless, moulded* and *spacious* begin arising. I begin the practice by arriving: in the space, in my body and in my practice. I start to shift my attention and awareness to my breath, the heartbeat pulsing in my belly, my lungs expanding with air, release my body into gravity. Attuning to sensations makes me more aware of the variations in my own body and in my own audiencing, which increase the fluctuations, actions and activities inside and outside of my body.

Shapeless

I audience the feelings and sensations of my dancing body. I always begin by audiencing my organs and the contents of my body. However, I don't perceive my face, my arms, my legs in their materiality. I cannot trace the boundaries of my body: it is a liquid, shapeless, malleable body. The gradations of this variation are as follows: attuning to the body, noticing an abundance of possibilities, and shaping the space with my movement. These gradations do not follow a linear nor progressive timeline.

> *When I yield into the floor, resting in awareness, I am at my best capacity to audience my dance from within. Horizontality is a very different orientation than verticality. My dance is in relationship with gravity, rather than an attempt to overcome it.*

Audiencing my own dance with a shapeless body feels like a never-ending spiral; I am engaged with what is happening while it occurs and I am not focusing on the way it looks, but rather on the way it feels.

ii Moulded

I am still focusing on the sensations, but I begin to audience the materiality of the body. I note the structure of my skeleton, my organs, my muscles and my skin; I keep it in the foreground. I am aware of where my body is in space, I perceive the limits and boundaries of my skeleton, but I can feel the dance going beyond the physical body. When I move this 'audiencing gaze' outside of my body, but still at the edges of it, I feel as if I am in two places at once. I can track the sensations of my body and follow the shapes and lines that my body makes, as if audiencing it from an audience member.

The gradations of this variation include noticing changes in my body and how these shift my movement. In audiencing my moulded body, I am in the liminal, chiasmic zone where I am in-between impressions and expressions. I must constantly stay present in the process, grounding myself and attending to the modifications in shape and alignment. I have to keep adapting, becoming soft and permeable, so that I can experience gravity and let the space support me.

iii Spacious

This variation occurs from a distance, and it includes the most space of the three. It almost feels as if I was audiencing my body as an outside witness. The focus is on the composition of the dance in relation to the room and, potentially, to others. My body attunes to other presences: my own dance, the lights, the sounds, the floor, and so on. The gradations of this variation come out of processing what I have audienced as 'shapeless' and audienced as 'moulded'. In this processing, I am notating the turning points, the lines and the expectations about the dance that might come up. When audiencing spaciousness, I often get stuck in an ideal image of what the dancing body and dance should look like. When I audience my dance in a spacious way, I am in dialogue with the internal editor/choreographer. In this variation of audiencing, I become more aware of movement choices and begin making choreographic decisions.

The three variations of audiencing are modes of somatic awareness. These practice-based concepts can support dancers and dance educators in becoming more attentive of how they gaze, or stare, at themselves and others. By learning to sense and feel the body, as opposed to just being or having a body, female dancers can reconnect with dancing without objectifying themselves.

Conclusive thoughts

In this chapter, I used disability studies and phenomenology as theoretical framework to analyse the notion of the gaze and the stare in ballet and contemporary dance training. I discussed my experience as a female dancer growing up in a studio environment that reinforced an objectification of my body. I challenged socio-politically inscribed ideals and ideas of bodies through somatic awareness and approaches. Particularly, I presented three somatic approaches to audiencing one's own dance, which I have developed through my own somatic dance practice, and distilled into a methodology that could be passed on to other dancers and choreographers. By moving towards this somatic approach to audiencing, dancers can finally be liberated from the gaze, and the stare, and in doing so, reclaim their bodies, rediscovering the pleasure and joy of dancing and of knowing themselves rather than presenting themselves as objects to others.

Note

1. Enrico Pitozzi describes 'gradations of presence' as a theoretical framework to discuss the notion of a presence of the body on stage in contemporary dance practices. In his analysis, he proposes that absence and presence are not a binary dichotomy, but rather, a spectrum. In an article published in 2007, Sarah Whatley (2007) describes different strategies that audiences use when they witness disabled dance performers. In the article, Whatley suggests a framework of five viewing strategies, which she developed by working with students and their responses to viewing dancers. The five viewing strategies are: passive oppressive, passive conservative, post-passive, active witness, and immersion.

References

Albright, A. C. (1997). *Choreographing difference: The body and identity in contemporary dance*. Wesleyan University Press.

Albright, A. C. (1998). Strategic abilities: Negotiating the disabled body in dance. *Disability, Art, and Culture, XXXVII*(3). http://hdl.handle.net/2027/spo.act2080. 0037.313

Arcelus, J., Witcomb, G. L. & Mitchell, A. (2014). Prevalence of eating disorders amongst dancers: A systemic review and meta-analysis. *Eur Eat Disord Rev, 22*(2), 92–101. http://dx.doi.org/10.1002/erv.2271

Batson, G. (2009). The somatic practice of intentional rest in dance education preliminary steps towards a method of study. *Journal of Dance & Somatic Practices, 1*(2), 177–197. http://dx.doi.org/10.1386/jdsp.1.2.177_1

Bergonzoni, C. (2021). Translations. A dance for the non-visual senses. *Danza e Ricerca, 13*, 217–230.

Bergonzoni, C. (2022). *A ravine of in-betweens: The body, dance, and writing into the excess* [Doctoral dissertation, Simon Fraser University. https://summit.sfu.ca/item/34905

Brooks-Gunn, J., & Warren, M. P. (1985). The effects of delayed menarche in different contexts: Dance and nondance students. *Journal of Youth and Adolescence, 14*(4), 285–300. http://dx.doi.org/10.1007/bf02089235

Burnidge, A. (2012). Somatics in the dance studio: Embodying feminist/democratic pedagogy. *Journal of Dance Education, 12*(2), 37–47. http://dx.doi.org/10.1080/15290824.2012.634283

Croft, C. (Ed.). (2017). *Queer dance*. Oxford University Press.

Davies, T. (2008). Mobility: AXIS dancers push the boundaries of access. *Text and Performance Quarterly, 28*, 43–63. http://dx.doi.org/10.1080/10462930701754309

Davis, L. J. (1995). *Enforcing normalcy*. Verso Books.

Davis, L. J. (2013). The end of identity politics: On disability as an unstable category. In L. J. Davis, *The disability studies reader* (4th ed., pp. 261–277). Taylor and Francis.

De Beauvoir, S. (2010). *The second sex*. (C. Borde & S. Malovany-Chevallier, Trans.). Vintage Books. (Original work published 1949).

Doria, N., & Numer, M. (2022). Dancing in a culture of disordered eating: A feminist poststructural analysis of body and body image among young girls in the world of dance. *PLoS ONE, 17*(1), 1–28. https://doi.org/10.1371/journal.pone.0247651

Eddy, M. (2009). A brief history of somatic practices and dance: Historical development of the field of somatic education and its relationship to dance. *Journal of Dance & Somatic Practices, 1*(1), 5–27. http://dx.doi.org/10.1386/jdsp.1.1.5_1

Eddy, M. (2017). *Mindful movement: The evolution of the somatic arts and conscious action*. Intellect.

Foucault, M. (2003). *The birth of the clinic*. (A. M. Sheridan, Trans.). Taylor & Francis. (Original work published 1963).

Fraleigh, S. (1987). *Dance and the lived body: A descriptive aesthetics*. University of Pittsburgh Press.

Fraleigh, S. (2010). *Butoh: Metamorphic dance and global alchemy*. University of Illinois Press.

Fraleigh, S. (2015). *Moving consciously*. University of Illinois Press.

Fraleigh, S. (2018). Phenomenology and life world. In S. Fraleigh (Ed.), *Back to dance itself. Phenomenologies of the body in performance* (pp. 11–26). University of Illinois Press.

Garland-Thomson, R. (1997). *Extraordinary bodies: Figuring physical disability in American culture and literature*. Columbia University Press.

Garland-Thomson, R. (2002). The politics of staring: Visual rhetorics of disability in popular photography. In S. L. Snyder, B. J. Brueggemann & R. Garland-Thomson (Eds.), *Disability studies: Enabling the humanities* (pp. 56–75). Modern Language Association of America.

Garland-Thomson, R. (2005). Feminist disability studies. *Signs: Journal of Women in Culture and Society, 30*(2), 1557–1587.

Garland-Thomson, R. (2006). Ways of staring, *Journal of Visual Culture, 5*(2), 173–192. 10.1177/1470412906066907

Garland-Thomson, R. (2009). *Staring how we look*. Oxford University Press.

Garland-Thomson, R. (2013). Integrating disability, transforming feminist theory. In L. J. Davis, *The disability studies reader* (4th ed., pp. 333–353). Taylor and Francis.

Garland-Thomson, R. (2017). *Extraordinary bodies: Figuring physical disability in American culture and literature*. Columbia University Press.

George, D. (2020). *The natural body in somatics dance training*. Oxford University Press.

Green, J. (2001). Socially constructed bodies in American dance classrooms. *Research in Dance Education, 2*(2), 155–173. http://dx.doi.org/10.1080/14647890120100782

Green, J. (2002). Somatics: A growing and changing field. *Journal of Dance Education, 2*(4), 113. http://dx.doi.org/10.1080/15290824.2002.10387218

Johnson, D. H. (2018). *Diverse bodies, diverse practices: Toward an inclusive somatics*. North Atlantic Books.

Lloyd, R. J., & Smith, S. J. (2021). A practical introduction to motion-sensing phenomenology. *Revue phénEPS / PHEnex Journal, 11*(2), 1–18.

Merleau-Ponty, M. (2012). *Phenomenology of perception*. (D. A. Landes, Trans.). Routledge. (Original work published 1945).

Mitchell, S. B., Cumming, S. P., & Haase, A. M. (2020). Experiences of delayed maturation in female vocational ballet students: An interpretative phenomenological analysis. *Journal of Adolescence, 80*, 233–241. http://dx.doi.org/10.1016/j.adolescence.2020.03.005

Mitchell, S. B., Haase, A. M. & Cumming, S. P. (2022). On-time maturation in female adolescent ballet dancers: learning from lived experiences. *The Journal of Early Adolescence*, 42(2), 262–290. http://dx.doi.org/10.1177/02724316211036752

Mitchell, S. B., Haase, A. M., Cumming, S. P. & Malina, R. M. (2017). Understanding growth and maturation in the context of ballet: A biocultural approach. *Research in Dance Education*, 18(3), 291–300. http://dx.doi.org/10.1080/14647893.2017.1387525

Online etymology dictionary (n.d.). Audience. In *Online etymology dictionary*. Retrieved September 8, 2023 from https://www.etymonline.com/word/audience#etymonline_v_18929

Pitozzi, E. (2012). Figurazioni: Uno studio sulle gradazioni di presenza. [Figurations: a study on the gradations of presence]. *Culture Teatrali*, 21, 107–127.

Reason, L., Reason, M. & Lindelof, A. M. (2016). *Experiencing liveness in contemporary performance: interdisciplinary perspectives*. Routledge.

Sandahl, C., & Auslander, P. (Eds.). (2005). *Bodies in commotion. Disability and performance*. University of Michigan Press.

Sartre, J. P. (2021). *Being and nothingness*. (S. Richmond, Trans.). Atria Books. (Original work published 1943).

Skantze, P. A. (2017). Take me the bridge, In N. Gansterer, E. Cocker & M. Greil, (Eds.), *Choreo-graphic figures: Deviations from the line* (pp. 175–179). Edition Die Angewandte University Press.

Snowber, C. (2016). *Embodied inquiry: Writing, living and being through the body*. Sense Publishers.

Snowber, C. (2018). Living, moving, and dancing: Embodied ways of inquiry. In P. Leavy (Ed.), *Handbook of arts-based research* (pp. 247–266). Guilford Press.

Snowber, C. N. (2022). *Dance, place, and poetics*. Springer International.

Whatley, S. (2007). Dance and disability: The dancer, the viewer and the presumption of difference, *Research in Dance Education*, 8(1), 5–25. http://dx.doi.org/10.1080/14647890701272639

Whatley, S., Garrett Brown, N. & Alexander, K. (Eds.). (2015). *Attending to movement: Somatic perspectives on living in this world*. Triarchy Press.

Williamson, A., Batson, G., Whatley, S., & Weber, R. (Eds.). (2014). *Dance, somatics and spiritualities: Contemporary sacred narratives*. Intellect.

Zoletić E., & Duraković-Belko E. (2009). Body image distortion, perfectionism and eating disorder symptoms in risk group of female ballet dancers and models in control group of female students. *Psychiatria Danubina*, 21(3), 302–309. PMID: 19794346

6

EMBODIED EXPERIENCE OF BODIES WITH BREASTS

Amelia Millward and James Brouner

Introduction

To begin, breasts, boobs, shoulder boulders, chest, mammary. The discussion of breasts can often be an uncomfortable or taboo topic. This discomfort and the fear of potential public repercussions are largely a result of the lack of research or published discourse on the topic. This chapter will push past the discomfort and discuss the topic of breasts, anatomy and the impact on dance through the lived experience of female dancers from a biomechanical lens.

In 2009, 17-year-old professional tennis player and winner of the French Open junior title Simona Halep underwent surgery to reduce the size of her breasts from 34DD to 34C, stating that not only was she uncomfortable in daily life, but the additional heavy weight from her breasts affected her reaction time when playing (Gatto, 2018). Many believed the decision made by Halep was made from aesthetic vanity, and she was met with scrutiny, scepticism, confusion, misogynistic objectification from the general public, and fear for her safety from family members. However, Halep's career quickly progressed to immense success after surgery, with a world Tennis Association (WTA) high rank of third in the world (World Tennis Association, n.d.). While it is impossible to determine her success if the reduction never occurred, Halep stands by her choice, reasoning her decision as a dedication to her sport. She stated that after the procedure, she felt less weighed down and had fewer back problems and less pain, allowing her to play to her highest standard (Murali, 2019). The experiences of Halep and many other elite female athletes seem to support the idea that having large breasts inhibits one's

DOI: 10.4324/9781003382874-8

athletic capabilities or, at the very least, creates an additional barrier to a high level of sports performance and success due to discomfort, pain, misogynistic history and the indoctrinated sexualisation of the female figure.

In the performing arts, it is a performer's role to elicit relationships between themselves and the viewer. However, they are often tasked with embodying or portraying concepts, identities, or characters different from themselves, meaning the connection between the audience and the dancer is only genuine as long as they remain committed to this portrayal. An emotional impact comes from making these interpersonal connections. A sense of power lies in the dancer's ability to control the audience's perceptions, which individuals may begin to crave off-stage (Kowal et al., 2017). Understanding how breast size can affect a dancer's physicality, mental health, career development and overall wellbeing is vital for practitioners and researchers alike. In this chapter, we explore these various aspects of breast size in female-presenting dancers and its impact on the dance world.

While still seen as a taboo subject, the understanding of the importance of the physical aesthetic is deeply ingrained in dance. Physical appearance is a key theme in *A Chorus Line,* which arrived on Broadway in 1975. Writers James Kirkwood Jr. and Nicholas Dante shone a light into the hidden spaces of show business and the lives of hopeful artists searching for jobs. One of these artists is Val, a dancer who regales audiences with the story of her arrival to the big city and the realisation of what it would take to get work. Her song and preceding monologue, 'Dance: 10—Looks: 3', leads viewers through a shared experience at an audition, where she is visibly and objectively a more proficient dancer than the other auditionees in the room yet still gets cut. After stealing an observation sheet from one of the casting panels, she learns they have given her 'on a scale of 1 to 10: for dance—10, for looks—3'. She leaves the audition and finds her way to a plastic surgeon who provides her with multiple body modifications, including breast augmentation, supporting her in finding a new space in her career and suddenly booking work (Hamlisch et al., 1977). This narrative implies that Val's success comes directly from her physical changes, Including a larger breast size. Her newfound success could be seen as perpetuating the notion that, in the performing arts, career progression for feminine identifying bodies is not dependent on pure talent alone but heavily relies on aesthetic vanity, societal idolisation, misogyny and the indoctrinated sexualisation of the female figure. These contradicting accounts of what it means to have a female-presenting body in physical occupations provide an insight into the frustrations that practitioners may feel.

Informed by previous qualitative and quantitative research, we look to explore the lived experience of performers and teachers to understand the impact of breasts on dance and the biomechanical difference in the performance of two comparable bodies with varying breast sizes during dance-specific movements, presenting an entirely original line of enquiry. Research surrounding the overarching topic of breasts in motion is limited. Until now, there was no published research on the physical relationship between breasts and dance practice. This is possibly due to the lack of general awareness and acknowledgement of the topic or from a sense of societal taboo surrounding the topic of breasts, which is deepened by a historical association of performing artists to heightened sexuality (Garafola, 1997).

The authors fully acknowledge that discussing the personal choices made by female-at-birth athletes concerning their bodies is not novel. Sociologists and gender studies experts continually study the differences in social acceptance within sport and gender and plead with the community to confront their biases toward what it means to be a woman in sport (Rintaugu & Ngetich, 2012). However, this discourse must still be more valued within the 'har" or more quantitative-driven sciences.

Breast anatomy

The study of breasts in clinical research is on the rise. Current knowledge of the breast's general anatomy, physiology and biomechanics has begun to focus on practical functionality and efficiency outside of disease and maladies. The structure of the breast consists of multiple layers of different tissues. While not proven, it is accepted that the breast is attached to the torso by Cooper's ligaments. The dermal skin of the breast comprises collagen and elastin fibres, which provide a flexible boundary for the underlying structure. Underneath the skin is a layer roughly 0.5—2cm thick of subcutaneous fat covering the fascia (Gefen & Dilmoney, 2007). Beneath the fascia is a mound of fibro-adipose tissue encompassing the corpus mammae and the underlying milk ducts and lobules (Huang et al., 2011). Due to the amount of fatty tissue in the breast anatomy, many claim that larger-breasted females will have a higher total body fat percentage, and some studies have found a correlation between chest size and body mass index (BMI) (Findikcioglu et al., 2007). However, additional studies suggest that the connection between breast size and total fat mass is inconsequential and biased (Katch et al., 1980; Brown et al., 2012; Wade et al., 2010). In addition, there is research showing that a heavier chest size impacts the posture of an individual, suggesting that the added mass of large breasts causes an increased forward inclination while standing compared to smaller breasts (Lapid et al., 2013; Mazzocchi et al., 2012a; Mazzocchi et al., 2012b).

MEDICAL STRUCTURE OF THE FEMALE BREAST

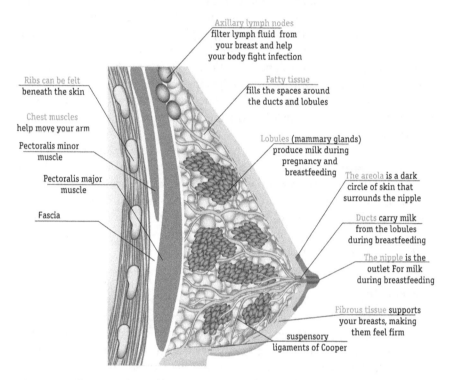

Axillary lymph nodes
filter lymph fluid from
your breast and help
your body fight infection

Ribs can be felt
beneath the skin

Fatty tissue
fills the spaces around
the ducts and lobules

Chest muscles
help move your arm

Pectoralis minor
muscle

Lobules (mammary glands)
produce milk during
pregnancy and
breastfeeding

Pectoralis major
muscle

The areola is a dark
circle of skin that
surrounds the nipple

Fascia

Ducts carry milk
from the lobules
during breastfeeding

The nipple is the
outlet For milk
during breastfeeding

Fibrous tissue supports
your breasts, making
them feel firm

suspensory
ligaments of Cooper

FIGURE 6.1 Cross section of breast anatomy. Copyright: Shutterstock 2023

Qualitative perspectives of breast impact on dance

> Perception is now understood to be a dynamic system of interaction with the world … in which our actions structure not only the how but also the what that we perceive.
>
> *(Albright in Kowal et al., 2017)*

The impact of breast size was examined in original research conducted by the authors of this chapter. The research was a mix-modelled examination of the impact of breast size for the performer from a psychological perspective and a quantitative understanding of breast size impact on a duel-focused case study looking at the biomechanical differences in performance between a performer with a small breast size versus a large breast size. An overview of the research outcomes is summarised in this chapter. It is important to note that the terms' small' and 'large' in relation to breast size in this chapter are defined as those below or above the measured average.

Breast size significantly impacts how a dancer is viewed externally by an audience from a stage or by teachers and peers within the studio. The general sexualisation and objectification of the female form, which is indoctrinated in the vast majority of Western society (Grabe et al., 2005; Suleiman, 1986), has a continued influence on the perceptions of art by the general population. Movement performance is often seen as a portrayal of sexual activity (Hanna, 1988). Because of the discomfort with physical expression in ordinary society and the disproportionate correlation between female anatomy and sexuality, a mover with overtly feminine attributes, such as large breasts, will be automatically specialised and seen as explicit or inappropriately sensual no matter what movement is being performed. As such, many choreographers and casting directors may be deterred from hiring a large-breasted dancer, no matter their skill level, because they feel audiences may be offended. However, the opposite is also true in many cases, specifically within the commercial dance industry. One of the few places where sexuality is accepted by society is within media such as movies, television and popular music (Berberick, 2010; Grossman, 2020; Karsay et al., 2019).

Many dancers with larger breast sizes find work within this industry through music videos or touring as backup dancers for musical artists. In these instances, the lack of a 'typical feminine body', as viewed through a Westernised social construct, can often lead to not booking work. Choreographers in this dance 'industry' sector often create work specifically to portray a certain level of sexuality. This is granted automatically to dancers with larger breasts, meaning a dancer with these attributes may not have to work as hard to create the so-called 'vibe' being sought. A large-breasted dancer is othered and specialised by viewers before they even begin to move, restricting the areas of dance where they can reach any level of professional success or even be welcomed, or experience overt sexualisation of their body based on their breast size. One participant from a survey of dance practitioners and teachers recalls:

> As a teen (with much smaller breasts than my current size, but still larger than average), I was singled out by different teachers in different institutions and dance styles about my breasts. Comments such as "only fat people have boobs" and my teacher getting angry because my size 6 body, with disproportionate DDs, barely squeezed into the pre-existing costumes, were detrimental to my confidence and resulted in a very unhealthy relationship with food.
>
> *(Participant A, 2019)*

Through the dissemination of misunderstood physiological and anatomical data, many people attribute being 'fat', or being a heavier weight, as inherently unhealthy and attribute being unhealthy to being incapable of physical exertion. Though this has been disputed by considerable research (Brochu, 2017; Dark, 2019; Fitzpatrick & Tinning, 2014; Rothblum, 2016; Wright & Leahy, 2016), contemporary Western society still struggles to let go of this idea. Since the dance community already struggles with weight management issues and the perpetuation of a specific 'dancer aesthetic' through the maintenance of outdated traditions (Arcelus et al., 2014), any dancer whose body deviates from this norm may be seen as less capable of dancing well or attaining specific dance skills. Results from responses show that many participants accept this as true because they believe most dance movements were created by and for a particular body type. These negative perceptions may influence how an instructor or choreographer treats large-breasted dancers, consciously or unconsciously.

Further results from the survey of dance practitioners and teachers showed a disconnect between dancers' interactions with their teachers and how teachers, choreographers and directors feel they interact with their performers. Many participants provided negative personal experiences wherein a teacher or director has made inappropriate, rude, graphic, demeaning, or condescending comments. These experiences are not limited to private conversations but have also been reported as happening while taking class and during rehearsals.

> I experienced rude, dismissive, and unprofessional comments from professors in college and firmly believe I was not cast in some productions due to my breast size. Rather than any discussion of my progress or future, my sophomore review was focused on a debate between two professors' debate about if I should have a reduction.
>
> *(Participant B, 2019)*

Teachers, however, report different experiences. Most teachers claim never to comment on a student's chest size unless privately and at the student's request. Those who admit to commenting say it is mainly done when making costuming decisions, intending to make the student feel comfortable and confident with the chosen attire. This disconnect could result from a need for more awareness on the part of the teacher. Many may make these comments in passing, giving little thought to the more significant repercussions, and then forget the comment was made. In contrast, the same comment may stay with students throughout their training, influencing their mental health and connection to dance. A deeper analysis of teacher responses showed that those who offered respectful and relevant commentary to students seemed to have personal experience of dancing with large breasts. This leads to the belief that unless instructors are confronted with these issues in a way that proves their value and relevance, these negative comments will remain a part of the studio environment.

Female dancers also struggle to live within a community focused on visual and aesthetic performance. Living with a body different from the ideal of the community of which you are a part can diminish an individual's body image, confidence and sense of self-efficacy. Dancers reported feeling no point in their passionate practice because their appearance would never be taken seriously or recognised within the art form. Even those with high hopes for affecting change may eventually encounter emotional burnout from the continual battle for progress against unwilling ears determined to maintain harmful traditions.

Internally, I had believed the societal narrative that said big-chested girls couldn't be ballerinas. No matter how much I wanted to believe that I could change the climate within the classical dance world, it was too heart-breaking to actually realise that change and it eventually got the better of me. I hope the culture in the studio and stage continues to change so that it becomes normalised to see and appreciates people's talents first and foremost, without their ability being perceived as a conditional secondary aspect of their appearance. (Participant C, 2019)

Quantitative analysis of the mechanical demands of breast size

Data was gathered on a match-paired case study design, comparing two female performers with similar dance experience and physical profiles except for breast size. The comparison criteria and data can be seen in Table 6.1.

Participant X was categorised as having a small relative breast size, and Participant Z was categorised as having a large relative breast size compared to each other and other previous study participants from which the matched pair was determined. Mechanical data was collected via 3D motion capture. Participants were taught a brief movement phrase comprising contemporary dance-based movement patterns, including lateral swings/undercurves, upper-body spirals, *pirouettes* and *sautés* in parallel. When the dancer felt comfortable with the movement and their ability to perform the phrase without coaching, they were asked to remove their tops or sports bras. They were given nipple covers to apply in the private changing space provided. Marker placement was determined following relevant bony landmarks (van Sint Jan, 2007) and necessary tissue landmarks specific to this research, such as the centre of the breast.

Markers placed on the sternum and left nipple were analysed, with the sternum providing a stable point of comparison to the nipple since there is little to no independent movement in this area. At the same time, consistency

TABLE 6.1 Comparative data of matched pair

Participant ID	Height (CM)	BMI	Jump Power (w/kg)	Jump Height (CM)	Band Measurement (CM)
X	168	21.8	13.89	11.6	31.5
Z	168	20.3	15.78	12.8	30

is maintained in the connective tissue and skin found on the torso, following previous research by Haake and Scurr (2010).

Acceleration during pirouette

Acceleration results for the nipple during the *pirouettes* saw Participant X display a higher maximum rate of acceleration than Participant Z (1.8 times higher), as well as a higher average rate of acceleration throughout the entirety of the rotation, with Participant X's average acceleration being 2.3 times that of Participant Z. There was also a difference in the total number of captured film frames needed for each participant to complete a full rotation. Participant X completed the rotation in 0.87 seconds, while Participant Z took 1.17 seconds.

Change in vertical position during *sautés*

With normalised vertical values for the nipple marker established during quiet stance, positive and negative vertical displacement was measured through a series of *sautés*. Figure 6.2 highlights the timing and displacement variance between Participants X and Z during the performance trials. Participant X maintained a much smaller vertical displacement, ranging from a positive average gain of 22.2cm to a negative of 8.9cm, while Participant Z saw a positive displacement of 29.4cm and a negative displacement of 9.6cm—resulting in a total average displacement for Participant X of 31.1 cm and Participant Z of 39.0 cm.

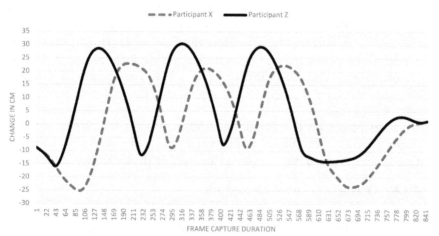

FIGURE 6.2   Displacement comparison of Participant X and Participant Z during *sautés*

Quantitative implications

Results suggest that larger breasts will move more slowly than smaller breasts, potentially due to the drag and resistance created by the additional weight of the mammary tissue. This was demonstrated during *pirouettes*, where the rate of acceleration was lower in total, and the amount of time needed to complete the rotation was longer for the larger-breasted participants. While other factors may influence the frame duration, such as each participant's training or personal stylistic choices, this holds practical application within the studio or performance environments as these differences in movement execution time could translate to visual differences. For example, two students may perform the same movement on the same counts. However, one may appear too slow or fast based on their breasts and how they compare to the other bodies in the room.

Jumping displacement results show that large breasts move independently from the rest of the body more often and more drastically than small breasts. This movement of heavy tissue could cause the pain and discomfort reported by participants in the qualitative survey. This study did not compare the timings of when the breast marker reached its apex position and when the dancer reached the visual apex of the jump. Assuming the acceleration conclusions from rotation apply to all movement, one could posit that there is an additional delay in the vertical movement of the breast compared to the sternum. In that instance, the moment the breast reaches its peak height would differ from when the dancer reaches the top of their jump. This could allow for the weight of the breast to slow the moment of initiation for the jump, potentially limiting the height that can be reached in any given amount of time. The breast tissue may, in turn, be pulled down harshly on the descent as it attempts to become in sync with the rest of the torso, causing increased pain or injury to the breast tissue, skin, or Cooper's ligaments. Breast pain has been related to increased displacement while moving. The pain was connected to the 'slapping' sensation created by the lag between the torso and breast in a larger movement and general breast bounce (McGhee & Steele, 2020). The drastic displacement also causes visual differences between dancers, not only in timing and visual height of jumps but also in the wholly aesthetic perceptions of audiences and viewers.

Conclusion

Students, performers and teachers can apply these findings directly in the studio and on the stage. By acknowledging the challenges they experience and striving to understand what causes them, students and performers are more likely to find efficient ways of altering movements as necessary and more quickly apply corrections received from instructors or choreographers. In addition, a more profound comprehension of these challenges allows dancers to address problems while also providing mutually beneficial solutions confidently and intelligently. Therefore, dancers will be better equipped to be advocates for themselves and others by feeling empowered to speak up in educational and professional settings.

An instructor's role is to provide dancers with the tools to improve their dance practice. By gaining a deeper understanding of the specific body challenges of their students, teachers can give this assistance and provide relevant, individualised feedback. Providing a dancer with objective, respectful and encouraging feedback creates a positive setting. It increases trust between students and teachers (Gilbert, 2018). This supportive environment encourages dancers to work more diligently and persist through moments of struggle. Without knowledge of or empathy with the challenges of a particular body, instructors have a limited range of tools they can provide for their students. This, in turn, limits the growth their students can realistically make while under their tutelage. With this help from an instructor, the likelihood of a dancer remaining in the art increases, too, due to a perceived lack of ability or emotional burnout from not progressing (Aujla et al., 2014). By better understanding the specific challenges faced by large-breasted dancers, there is increased opportunities for technical and professional development of different body types and elevated levels of self-worth for dancers within their community. Further research is needed to continue developing this understanding and ways to counteract adverse effects. Consider looking into the development of more effective dancewear attire, or the external perspectives of society outside of the dance community. The need and opportunities for growth in this topic are endless as we have just begun to break to the surface.

References

Albright, A. C. (2010). *Choreographing difference: The body and identity in contemporary dance*. Wesleyan University Press.

Arcelus, J., Witcomb, G. L. & Mitchell, A. (2014). Prevalence of eating disorders amongst dancers: A systemic review and meta-analysis. *European Eating Disorders Review*, 22(2), 92–101. https://doi.org/10.1002/erv.2271

Aujla, I. J., Nordin-Bates, S. & Redding, E. (2014). A qualitative investigation of commitment to dance: Findings from the UK Centres for Advanced Training. *Research in Dance Education, 15*(2), 138–160. https://doi.org/10.1080/14647893.2013.825764

Berberick, S. N. (2010). The objectification of women in mass media: Female self-image in misogynist culture. *The New York Sociologist*, 5(2), 1–15.

Brochu, P. M. (2017). Addressing weight bias in a clinical psychology training program. Presented at the 5th Annual Weight Stigma Conference, Prague, Czech Republic.

Brown, N., White, J., Milligan, A., Risius, D., Ayres, B., Hedger, W. & Scurr, J. (2012). The relationship between breast size and anthropometric characteristics. *American Journal of Human Biology, 24*(2), 158–164. https://doi.org/10.1002/ajhb.22212

Dark, K. (2019). Exposure and erasure: Fat kids in gym class, fat adults as athletes. *Fat Studies, 8*(2), 127–134. https://doi.org/10.1080/21604851.2019.1552063

Findikcioglu, K., Findikcioglu, F., Ozmen, S. & Guclu, T. (2007). The impact of breast size on the vertebral column: A radiologic study. *Aesthetic Plastic Surgery, 31*(1), 23–27. https://doi.org/10.1007/s00266-006-0178-5

Fitzpatrick, K., & Tinning, R. (2014). Health education's fascist tendencies: A cautionary exposition. *Critical Public Health, 24*(2), 132–142. https://doi.org/10.108 0/09581596.2013.836590

Garafola, L. (1997). *Rethinking the Sylph: New perspectives on the romantic ballet.* Wesleyan University Press.

Gatto, L. (2018). Simona Halep breast reduction was her biggest sacrifice. Tennis World Foundation. Retrieved January 12, 2024 from https://www.tennisworldusa. org/tennis/news/Tennis_Interviews/55391/simona-halep-breast-reduction-was-her-biggest-sacrifice/

Gefen, A., & Dilmoney, B. (2007). Mechanics of the normal woman's breast. *Technology and Health Care, 15*(4), 259–271. http://dx.doi.org/10.3233/thc-2007-15404

Gilbert, A. G. (2018). Brain-compatible dance education (2nd ed). Human Kinetics.

Grabe, S., Routledge, C., Cook, A., Andersen, C. & Arndt, J. (2005). In defense of the body: The effect of mortality salience on female body objectification. *Psychology of Women Quarterly, 29*(1), 33–37. https://doi. org/10.1111/j.1471-6402.2005.00165.x

Grossman, D. (2020). Sexuality and Popular Culture. In N. Naples (Ed.) *Companion to sexuality studies.* John Wiley and Sons Ltd. https://doi. org/10.1002/9781119315049.ch15

Haake, S., & Scurr, J. (2010). A dynamic model of the breast during exercise. *Sports Engineering, 12*(4), 189–197. https://doi.org/10.1007/s12283-010-0046-z

Hamlisch, M., Noeltner, R. H., Kleban, E., Kirkwood, J. & Dante, N. (1977). *A chorus line.* Larry Shayne Enterprises Group.

Hanna, J. L., & Jowitt, D. (1988). *Dance, sex, and gender: Signs of identity, dominance, defiance, and desire.* University of Chicago Press. https://doi.org/10.2307/1478390

Huang, S., Boone, J. M., Yang, K., Packard, N. J., McKenney, S. E., Prionas, N. D., Lindfors, K. K. & Yaffe, M. J. (2011). The characterization of breast anatomical metrics using dedicated breast CT. *Medical Physics, 38*(4), 2180–2191. https://doi. org/10.1118/1.3567147

Karsay, K., Matthes, J., Buchsteiner, L. & Grosser, V. (2019). Increasingly sexy? Sexuality and sexual objectification in popular music videos, 1995–2016. *Psychology of Popular Media Culture, 8*(4), 346. https://doi.org/10.1037/ppm0000221

Katch, V. L., Campaigne, B., Freedson, P., Sady, S., Katch, F. I. & Behnke, A. R. (1980). Contribution of breast volume and weight to body fat distribution in females. *American Journal of Physical Anthropology, 53*(1), 93–100. https://doi. org/10.1002/ajpa.1330530113

Kowal, R. J., Siegmund, G. & Martin, R. (2017*). The Oxford handbook of dance and politics.* Oxford University Press.

Lapid, O., de Groof, E. J., Corion, L. U., Smeulders, M. J. & Van Der Horst, C. M. (2013). The effect of breast hypertrophy on patient posture. *Archives of Plastic Surgery, 40*(5), 559. https://doi.org/10.5999/aps.2013.40.5.559

Mazzocchi, M., Dessy, L. A., Di Ronza, S., Iodice, P., Saggini, R. & Scuderi, N. (2012a). A study of postural changes after breast reduction. *Aesthetic Plastic Surgery, 36*(6), 1311–1319. https://doi.org/10.1007/s00266-012-9968-0

Mazzocchi, M., Dessy, L. A., Iodice, P., Saggini, R., & Scuderi, N. (2012b). A study of postural changes after breast augmentation. *Aesthetic Plastic Surgery, 36*(3), 570–577. https://doi.org/10.1007/s00266-011-9841-6

McGhee, D. E., & Steele, J. R. (2020). Breast biomechanics: What do we really know? *Physiology, 35*(2), 144–156. https://doi.org/10.1152/physiol.00024.2019

Murali, M. (2019). Simona Halep opens up on breast surgery ahead of Australian Open 2019. Essentially Sports. Retrieved January 12, 2024 from https://www.essentiallysports.com/simona-halep-opens-up-on-breast-surgery-ahead-of-australian-open-2019/\

Rintaugu, E., & Ngetich, E. (2012). Motivational gender differences in sport and exercise participation among university sport science students. *Journal of Physical Education and Sport, 12*(2), 180.

Rothblum, E. D. (2016). Seven: Weapons of mass distraction in teaching fat studies: 'But aren't they unhealthy? And why can't they just lose weight?' *Counterpoints, 467*, 71–79. http://dx.doi.org/10.3726/978-1-4539-1784-8/20

Suleiman, S. R. (1986). *The female body in Western culture: Contemporary perspectives* (Vol. 6, Issues 1–2). Harvard University Press.

Van Sint Jan, S. (2007). *Color atlas of skeletal landmark definitions e-book: Guidelines for reproducible manual and virtual palpations*. Elsevier Health Sciences.

Wade, T. D., Zhu, G., & Martin, N. G. (2010). Body mass index and breast size in women: Same or different genes? *Twin Research and Human Genetics, 13*(5), 450–454. https://doi.org/10.1375/twin.13.5.450

Wright, J., & Leahy, D. (2016). Fourteen: Moving beyond body image: A socio-critical approach to teaching about health and body size. *Counterpoints, 467*, 141–149. http://dx.doi.org/10.3726/978-1-4539-1784-8/28

WTA Official. (n.d.). Simona Halep | ranking history | weekly and yearly rankings—Women's Tennis Association. Retrieved September 27, 2021, from https://www.wtatennis.com/players/314320/simona-halep/rankings-history

PART II

Moving through change

7

STRENGTH TRAINING CONSIDERATIONS FOR FEMALE DANCERS

Claire Farmer

Introduction

Different dance genres have differing demands and different aesthetics but strength is not a word often associated with female dancers. On the contrary, a female dancer's physique, particularly in dance forms of the Western canon, have been described as lithe and ethereal in ballet (Liiv et al., 2013) and of a slightly more muscular physique within modern dance (Chatfield et al., 1990).

Female dancers are often directed towards Pilates and yoga or low resistance exercise in order to gain 'long, lean muscles' due to the preconception held in the dance sector that strength training will increase muscle girth and therefore negatively impact the aesthetics of their dance performance (Koutedakis et al., 2005, 2007; Twitchett et al., 2009) despite evidence to the contrary (Koutedakis et al., 2005). Recent research (Farmer & Brouner, 2021; Rosenthal et al., 2021) has also demonstrated that there is a desire among current dance students and professional dancers to include strength training in their programmes. However, a lack of time within dancers' training or performance schedules, and a lack of specific guidance from qualified strength and conditioning coaches within schools and companies restricts this. Additional barriers to participating in strength training may also include feelings of intimidation entering a gym space, particularly for those who do not have access to a dedicated fitness training space within their dance institution. Gyms remain gendered spaces that are often perceived as masculine environments, particularly in relation to weight training (Coen et al., 2018; Turnock, 2021). This may make dancers feel uncomfortable entering these spaces to train, and therefore reduce participation in strength training that

DOI: 10.4324/9781003382874-10

could enhance their dance performance. Dance students also recognised the need for parity of access, noting that strength training is neither a male nor female activity (Farmer et al, 2024). Therefore, these training environments need to feel equally open and accessible to all.

The choreographic demands placed upon dancers are increasing, with more extreme athletic abilities required (Wyon et al., 2016) such as handstands, controlled falls to the floor and other inverted movements that require upper body strength and endurance. More extreme ranges of motion are popularised and higher, more technically demanding jumps and tricks with great athletic demand. This requires an increased level of physical tolerance and capacity to be able to withstand this demand. This chapter will explore the social-cultural, structural and emotional barriers to participation in strength training and the physiological differences that need to be considered when training female dancers. It should be noted that this chapter will explore female both as sex in relation to biological outcomes, and as gender in relation to the experiences of the female dancer in strength training spaces.

Female athletic participation and performance

Historically females have been discouraged or even prohibited from participating in sports (Forsyth & Roberts, 2019; McGregor, 2020) with only 2.2% of Olympic competitors in 1900 being female (Costello et al., 2014; Elliott-Sale et al., 2021). Since then, there has been a significant increase in female participation in sports and physical activity, reaching 44.2% of total participants in London in 2012 (Costello et al., 2014) with females now participating in sports in record numbers (Sims & Heather, 2018). Despite this increase in participation, there are currently no sport and exercise related guidelines for training and nutrition that are customised to the female athlete (Elliott-Sale et al., 2021). As such, female training is often formulated based on guidelines for male athletes and does not account for known biological differences between sexes and the female training environment (Emmonds et al., 2019).

Females require different guidelines relating to nutrition, performance, recovery and injury prevention that consider biological, psychological, biomechanical and environmental differences with male athletes and dancers (Emmonds et al., 2019). Sports/dance scientists and coaches working with athletes and dancers aim to provide evidence-based practice, utilising current research to inform the way they train, treat or coach females (Emmonds et al., 2019). However, the use of research that has been carried out predominantly on male participants is concerning for the female athlete as they have been shown to experience different symptoms, prevalence and outcomes to injuries when compared with male athletes. For example, it has been proposed that females are more prone to anterior cruciate ligament (ACL) injuries, with a disproportionate increase in female ACL injuries after the onset of puberty (Sutton & Bullock, 2013). Females may also be more susceptible to concussion than their male counterparts and experience prolonged symptoms post-concussion (Covassin et al., 2013; McGroarty et al., 2020). It has been suggested that these differences are as a result of biomechanical and hormonal differences, although there is currently a paucity of data to support this assertion. However, these differences highlight the need for sex-specific guidelines in the prevention, and treatment of injuries, as well as the way in which we train female dancers.

Many different factors may impact females' experience of training throughout their lifetime, including puberty, menstrual cycle, pregnancy, perimenopause, menopause, lack of female coaches and differences in body composition in comparison to male athletes. Without recognising these fundamental differences, and continual fluctuations and changes within a female's training and professional life cycle, we may be impeding their progress and performance ability. Female dancers' full athletic and creative potential may not be fully achieved if we continue to apply male focused research to females (Elliott-Sale et al., 2021; Emmonds et al., 2019) and do not address the many barriers to participation in strength training. It therefore may also be possible to achieve marginal gains in female training outcomes through implementation of sex-specific training (Elliott-Sale et al., 2021; Nuzzo, 2023).

Muscle hypertrophy

Skeletal muscle plays an important role in the functioning of the human body during movement, specifically in this instance relating to athletic (Lim et al., 2022) and dance performance. Muscle hypertrophy refers to an increase in the axial cross-sectional area (CSA) of skeletal muscle (Lim et al., 2022). A commonly held misconception among dancers, particularly female dancers, is that strength training will elicit significant increases in muscle CSA and therefore negatively impact dance aesthetics, despite evidence to the contrary (Koutedakis et al., 2005). Indeed, initial strength increases have been suggested to be as a result of neuromuscular adaptation, and thus hypertrophy is not a significant concern in the early stages of strength training (Koutedakis & Jamurtas, 2004). The ability to increase muscle CSA also differs for females due to a range of physiological and hormonal differences.

Muscle contraction relies on the contractile properties of the muscle tissue. Muscle length plays an important role in the ability to exert force due to the optimal crossover of actin and myosin filaments and ability of the muscle to exert force (Katch et al., 2015). Due to the presence of the male sex hormone, androgen/testosterone, men possess a greater degree of muscle mass and thus greater strength overall, but to a bigger degree in the lower limbs than females (Forsyth & Roberts, 2019; Nuzzo, 2023).

TABLE 7.1 Absolute and relative strength comparison

Dancer 1	*Dancer 2*
Body mass = 58kg	Body mass = 80kg
Deadlift = 70kg	Deadlift = 70kg
Absolute strength = 70kg	Absolute strength = 70kg
Relative strength = 1.21 kg/kg of body mass	Relative strength = 0.88 kg/kg of body mass

Muscular strength can be discussed as either 'absolute strength' or 'relative strength'. Absolute strength refers to the total amount of weight lifted. However, relative strength provides a measure of strength in relation to your own body mass. For example, in Table 7.1 you can see an example of two dancers who have a different body mass but are both able to deadlift a maximum of 70kg (1 Repetition Max). While the absolute strength of both dancers is the same at 70kg, when we compare their strength in relation to body mass, Dancer 1 is stronger, as they are able to lift more kilograms per kilograms of body mass. This can be particularly useful in comparing the strength of a group of athletes or dancers who each have a different body mass or in weight category sports such as Powerlifting.

Women have been shown to possess 40%–50% of absolute strength in the upper body (elbow flexion and extension) in comparison to men and 50%–80% of absolute strength in the lower body (knee flexion and extension) (Nuzzo, 2023). However, there are no sex differences when strength is expressed relative to CSA, suggesting there is no difference in strength per unit between sex. Men and women also likely have difference strength-related training outcomes; however the degree to which these differences occur and how they may differ between different muscle groups and contractions is not yet fully understood (Nuzzo, 2023).

Hormones play an important role in the maintenance of skeletal muscle. Testosterone levels in men remain relatively stable from day to day, and therefore do not fluctuate across a training cycle in the same way that female hormones (oestrogens) do, although testosterone levels may fall as a result of overtraining (Sims & Heather, 2018). The fluctuations of female hormones throughout the menstrual cycle have been suggested to have a minor impact upon components of fitness including strength. However there is currently limited research of moderate quality and with different methodologies which means this is difficult to substantiate (Colenso-Semple et al., 2023; Ekenros et al., 2022). More long-term decreases in hormone levels such as the drop in oestrogen associated with the menopause, may however have greater impact on muscular strength. Resistance training throughout the life cycle can therefore have beneficial outcomes for female dancers in order to develop and maintain muscular strength.

Resistance training

Resistance training (also known as strength or weight training) is an external stimulus for increasing skeletal muscle mass (Lim et al., 2022). However, this is also impacted by other internal factors. Early strength gains in untrained individuals may occur from neural adaptations, whereby there are improvements in movement co-ordination and effective engagement of muscle fibres (Wyon & Clarke, 2021). This can be seen in rapid increases in strength during the initial weeks and months of a training programme. Further strength gains after this are related to an increase in muscle CSA (hypertrophy) (Bird et al., 2005). However, this is likely to appear as more muscle definition and tone rather than the significant changes in muscle size often seen in body builders. The dramatic increase in CSA in this population occurs as a result of specific hypertrophy training regimes, for example 10RM with 1-minute rest periods, which has been shown to increase anabolic hormones as well as providing greater total work and blood lactate concentrations (Bird et al., 2005). These practices are unlikely to occur in a dancers' strength training programme and therefore dramatic increases in muscle CSA are improbable unless the strength training programme undertaken is designed with a hypertrophy goal in mind.

Females are often directed to low intensity bodyweight exercises, Pilates or yoga to avoid increases in muscle girth, with an assumption that picking up heavier weights will cause sudden muscle bulk. As discussed above, initial increases in strength may be derived from neuromuscular adaptation, therefore these lower intensity practices may be beneficial in the initial stages of training. However, without continual progressive overload, strength gains will begin to plateau, and training will focus on muscular endurance instead. While muscular endurance is beneficial for dance performance, building physical capacity through strength training can aid in stability of joints and building physical tolerance for choreographic demands. Current research into Pilates has demonstrated mixed methodologies and thus physiological outcomes are currently difficult to ascertain (Bernardo & Nagle, 2006), although benefits to neuromuscular control and abdominal strength for postural control have been noted (Ahearn et al., 2018). The impact on global strength has yet to be determined however.

Progressive overload relies on a regular increase of volume, intensity or frequency in order to stimulate muscular adaptation (Bird et al., 2005), thus dancers must regularly alter their training programmes to see continual progression in fitness parameters such as muscular strength. In order to increase muscular strength ≤6 repetitions are recommended at 85% of your one repetition maximum (1RM)—the maximum amount of weight you can lift for one repetition. Recent research however, has instead suggested utilising RM, 'the greatest amount of weight lifted with correct technique for a specified number of repetitions' (Bird et al., 2005, p. 844) to avoid the need for testing 1RM which can be unsafe for those unfamiliar with the specific lift (commonly used measures include the back squat, bench press or overhead press). For example, a 3- or 5-RM may be a safer option (Wyon & Clarke, 2021). For those new to strength training, exercise programmes may begin as three to five repetitions with just your bodyweight such as a squat, push up (or modified variation). These are examples of compound movements that utilise multiple muscle groups collaboratively and form a strong foundation for further strength training work.

As with all exercises, including dance movements, it is important to ensure correct form before progressing and loading them with more weight, therefore beginning with these body weight exercises can allow time for neuro-muscular adaptation in preparation for implementing progressive overload. Increases in load might take the form of dumbbells, kettlebells, barbells or utilising resistance training machines at the gym. If you are unsure where to begin with this equipment it is always best to seek the advice of a qualified professional in setting up the equipment safely and to suit your own body.

Environmental barriers to participating in strength training

Females are less likely to meet national guidelines for physical activity in the UK (Sport England, 2023) and North America (Coen et al., 2018). Lack of access to strength training professionals and safe, welcoming spaces may also be responsible for the lack of female participation in strength training. Gendered norms around what is perceived as a 'healthy' or 'fit' body are widely promoted, particularly within the commercial sector as more in line with heterosexualised and patriarchal images of female fitness (Turnock, 2021). This 'body privilege' can lead many to feel marginalised, especially from physical fitness spaces such as gyms if they do not fit these predefined body images (Turnock, 2021), and has been linked with limited female engagement in sports such as weightlifting (Coen et al., 2018).

Gym spaces remain heavily gendered spaces, often perceived as 'hyper-masculine' (Coen et al., 2018; Turnock, 2021), with the gym floor often separated into cardiovascular spaces (perceived female) and weight training spaces (perceived male) (Coen et al., 2018). Women have also reported feeling intimidated entering free-weights areas within gym environments that are often heavily male-populated, or do not feel able to approach gym staff for guidance (Turnock, 2021). These social-cultural and structural barriers are also reflected in the current sports and exercise research and strength recommendations for women, and may be related to lower levels of participation in physical activity, specifically strength training, than men (Coen et al., 2018).

Recent research has suggested that dancers are keen to participate in strength training (Farmer & Brouner, 2021) and that dance students perceive strength training as important for all genders and should not be the domain of men only (Farmer et al., 2024). However, dancers often lack access to qualified strength and conditioning coaches to guide them in specific training programmes, and are often taught strength training by a dance teacher, personal trainer or via online video tutorials. It is important for dancers, particularly those at the beginning of their strength training journey, to be able to access guidance and equipment that can allow them to safely develop their physical fitness and in a way that is specific to their individual body and choreographic requirements. However, barriers to physical gym spaces and engaging with gym staff can make this difficult for all dancers to access.

Demystifying strength training programmes and equipment can open these spaces to females. Potential avenues to achieving this can be the through the inclusion of strength training coaches within dance schools and company staff teams, providing a multi-disciplinary approach to dance training, as well as opportunities to work with peers during strength training for motivation and support. Parity of education and access should also be given to both male and female dancers with regards to setting up gym equipment, technique guidance and ongoing training advice. Designated time should also be provided within timetables for focused strength and conditioning with qualified coaches, allowing artistic staff to focus on technique, artistry and creativity.

Injuries in dance

Injury rates in dance have been suggested to be high in comparison to other sports with a high prevalence of lower extremity injuries including ankle, knee and lower back. It should be noted however that current dance injury research lacks consistency in injury definition, diagnoses and calculation of incidence (Mattiussi et al., 2021). Research into injury incidence and characteristics in musical theatre dance students (Stephens et al., 2021) and modern dancers (Bronner, 2021) showed no significant sex differences. Although the demands of choreography are continually developing, with blurring of gender divides, current training and roles still perpetuate specific movements dependent on gender. This sees female ballet dancers, for example, spending more time on pointe with a higher potential for ankle injuries, compared with male ballet dancers who are expected to demonstrate powerful, explosive movements such as jumps. Hip-hop dancers have been shown to employ many weight-bearing movements that are at end range of motion (Bronner et al., 2015) and sustain a greater number of injuries than modern dancers (Uršej & Zaletel, 2020). Research on ballroom dance sport has demonstrated a higher prevalence of head and neck injuries in female dancers than their male partners (Keijsers et al., 2023). Finally, those participating in pole dancing sustain more injuries to the shoulder and thigh, specifically the hamstrings (Nicholas et al., 2022). Based on this research it should be considered that the location and mechanism of an injury will be specific to the dance genre and broad assumptions in relation to 'dance' should be avoided.

Women with higher concentrations of relaxin, which has been noted to peak around the luteal phase of the menstrual cycle (Emmonds et al., 2019), as well as higher concentrations during pregnancy, may experience increased range of motion due to the effects of relaxin on tissue laxity. Dancers in particular may be tempted to utilise this additional range which may put ligaments and joints at risk and predispose them to potential injury. Therefore, stabilising these joints through strength training may be beneficial. It has also been suggested that women are more prone to ACL injuries than men (Sutton & Bullock, 2013). In comparison to sports however, incidence of ACL injuries has been shown to be relatively low in dance with 0.2% in ballet and 0.4% in contemporary dance over the course of a five-year study and an overall incidence rate of 0.009 ACL injuries per 1,000 dance exposures (Liederbach et al., 2008).

Although data are inconsistent, it is apparent that dancers of all genres are at risk of injury, potentially due to fatigue, incorrect technique, or other extrinsic factors. Consideration should therefore be given to the demands of any upcoming choreography with training planned to mitigate this injury risk where possible.

How strength training can benefit the female dancer

Although there is currently very little research relating to the strength demands of choreography and benefits on dance performance from strength training, it has been suggested that strength training can be beneficial in stabilising joints, thus reducing the risk of injury and increasing physical tolerance (Angioi et al., 2009; Moita et al., 2017). However, differing and weak research methodologies mean the relationship between strength and dance injuries is still unclear (Moita et al., 2017).

Research has however also indicated that dancers have lower isokinetic torque values than other athletes and similar or lower levels than some untrained individuals (Koutedakis et al., 2005), and that female ballerinas have the least muscular strength (Koutedakis & Jamurtas, 2004). It should be noted though, that strength research in dance has to date focused predominantly on the lower body and within ballet and contemporary dance genre.

Although research has yet to explore a definitive link between strength and injury, it stands to reason that increased physical capacity will enhance tolerance to choreographic demand and potentially mitigate injury risk (Koutedakis et al., 2005). It has been posited that dance class does not place sufficient demand on the physiological systems to elicit any adaptation, including increases in muscular strength (Koutedakis et al., 2005). Therefore, in order to see any increases in strength, dancers must also include specific strength training in their routine. Note that I do not describe this as supplementary training, as this should be an integral part of dance training rather than an optional addition. Building physical tolerance in all fitness parameters, including muscular strength will allow you to explore more diverse and demanding choreography within class, and focus on creativity and expression rather than worrying about tired muscles.

Strength training can also help to stabilise joints, particularly for those who have hypermobility spectrum disorder (HSD) or Hypermobile Ehlers Danlos Syndrome (hEDS) and therefore may require more stability around their joints to control extreme range of motion and reduce risk of recurrent joint dislocations (Coussens et al., 2022). Coussens et al. (2022) measured strength and endurance in females with HSD and hEDS and reported lower levels of strength in the lower limbs than control groups. The authors therefore suggested that individualised strength and endurance training be included in treatment of those with HSD and hEDS. However, strength training requires moving heavy loads of ≤60% 1RM in untrained individuals, or ≤80% in active individuals, and there have therefore been safety concerns with lifting such heavy loads, and testing 1RM with those with HSD or eEDS (Zabriskie, 2022).

Strength training also provides a myriad of health benefits including increased bone mass, reduced blood pressure, reduced body fat and increased muscle and connective tissue CSA for those with and without HSD/eDS (Bird et al., 2005; Zabriskie, 2022). Increases in bone mass can be of particular importance for those experiencing osteopenia or osteoporosis, either due to the impact of REDs or as a result of decreases in oestrogen post-menopause. Therefore, for the older dancer, participating in strength training may increase career longevity as well as general improved health outcomes.

The benefits of participating in strength training therefore appear to outweigh any fear of changes to the dance aesthetic. Thus, excluding female dancers from strength training programmes, or not providing parity of access for all dancers, may hinder performance and put dancers at risk of injury from lack of strength. Incorporating strength training, by qualified professionals, into dance training and performance programmes could help to mitigate these risks and greater stronger, more resilient dancers.

Strength training recommendations for female dancers

- Consider the choreography you are currently being asked to perform. Which muscle groups have the most demand? Would developing strength in these muscles aid your performance?
- Seek the support of a strength and conditioning coach to design a plan that is specific to you and the choreography you are working on.

- Ask a member of the gym staff or a friend to show you the gym and how to set up a squat rack or use a specific piece of equipment. Then you can feel confident moving in these spaces.
- Find a gym buddy. This can help you to feel more confident in gym spaces, provide motivation and help you feel more confident.
- Although it can be difficult, try to focus on the functionality of your body rather than the aesthetic component of exercise. Your training is about preparing it to perform the amazing choreography you are aiming for!

References

Ahearn, E. L., Greene, A. & Lasner, A. (2018). Some effects of supplemental Pilates training on the posture, strength, and flexibility of dancers 17 to 22 years of age. *Journal of Dance Medicine & Science: Official Publication of the International Association for Dance Medicine & Science*, 22(4), 192–202. https://doi.org/10.12678/1089-313X.22.4.192

Angioi, M., Metsios, G. S., Twitchett, E., Koutedakis, Y. & Wyon, M. (2009). Association between selected physical fitness parameters and esthetic competence in contemporary dancers. *Journal of Dance Medicine & Science : Official Publication of the International Association for Dance Medicine & Science*, 13(4), 115–123. https://pubmed.ncbi.nlm.nih.gov/19930813/

Bernardo, L. M., & Nagle, E. E. (2006). Does Pilates training benefit dancers? *Journal of Dance Medicine & Science*, 10(1/2), 46–50. http://dx.doi.org/10.1177/1089313x06010001-210

Bird, S. P., Tarpenning, K. M. & Marino, F. E. (2005). Designing resistance training programmes to enhance muscular fitness: A review of the acute programme variables. *Sports Medicine*, 35(10), 841–851. https://doi.org/10.2165/00007256-200535100-00002/FIGURES/TAB1

Bronner, S. (2021). Injury characteristics in pre-professional modern dancers – prospective study of differences due to sex, training year, and external causal mechanisms. *Journal of Dance Medicine & Science: Official Publication of the International Association for Dance Medicine & Science*, 25(2), 117–130. https://doi.org/10.12678/1089-313X.061521G

Bronner, S., Ojofeitimi, S. & Woo, H. (2015). Extreme kinematics in selected hip hop dance sequences. *Medical Problems of Performing Artists*, 30(3), 126–134c. https://doi.org/10.21091/MPPA.2015.3026

Chatfield, S. J., Byrnes, W. C., Lally, D. A. & Rowe, S. E. (1990). Cross-Sectional Physiologic Profiling of Modern Dancers. *Dance Research Journal*, 22(1), 13. https://doi.org/10.2307/1477737

Coen, S. E., Rosenberg, M. W. & Davidson, J. (2018). 'It's gym, like g-y-m not J-i-m': Exploring the role of place in the gendering of physical activity. *Social Science & Medicine*, 196, 29–36. https://doi.org/10.1016/J.SOCSCIMED.2017.10.036

Colenso-Semple, L. M., D'Souza, A. C., Elliott-Sale, K. J. & Phillips, S. M. (2023). Current evidence shows no influence of women's menstrual cycle phase on acute strength performance or adaptations to resistance exercise training. *Frontiers in Sports and Active Living*, 5, 1054542. https://doi.org/10.3389/FSPOR.2023.1054542/BIBTEX

Costello, J. T., Bieuzen, F. & Bleakley, C. M. (2014). Where are all the female participants in sports and exercise medicine research? *European Journal of Sport Science*, *14*(8), 847–851. https://doi.org/10.1080/17461391.2014.911354

Coussens, M., Lapauw, B., Banica, T., De Wandele, I., Pacey, V., Rombaut, L., Malfait, F. & Calders, P. (2022). Muscle strength, muscle mass and physical impairment in women with hypermobile Ehlers-Danlos syndrome and hypermobility spectrum disorder. *Journal of Musculoskeletal & Neuronal Interactions*, *22*(1), 5. http://dx.doi.org/10.1016/j.bone.2022.116583

Covassin, T., Elbin, R. J., Crutcher, B. & Burkhart, S. (2013). The management of sport-related concussion: Considerations for male and female athletes. *Translational Stroke Research*, *4*(4), 420–424. https://doi.org/10.1007/S12975-012-0228-Z

Ekenros, L., von Rosen, P., Solli, G. S., Sandbakk, Ø., Holmberg, H. C., Hirschberg, A. L. & Fridén, C. (2022). Perceived impact of the menstrual cycle and hormonal contraceptives on physical exercise and performance in 1,086 athletes from 57 sports. *Frontiers in Physiology*, *13*, 954760. https://doi.org/10.3389/FPHYS.2022.954760/BIBTEX

Elliott-Sale, K. J., Minahan, C. L., de Jonge, X. A. K. J., Ackerman, K. E., Sipilä, S., Constantini, N. W., Lebrun, C. M. & Hackney, A. C. (2021). Methodological considerations for studies in sport and exercise science with women as participants: A working guide for standards of practice for research on women. *Sports Medicine (Auckland, N.Z.)*, *51*(5), 843–861. https://doi.org/10.1007/S40279-021-01435-8

Emmonds, S., Heyward, O., & Jones, B. (2019). The challenge of applying and undertaking research in female sport. *Sports Medicine – Open*, *5*(1), 1–4. https://doi.org/10.1186/S40798-019-0224-X/FIGURES/1

Farmer, C., & Brouner, J. (2021). Perceptions of strength training in dance. *Journal of Dance Medicine & Science*, *25*(3), 160–168. https://doi.org/10.12678/1089-313x.091521a

Farmer, C., De'Ath, S. & Brouner, J. (2024). Strength training perceptions amongst vocational circus and dance students. *Journal of Dance Medicine & Science*, *28*(1), 37–42. https://doi.org/10.1177/1089313X231204164

Forsyth, J. J., & Roberts, C.-M. (2019). *The exercising female: Science and its application*. Routledge.

Katch, V., Katch, F. & McArdle, W. (2015). *Essentials of exercise physiology* (5th ed.). LWW.

Keijsers, P. J. H., Busscher, I., Crijns, H. J. M. J. & Ewals, R. C. T. (2023). Injuries in ballroom dance sport: A retrospective study on prevalence and relation with demographic data. *Journal of Dance Medicine & Science: Official Publication of the International Association for Dance Medicine & Science*, 1089313X2311780. https://doi.org/10.1177/1089313X231178090

Koutedakis, Y., Hukam, H., Metsios, G., Nevill, A., Giakas, G., Jamurtas, A. & Myszkewycz, L. (2007). The effects of three months of aerobic and strength training on selected performance and fitness-related parameters in modern dance students. *Journal of Strength and Conditioning Research*, *21*(3), 808–812. https://doi.org/10.1519/R-20856.1

Koutedakis, Y., & Jamurtas, A. (2004). The dancer as a performing athlete: Physiological considerations. In *Sports Medicine* (Vol. 34, Issue 10, pp. 651–661). Springer. https://doi.org/10.2165/00007256-200434100-00003

Koutedakis, Y., Stavropoulos-Kalinoglou, A. & Metsios, G. (2005). The significance of muscular strength in dance. *Journal of Dance Medicine & Science, 9*(1), 29–34. http://dx.doi.org/10.1177/1089313x0500900106

Liederbach, M., Dilgen, F. E. & Rose, D. J. (2008). Incidence of anterior cruciate ligament injuries among elite ballet and modern dancers: A 5-year prospective study. *The American Journal of Sports Medicine, 36*(9), 1779–1788. https://doi.org/10.1177/0363546508323644

Liiv, H., Wyon, M. A., Jürimäe, T., Saar, M., Mäestu, J. & Jürimäe, J. (2013). Anthropometry, somatotypes, and aerobic power in ballet, contemporary dance, and DanceSport. *Medical Problems of Performing Artists, 28*(4), 207–211. http://dx.doi.org/10.21091/mppa.2013.4041

Lim, C., Nunes, E. A., Currier, B. S., McLeod, J. C., Thomas, A. C. Q. & Phillips, S. M. (2022). An evidence-based narrative review of mechanisms of resistance exercise-induced human skeletal muscle hypertrophy. *Medicine and Science in Sports and Exercise, 54*(9), 1546. https://doi.org/10.1249/MSS.0000000000002929

Mattiussi, A. M., Shaw, J. W., Williams, S., Price, P. D. B., Brown, D. D., Cohen, D. D., Clark, R., Kelly, S., Retter, G., Pedlar, C. & Tallent, J. (2021). Injury epidemiology in professional ballet: A five-season prospective study of 1596 medical attention injuries and 543 time-loss injuries. *British Journal of Sports Medicine, 55*(15), 843–850. https://doi.org/10.1136/BJSPORTS-2020-103817

McGregor, Angela. J. (2020). *Sex matters: How male-centric medicine endangers women's health and what we can do about it.* Quercus.

McGroarty, N. K., Brown, S. M. & Mulcahey, M. K. (2020). Sport-related concussion in female athletes: A systematic review. *Orthopaedic Journal of Sports Medicine, 8*(7). https://doi.org/10.1177/2325967120932306/ASSET/IMAGES/LARGE/10.1177_2325967120932306-FIG1.JPEG

Moita, J. P., Nunes, A., Esteves, J., Oliveira, R. & Xarez, L. (2017). The relationship between muscular strength and dance injuries: A systematic review. *Medical Problems of Performing Artists, 32*(1), 40–50. https://doi.org/10.21091/MPPA.2017.1002

Nicholas, J., Weir, G., Alderson, J. A., Stubbe, J. H., van Rijn, R. M., Dimmock, J. A., Jackson, B., Donnelly, C. J. & Nicholas, J. (2022). Incidence, mechanisms, and characteristics of injuries in pole dancers: A prospective cohort study. *Medical Problems of Performing Artists, 37*(3), 151–164. https://doi.org/10.21091/MPPA.2022.3022

Nuzzo, J. L. (2023). Narrative review of sex differences in muscle strength, endurance, activation, Size, fiber type, and strength training participation rates, preferences, motivations, injuries, and neuromuscular adaptations. *Journal of Strength and Conditioning Research, 37*(2), 494–536. https://doi.org/10.1519/JSC.0000000000004329

Rosenthal, M., McPherson, A. M., Docherty, C. L. & Klossner, J. (2021). Perceptions and utilization of strength training and conditioning in collegiate contemporary and ballet dancers a qualitative approach. *Medical Problems of Performing Artists, 36*(2), 78–87. https://doi.org/10.21091/mppa.2021.2012

Sims, S. T., & Heather, A. K. (2018). Myths and methodologies: Reducing scientific design ambiguity in studies comparing sexes and/or menstrual cycle phases. *Experimental Physiology, 103*(10), 1309–1317. https://doi.org/10.1113/EP086797

Sport England. (2023). *Active Lives Adult Survey November 21–22 Report*. Retrieved January 12, 2024 from https://www.sportengland.org/research-and-data/data/active-lives

Stephens, N., Nevill, A. M. & Wyon, M. A. (2021). Injury incidence and severity in musical theatre dance students: 5-year prospective study. *International Journal of Sports Medicine, 42*(13), 1222–1227. https://doi.org/10.1055/A-1393-6151

Sutton, K. M., & Bullock, J. M. (2013). Anterior cruciate ligament rupture: Differences between males and females. *The Journal of the American Academy of Orthopaedic Surgeons, 21*(1), 41–50. https://doi.org/10.5435/JAAOS-21-01-41

Turnock, L. A. (2021). 'There's a difference between tolerance and acceptance': Exploring women's experiences of barriers to access in UK gyms. *Wellbeing, Space and Society, 2*, 100049. https://doi.org/10.1016/J.WSS.2021.100049

Twitchett, E. A., Koutedakis, Y. & Wyon, M. A. (2009). Physiological fitness and professional classical ballet performance: A brief review. *Journal of Strength and conditioning research / National Strength & Conditioning Association, 23*(9), 2732–2740. https://doi.org/10.1519/JSC.0b013e3181bc1749

Uršej, E., & Zaletel, P. (2020). Injury occurrence in modern and hip-hop dancers: A systematic literature review. *Zdravstveno Varstvo, 59*(3), 195–201. https://doi.org/10.2478/SJPH-2020-0025

Wyon, M., Allen, N., Cloak, R., Beck, S., Davies, P. & Clarke, F. (2016). Assessment of maximum aerobic capacity and anaerobic threshold of elite ballet dancers. *Medical Problems of Performing Artists, 31*(3), 145–150. https://doi.org/10.21091/MPPA.2016.3027

Wyon, M., & Clarke, S. (2021). *Strength and conditioning for dancers*. Crowood Press.

Zabriskie, H. A. (2022). Rationale and feasibility of resistance training in hEDS/HSD: A narrative review. *Journal of Functional Morphology and Kinesiology, 7*(3), 61. https://doi.org/10.3390/JFMK7030061

8

PELVIC FLOOR CONSIDERATIONS FOR FEMALE DANCERS THROUGH THE LIFESPAN

Brooke Winder

Introduction to pelvic floor anatomy and function

The pelvic floor refers to the region of the body containing the base of the pelvic bones, the sacrum, pelvic floor muscles and associated organs, connective tissue, nerves and blood vessels. The pelvic floor serves many important functions for a dancer, both in daily life and in dance training and performance.

To visualise pelvic floor anatomy, begin by imagining the two pelvic bones (the os coxae) joining in the front at the pubic region (forming a joint called the pubic symphysis) and joining at the back by hugging either side of the triangular sacral bone (forming a right and left sacroiliac joint.) The pelvis forms a heart-shaped bowl, with the base of the bowl being the pelvic floor.

The muscles of the pelvic floor span from front to back (pubic symphysis to tailbone, or coccyx), and from side to side, between the sitz bones (ischial tuberosities), like a hammock. There are three layers of muscle that make up this hammock. The most superficial layer (closest to the surface of the body) and the middle layer consist of muscles that serve mainly as sphincters, including the external urethral sphincter and external anal sphincter. These muscles help close the openings of the body (i.e. the urethra and rectum) to control the flow of urine and faeces, and they relax to allow for urination and bowel movements. The deepest (farthest from the surface and closer to the abdominopelvic cavity) layer consists of the muscles known as the 'pelvic diaphragm', including the levator ani (pubococcygeus, puborectalis and iliococcygeus) and the coccygeus. These muscles serve as the deep, broad support for the organs of the pelvis (Eickmeyer, 2017) (Figures 8.1 and 8.2).

When the pelvic floor muscles contract, they pull toward the centre of the perineum (the fleshy area between the sitz bones) as well as upwards towards

DOI: 10.4324/9781003382874-11

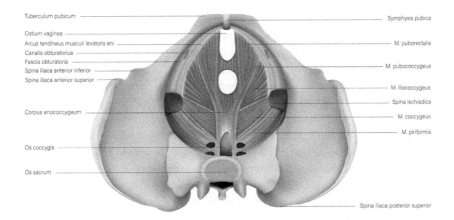

Tuberculum pubicum
Ostium vaginae
Arcus tendineus musculi levatoris ani
Canalis obturatorius
Fascia obturatoria
Spina iliaca anterior inferior
Spina iliaca anterior superior
Corpus anococcygeum
Os coccygis
Os sacrum

Symphysis pubica
M. puborectalis
M. pubococcygeus
M. iliococcygeus
Spina ischiadica
M. coccygeus
M. piriformis
Spina iliaca posterior superior

FIGURE 8.1 Superior view of the pelvic floor (deepest layer/pelvic diaphragm)

PELVIC FLOOR MUSCLES

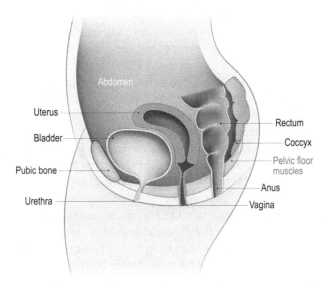

Abdomen
Uterus
Bladder
Pubic bone
Urethra
Rectum
Coccyx
Pelvic floor muscles
Anus
Vagina

FIGURE 8.2 Lateral view of pelvic floor muscles' relationship to the pelvic organs. Copyright Shutterstock

the inside of the body. This contraction is often referred to as a kegel. When the muscles relax, they soften back downwards.

To practice a kegel, begin in a sitting position to feel your sitz bones and perineum underneath you. Then, inhale and imagine softening and slightly expanding the hammock of pelvic floor muscles into the chair. As you exhale, pull your perineum up away from the chair. Example imagery can include 'suck up a thick milkshake through a straw with your muscles' or 'use the muscles to grasp a tiny imaginary blueberry and lift it up inside your body.' You may feel a gentle abdominal contraction when this occurs, and that is great—however, try to avoid clenching your buttock or sucking in the abdomen intensely. After the contraction occurs, make sure to finish with a full relaxation of the muscles down toward the chair. Imagery to encourage relaxation can include 'let the pelvic floor muscles melt like butter,' or 'imagine the space between your sitz bones expanding.' The pelvic floor muscles can also bulge outward and downward, which is the bearing down necessary during bowel movements or, on a larger scale, during vaginal birth.

The muscles of the pelvic floor work together with the endopelvic fascia, which provides connective tissue support to the bony structures, muscles and organs of the pelvis. Sitting just above the pelvic floor muscles and suspended by the fascia are the bladder, rectum and uterus (or prostate) if present. Several important nerves feed the pelvic floor region, including nerves from the autonomic nervous system (the system that regulates homeostasis) and nerves that control muscle activation and sensation, such as the pudendal nerve (Betschart et al., 2019; Roch et al., 2021).

There are five 'S' functions of the pelvic floor: sphincteric, sexual, 'sump pump', support and stability. The sphincteric function means that these muscles help to 'close the openings' of the body to maintain continence (avoiding urine or bowel leakage), and they relax for urination and bowel movements. These muscles support sexual function by contributing to arousal and orgasm. The 'sump pump' function means that the pelvic floor helps move lymph fluid and blood through the pelvis and up into the trunk. Support refers to the pelvic floor supporting the organs against the downward pressure produced by coughing, laughing, jumping, landing and other impact activities. And last, stability refers to the pelvic floor's contribution to stabilisation across the pelvis, otherwise referred to as 'force closure', allowing a stable pelvic base for the forces dancers encounter from the lower body up through the spine.

The pelvic floor also holds important roles in breathing, pressure management and core function, which are integral to efficient dance movement. The pelvic floor works closely with the respiratory diaphragm and the glottis (the middle of the larynx where the vocal cords open and close) during inhalation and exhalation, vocalisation and singing, and in movement to adjust pressure throughout the trunk, ribs and pelvis. When inhaling occurs during relaxed breathing, the diaphragm moves downward into the abdominal cavity, and the pelvic floor also descends downward. During a relaxed exhalation, both the diaphragm and pelvic floor move upward (Kocjan et al., 2017; Talasz et al., 2011).

Because the pelvic floor responds to and works with the diaphragm, one of the easiest ways to encourage improved pelvic floor movement and function is for dancers to train a variety of breathing strategies. Many dancers tense their core so much during dancing that they can restrict adequate diaphragm and pelvic floor movement and function. To counteract this habit, you can practise expansive breathing in a variety of restful or stretching positions. Imagine your inhales expanding to the sides and back wall of your ribcage and your lower belly in a three-dimensional manner, and long exhales softening down the front of your chest and ribs.

The pelvic floor muscles are key players in a dancer's core stabilisation. The trunk and pelvis act as a pressure-filled canister, with the diaphragm as the lid, abdominal wall at the front, back extensor and spinal stabiliser muscles along the back, and the pelvic floor as the base. This canister serves as a dynamic and responsive system that adjusts to pressure and impact, mostly automatically. During more intense demands, such as strong vocalisation or singing, landing from a jump, or lifting a partner, the muscles around the canister produce tension to increase pressure and spinal stiffness—and the pelvic floor will activate to meet the pressure produced by the trunk muscle stiffening from above. You can sense how automatic this is by trying to sing loudly or pick up a heavy object—the whole canister will naturally stiffen, and you may feel a slight 'lift' from the pelvic floor. Efficient core and pelvic floor function does NOT, however, mean you should just 'pull up the pelvic floor' the entire time you dance. Instead, the pelvic floor should respond with some tension *and* some give. Almost like a trampoline that catches the weight of a person jumping and landing, the pelvic floor responds to increased pressure like a cough or a landing from a jump with a tiny bit of give and a responsive stiffening. A common non-optimal strategy dancers may employ is over-recruiting the abdominal wall and pelvic floor with a very rigid lift in the name of using a strong core. But, when the pelvic floor is held too stiff, and/or there is too much pressure above it from overly tightened abdominals, this can contribute to urine leakage for some dancers (more on this later).

Functionally and anatomically, the muscles of the pelvic floor are directly connected to the deep outward rotator muscles of the hip—in particular, to the obturator internus muscle (Figure 8.1). Therefore, tension produced by contraction of the hip muscles will impact the pelvic floor muscles and vice versa. For the hips to feel as 'open' and mobile as you may want, your pelvic floor muscles need to be able to relax and eccentrically lengthen optimally. And, to optimise pelvic floor function and decrease risk of pelvic floor symptoms, good strength and mobility of the surrounding hip muscles, including the deep hip rotators and gluteal muscles, is ideal (Foster et al., 2021).

Pelvic floor dysfunction in dancers: What are the symptoms?

The following is a list of potential symptoms you may experience if an issue arises(Bo et al., 2017). It is important to note that such symptoms are common in female athletes, including dancers:

Bladder-related symptoms

- Urine leakage: this is also known as urinary incontinence (UI). Stress urinary incontinence refers to the experience of leaking with coughing, laughing, sneezing or exercise/impact. Urge urinary incontinence is a very strong urge to urinate, followed by leakage. Some dancers may experience one or the other, and some may experience both types.
- Urinary incontinence is much more common in dancers than you might think! In fact, a study by Winder et al. (2023) revealed that 34.6% of female professional dancers experience urinary incontinence, with stress incontinence being the most common type. Most of the dancers in this study were having leakage issues without ever having been pregnant or given birth. These rates were very similar to rates of leakage in other high-level female athletes (Winder et al., 2023).
- Urinary frequency: this refers to having to go to the toilet more frequently than every 2–4 hours or getting up more than once during the night to urinate. Dancers experiencing frequency may feel unable to sit through a long flight or get through a whole dance class due to this symptom.
- Feelings of incomplete ability to start the urine flow or to empty the bladder completely. Dancers may feel like they need to 'go' again almost immediately after emptying, or even notice some dribble a few seconds or minutes after finishing urination.
- General bladder irritability: Feeling like there might be a urinary tract infection but testing negative repeatedly.

Bowel-related symptoms

- Anal/faecal incontinence: The involuntary loss of faeces or gas (the most common being involuntary loss of gas).
- Constipation: decreased frequency of or needing to strain for bowel movements, feeling 'backed up'.
- Painful bowel movements, or the relief of pelvic pain with bowel movements.

Pressure symptoms

- Feeling a bulge or pressure in the vaginal area.
- Feeling like a tampon is falling out, or feeling like organs are falling/descending.

- These symptoms can be caused by a variety of factors (including an overly tensioned pelvic floor), but one factor can be pelvic organ prolapse (POP). POP refers to a laxity of the supportive connective tissue around the bladder, uterus/cervix, or rectum that contributes to descent of the pelvic organs into the vaginal walls.

Pelvic pain

- Pelvic floor myofascial pain is typically related to overly tensioned or chronically irritated pelvic floor muscles or nerves. Symptoms can include pain in the vagina or vulva, the perineum, the pubic bone, rectum, or tailbone, as well as pain with sexual activity/intercourse. In fact, a study of female professional dancers revealed that nearly 45% of dancers experienced pain with sexual activity/intercourse (Winder et al., 2023).
- Pain produced by the pelvic floor muscles can also 'refer' to the lower abdominals, low back, groin, buttock, or posterior thigh, and can exacerbate menstrual pain as well.

Pelvic floor dysfunction can negatively impact a dancer's daily life, body image and relationships as well as limit participation in dance. Dancers experiencing urinary incontinence, for example, may be distressed about managing this leakage in terms of clothing/costuming choices, wearing padding to absorb leakage, limiting water intake before dancing, or restricting dance movements that are aggravating. Because of the sensitive nature of these symptoms, dancers may also be hesitant to report them to others, including healthcare providers.

It is important for dancers to know that there are many ways to decrease the risk of developing pelvic floor issues, as well as successful treatment and management options available should a problem arise. To understand this further, it can help to explore possible contributing factors to pelvic floor symptoms in dancers.

Contributing factors to pelvic floor dysfunction in dancers and what to do about them

General health factors

The health of the pelvic floor is inextricably linked to a dancer's general health and wellness, including optimal nutritional and hormonal status. Studies have shown that disordered eating and/or Relative Energy Deficiency in Sport (REDs) is linked to increased risk of urinary incontinence in female athletes (Carvalhais et al., 2019; Whitney et al., 2021). When energy deficiency contributes to hormonal dysfunction, including irregularity or complete cessation of the menstrual cycle, the pelvic floor can be greatly impacted, especially because the health of vulvar and vaginal tissues depends on optimal levels of hormones like oestrogen. So, when such levels are non-optimal, urinary incontinence, pelvic pain or bladder irritability can increase. Other issues related to energy deficiency, such as low vitamin D status (common in the dance population), may interfere with the body's ability to maintain optimal muscle strength and function, including in the pelvic floor muscles.

Therefore, a pillar of pelvic floor health is maintaining adequate fuelling to support your dance training. If you are unsure how to manage your nutritional needs, it is best to consult experts including registered dietitians, physicians and/or psychologists to manage this area of health. You should also pair your fuelling with adequate hydration because a dehydrated bladder is often much more irritable and sensitive. You may find it helpful to decrease symptoms of leakage by limiting water or caffeine intake just prior to dance class; however, you should be sure that this is offset by improved water intake throughout the rest of the day to ensure proper hydration and decrease bladder irritability. A dancer's gastrointestinal (GI) health is also strongly linked to pelvic floor health, as gut discomfort and/or constipation can exacerbate existing pelvic floor symptoms. Constipation is considered a risk factor for urinary incontinence in female athletes (Sorrigueta-Hernández et al., 2020). This is likely because the rectum sits very close to the bladder within the pelvis, so stool backed up in this area can put more pressure on the bladder and contribute to leakage, urgency or frequency. Common tips for optimising GI function to help the pelvic floor include consuming adequate amounts of fibre (too much or too little can cause constipation), hydrating for optimal stool consistency, chewing all food thoroughly and without rushing (this helps to initiate better digestion), abdominal massage techniques, propping the feet up on a stool for bowel movements to decrease the need for straining, and listening to the urge to have a bowel movement. This might mean you need to plan to wake a few minutes earlier in the morning, consume some breakfast and leave enough time for a bowel movement before rushing through the day without an opportunity to empty.

The health and regulation of a female dancer's nervous system can also have a large impact on pelvic floor health. The pelvic floor is directly connected to nerves of the autonomic nervous system—the system that maintains homeostasis and includes both the sympathetic (fight, flight, freeze and fawn) and the parasympathetic (rest and digest) nervous systems. If a dancer experiences chronic stress responses and/or high anxiety, there can be excessive drive from the sympathetic nervous system. This is often associated with increased gripping, tension or pain in the pelvic floor region, and can also increase bladder urgency and frequency or constipation. You can incorporate practices to manage stress and calm your nervous system in many ways, including slow, meditative breathing, restorative yoga poses, humming or singing, journalling, cold exposure, meditation, mindfulness, and/or connecting regularly with friends.

Last, dancers with hypermobility, particularly those with hypermobility spectrum disorders or Ehlers Danlos Syndromes, can also be at higher risk for pelvic floor dysfunction—including bladder or bowel-related symptoms, pelvic organ prolapse, or pelvic pain (Gilliam et al., 2020). If hypermobility is a significant issue, targeted cross training to improve strength, proprioception and stability, pacing and workload management, taping or bracing as needed for areas of pain or instability, and medical support for autonomic dysregulation or histamine reactivity can be helpful tools (Callahan et al., 2022). Also, female dancers with diagnoses such as endometriosis, polycystic ovarian syndrome (PCOS), chronic yeast infections, recurrent urinary tract infections, recurrent bacterial vaginosis and/or irritable bowel syndrome can all be at higher risk for experiencing pelvic floor issues.

Movement/mechanical factors

Many people assume that pelvic floor dysfunction such as urinary incontinence is simply due to a weak pelvic floor. While this can certainly be a contributor to symptoms, this is often not the main issue with dancers. We've seen from research that relatively young professional dancers who have never been pregnant or given birth can experience urinary incontinence (Winder et al., 2023). It is unlikely that their pelvic floor muscles would be specifically weakened out of nowhere unless the dancer has had injury or surgery that has impacted tissue strength and support in the region.

Dancers should also consider that leakage can occur in part due to excessive tone or tension of the pelvic floor that interferes with the muscles' ability to produce optimal contraction, relaxation and coordination. Dancers are often (but not always) trained to pull their abdominal wall and pelvic floor region up and in consistently, which can lead to habits of excessive tension and gripping in pelvic floor over time. This habit can also be paired with extreme demands on the hip, including end-range positions and repetitive recruitment of the deep hip rotators and adductors. This demand on the hip may continually compound tension on the pelvic floor. Some dancers who use turnout consistently in their dance forms might also be training their posterior pelvic floor muscles in a chronically shortened position—especially if this includes compensatory turnout strategies like tucking or gripping the buttocks or is not balanced out with equally training internal rotation of the hip. Therefore, many dancers can benefit from incorporating a focus on pelvic floor length and relaxation into their training. Imagery such as 'send your breath gently toward your pelvic floor and untuck your tail' can be used in child pose, happy baby pose, or deep supported yoga squats to encourage pelvic floor relaxation.

Dancers may also experience pelvic floor symptoms as a result of poor strength and conditioning to meet the demands of dance, or even as a result of overtraining. One common thread in rates of female athletes who leak is repetitive impact and higher hours of training (Parr et al., 2023). Studies have also shown fatigue to be a factor in athletes experiencing pelvic floor symptoms like urinary leakage (Thomaz et al., 2018). When fatigue sets in, the pelvic floor will demonstrate poorer ability to tolerate loads. Therefore, if a dancer tries to tackle the high demands and impact of dance, but her overall body strength and cardiovascular tolerance is relatively low, she will hit fatigue faster and more often. The pelvic floor is just one of many areas that might experience symptoms due to under-preparation for overall dance load. Similarly, if a dancer trains a high number of hours at intense loads and does not incorporate enough rest and recovery into her training, overtraining fatigue can be problematic for the pelvic floor. You can mitigate this risk by seeking appropriate cross training to handle dance loads and incorporating intentional rest and recovery through appropriately periodised programmes. If unsure how to approach this, consult a trained strength and conditioning or rehabilitation professional for guidance.

Last, pelvic floor issues like urinary incontinence are also highly correlated with low back pain and injury as well as hip pain and injury, which are common orthopaedic issues for dancers (Welk & Baverstock, 2020). If you are experiencing low back and/or hip pain or injury, it is important to consider that issues with the pelvic floor may commonly arise as well and should be addressed.

Help is available if problems arise

Though female dancers, like other high-level female athletes, are at an increased risk of experiencing pelvic floor dysfunction, it is important for dancers to know that they are not alone and that there is effective treatment available to help with these symptoms. Research has shown that pelvic floor rehabilitation is the first-line intervention for managing pelvic floor symptoms and is quite effective (Balakrishnan & Thomas, 2022; Sorrigueta-Hernández et al., 2020). Pelvic floor rehabilitation provided by a trained professional can include pelvic floor muscle training (strength, length and coordination training), education in improved bladder and bowel habits, myofascial release techniques, mindfulness and relaxation training, whole-body strength and mobility training, and collaboration as needed with other medical and health practitioners who help manage nutritional, hormonal and mental health needs unique to dancers.

Considerations across a dancer's lifespan

There are particular life phases that can impact a dancer's pelvic floor greatly. One important phase occurs during pregnancy and the postpartum period.

In fact, two of the biggest risk factors for pelvic floor dysfunction for females are pregnancy and vaginal birth (Van Geelen et al., 2018).

During pregnancy, a dancer's body experiences a multitude of expected hormonal and mechanical changes as the body prepares for birth. The pelvic fascial structures become less strong and more compliant to stretch. Growing pressure from the pregnant uterus on the bladder and pelvic floor can contribute to urinary frequency and stress incontinence. Incontinence during pregnancy is also impacted by genetics and hormonal changes, so every pregnant dancer's experience will differ. Pregnancy-related pelvic girdle pain can also be common and can interfere with a dancer's comfort with daily activities, training and performance. Pelvic floor muscle training and individualised exercise and pain management plans can be effective to manage symptoms (Mørkved & Bø, 2014; Pires et al., 2020). Pelvic floor/perineal stretching and breath-specific training can also be helpful in assisting a dancer in preparing for the birthing process.

Vaginal delivery requires stretching the connective tissues and skeletal muscles of the pelvic floor beyond their typical physiological limits, which can contribute to overstretching trauma or tearing of the levator ani muscles, and/or disruption of the anal sphincter, as well as neural damage. In most women postpartum, reinnervation, wound healing and muscle hypertrophy assist pelvic floor recovery, and pelvic floor muscle function recovers within a year following vaginal delivery. In a small number (5–20%) of women, major pelvic floor injury (tears or avulsions) and nerve injury may lead to more significant postpartum symptoms. Common issues postpartum are stress incontinence and pelvic organ prolapse (Urbankova et al., 2019; Van Geelen et al., 2018). Though vaginal birth is a higher risk factor for postpartum pelvic floor symptoms, dancers who birth via caesarean section can also experience pelvic floor issues that may in part be due to the experience of pregnancy itself. Dancers may also experience residual pain or sensitivity from the C-section scar that can contribute to urinary urgency or bladder discomfort.

In terms of the pelvic floor, returning to dance postpartum is an individual journey for each dancer. Some dancers may feel that returning to exercise and light dancing can happen relatively quickly postpartum, and others may need more healing time before tolerating a progressive return to dance. The pace of returning to dance can be impacted by the degree of perineal tearing that during vaginal birth (these tears are graded on a scale of 1–4, with 4 being the most severe or involved), levels of postpartum bleeding, C-section healing times and restrictions or any complications that may have been involved in the birthing process. Other factors in postpartum healing include adjusting to parenting a newborn, sleep deprivation, nutritional concerns, breastfeeding challenges and/or postpartum mental health concerns.

Ideally, once medically cleared for return to exercise, a dancer should undergo at least a screening by a healthcare practitioner for any pelvic floor symptoms or concerns, and an assessment of pelvic floor strength or any pelvic organ prolapse. This may reveal specific needs that should be addressed with pelvic floor rehabilitation (pelvic floor strength, length and coordination training, biofeedback and/or perineal or C-section scar tissue mobilisation as applicable) to help mitigate the development of symptoms when returning to dance (Hadizadeh-Talasaz et al., 2019; Mørkved & Bø, 2014). Dancers with bothersome pelvic organ prolapse symptoms can be guided in exploring supportive options such as pessaries, which are devices worn inside the vagina to support the tissues displaced by the prolapse. Because women with symptoms of pelvic floor dysfunction postpartum are more likely to suffer depression and anxiety, and because pelvic floor symptoms can interfere with return to dance, pelvic floor considerations should *always* be assessed for postpartum dancers. Pelvic floor assessments should be paired with assessment of any postpartum abdominal wall concerns such as diastases recti or even simply the need to reconnect with abdominal function after the significant stretching of the abdominal wall during pregnancy. During the postpartum period, dancers can also experience temporary symptoms of vaginal dryness and pain, particularly if they are breastfeeding, due to low levels of oestrogen. Increased use of lubricants and possible use of low-dose vaginal oestrogen may be helpful options for these dancers as their hormones re-regulate postpartum.

Another significant life phase for female dancers and their pelvic floor health involves perimenopause, the menopause transition, and post menopause. Perimenopause refers to the normal transitional time of life from regular periods (with ovulation and hormone cycles) to menopause. Perimenopause typically begins around the age of 40 and can last up to ten years. During this phase, menstrual cycles become irregular, with ovulation occurring some months and not in others. Associated symptoms of perimenopause are due to fluctuating hormones, particularly levels of oestrogen and progesterone. The menopause transition occurs at the point in time when the ovaries 'retire'. Menopause is retrospectively 'diagnosed' because it occurs when there have been 12 months without menstruation (Marlatt et al., 2022). The average age of menopause is between 45 to 55 years, but there is a large variation of experiences due to an individual's genetics.

Concerning the pelvic floor, female dancers should know that one common set of symptoms for post-menopausal women (though these symptoms can begin in perimenopause) is genitourinary syndrome of menopause. The drop in oestrogen that occurs at menopause affects the tissues of the vagina and vulva, and can contribute to symptoms of vaginal dryness, burning, irritation, lack of lubrication, discomfort and pain, as well as increased risk of urinary incontinence, urinary urgency and urinary tract infections (Erekson et al., 2016). Dancers who experience these symptoms may find that they interfere with their comfort during exercise and dancing. They can also severely impact daily life and sexual function. It is important for dancers to understand that these symptoms are common in this phase of life, and that overall strength training, pelvic floor muscle training, hormone replacement therapy, and/or vaginal oestrogen as appropriate can be very helpful in managing symptoms.

Pelvic floor health for transfeminine dancers

Transfeminine dancers (dancers who were assigned male at birth but identify with femininity—including trans women, as well as nonbinary and gender fluid dancers who seek to present femininely, identify as more female than male, or wish to transition to look more feminine) may experience pelvic floor concerns due to any of the factors already addressed in this chapter and may be impacted by unique experiences as well.

Transfeminine dancers may choose to use gender-affirming approaches such as genital tucking (moving the penis and scrotum out of the way for a more feminine appearance of the pelvic area). For many people, tucking is immensely helpful in relieving gender dysphoria, allowing dancers to wear clothing that affirms their gender, and/or improving safety in social situations. Other dancers may use genital tucking to wear drag and perform in drag shows. There are a wide variety of methods used to tuck, involving the use of tape, tight underwear, and/or specialised supportive undergarments called gaffs. Pelvic floor-related symptoms can arise with tucking and can include:

- Testicular pain, scrotal pain, penile pain or other pelvic pain
- Urinary tract infections or urinary discomfort due to decreased frequency of urination during tucking
- Inguinal hernia
- Prostatitis, cystitis

Taking breaks from tucking, decreasing the time spent tucking, using gaffs or other supportive undergarments instead of taping, and exploring alternating tucking techniques may be options for dancers who are experiencing pain or urinary symptoms (Crossway et al., 2023).

Transfeminine dancers may also use gender-affirming hormonal regimens including oestrogen, progesterone and/or androgen blockers. Dancers using these regimens might experience that some androgen blockers can cause increased urinary frequency.

There are also voice considerations for transfeminine dancers in terms of demand on the pelvic floor. If transfeminine dancers want to explore higher pitches in voice, the diaphragm and pelvic floor need to support those demands to decrease stress on the vocal folds—this may pose a need for some targeted pelvic floor and core training. Dancers can also explore postures that optimise pelvic floor and core activation (such as a forward weight shift or a more upright posture) in order to better support the demands of a higher pitch. If you are finding that the desired pitch you want to explore is challenging for your body, consulting voice coaches, speech therapists and/or pelvic floor professionals can be helpful.

Last, for any transfeminine dancers who undergo gender-affirming surgeries such as bottom surgery, specific post-surgical protocols and pelvic floor rehabilitation can help to manage optimal healing and function for the future (Crossway et al., 2023; Jiang et al., 2019).

In summary: Pelvic floor takeaways and tips for female dancers

- Get to know your pelvic floor—learn where it is, how to kegel, and how to relax the pelvic floor.
- Work on three-dimensional breathing, expanding your ribcage, belly and pelvic floor in various positions and stretches.
- When dancing, envision the pelvic floor and core as a dynamic, responsive system that matches its tension to the difficulty of an activity or movement.
- Cross train to maintain overall body strength and conditioning, with a focus on hip strength and control.
- Fuel adequately (including fibre) and hydrate well for optimal energy availability and GI function, as well as a happier bladder.
- Make time for bowel movements, and prop your feet to reduce straining while emptying.
- Pelvic floor symptoms are relatively common in dancers and can be affected by various risk factors and life phases. Understand and care for your pelvic health early and often, and advocate for more conversations around pelvic health.
- If pelvic floor symptoms are bothersome, seek guidance from a trained pelvic floor rehabilitation professional.

References

Balakrishnan, P., & Thomas, A. (2022). Stress urinary incontinence among young nulliparous females – a systematic review. *Journal of Pharmaceutical Negative Results*, 13(5), 1384–1389. https://doi.org/10.47750/pnr.2022.13

Betschart, C., Singer, A. & Scheiner, D. (2019). Female pelvic floor: Anatomy and normal function. *Therapeutische Umschau. Revue Therapeutique*, 73(9), 529–534. https://doi.org/10.1024/0040-5930/A001035

Bø, K., Frawley, H. C., Haylen, B. T., Abramov, Y., Almeida, F. G., Berghmans, B., Bortolini, M., Dumoulin, C., Gomes, M., McClurg, D., Meijlink, J., Shelly, E., Trabuco, E., Walker, C. & Wells, A. (2017). An International Urogynecological Association (IUGA)/International Continence Society (ICS) joint report on the terminology for the conservative and nonpharmacological management of female pelvic floor dysfunction. *International Urogynecology Journal, 28*(2), 191–213. https://doi.org/10.1007/S00192-016-3123-4/FIGURES/9

Callahan, A., Squires, A. & Greenspan, S. (2022). Management of hypermobility in aesthetic performing artists: A review. *Orthopaedic Physical Therapy Practice, 3*, 134–145.

Carvalhais, A., Araújo, J., Natal Jorge, R. & Bø, K. (2019). Urinary incontinence and disordered eating in female elite athletes. *Journal of Science and Medicine in Sport, 22*(2), 140–144. https://doi.org/10.1016/J.JSAMS.2018.07.008

Crossway, A., Rogers, S., Hansen, A., Lopez, R. M., Sturtevant, J. & Moffit, D. (2023). The role of the athletic trainer in providing care to transgender and gender diverse patients: Considerations for medical affirmation – part II. *Journal of Athletic Training*. https://doi.org/10.4085/1062-6050-0313.22

Eickmeyer, S. M. (2017). Anatomy and physiology of the pelvic floor. *Physical Medicine and Rehabilitation Clinics of North America, 28*(3), 455–460. https://doi.org/10.1016/j.pmr.2017.03.003

Erekson, E. A., Li, F. Y., Martin, D. K. & Fried, T. R. (2016). Vulvovaginal symptoms prevalence in postmenopausal women and relationship to other menopausal symptoms and pelvic floor disorders. *Menopause (New York, N.Y.), 23*(4), 368. https://doi.org/10.1097/GME.0000000000000549

Foster, S. N., Spitznagle, T. M., Tuttle, L. J., Sutcliffe, S., Steger-May, K., Lowder, J. L., Meister, M. R., Ghetti, C., Wang, J., Mueller, M. J. & Harris-Hayes, M. (2021). Hip and pelvic floor muscle strength in women with and without urgency and frequency predominant lower urinary tract symptoms. *Journal of Women's Health Physical Therapy, 45*(3), 126. https://doi.org/10.1097/JWH.0000000000000209

Gilliam, E., Hoffman, J. D. & Yeh, G. (2020). Urogenital and pelvic complications in the Ehlers-Danlos syndromes and associated hypermobility spectrum disorders: A scoping review. *Clinical Genetics, 97*(1), 168. https://doi.org/10.1111/CGE.13624

Hadizadeh-Talasaz, Z., Sadeghi, R. & Khadivzadeh, T. (2019). Effect of pelvic floor muscle training on postpartum sexual function and quality of life: A systematic review and meta-analysis of clinical trials. *Taiwanese Journal of Obstetrics and Gynecology, 58*(6), 737–747. https://doi.org/10.1016/J.TJOG.2019.09.003

Jiang, D. D., Gallagher, S., Burchill, L., Berli, J. & Dugi, D. (2019). Implementation of a pelvic floor physical therapy program for transgender women undergoing gender-affirming vaginoplasty. *Obstetrics and Gynecology, 133*(5), 1003–1011. https://doi.org/10.1097/AOG.0000000000003236

Kocjan, J., Adamek, M., Gzik-Zroska, B., Czyżewski, D. & Rydel, M. (2017). Network of breathing. Multifunctional role of the diaphragm: A review. *Advances in Respiratory Medicine, 85*(4), 224–232. https://doi.org/10.5603/ARM.2017.0037

Marlatt, K. L., Pitynski-Miller, D. R., Gavin, K. M., Moreau, K. L., Melanson, E. L., Santoro, N. & Kohrt, W. M. (2022). Body composition and cardiometabolic health across the menopause transition. *Obesity, 30*(1), 14–27. https://doi.org/10.1002/OBY.23289

Mørkved, S., & Bø, K. (2014). Effect of pelvic floor muscle training during pregnancy and after childbirth on prevention and treatment of urinary incontinence: A systematic review. *British Journal of Sports Medicine, 48*(4), 299–310. https://doi.org/10.1136/BJSPORTS-2012-091758

Parr, R. E., Jones, E., Figuers, C. & Ewen, H. H. (2023). Relationship of sport variables on stress urinary incontinence in nulliparous collegiate athletes. *Journal of Women's Health Physical Therapy*, 47(2), 96–102. https://doi.org/10.1097/JWH.0000000000000259

Pires, T. F., Pires, P. M., Costa, R. & Viana, R. (2020). Effects of pelvic floor muscle training in pregnant women. *Porto Biomedical Journal*, 5(5), e077. https://doi.org/10.1097/J.PBJ.0000000000000077

Roch, M., Gaudreault, N., Cyr, M. P., Venne, G., Bureau, N. J. & Morin, M. (2021). The female pelvic floor fascia anatomy: A systematic search and review. *Life*, 11(9), 900. https://doi.org/10.3390/LIFE11090900

Sorrigueta-Hernández, A., Padilla-Fernandez, B. Y., Marquez-Sanchez, M. T., Flores-Fraile, M. C., Flores-Fraile, J., Moreno-Pascual, C., Lorenzo-Gomez, A., Garcia-Cenador, M. B. & Lorenzo-Gomez, M. F. (2020). Benefits of physiotherapy on urinary incontinence in high-performance female athletes. Meta-analysis. *Journal of Clinical Medicine*, 9(10), 3240. https://doi.org/10.3390/JCM9103240

Talasz, H., Kremser, C., Kofler, M., Kalchschmid, E., Lechleitner, M. & Rudisch, A. (2011). Phase-locked parallel movement of diaphragm and pelvic floor during breathing and coughing-a dynamic MRI investigation in healthy females. *International Urogynecology Journal*, 22(1), 61–68. https://doi.org/10.1007/S00192-010-1240-Z/TABLES/3

Thomaz, R. P., Colla, C., Darski, C. & Paiva, L. L. (2018). Influence of pelvic floor muscle fatigue on stress urinary incontinence: A systematic review. *International Urogynecology Journal*, 29(2), 197–204. https://doi.org/10.1007/S00192-017-3538-6/TABLES/1

Urbankova, I., Grohregin, K., Hanacek, J., Krcmar, M., Feyereisl, J., Deprest, J. & Krofta, L. (2019). The effect of the first vaginal birth on pelvic floor anatomy and dysfunction. *International Urogynecology Journal*, 30(10), 1689–1696. https://doi.org/10.1007/S00192-019-04044-2/TABLES/4

Van Geelen, H., Ostergard, D. & Sand, P. (2018). A review of the impact of pregnancy and childbirth on pelvic floor function as assessed by objective measurement techniques. *International Urogynecology Journal*, 29(3), 327–338. https://doi.org/10.1007/S00192-017-3540-Z

Welk, B., & Baverstock, R. (2020). Is there a link between back pain and urinary symptoms? *Neurourology and Urodynamics*, 39(2), 523–532. https://doi.org/10.1002/NAU.24269

Whitney, K. E., Holtzman, B., Cook, D., Bauer, S., Maffazioli, G. D. N., Parziale, A. L. & Ackerman, K. E. (2021). Low energy availability and impact sport participation as risk factors for urinary incontinence in female athletes. *Journal of Pediatric Urology*, 17(3), 290.e1–290.e7. https://doi.org/10.1016/J.JPUROL.2021.01.041

Winder, B., Lindegren, K. & Blackmon, A. (2023). Prevalence of urinary incontinence and other pelvic floor-related symptoms in female professional dancers. *Journal of Dance Medicine & Science*, 27(1), 50–55. https://doi.org/10.1177/1089313X231176629

9

IMPROVISING WITH THE PAIN(S) OF ENDOMETRIOSIS

Kate March

Introduction: Dancing with endometriosis

Throughout my tumultuous journey with endometriosis, accumulated insights from a performing arts practice have supported the cultivation of resilience, strength and presence. Dancing with endometriosis has inspired my profound trust in the body as powerful storyteller and likewise, has revealed the creative process as transformational healer. Drawing from these revelations, this chapter homes in on my recent research exploring the meaningful ways the body voices its own story or others' stories of disability, disease and pain. Specifically, I unravel how enduring, recalling or expressing the pain(s) of endometriosis informs both approaches to and manifestations of art-making. Emerging from a life perspective and artistic practice influenced by improvisation, I highlight temporalities; physical vocabularies or spatial trajectories; and other performance elements shaped and birthed from lived body endometriosis experiences. In this writing I address how one might navigate time, space, energy and comportment when encountering chronically, cyclically or temporarily altered physicalities or indeed, the embodied memories of such. This intimate personal essay, entwined with academic scholarship, reveals the ways in which my worlds of gendered disability, pain and artistic voice collide. I invite the reader into this intersection where pain is disruptor and improvisation is arbiter; a robust place honouring the reconfiguration of the body's crip[1] relationship to time, space, energy and ultimately, expression.

Improvisation and endo

My body is a battleground. For 25 years, marked by my menarche, I have endured stabbing, throbbing, aching, nauseating, devastating sensations that

DOI: 10.4324/9781003382874-12

originate in my pelvis. The pain radiates through my lower stomach, lower back or hips and frequently might manifest as a migraine. The embarrassing, shameful, agonising, traumatising, recurring pain experiences (can any words accurately describe it?) were finally diagnosed as endometriosis following my first gynaecological laparoscopic surgery, eight years ago, at the age of 30. The ongoing battle with endometriosis has been waged through seven surgeries and seven recovery periods; multiple emergency room visits; three IVF cycles (one successful and two failed); and hundreds of hours of physical and psychological suffering before, during and after menstruation. At times, this disease has severed me: I am as broken as I am whole.

Endometriosis, often referred to as 'endo', has been described as 'a riddle wrapped in a mystery inside an enigma' (Ballweg, 1995, p. 275); and impacts at least 1 in 10 women globally (Zondervan et al., 2020). Though a comprehensive review of endo and other gendered disabilities is beyond the scope of this writing, common traits and lived experiences are referenced throughout. For instance, although endo manifests uniquely in any given body, delayed diagnosis resulting in inadequate treatment response and prolonged suffering, is unfortunately, a prevalent pattern (Greene et al., 2009). Besides the cardinal symptom of severe pelvic pain which often peaks around menstruation, frequently cited symptoms may include, but are not limited to painful menstruation; acyclic pelvic pain; abdominal cramping; diarrhoea; painful bowel movements; other intestinal upset at the time of the period; painful sex; urinary issues; infertility; somatosensory amplification; and fatigue (Ballweg, 2004; Zondervan et al., 2020). Endo has no cure; treatment for pain or any of the myriad of aforementioned symptoms varies in success with high recurrence despite surgical removal; and in general, female pain has been and still is trivialised as a result of ingrained gender biases. Finding relief from the grip of this disease and other similar conditions requires true grit.

Ironically, as a professional performance artist I have perpetually depended on my body as the most essential channel and vehicle for creative expressions. In a career spanning nearly two decades and multiple continents, I have developed and performed in works which have required technical expertise in contemporary dance, experiential physical theatre and movement improvisation. Indeed, despite being a source of pain and challenge, my body has always been and remains an invaluable instrument and the root of my greatest joys. I embrace the ways in which my experience as a movement artist, particularly, an improviser, primes me for wrestling with the unpredictability and uncertainties of chronic pain or disease. As I metaphorically and literally dance my way through time and space, I am both interrupted *and* sustained by my body; I oscillate between a woman in pain and a woman remembering pain.

For movement artists especially, endo's corporeal interruptions interfere significantly with career trajectory. Throughout my early dance years as a teenager, an undergraduate or even a graduate student, sometimes pain would force me to miss or observe class. Despite my obvious commitment and passion for dance, it was clear these periods of rest or absence were frequently frowned upon by teachers and some professors. Comparable to experiences in the medical context, my pain was frequently downplayed or dismissed altogether. Although the reason I was doubled over or sick in bed on a regular cyclical basis was never explicitly addressed, others' casual responses conveying disbelief, judgement, or suspiciousness towards my cyclically ailing body, made me feel misunderstood and perceived as weak.

Following graduate school, the pain that was considered a mere nuisance by educators transformed into a looming burden haunting my professional development. My body's anticipated debilitation dictated scheduling and participation in performance or choreographic opportunities made available to me. In several instances while working abroad, I lost consciousness during meetings or rehearsals as a result of prioritising my desire for achievement rather than considering my body's needs. In many cases, choosing to conceal rather than openly reveal and honour my body's story, I suffered more intensely. Over time, as the endo became more aggressive, the pain was present throughout the entire menstrual cycle, necessitating more stillness than movement. The merciless pain inevitably required surgeries and post-surgical recoveries. Of course, repeated medical treatment and associated lengthy healing intervals are not ideal circumstances for a professional artist accustomed to relying on her body. Undoubtedly, all this disruption and uncertainty has shaped my artistic career, but not in an entirely undermining way.

Perhaps the most productive outcome of my endo experiences has been a deepened devotion and reliance on improvisation both in life and in art-making. The physical, psychological, spiritual and emotional pain of endo prompts shifts and negotiations: time, space and energy are impacted in both practical and artistic ways. The pain(s) of endo demand pliability in the form of a spontaneous and intuitive responsiveness, not unlike artistic improvisation itself. After years of corporeal disruptions, I have, out of necessity, adapted and learned to flow with the pain, listening to my body in a manner akin to improvising, enabling 'new ways of considering and acting' (Midgelow, 2019, p. 10). Leveraging improvisation-based principles like presence and adaptability, I move in life and art unapologetically as the individual I am, broken and whole, and with the pain or relief I feel in a given moment. Beyond how improvisation has creatively appealed to me, it empowers and transforms in ways that traditional forms of medicine have historically failed.

Interruption and adaptation (TIME)

No matter the profession, endo interrupts the body's experience of time—unpredictably, exhaustingly, chronically. The unrelenting disruptions of endo can be framed in a similar way to maternal experiences of interruption elaborated on by Lisa Baraitser. For example, women are expected to have sustained presence and perseverance regardless of the 'nightmarish intensity' of repetitious disruption (Baraitser, 2009, p. 67). Being thrust into and pulled out of a durational experience, an individual suffering from endometriosis is expected to and indeed, must, in order to overcome the disruption, 'right herself' over and over again (Baraitser, 2009, p. 68). The constant and vicious cycle of re-balancing and re-negotiating time and space is daunting. Likewise, the energy devoted to containing this dauntingness behind a veil of secrecy for the sake of maintaining sociocultural norms can be all consuming. The pain, as if an infant or young child, demands the woman to 'respond to me' and 'deal with me' not later, but now, in the immediate instant (Baraitser, 2009, p. 68).

In suffering from endo and other recurring pain conditions, we are ripped from the natural rhythm and passage of time and must move instead within the here and now. This repeated reconnection and pivot to the present moment is analogous to the way one might engage with time in an improvisational arts practice. In both cases, the body's relationship to time carries a sense of immediacy and instability. For the sake of innovation and authenticity, the improvising body must create by abandoning expectation and judgement. In seeking relief, the endo body must meet particularly challenging moments with spontaneity and intuition. Being in this world in such a way requires an attuning and awareness reminiscent of the distinctive embodiment and orientation to space and time described by many improvisation-based artists or performing arts practitioners as 'presence' (Biasutti & Habe, 2021). For instance, in discussing dance improvisation and uncertainty, Louise McDowall elaborates upon the many ways dance improvisation involves 'presencing' a polyattentive body, conversing with ambiguity, uncertainty, potentiality, and choice' (McDowall, 2019, p. 185). McDowall cites a wide range of various dance practitioners' and philosophers' accounts or definitions of the experiencing of 'this moment' or 'presence' aided by descriptions such as 'feeling lost', 'disorientated', 'dazed', 'elsewhere', 'transported somewhere', 'a zen or zen-like state', or having a sense of 'presence/present-ness' (McDowall, 2019, pp. 185–188). Although the exact words vary, 'presence' seems to inevitably connect an improvising body with a different experience of space and time.

Additionally, improvisation can induce participants to construct another world in which intricate processes and feelings are actuated (Kloppenberg, 2010; Minton, 1997; Morgenroth, 1987). Likewise, in the world of dance improvisation, movers can become so attentive and concentrated beyond distractions, that their complete absorption in the movement or performance may 'enhance a loss of self-consciousness and time' (Hefferon & Ollis, 2006, p. 144). Some of these aspects are prerequisites and manifestations of presence or presence functioning at its highest level, flow. Flow, which in dance is essentially a heightened sense of presence, is most basically defined as 'a state in which people are so involved in an activity that nothing else seems to matter' (Csikszentmihalyi, 1990, p. 4).

Of course, accessing or entering states of presence or flow is much different in moments of excruciating pain compared to artistic practice. However, I find that the same unique consciousness of body and erasure of past and future exists. In the midst of corporeal interruptions, the embodiment of improvisation as 'a kind of deliberate staying in the present' may allow for moments of surprise, of self-knowing without rigid meanings, of heightened sentience and of challenging preconceived notions of productivity or contentment (Baraitser, 2009, p. 4). As our bodies improvise with and against the rhythms of interruption, our attention can become more grounded in cultivating a new, changed relation with ourselves and less grounded in trying to defeat the disturbance of our time. Instead of 'trying to get back' to what she was saying, thinking, or doing, the woman suffering from cramps or a migraine, accepts the interrupted time as an experience 'beside herself'—a moment of coming undone and coming back together anew (Baraitser, 2009, p. 75). This improvisational perspective, which itself takes tenacity, commitment and repetition to embody, is what Baraitser seems to be calling for in order to realise the generative potential of interruption.

My body's relationship to time has directly impacted how I make art. As a result of adapting to the chaos of pain and disease, one of the ways I have and continue to work within the improvisational currents of spontaneity and presence is by creating in quick fire bursts of action. When pain-free, uninterrupted time is at my disposal, I pursue a state of improvisational flow with a sense of urgency and attack acknowledging that at any given moment, I might not be able to freely explore certain impetuses. If flow seems unattainable within these pursuits, I aim to, at the very least, carve out concentrated moments of presence. This burst action is a form of 'anticipatory scheduling' characteristic of some versions of 'crip time'[2] and as such, is a key component of my personal art-making which might be viewed as a 'crip performance practice' (Kafer, 2013, pp. 25–46).

This burst action characteristic of my artistic practice, is also described by performance artist Dr Sarah Hopfinger who suffers from a chronic pain condition and must write in 'short stints as I am unable to sit or stand still for more than one hour at a time' (Hopfinger, 2021, p. 123). She elaborates on her experiences indicating how the 'disruptions from muscle pain, stiffness, inflammation, aches, nerve pain, and so on' determine not only her thinking and articulation of ideas, but also the punctuated nature of her daily creative practices (Hopfinger, 2021, p. 123). Hopfinger's performance, research and writing practice are in dynamic response and embrace of her body's fluctuating needs and demands, and interestingly, the outcomes of such also are shaped by this. Bodily pain is written into our artistic practices or outcomes because of how we must negotiate time. Engaging with both the interrupted and uninterrupted windows of time through the lens of improvisation allows for a new model of endometriosis pain, menstrual pain or chronic diseases as not just disabling and disruptive, but potentially generative and complex. Situating pain in the context of improvisation, reimagines ableist temporalities and problematises ableist narratives of betterment.

Externalising interiors and downward trajectories (SPACE)

Individual pain experiences determine not only when and how art is made, but also, *how* the body moves (or does not move) within the practice itself. Improvising with pain, in life and art, means being open to experiencing and using time differently and being amenable to how a fluctuating body experiences or carves space. As Hopfinger (2021) eloquently discusses, cripping the aesthetics and methods of choreographic and performance practices may shift how pain narratives are expressed and received by audiences:

> taking an affirmative approach is not about denying the difficulties of chronic pain experience but rather it is about (re)claiming the chronic pain body as a valid and knowledgeable body, where the complexities of chronic pain experience can be respected and drawn from.
>
> *(pp. 125–126)*

For example, harnessing an improvisational approach in the artistic exploration of my endo body has allowed me to reframe emerging body vocabularies and mediations with space as novel and indicative of various interiorities rather than dismiss them as limited or tedious. In celebrating the body's differences through creative expression, pain is both articulated and honoured as a crucial experience garnering compassion, empathy and inquiry.

Intentionally aiming to move beyond 'internalised able-bodied assumptions' by embracing and emphasising the uniqueness of certain postures or trajectories of my endo body, allows for various niche vocabularies to emerge (Hopfinger, 2021). As a whole, these vocabularies tell a story of resilience and express the embodied wisdom of a body impacted by endometriosis. Resilience in this case refers not to pushing through pain or hiding pain for the sake of an aesthetic representing able bodies, normalcy or idealised notions of beauty. Resilience defined from this more affirmative perspective emerges through creating with and through 'the expertise of an [impaired] body to move in unique and creative ways' (Hopfinger, 2021, p. 125).

For example, during recent windows of uninterrupted time, my movement research focuses on positionings which express lived body experiences of endometriosis such as enduring severe menstrual cramps, migraines, back pain, surgery or recovery. Through these movement explorations, specific choreographic ideas materialise and develop in conjunction with associated written reflections, kinetic paintings, films, or poetry; a nuanced movement vocabulary related to endometriosis is revealed. In particular, key postures according to specific pain inflictions have emerged: a non-vertical/grounded body, a body doubled over, a body in foetal position, or a body in a bracing position. Being slumped over or horizontal, moving slowly, or not at all, might be typically considered antithesis expressions of a typical dance practice, however, I argue they can be viewed as choreographic tools and highlight a crip performance 'practice of care and resilience' (Hopfinger, 2021, p. 125).

Embodying endometriosis pain, I find myself more likely to be closer to the ground and often on the ground in positions that require support from the floor or other structures in the space (a toilet, a bed, a chair). The trajectory of pain is downward and instead of one motion of falling, the body is often caught in a liminal space between vertical and horizontal. While many performance artists and dancers have worked with the action of falling and the illusion of falling in the context of performance and movement expression, occupying a limbo body space is often less of a focus. However, exploring the concept of falling and its performative and embodied implications is a necessary segue into analysing and honouring this limbo body in pain.

Indeed, considering the four-phased embodiments of falling as defined by psychotherapist and dance artist Emilyn Claid (2013) (face-to-face, stooping, kneeling and lying), subsequently leads to associations of vulnerability/disease and then, poise/resiliency. Relatedly, the grotesqueness of the position, at least partially, originates in what non-vertical bodies represent in Western culture. For instance, a vertical body or the more upright body tends to assume some level of power over a physically lower body. Western definitions of prosperity and achievement are often culturally framed along an upward curve so that '...downward mobility becomes exclusively associated with shame...Every fall from the ladder becomes a fall from grace' (King, 2004, p. 35). The sociocultural tendency towards upward-ness is akin to a tendency towards perfection and able-bodiedness: 'Physically slumping symbolises a lower status, provokes shame, loss of dignity, inferiority and failure' (Claid, 2013, p. 78). However, to embrace the horizontal body, the downward body or the slumping body wavering between vertical and horizontal, is to accept our own imperfections, our fallible humanity, and importantly, our resilience. Indeed, in movement expression perhaps falling or stooping reveals the 'precariousness of life' (Sharrocks, 2013, p. 48) and offers an opportunity to 'rejoice in a freedom from uprightness' without the shackles of shame (p. 52).

Beyond the performative embodiment, personal and cultural meaning can be ascribed to various downward body postures when the stages of falling are scrutinised with focus and attention. For instance, in her artistic research practice, Claid (2013) acts as a dynamic witness to a dancer as he intentionally and slowly falls in front of her. Claid reads his slumping body as uncomfortable and faltering and her reflections resonate with how I witness and personally embody endometriosis pain as she declares, 'Kuldip's body posture of stooping affects me kinaesthetically. I feel a social responsibility to fix this discomfort—for us both' (Claid, 2013, p. 76). In her own body she seems to feel haunted by the pursuit of verticality as she writes, 'Kuldip's slumping evokes my shame—a persistent ghost from my training as a ballet dancer' (Claid, 2013, p. 78). Even though the dancer is performing a slow-motion fall without risk of injury and without pain as an origin, a lurking sense of aloneness, isolation and instability emits from the limbo body as it slumps and stoops (Claid, 2013).

The body in a 'doubled over' or 'hunched over' posture is a position reiterated by myself and other endo suffers repeatedly. This posture, akin to a monstrous hunchback, asserts itself within reflective writing, dancing and dialoguing within my collaborative research with five women with endo. Such body positioning seems to represent a myriad of endometriosis embodiments: low back pain, pelvic pain, uterine cramping, mental defeat, shame or total depletion. The pain-induced transformation from upright, poised, athletic, professional dancer to awkwardly hobbling, inelegant, out-of-body creature is dramatic and abrupt. Moving in and out of this estranged physicality, a different embodiment from my customary able-bodiedness, the invisible seems to become visible. The body's centre can no longer support the weight of the torso and being stooped over or proximate to horizontality brings at least minimal relief. Through this hunchback body posturing, and the way the body must re-negotiate space, the distortions and contortions that are so readily felt internally are finally seen. The inner grotesque disease, the monster living within, discovers a way to be external and present outside of the self, even if only allowing a glimpse of its malevolence. The invisibility of endometriosis as a disability or bodily difference cloaks the feelings of abnormality, deformity or monstrosity that those of us who suffer might experience towards our own bodies. Through intentional improvisational movement explorations, which then become distilled into a vocabulary, the inner grotesqueness may find ways to be partially unveiled. In this sense, the performative incarnations as well as the natural embodiments of endometriosis coalesce, opening possibilities for the unseen and unheard aspects of disease.

Claid discusses this lowered position and the eventual fall in depth but fails to ask a few pertinent questions related to a disabled body. What if a body remains or temporarily halts in this slumped position? What if the collapsed body cannot comfortably or swiftly return to an upright position? What if the stooped position is not from an intentionally designed choreographic task, but is caused by illness, disease, or disability? Sometimes, being stooped over, slumped, hunched or caught in between upward and downward is an endo body's unrelenting duet with gravity and with pain. My interest in the artistic and theoretical questions posed by this in-between and horizontal space, its relationship to pelvic or back pain, and the metaphorical associations with a downward trajectory continue to challenge and contribute to the evolution of my artistic voice as well as the development of an aesthetic expressing female pain.

Stillness, slowness and the aesthetics of repair (ENERGY)

As described, pain might shape how the body moves in space. It can also dictate how the body does *not* move and similarly, by literally and artistically improvising with endo I have witnessed how trauma or pain changes how the body energetically executes various trajectories or locomotions. In the past, when I have experienced menstrual pain or other physical sensations like migraines; surgery and surgical recuperation; or an IVF cycle, my body physically requires me to participate in certain qualities of expression. Typically, the idiosyncratic dynamics of endometriosis that have recurrently manifested in and through my improvisational practice include stillness, a decreased pace of movement or seeking comfort through repetition and ritual. These qualitative shifts especially occur in the aforementioned downward trajectories or lower, horizontal positions. Deepening artistic experimentation with these energetic variations might bring about new presentation formats or relationships with the audience.

Frequently, whether representing embodied trauma or suffering pain, I have felt a sense of defeat as my body urges a more subdued energy level or rest. For instance, compelled to lower myself to a more supported horizontal position, I may initially try to execute floor work without hesitancy and with a liberated sense of abandon. However, if pain or heavy fatigue disrupts this style of movement engagement, then I slow down or find stillness as a response. I know firsthand that stillness or slowness happening without a choice, whether in dance or other settings, often does not feel productive nor restful. Being forced to sustain or repeat various modified body positions, gestures, rhythms or pace, an individual can easily feel powerless or perceived as weak. Additionally, a body paused in horizontal or foetal positioning can conjure feelings of devastation, failure and inferiority (Albright, 2019). Specifically, in the context of dance or performance art, in such states, it is often assumed by bystanders that the body will rise and return vigorously back to verticality (Albright, 2019).

Such moments necessitate the further cultivation of an improvisational perspective and practice in order to make space for creative discovery despite and indeed, fed by disruption. For instance, in embracing the new vantage point offered by non-traditional relationships between time, space and body, one might reject a quick return to the realm of uprightness. Engaging purposefully in a full descending motion, the body is participating in and representing the experience of lowering to positions re-conceived as resistance, rest, recovery and repair (Albright, 2019; Sharrocks, 2013). In this trajectory, staying low presents opportunities for self-preservation and healing as well as new expressive vocabulary (Albright, 2019). Indeed, being grounded might offer a place of rich self-discovery and pause. In embracing horizontality, perhaps some bodies can better realise a journey towards recovery and true resilience.

In an attempt to embody this viewpoint creatively and practically, I intentionally engage in supine, prone or foetal positions for extended durations and focus on intricate gesturing with the less disease-impacted body parts like hands, fingers, toes, shoulders or arms. Likewise, soft and stretched out choreography within certain positions makes a statement of its own or it can be reworked into a new rhythmic score when the body feels ready. In the case of the latter, I have used durational movement to inform the development of momentum driven or syncopated choreography. Often, I rephrase grounded movements using different body postures or relationships with space.

Energetic variations impact how artistic explorations of time and space are perceived by the audience and felt in my or collaborators' bodies. Thus, as a part of the creative development of an endo-informed body vocabulary, I might more deeply consider how the relationship between my body, other bodies, and/or the physical environment might challenge the way my story is heard, seen or felt by others. A body's more 'dissonant' energies might be perceived differently when traditional boundaries are blurred; engrained perceptions of beauty or strength may be redefined and challenged in specific settings. For example, in an effort to realise the power of these postures and gestures and the accompanying dynamics, I often will place a performing body or bodies in alternative performance spaces providing intimate proximity between audience and performers. Unrelenting eye contact or the tension and release seen between muscles and skin from small gestural actions can reveal courage, vulnerability, intensity and passion. Perhaps, moving slowly or repetitively from one recuperative posture to another, especially up close, invites both the audience and performer to co-behold a creative metamorphosis with deepened presence and attention. In this way, as part of a crip performance practice, the artist supports the audience in becoming '... attuned to the small shifts of pain breath, or fluttering fingers, or a furrow building between the eyes' whether or not they themselves have suffered from chronic pain or disease (Kuppers, 2006, para. 4). My body's adhesions, lesions, scar tissue and damaged organs might not be seen, but they can be sensed through how and where I express energy.

Conclusion: The whole broken story

Improvisation invites alternative relationships to time, space and energy for a spectrum of bodies and identities. Personally, I improvise in order to honour and reclaim my body's story: its battles and victories, its needs and aspirations. Artistically engaging with and embodying my multidimensional story in relatively pain-free moments allows me to reaffirm body control and appreciation for my endo body. I have learned that by emphatically working with and referencing disruption, I can discover and embrace new ways of creating, moving, pausing and presenting, with my body's uniqueness. Inevitably, when pain erupts or disease flares, many of the punctuations and compromises in time, space and energy occur without the freedom of choice. In these moments, if I truly dial into improvisation, my somatic presence feels somehow altered. If only for an instant, I am able to meet my own pain more objectively as creative material. Improvisation and creative expression may not excise pain or cure disease, but they allow for a narrative shift. Perhaps in the reinterpretation of our body's suffering, we can discover a sense of metamorphosis and healing.

Embracing various principles of improvisation in life perspective, artistic expression and research methodology has supported my body's journey and provided a path for flourishing with light despite darkness. And although the modalities and mindsets briefly mentioned in this chapter are certainly not the only way to mitigate pain or move with disability, they might represent an inspiring approach for menstruators who do not have endometriosis, but who nonetheless suffer from painful cramps, PMS, back pain, or migraines. Likewise, artists with a similar body story, whether in dance or other disciplines, might also benefit from incorporating experimentation, intuition, spontaneity, adaptability and presence into a distinctive arts practice. Decidedly, when our bodies' natural impulses are affirmed as provocative and interesting, our stories become the foundation and architecture for uncompromised artistic expression, authentic exchange and beautiful innovation.

Notes

1. Crip, originating from the word 'crippled' is an expansive, inclusive and flexible term with currency in disability culture/studies intended to include 'not only those with physical impairments but those with sensory or mental impairments as well' (Kafer, 2013; Sandahl, 2003). Notably, 'cripping' something means applying a disability justice lens to it as a form of identity reclamation. As a whole, rather than focus on medical diagnosis, symptomatology or social constructions of disability, crip poetry intends to express the fluid and ever-changing experiences and realities of bodies that might differ from an unmarked norm. For further examples and descriptions of the power of crip poetry as an art form look into the work of scholar and artist Petra Kuppers or Emilia Nielsen.

2. Crip time is discussed in Alison Kafer's seminal work about crip theory. Crip time is a non-normative way of orienting one's self to the linearity and futurity of time. Crip time refuses to define itself in terms of either the ideal or the average, shaped instead by individual needs, desires and abilities (Kafer, 2013).

References

Albright, A. (2019) 'Life practices'. In V. Midgelow (Ed.) (2019) *The Oxford handbook of improvisation in dance* (pp. 25–35). Oxford University Press.

Ballweg, M. L. (1995). The puzzle of endometriosis. In C. R. Nezhat, G. S. Berger, F. R. Nezhat, V. C. Buttram & C. H. Nezhat (Eds.), *Endometriosis: Advance management and surgical techniques,* (pp. 275–285). Springer.

Ballweg, M. L. (2004). *Endometriosis: The complete reference for taking charge of your health.* McGraw-Hill.

Baraitser, L. (2009). *Maternal encounters: The ethics of interruption.* Routledge.

Biasutti, M., & Habe, K. (2021). Teachers' perspectives on dance improvisation and flow. *Research in Dance Education, 24*(3), 1–20. https://doi.org/10.1080/146478 93.2021.1940915

Claid, E. (2013). Can I let you fall? *Performance Research, 18*(4), 73–82. https://doi.org/10.1080/13528165.2013.856090

Csikszentmihalyi, M. (1990). *Flow: The psychology of optimal experience.* Harper and Row.

Greene, R., Stratton, P., Cleary, S. D., Ballweg, M. L. & Sinaii, N. (2009). Diagnostic experience among 4,334 women reporting surgically diagnosed endometriosis. *Fertility and Sterility, 91*(1), 32–39. https://doi.org/10.1016/j.fertnstert.2007.11.020

Hefferon, K. M., & Ollis, S. (2006). 'Just clicks': An interpretive phenomenological analysis of professional dancers' experience of flow. *Research in Dance Education, 7*(2), 141–159. https://doi.org/10.1080/14647890601029527

Hopfinger, S. (2021). Chronic pain, choreography and performance: Practices of resilience. *Research in Drama Education: The Journal of Applied Theatre and Performance, 26*(1), 121–136. https://doi.org/10.1080/13569783.2020.1820859

Kafer, A. (2013). *Feminist, queer, crip.* Indiana University State Press.

King, J. (2004). Which way is down? Improvisations on black mobility. *Women in Performance, 14*(1): 25–47. https://doi.org/10.1080/07407700408571439

Kloppenberg, A. (2010). Improvisation in process: 'Post-control' choreography. *Dance Chronicle, 33*(2), 180–207. https://doi.org/10.1080/01472526.2010.485867

Kuppers, P. (2006). Disability culture poetry: The sound of the bones. A literary essay. *Disability Studies Quarterly, 26*(4). https://doi.org/10.18061/dsq.v26i4

McDowall, L. (2019). Exploring uncertainties of language in dance improvisation. In V. Midgelow. (Ed.), *The Oxford handbook of improvisation in dance* (pp.185–206). Oxford University Press.

Midgelow, V. (2019). Improvising dance: A way of going about things. In V. Midgelow (Ed.), *The Oxford handbook of improvisation in dance* (pp. 1–15). Oxford University Press.

Minton, S. C. (1997). *Choreography: A basic approach using improvisation* (2nd ed.). Human Kinetics.

Morgenroth, J. (1987). *Dance improvisations.* University of Pittsburgh Press.

Sandahl, C. (2003). Queering the crip or cripping the queer? Intersections of queer and crip identities in autobiographical solo performance. *GLQ: A Journal of Lesbian and Gay Studies 9*(1), 25–56. Duke University Press. https://doi.org/10.1215/10642684-9-1-2-25

Sharrocks, A. (2013). An anatomy of falling. *Performance Research, 18*(4), 48–55. https://doi.org/10.1080/13528165.2013.814368

Zondervan, K. T., Becker, C. M. & Missmer, S. A. (2020). Endometriosis. *The New England Journal of Medicine, 382*(13), 1244–1256. https://doi.org/10.1056/NEJMra1810764

10

THE PREGNANT DANCER

Chloe Hillyar

Introduction

Dance and pregnancy impose extreme physical demands. Dancers undergo athlete-level training in pursuit of excellence (Redding, 2019), and pregnancy causes significant morphological changes that have the potential to limit physical activity (PA) (Szumilewicz et al., 2022). Together, the two are perceived as fundamentally incompatible (Jackson et al., 2022). As such, one of the most common questions dancers ask when they become pregnant is, 'Is it safe to dance?' Given the elite level of training dancers engage in, this is not a straightforward 'yes' or 'no' answer. For the majority of people, it is safe to continue engaging with pre-pregnancy physical activity levels—in fact, it is encouraged. Antenatal PA is a critical component of a healthy pregnancy with moderate intensity training conferring profound benefits (Wowdzia et al., 2023). However, professional dancers easily exceed moderate intensity levels of physical activity and often feel that general PA guidelines do not account for their high levels of training or make dance-specific recommendations. This is due to a lack of scientific evidence supporting the safety of vigorous and near-maximal exercise during pregnancy. Such paucity of evidence leads to assumptions being made about what pregnant dancers can and cannot do based on pre-conceived ideas about the female body. Consequently, pregnant dancers are seen as less employable and at risk of illegal or discriminatory behaviour due to arbitrary perceptions of pregnancy-appropriate activity.

However, research on pregnant athletes has found no correlation between high intensity exercise and adverse foetal outcomes. In fact, there is a growing body of evidence demonstrating the potential health benefits available at higher levels of physical activity, such as an improved foetal-placental perfusion, a greater tolerance for sub-maximal cardiovascular training (for a short time

DOI: 10.4324/9781003382874-13

after birth) and a quicker return to physical activity postpartum (Bung & Huch, 1991; Kardel, 2005; Kehler & Heinrich, 2015; Bø et al., 2016; Erdener, 2016; Wowdzia et al., 2021; Jackson et al., 2022). As such, recent data is countering previous recommendations to avoid all high intensity activity which unlocks new opportunities for dancers to continue dancing at a professional level during pregnancy (De Vivo et al., 2022). This chapter considers the multiple physiological variables at play throughout pregnancy relevant to professional dancers with the aim of empowering pregnant dancers to make autonomous, well-informed decisions about the type, frequency and intensity of dance training they wish to engage in.

Transgender women and women with differences in sexual development have not yet been characterised within the academy (Elliot-Sale et al., 2021). Females, however, are defined based on ovarian steroid concentrations. Therefore, this chapter will use the term 'female' to refer to populations who have the biological ability to carry and birth a child.

How is this relevant to me?

Regardless of whether you have the ability or desire to become pregnant, learning about the implications of pregnancy is important because you may become the partner, teacher, employer and/or employee of a pregnant dancer. If the UK dance sector is interested in endorsing more inclusive dance practices, everyone is responsible for rejecting discriminatory attitudes that have so far prevented pregnant dancers from professionally participating. The perception that pregnant dancers pertain a risk to employers is propagated by a male-bias system that has neglected the needs of women. Much like feminist and anti-racism movements, cultural shifts in gender equality require a unanimous effort to dismantle harmful social hierarchies that seek to oppress those who do not conform to the status quo. What's more, including pregnancy in dance can yield expanded ideas of the female body in performance and increase the potential for diverse bodies to appear in all dance contexts. Put simply, so long as women continue to participate in dance, the subject of pregnancy concerns the entire dance workforce.

Systemic consequences

Failure to consider sex-specific differences within wider society has resulted in a default male bias prevailing in sectors oversaturated with women—such as dance. Male-bias systems fail to understand or support the needs of female dancers, especially regarding health-related matters. For example, the lack of maternal support available results in mother dancers leaving the profession either in search of more secure, parent-friendly and financially viable work (Dance Mama, n.d.), or to dedicate themselves solely to their child

(Massey & Whitehead, 2022). Consequently, many women are unable to achieve leadership positions which results in a disproportionate number of men leading a female dominated industry. If leaders are not representative of the population they are serving, they are not going to be able to understand or satisfy the requirements of their workforce.

Motherhood

While this chapter will discuss pregnancy-specific considerations, it is also important to remember that motherhood cannot be essentialized to only include people who have carried and delivered a baby (Duffy, 2023). In vitro fertilisation (IVF), adoption, surrogacy, fostering, step-parenting and caregiving all encompass unique and complicated procedures that will have an impact on a dancer's ability to professionally participate in sector. Achieving pregnancy is not always straightforward and it is important to use inclusive language that validates all experiences of motherhood.

Pregnancy and the dancer

Modification over cessation

Pregnancy is not a time to stop being physically active. Previously fit women may continue with the same level of exercise intensity, frequency and genre they were engaging with before pregnancy (Mottola et al., 2019). Conversely, pregnancy is also a time for maintenance and modification; when it becomes too difficult to maintain the same level or type of exercise, this indicates that it is time to modify in a way that keeps the exercise comfortable yet challenging.

It is important to remember that pregnancy acts as a form of cardiovascular training in and of itself. The increases in cardiac output (40%), stroke volume (10%) and blood volume (50%) essentially subjects the female body to a nine-month training regime whereby cardiorespiratory ability is continuously improving (Cram, 2023). This means that the body is already under considerable stress even before engaging in physical activity and dancers shouldn't feel disheartened if they are unable to achieve pre-pregnancy results. In fact, improvements made to the cardiorespiratory systems are such that postpartum individuals may experience a greater tolerance for sub-maximal cardiovascular training for a short time after birth (Ingham, 2020).

In addition to the above cardiovascular benefits, pregnancy also improves strength. As gestation progresses, the load pregnant dancers have to work with increases. The weight of the increased blood volume (3–4lbs/1.4–1.8kg), uterus (2lb/0.9kg), increased extracellular fluid (3–4lbs/1.4–1.8kg), enlarged breasts (1–2lbs/0.4–0.9kg), necessary fat stores (5–8lbs/2.3–3.6kg), placenta (1–1.5lbs/0.50.7kg), amniotic fluid (2lbs/0.9–1kg) and the baby

(7–8lbs/3–3.6kg) can result in an additional c.31.5lbs/14.3kg of physical load (Bø et al. 2016). As such, exercising during pregnancy is like putting on a rucksack that is getting heavier each week and it is important to modify workloads in order to maintain the activity at hand.

Physical activity guidelines

Pregnant individuals are physically capable of much more than previously thought. Up until the mid-1980s, exercise and pregnancy guidelines had little scientific basis and reinforced the notion that pregnant women were weak and fragile (Kehler & Heinrich, 2015). Exercise guidelines for pregnancy discouraged most forms of fitness-improving activities and promoted gender-stereotypes by endorsing domestic housework as a way of staying active (Vertinsky, 1987 in Kehler & Heinrich, 2015). This school of thought remained relatively unquestioned until the late 1960s when physicians Michael Bruser and Ernst Jokl began to revolutionise medical thought about the physical capabilities of pregnant women (Jette, 2011 in Kehler and Heinrich, 2015). However, it wasn't until 1985 when the first evidence-based exercise guidelines for pregnant women were published by the American College of Obstetricians and Gynaecologists (ACOG) and pregnancy was no longer considered a cause for confinement.

Physical activity (PA) guidelines for pregnancy have evolved since ACOG's seminal publication and it is currently recommended that general pregnant populations engage in 150 minutes of moderate intensity PA and two days of strength training each week (Department for Health and Social Care, 2021). This level of physical activity confers numerous health benefits such as a reduction in the occurrence of gestational diabetes mellitus, gestational hypertension disorders, macrosomia, excess weight gain, as well as shorter labours and improved mood (De Vivo et al., 2022). While these guidelines have led to increased awareness, promotion and engagement of PA among the general pregnant public, specific support for elite exercisers who will exceed these guidelines are lacking (De Vivo et al., 2022)—but that is beginning to change.

Since the turn of the century there has been a growing number of women participating in elite-level sport and a consequential increase in sportswomen competing during and after pregnancy (Massey & Whitehead, 2022). As more female athletes train and compete during their reproductive years (Davenport et al., 2022), there has been growing investment in studies evaluating the impact of high intensity PA on pregnant athletes. However, not enough research exists to create PA guidelines for the physically elite, leaving those with physically strenuous occupations at risk of uncertainty, injury and drop-out. Similarly, there is a lack of research investigating the impact that pregnancy has on the dancing body, and vice versa; dance-specific PA guidelines are equally absent.

In the absence of dance-specific PA guidelines, the remainder of this chapter will delineate what dance activities are safe and even beneficial for the mother and her baby, as well as potential contraindications. The advice to anyone using this chapter as a guide for safe physical participation is to first fill in the 'Get Active Questionnaire for Pregnancy' created by the Canadian Society for Exercise Physiology, British Association of Sport and Exercise Science and the Active Pregnancy Foundation. This self-administered tool is a practical and affordable way of helping you decide whether seeking medical advice is necessary before participating in PA. Conversely, if no contraindications[1] are identified you may begin or continue physical activity as early as the first week of gestation.

Trimester-specific guidance

The American College of Obstetricians and Gynecologists committee advises that the type and volume of training modality should be considered between trimesters because of the anatomical and physiological variability of pregnancy (Jackson et al., 2022); hence why the following adaptations have been separated into trimesters. It is important to remember that one size does not fit all, and pregnant dancers should use the following as a guide to facilitate flexible person-centred strategies that accommodate the many changes associated with the maternal period.

First trimester

There are numerous endocrinological, cardiovascular and haematological changes that occur throughout pregnancy from the first trimester (Perales et al., 2022). While these changes have the potential to impact a dancer's ability to fully engage with PA when compared with non-pregnant values (NPVs), none of the following changes contraindicates dancers with healthy pregnancies from engaging in dance-specific PA (Perales et al., 2022).

Endocrinological changes

Many endocrinological changes occur during pregnancy but some of the most pertinent to dancers include those relating to ligamentous laxity. For example, the hormone relaxin increases the laxity of ligaments to prepare the pelvis for childbirth. It is produced as early as the second week of pregnancy (Quin et al., 2015) and peaks in the first and third trimester (Jackson et al., 2022). While it is produced by the corpus luteum, decidua and placenta, it is not localised to the pelvic-region and has the potential to increase the laxity of all ligaments in the body (Soma-Pillay et al., 2016). Several authors have asserted relaxin as a risk for dancers, specifically for its potential to tempt dancers into stretching beyond their limits (Keay, 2022; Quin et al., 2015; McCoid & Rafiefar, 2013). This is because flexibility is a valued commodity and a quintessential skill among dancers. Some authors postulate that without adequate flexibility dancers are unlikely to achieve professional standards (Deighan, 2005 in Quin et al., 2015). Naturally, dancers with professional ambitions are concerned with increasing their flexibility and are therefore at greater risk of abusing their newfound flexibility during pregnancy. There is limited research on flexibility training during pregnancy but it is recommended for pregnant populations to stretch to a comfortable range of movement 'in a slow and controlled manner' (Szumilewicz et al., 2022). The joints at most risk of injury from relaxin are the symphysis pubis, sacroiliac joint, labrum and meniscus (Quin et al., 2015). During pregnancy, emphasis should be placed on strengthening the muscles around these joints to offset the slackening ligaments and maintain stability.

Other endocrinological changes include a gradual increase in progesterone, oestrogen, prolactin and oxytocin (Jackson et al., 2022). The increase in progesterone is particularly pertinent for dancers as it has an influence on respiratory function. Changes in the respiratory system begin from the first trimester and include variations in lung dimension and capacity, and respiratory mechanisms (Perales et al., 2022). At the beginning of pregnancy, the increase in progesterone will cause the woman to breathe more deeply but not more frequently (Perales et al., 2022). The amount of air that moves in or out of the lungs with each respiratory cycle is known as tidal volume. The higher tidal volume results in a decreased expiratory reserve (the amount of air available to exhale after normal exhalation). This means that there is less extra volume of air that can be expired (exhaled) with maximum effort during pregnancy (Perales et al., 2022). In relation to dancing, the respiratory modifications may result in pregnant dancers feeling short of breath at the beginning of PA. Conversely, dyspnoea (the feeling of running out of breath) and respiratory effort will decrease during sub-maximal steady-state exercise (Jackson et al., 2022).

Cardiovascular and hemodynamic changes

Essential structural and functional cardiovascular changes begin around the fifth week of gestation to ensure sufficient blood supply to both mother and foetus throughout pregnancy (Jackson et al., 2022; Perales et al., 2022). There is an increase in maternal heart rate (HR) of between 15–20 beats per minute (bpm) above NPVs (Mottola, 2019) and an increase of blood volume (up to 40–45% by the 16th–20th week of gestation) (Perales et al., 2022). To minimise the stress on the heart from the increase in blood volume, eccentric hypertrophy of the left ventricular begins from the first week of gestation. The increase in maternal HR means that maximal maternal HR is lower, resting HR (RHR) is higher and heart rate reserve (HRR) is reduced. Mottola et al. (2006) recommend previously active women and athletes to train at 50–60% of their maximal heart rate (MHR).

Due to the variability in maternal HR, prescribing PA intensity based exclusively on HR is not recommended because it may not accurately correlate with exertion levels. Instead, additional subjective measures should be used to control PA intensity. There are two inexpensive and effective measures that can be administered alongside HR monitors within the dance studio. First, the rate of perceived exertion (RPE) is a positive example of a free-to-use resource that empowers pregnant dancers to make autonomous decisions about their intensity levels as they are dancing. While there are different types of RPE scales, Borg's Rating of Perceived Exertion is popular among athletes due to its numerical correlation with HR where 6 represents no exertion (equivalent to a RHR of 60bpm) and 20 represents maximal exertion (equivalent to a MHR of 200bpm) (Santos-Rocha et al., 2022). If the goal is to reach light-to-moderate intensities, an RPE between 11–13 is recommended as it corresponds with approximately 60% of the estimated MHR.

Second, the 'talk test' is another accessible measure of exercise intensity whereby the pregnant individual should be able to carry out a conversation during moderate intensity PA. Vigorous PA is associated with substantial increases in breathing, perspiration and the inability to carry out a normal conversation easily (Santos-Rocha et al., 2022). The literature recommends pregnant individuals work at a level that causes a sensation of increased breathing but allows for complete sentences comfortably (Santos-Rocha et al., 2022).

Thermoregulatory changes

The pregnant body is very efficient at regulating body temperature. This is caused by a downward shift in body temperature threshold initiating

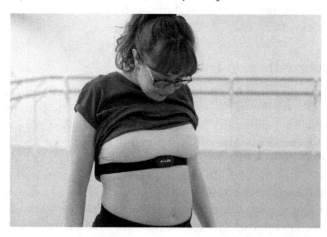

FIGURE 10.1 HR Monitor © Chloe Hillyar PhD. Photographer: Phoebe Pullinger

evaporate heat loss via sweating at a lower body temperature (Bø et al., 2016). Pregnant individuals may engage in various intensities of PA while remaining below the critical core temperature of 39°C (102.5°F), above which teratogenic (physiological abnormalities) effects can occur (Sanders, 2008). However, pregnant individuals are advised against exercising in warm environments especially during early pregnancy. This is because the foetal neural tube develops within the first 35–42 days of gestation. Raising maternal body temperature above 39°C during this period increases the risk of neural tube defect. As such, employers and teachers of pregnant dancers should ensure studio environments are ventilated and air conditioned, and for exercise to occur when the weather is below 27°C (80.6°F) (Quin et al., 2015). Exercising in the early morning or late evening can also improve heat dissipation (Quin et al., 2015).

Second trimester

Locomotor changes

Changes in the locomotor system will begin to limit a pregnant dancer's balance and physical ability. As gestation progresses, the weight of the growing uterus and baby results in the pregnant dancer deviating from her centre of gravity (Perales et al., 2022). To compensate for the forward weight, the craniocaudal axis shifts backwards which results in lumbar lordosis (Quin et al., 2015). This new posture is responsible for many common symptoms during pregnancy that might limit a pregnant dancer's ability to perform, including lumbo-sciatica, anterior pelvic tilt and kyphosis (Quin et al., 2015). Poor postural hygiene can amplify the risk of falling; pregnant individuals are two to three times more likely to fall than NPVs (Jackson et al., 2022) and will impact movements that require a good sense of balance such as *pirouettes*, dynamic changes in direction and single-leg balances (e.g. *arabesques and attitudes*). Pregnant dancers should also be aware that their reduced balance will impact their ability to effectively manage vertical impact forces such as *grande battements* and jumps. These altered biomechanics may be an indication to start incorporating modifications where necessary.

Third trimester

Abdominal separation

Pregnant individuals would have lost their ability to fully engage their abdominal muscles from the second trimester. As pregnancy reaches the third trimester, the two lengths of the rectus abdominals begin to separate at the linea alba, meaning that the uterus is only covered by a thin layer of peritoneum, fascia and skin (Perales et al., 2022). There is some inconsistency as to whether total separation, referred to as diastasis recti, occurs in all pregnancies. Many sources have stated that diastasis recti is an 'occasional' occurrence in pregnant individuals (Quin et al., 2015; Perales et al., 2022; Bø et al., 2022). Others have suggested that this is an inevitable occurrence that will manifest by the 37th week of gestation in 100% of pregnancies (Jackson et al., 2022). Regardless of prevalence, it is important for pregnant women to cease abdominal work once separation occurs. Abdominal work (such as sit-ups, crunches or the plank) can cause the linea alba to bulge and protrude through the rectus abdominus, thus creating a barrier between the two lengths of abdominal wall and possibly preventing unification postpartum (Quin et al., 2015). Not only will this prolong postpartum recovery, but it could further weaken and separate the abdominal walls (McCoid & Rafiefar, 2013).

Supine position

The supine position describes a horizontally lying position with the anterior side of the frontal plane facing up and the posterior side facing down, in contact with the floor. Pregnant individuals are advised against lying in the supine position after the 20th week of gestation due to the weight of the gravid uterus obstructing the aorta and the inferior vena cava, resulting in a decreased venous return from aortocaval compression (Mottola et al., 2019). The body produces natural warning signs to alert the mother of aortocaval compression. Symptoms include dizziness, sweating, nausea and increased HR and will usually occur within 3–10 minutes of lying in the supine position but will resolve when supine lying ceases. However, pregnant dancers may be asymptomatic due to the sympathetic compensation that can occur in healthy pregnant individuals and therefore should avoid engaging in supine rest. Supine rest is associated with maternal hypotension (low blood pressure) and foetal bradycardia (a slower than normal heartbeat) as a result of lower foetal oxygenation (Mottola et al., 2018). However, there is insufficient evidence to determine whether supine exercise is associated with the same adverse outcomes as supine rest; given the potential clinical issues associated with supine rest, it is plausible there could be a relationship (Mottola et al., 2018). As such, health care providers and PA guidelines have cautioned pregnant populations away from occupying the supine position (for rest and exercise) from the first trimester onwards on the basis of caution rather than explicit scientific evidence (Mottola et al., 2018).

Albeit limited, some studies suggest that supine exercise may not be harmful (Nesler et al., 1988; Jeffreys et al., 2006; Avery et al., 1999 in Mottola et al., 2018). In fact, a study by Jeffreys et al. (2006) found that venous return, cardiac output and blood pressure increases during supine exercise which increases the uterine blood flow to a level that is significantly above that observed at supine rest in healthy, fit, late-pregnant women. Furthermore, the foetus develops its own protective mechanism in order to adapt to mild hypoxic stress. In the event of reduced placental perfusion, the foetus enters a low-oxygen-consuming state as a protective adaptation. While this indicates that supine exercise may be safe for pregnant dancers to engage in, the low quality and quantity of evidence positing that supine exercise is safe beyond any reasonable doubt means that pregnant dancers should exercise caution when assessing whether to engage in supine exercise, especially after the first trimester.

After childbirth

Discussing the postpartum impact on pregnant dancers goes beyond the scope of this chapter—however, I will touch upon it briefly. While many of the above adaptations normally resolve naturally after childbirth, some adaptations can persist beyond 12 months postpartum (Thein-Nissenbaum, 2016 in Jackson et al., 2022). This could present significant challenges for dancers returning to work.

The time taken to recover from pregnancy and childbirth can vary depending on gestational complications, mode of delivery (vaginal, instrumental or caesarean section), pelvic floor dysfunction, pain and/or psychological well-being. After an uncomplicated pregnancy and vaginal birth, it is possible for women to return to low-impact physical activity in less than 12 weeks postpartum (Jackson et al., 2022). However, dancers who return to training prematurely are at risk of becoming injured due to insufficient rehabilitation and recovery time following childbirth. Musculoskeletal soft tissue injuries require 12 weeks to heal. Therefore, it is recommended that postpartum women with soft tissue trauma wait until they are at least 12 weeks postpartum before resuming high-impact activities (Jackson et al., 2022).

Conclusion

Pregnancy constitutes a significant transition in the careers of many female dancers. Becoming pregnant can result in female dancers stepping away from dance due to many compounding challenges. The absence of dance-specific guidelines means that dancers and their employers are unsure about what is safe to engage with in a dance-work environment. This chapter has delineated some high intensity activities of interest to the pregnant dancer that have been proven to be safe in the field of Sport and Exercise Science. We must apply this knowledge in the dance field to retain our talented, maturing female dancers. To that end, there needs to be a call to action for more scientific evidence supporting the safety of dance-specific activity during pregnancy. This will afford female dancers the scope and flexibility to start a family during their performative years, which will facilitate a more sustainable and inclusive future for the dance ecology.

Note

1 A contraindication refers to a condition or circumstance where exercise is not recommended. There are two types of contraindications: relative and absolute. A relative contraindication warrants discussion between the pregnant individual and her obstetric health care professional about the potential risks and benefits of pre-natal exercise (there may be circumstances where the benefits of exercise outweigh the risks or vice versa). Absolute contraindications refer to a medical condition where exercise is unequivocally discouraged. To learn more about which medical conditions constitute absolute or relative contraindications, please see Meah et al., 2020.

References

Bø, K., Artal., R, Barakat, R., Brown, W., Davies, G. A., Dooley, M., Evenson, K. R., Haakstad, L. A., Henriksson-Larsen, K., Kayser, B., Kinnunen. T. I., Mottola, M. F., Nygaard, I., van Poppel, M., Stuge, B. & Khan, K. M. (2016). Exercise and pregnancy in recreational and elite athletes: 2016 evidence summary from the IOC expert group meeting, Lausanne. Part 1—exercise in women planning pregnancy and those who are pregnant. *British Journal of Sports Medicine, 50*, 571–589. http://dx.doi.org/10.1136/bjsports-2016-096218

Bø, K., Brit, S. Hilde, G. (2022). Specific musculoskeletal adaptations in pregnancy: Pelvic floor, pelvic girdle, and low back pain Implications for physical activity and exercise. In R. Santos-Rocha (Ed.), *Exercise and physical activity during pregnancy and postpartum. Evidence-based guidelines* (pp. 135–155). Springer. http://dx.doi.org/10.1007/978-3-031-06137-0_6

Bung, P., Hutch, R. & Hutch, A. (1991). Maternal and foetal heart rate patterns: a pregnant athlete during training and laboratory exercise test: A case report. *European Journal of Obstetrics & Gynecology and Reproductive Biology, 39*(1), 59–62. http://dx.doi.org/10.1016/0028-2243(91)90143-9

Cram, C. (2023). Training during pregnancy—with Catherine Cram. [Fast Talk Femmes Podcast]. Retrieved January 12, 2024 from https://www.fasttalklabs.com/fast-talk-femmes/fast-talk-femmes-podcast-training-during-pregnancy-with-catherine-cram/

Davenport, M., Ray, L., Nedsoly, A., Thornton, J., Khurana, R. & McHugh, T. F. (2022). We're not superhuman, we're human: A qualitative description of elite athletes' experiences of return to sport after childbirth. *Sports Medicine, 53, 269–279*. http://dx.doi.org/10.1007/s40279-022-01730-y

Department for Health and Social Care (DHSC). (2021). Women's Health Strategy for England. Retrieved January 12, 2024 from https://www.gov.uk/government/publications/womens-health-strategy-for-england/womens-health-strategy-for-england

De Vivo, M., Atkinson, L., Donnelly, G., Elliot-Sale, K., Hillyar, C., Rand, S. and Roberts, C. (2022). A bump in the road? The BASES expert statement on pregnant and postpartum athletes. *The Sport and Exercise Scientist, 74*, 8–9.

Duffy, A. (2023). *Dancing motherhood*. Routledge.

Erdener, U., & Budgett, R. (2016). Exercise and pregnancy: focus on advice for the competitive and elite athlete. *British Journal of Sports Medicine, 50*, 567. http://dx.doi.org/10.1136/bjsports-2015-095680

Hallett, S., Toro, F. & Ashurst J. V. (2023). *Physiology, tidal volume.* StatPearls [Internet]. Treasure Island (FL): StatPearls. Retrieved January 12, 2024 from https://www.ncbi.nlm.nih.gov/books/NBK482502/

Ingham, S. (2020). The pregnant dancer. Arts Council England.

Jeffreys, R. M., Stepanchak, W., Lopez, B., Hadis, J. and Clapp, F. (2006). Uterine blood flow during supine rest and exercise after 28 weeks of gestation. BJOG: An International Journal of Obstetrics and Gynaecology, *113*(11), 1239–1247. https://doi.org/10.1111/j.1471-0528.2006.01056.x

Jackson, T., Bostock, E. L., Hassan, A., Greeves, J. P., Sale, C. & Elliot-Sale, K. (2022). The legacy of pregnancy: Elite athletes and women in arduous occupations. *Exercise Sports Science Review, 50,* 14–24. http://dx.doi.org/10.1249/jes.0000000000000274

Kardel, K. R. (2005). Effects of intense training during and after pregnancy in top-level athletes. *Scandinavian Journal of Medicine and Science in Sports, 15,* 79–86. http://dx.doi.org/10.1111/j.1600-0838.2004.00426.x

Keay, N. (2022). *Hormones, health and human potential.* Sequoia Books.

Kehler, A. K., & Heinrich, K. M. (2015). A selective review of prenatal exercise guidelines since the 1950s until present: Written for women, health care professionals, and female athletes. *Women Birth, 28,* e93–8. http://dx.doi.org/10.1016/j.wombi.2015.07.004

Massey, K. L., & Whitehead, A. E. (2022). Pregnancy and motherhood in elite sport: The longitudinal experiences of two elite athletes. *Psychology of Sport and Exercise, 60.* http://dx.doi.org/10.1016/j.psychsport.2022.102139

McCoid, F., & Rafiefar, R. (2013). *Pregnancy and the dancer.* One Dance UK.

McCrudden, L. (n.d.). Dance mama. Retrieved January 12, 2024 from https://www.dancemama.org/

Meah, V., Davies, G. A. and Davenport, M. (2020). Why can't I exercise during pregnancy? Time to revisit medical 'absolute' and 'relative' contraindications: systematic review of evidence of harm and call to action. *British Journal of Sports Medicine, 54,* 1395–1404. http://dx.doi.org/10.1136/bjsports-2020-102042

Mottola, M., Davenport, M., Ruchat, S., Davies, G., Poitras, V., Gray, C., Jaramillo Garcia, A., Barrowman, N., Adamo, K., Duggan, M., Barakat, R., Chilibeck, P., Fleming, K., Forte, M., Korolnek, J., Nagpal, T., Slater, L., Stirling, D., Zehr L. (2019). No. 367–2019 Canadian guidelines for physical activity throughout pregnancy. *Journal of Obstetrics and Gynaecology Can, 40,* 1528–1537. http://dx.doi.org/10.1016/j.jogc.2018.07.001

Perales, M., Nagpal, T. & Barakat, R. (2022). Physiological changes during pregnancy. Main adaptations, discomforts and implications for physical activity and exercise. In R. Santos-Rocha (Ed.), *Exercise and physical activity during pregnancy and postpartum. Evidence-based guidelines* (pp. 47–59). Springer.

Quin, E., Rafferty, S. & Tomlinson, C. (2015). *Safe dance practice.* Human Kinetics.

Redding, E. (2019). The expanding possibilities of dance science. In H. Thomas & S. Prickett. (Eds.), *The Routledge companion to dance studies* (1st ed.). Routledge.

Sanders, S. G. (2008). Dancing through pregnancy activity guidelines for professional and recreational dancers. *Journal of Dance Medicine & Science, 12,* 17–21.

Santos-Rocha, R., Fernandes de Carvalho, M., Prior de Freitas, J., Wegrzyk, J. & Szumilewicz, A. (2022). Active pregnancy: A physical exercise program promoting fitness and health during pregnancy—development and validation of a complex intervention. *International Journal of Environmental Research and Public Health*, *19*(8), 4902. http://dx.doi.org/10.3390/ijerph19084902

Soma-Pillay, P., Nelson-Piercy, C., Tolppanen, H. & Mebazaa, A. (2016). Physiological changes in pregnancy. *Cardiovascular Journal of Africa, 27*. http://dx.doi.org/10.5830/cvja-2016-021

Szumilewicz, A., Worksa, A., Santos-Rocha, R. and Oviedo-Caro, M. (2022). Evidence-based and practice-oriented guidelines for exercising during pregnancy. In R. Santos-Rocha (Ed.), *Exercise and physical activity during pregnancy and postpartum. Evidence-based guidelines* (pp. 177–217). Springer,

Wowdzia, J., Hazell, T., Vanden Berg, E., Labrecque, L., Brassard, P. & Davenport, M. (2021). Elite athletes and pregnancy outcomes: A systematic review and meta-analysis. *Medicine and Science in Sports and Exercise, 53*, 534. http://dx.doi.org/10.1249/mss.0000000000002510

11

FASCIA ILLUMINATED

May Kesler

Introduction

The first time I experienced a massage I was about ten years old. I had just grown a significant amount—and that was quite memorable, as I was always the shortest one in the class. The other reason I know my age was because we had just started pointe shoes, and my legs were so sore at night I couldn't sleep.

My mom was a paediatrician, and she worked to exhaustion most days. She occasionally hired a massage therapist to come to the house to work on her. I watched the masseuse work with all the fascination of a child watching cookies being made. I wanted one too.

I wish for many things in my life—for my mother to have lived a full life, as we lost her to breast cancer when I was 17. I wish I was tall and slim and had hips so flexible I could kiss my knees in my sleep. Those wishes can't come true now. But there is a wish that I know is possible, and it is this: that we realise that for all ages the benefits of bodywork go far beyond relaxation.

When I got that first massage I almost cried with relief. I never forgot it and sought out bodywork later in life to figure out what was happening. My right calf and ankle especially always seemed to give me problems, from the first time I sprained it in later childhood, to the hip pain I had when I was pregnant with my daughter. I remember I walked pigeon toed as a child, and that's why my mother sent me to ballet class. I also danced incessantly to the same ballet record. It seems I always loved to feel my body move.

That experience of massage as a child led me to become a physical therapist, specialising in bodywork, which has been my lifesaver and my life's work. I studied many methods throughout my 64 years of dancing and

DOI: 10.4324/9781003382874-14

41 years as a physical therapist: including myofascial release, craniosacral therapy, visceral manipulation, pelvic floor, lymphatic drainage, osteopathic methods and somatic/movement re-education.

Physical therapy and dance

Learning about anatomy answered the first of my questions. But anatomy books don't show how the body looks in a living being, and don't take into consideration how the body's systems work together. Anatomy was mainly studied until recently on dehydrated stiffened cadavers. Information about the inside of the living body, which is therefore in motion, was hardly available until microsurgery, and videos on smart phones in the last 20 years (Guimberteau, 2015; UKyOrtho, 2014). Though fascia was always identified as a sheath of tissue surrounding organs and muscles, details about it as a new organ and how it connects and unifies us was recently described by Dr Neil Theise (Benias et al., 2018).

The discovery of fascia and biotensegrity began to dominate my physical therapy work since studying Barnes myofascial release. I attended the British Fascia Symposium, and then Fascia Research Society conferences. I heard lectures there on biotensegrity, the science of how complex living structures from molecules to the entire body moves, and the continually changing balance between tension and compression within our self-organising systems (Scarr, 2014). I took these concepts and explored biotensegrity and its effect on fascia through choreography, giving workshops on 'Fascia through the lens of dance'.[1]

I came to realise that the movement properties and texture of our structure is multifaceted: a muscle embedded in fascia moves differently from organs, bone, lymph or blood. Yet all those systems are working in concert. If one is off balance, it alters the mechanics of the larger system. For example, I recently worked on a young female dancer, who had Achilles tendonitis, and though she is hypermobile, couldn't do a split. I worked on her neck and lower back—not her hamstrings – and it seemed like magic when her leg rose 30 degrees higher after a few minutes. I then worked on her whole leg, showing her how to unwind the tissue restrictions from overuse. I taught her specific somatic-informed exercises to give her more choices of movement, with the aim to reduce injury recurrence by repatterning the movement dynamics through which the injury had manifest.

Fascia—a new point of view

What is fascia, and how does it affect our movement?

Fascia is a three-dimensional (or four-dimensional if you count its motion) spider weblike tissue of light filled, fluid filled collagen tubules, creating a matrix for the cells within us (Avison, 2021). There is a thread of the fascial fabric that surrounds and infiltrates every cell, called the interstitium (Benias et al., 2018). The result is that every cell is surrounded by this mucous like stringy web, whether it is muscle, ligament, bone, or organ tissue. It also means that all our tissues, from heart cell to neuron, are interconnected and communicate with each other.

I had experienced human cadaver dissection before, in physical therapy school, on a formaldehyde preserved body, where tissues are like a dried leaf in the fall. I went to Dundee, Scotland, in 2017, to attend my first dissection course. The cadavers were preserved by Thiel method, or saline preservation, giving the body tissues a completely different texture—more like a new leaf in spring. The Thiel preserved fascia is more hydrated and malleable, the joints and connections between bones and organs able to be manipulated more easily. Just under the superficial layer of skin, there is a continuous sheath of gelatinous slimy tissue. There are no divisions, angles, or clear margins. If you look closely, you can see the collagen fibres become part of the tendon, which becomes integrated with the bone. Bone can be seen as stiffened calcified fascia (Sharkey, 2021). The brain is a gelatinous patterned mass of neurons within a slimy shiny network, cradled in a denser sheath of fascia. The digestive system is a series of tubules. Muscles are not a clean red shape but are enveloped in what looks like continuous saran wrap. There are no empty spaces, no beginnings or endings of this omnidirectional tissue inside the body.

For example, the tongue forms thick bands that join the front of the cervical spine, then down through the oesophagus, and then form into the pericardium that surrounds the heart. So, speaking from your heart is a truism! While dancing, the position of your tongue will affect how your neck, back and organs all the way to your feet are aligned. There are many other intricate and fascinating connections—supporting your arms with your back directly affects the alignment of your pelvis, through the lumbodorsal fascia from the shoulder to the lower back. The digestive organs' fascia interconnect with the front of the spine, affecting alignment.

How did it form that way? In embryonic development, fascia is formed first after the first ring of cells. The movement of the fascia, and other external and internally generated forces, dictates the genesis of many cell types resulting in specialisation (Van der Wal, 2021). The embryo as it grows folds over itself, invaginating over and over until there are tubules for nerves, bones, pockets that form organs (Sharkey, 2021).

As an embryo, the first buds for the legs and arms are the buds of toes and fingers. The spiralling tension of the toes, then feet as the embryo grows lead to the growth of the lower leg, knee, upper leg. The shape and use of your foot mirrors the way one uses their pelvis because it grew out of your pelvis (Avison, 2021). The same process happens for the arms.

The connections your body makes as it grows are unique to you, your body's physical attributes, and everything that has happened in your life. The quality and movement of everyone's fascia is unique to that person, and because we are living moving beings, this is never the same at any one moment.

Hypermobility

Hypermobility, as an example of above average flexibility, is more common in female dancers. It can be seen as talent in a dancer, while less flexibility may deny a career in dance with today's aesthetic. There is less joint stability in those with hypermobility, which leads to the muscle tissue being used to provide stability rather than the joint capsule, causing tightness in deep muscles and creating conditions for osteoarthritis and joint subluxations. My more tightly woven fascia gives me strength and stability in some areas, and restrictions in others. But being tight isn't a bad word—we need tension in our body to maintain our shape to move other areas more freely (Avison, 2021). It isn't bones that give us our humanoid shape; the tension integrated with compression in our fascial web gives us our shape. Imagine doing an *arabesque* without tension—it isn't possible!

Training to have a balance between fascial flexibility and stability, with just the right amount of tensional integrity in the tissues, can be described as the hallmark of any great dancer. Methods that assist with this concept combine somatic and interoceptive training with stability while increasing flexibility.

> *Use your inner sense of interoception to become aware that inside of us is an interconnected 3-dimensional moving fabric inside. When one part of the web moves, the whole fabric that is us shifts. Try it with your clothing. Pull one part, say near your waist. Notice where you actually feel the tension—the other side of your waist, or your back or your shoulder, all depending on the type of fabric, the position you are in, the design of your clothing, the shape of your body. Then imagine this effect all the way through your body, as if the clothing is inside you, front to back, top to bottom, side to side. Even if you only pull the smallest thread, the shape of your clothing changes.*

Fascia moves microscopically like a hand with fingers. In a shortened position, the fibres are closer together and look like one thick strand. When lengthening in the body is needed—for example the hamstrings in a *developpé*—the fibres spread out like a jazz hand. The tissues, also are known to glide through what looks like layers, so a deeper area of myofascial tissue will glide under a more superficial one as the movement happens, as you would see in the turning of your forearm in port de bras. The collagen fibres that make up fascia are like a closed Slinky. When lengthening is needed—the gastrocnemius soleus complex in a *plié*—the Slinky opens, thus giving it a rebound effect in the jump that may follow.

All of this means there is a lot more happening than just a muscle contraction in movement:

> Fascia recoil plays an impressive role in human movements. How high you jump...depends not only on the contraction of your muscle fibers, it also depends to a large degree on how well the elastic recoil properties of your fascial network are supporting your movements.
> *(Schleip, 2015, cited in Avison, 2021, p. 224)*

Muscles contract and relax in synergistic fashion, not in a big group, shimmering when their contraction is seen in slow motion, creating a flow of movement.

It starts to explain how we can do such incredible feats like multiple *pirouettes*, quick changes in movement, complex phrases and superhuman balances. It's remarkable that we can dance at all! How do we even walk and not fall into a messy heap of tangled strands?

Biotensegrity in fascial movement aka fasciategrity

The science of biotensegrity, how fascia moves in living beings, attempts to explain some of this. A tensegrity structure, which is a set of compression struts that appear to float within a network of tensioned cables, creating a stable balanced three-dimensional structure, with volume that will hold its shape without being affected by gravity. There is a large one by Kenneth Snellson at the Hirshorn Museum in Washington DC. Dr Stephen Levine (Biotensegrity Archive, 2021) theorised it is as a model for the multi-dimensional structure of tension/compression that we have in the fascial web. Fasciategrity was created as a term to explain how fascia organises itself with a biotensegrity relationship (Avison, 2021).

Gerald De Jong, a tensegrity model maker, developed the models I used in the Fascia Illuminated dance.[2] I used De Jong's models, and fabric, as extensions of the body, amplifying what we are sensing inside us. It is accompanied by the reading of anatomist Gil Hedley's *The Seeming Space* poem (Hedley, 2021). Rudolf Laban and William Forsyth also integrate the use of a moving cube-like icosohedrons as a tensegrity model in their movement studies. That model also works for describing movement between cells, or between organ systems. It is fascinating to do a movement improvisation on this micro to macro concept!

> *Move as if you are moving from the point of view of one cell inside you, surrounded by the tension of fascia around it; then move as if your whole body is one cell. Then imagine brain cells interacting with a digestive*

organ cell, or reproductive organ cell with a muscle cell. This may add an emotional charge as you recall issues in these areas of your body.

I also like using fabric as a biotensegrity model.

Find a piece of tulle or knitted blanket. Imagine the tiny spaces in the fabric to be where the icosahedron is, filled with a cell surrounded by pockets of fluid. Notice how if you pull one tiny corner of it, the whole shape changes almost instantly. If you shake or vibrate one corner, sense that vibration immediately in any other area of the fabric. In that line of tension you created, note the folds of relaxation or compression below and above the line. Twist the fabric and imagine the cells within the small spaces. The cells would then be squeezed, dehydrated, their shape changed, but more importantly the pressure needed to move nutrients is no longer there, and so the cell can't function. Notice that if you want to straighten out the folds in the fabric, pulling it at the horizontal ends unfurls it the quickest.

If we are all connected internally, then if one tiny cell moves, everything else must move in relation to it. If I shift my finger to the right, my left hip knows it must stabilise, communicating through the system of struts and pulleys tension and compression to allow the volume of my whole fabric to respond. It doesn't only go through the brain; it connects through the highly innervated fascial system. More exciting than that, scientists are now finding there are many intricate communication systems in the body (Oschman, 2016).

Fascia and dancing

What does this have to do with dancing?

I was taught both in dance class and physical therapy school at Columbia University that it is muscles that move the body. Physical therapy began as

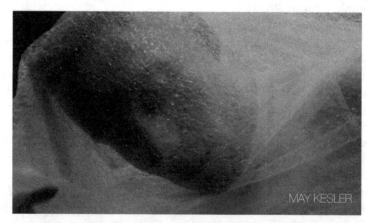

FIGURE 11.1   Max Maisey, dancer, enveloped in fascia like fabric, showing the folds of tension/compression. Copyright May Kesler, 2019

a profession to evaluate specific muscles in polio patients. Movement was described as; the brain sends nerve signals to the muscle to contract, and the muscle interlocks filaments; the shortened fibres pull on the bone, creating lever-like movement.

But the relatively slower speed of nerve conduction creating movement is not fast enough to allow for our bodies' complex interactions. All our bones are floating in the fascial matrix—they are all sesamoid bones (Sharkey, 2021). Joints and bones don't move linearly or create angles with contraction (Scarr, 2014), but they move in curves and spirals (Lowell de Solórzano, 2021). We can now look at the body as a continuous biotensegral interconnected system. An injury is never isolated; it always affects other areas.

Accessing fascia can dramatically change the quality of dancing. When doing an *arabesque*, for example, the dancer raises their leg to the back. But a more expressive *arabesque* can be executed when the dancer is aware of involving their whole body. The balanced amount of tension and torque in the foot, ankle, knee, hip of the standing leg, with the spiralling into turnout of both standing and working legs, the abdominals supporting the front of the spine, the coordination of the arms all feed into the system of this motion. Even adding the emotion can add a tension that evokes the desired expression. Try that yourself now—an academically executed *arabesque*, and then an *arabesque* thinking of involving your fascial web, then adding an emotional component. What do you feel inside that changes how you execute it?

I learned to access this feeling for myself as a dancer from Jennifer Muller. She used imagery of motion and texture in teaching. The resulting dancing was exhilarating to do, enhancing flow and emotion.

What's happening inside the body can be compared to choreography. If one dancer changes their timing of a step, it can change the meaning of the dance, making it asynchronous. A conductor adding even one count to the music implicates changes through the whole dance. Notice that in a living system of a group of dancers, the overall structure allows us to adapt and correct the timing.

The constant movement of blood, hormones, nerves, muscles, digestion, musculoskeletal systems all interact, interconnecting, flowing. From the outside of our body, we are influenced by the air we are breathing, the emotional relationships within our environment, the physical nature of the chair you are sitting in, and the sunshine letting you know it's daytime. The floor you are dancing on, the music and its vibrations, the costume, affect how you will dance. We change movement depending on the lights, the audience, the choreographer's instructions, what you ate and drank that day, what the temperature and humidity are, not to mention your fellow dancers being on cue and remembering the phrases!

Like the cloud of a group of birds flying together, all the systems in our body move as one (Theise, 2023). Perhaps the shift in our inner light, a wave of air is enough for our bodies to sense others we are working in concert with. Studying with the Pilobolus Dance company at the American Dance Festival in North Carolina, we used flocking[3] as a choreographic device. Attuning myself to the dancers around me to move as close to the moment that they moved demonstrated that we sense each other, and our own movements so quickly and precisely! If you add a partner with contact to dancing, the interaction becomes exponentially more complicated, yet we do it with ease after some practice. When you dance in a group, isn't it magical how everyone moves so seamlessly together?

Fascia injury and recovery

I went to one of the best dance workshops of my life at American University in 1976. Dancing eight hours a day with the Twyla Tharp, and Merce Cunningham companies, it was dance heaven. One night we went to Wolftrap Performing Arts Center for a dance performance. It was delightfully cool after a hot day in Washington DC. At intermission, I stood up, and felt a sharp electric pop in my right calf. I shouted from the shock and pain, grasping my leg. I ended up in the emergency room, where an X-ray showed no fracture. They gave me crutches at my request, as they assessed I could walk, though I clearly couldn't. My calf had swollen to the shape of an odd balloon, and it was painful to put weight on my foot.

I had torn part of my gastrocnemius muscle. Knowing what I know now, I believe it was set up by my uneven pelvic alignment, and scoliosis. The twist and spiralling of all my tissues, the overwork, probable dehydration in the summer heat, the cool air, sitting still in a shortened position, along with a rather sudden lengthening of them by standing up, pulled on the tissues enough to tear them.

It took me a good year to recover from my calf injury, mostly because I never saw a dance medicine specialist of any kind. There was no internet, and finding someone was through a phone book, or word of mouth. Eventually I went to a physiatrist, who told me to use a whirlpool bath on my calf, wear supportive shoes, massage the whole calf, knee and foot, and do careful slow ankle circles, and slowly progress to toe raises, and no stretches. If that injury had happened now, I would have just gone to see a physical therapist—in most US states physician referrals are not needed for an initial visit. That's important, because getting treatment after an injury quickly can speed up recovery time dramatically. Even if an area is overly sensitive for manual therapy, there is much that can be done to enhance healing through unwinding other areas of the body.

When there is inflammation, whether due to an injury, illness, or overuse, the ground substance becomes sticky and forms a gel, and the web forms adhesions, what feels like knots (when tissues stiffen together), twisting in its fabric, dehydrating the cells, causing more inflammation and restrictions.

The twisting along with those factors can be enough force to tear the soft tissues. The fascial tension can create 2,000 lbs. of pressure per square inch on the tissues it surrounds (Barnes, n.d.). The injured structures, whether musculoskeletal or organ, are stuck as if in a traffic jam—they can't move as they were meant to.

When there is an injury, there are areas of higher tension and lower compression or lack of tension, disrupting the tensional balance in our system. However, the amount of volume we take up from our width, length and volume one end of us to the other stays the same—that is your physiological volume. We can change shape within volume, and we constantly do, but we can never really get longer or shorter. This means that stretching isn't really stretching. Dynamic stretching has been found to be most useful in unwinding your tissues to their full length without injury. Static stretching can be unfolding the Slinky to a point, and it can be unravelling restrictions or congestion, but actual stretching of our tissues to a line of tensional pain can be injurious to them. If working the hip to open past the range a hip joint can accommodate, the hip joint capsule can wear down, or not grow correctly. Overstretching softer tissues can literally tear the fascial tubules if the tension becomes too great. The spaces within the fascial fabric, some of which contained water droplets, break open, creating free water which shows as swelling. The tear signals biochemicals for inflammation, which is necessary to contain the injury. Ice is no longer recommended, nor are anti-inflammatories, as this decreases the body's natural healing response, and increases recovery time. The inflammation biochemicals become a sticky gel, which creates scar tissue. The fibres in that area stick together, and the fascia regrows; stem cells enter and recreate the type of cells that were injured.

For the female dancer, this is made more complex by menstruation, widening hips changing the angle of hip to knee in adolescents, and then childbearing and menopause. When there is an area of looseness, there is an area of tightness in relation to it. This creates an unevenness in extensibility/stability/flexibility.

Scar tissue is more than a line of repair on your skin—there is also scaring internally from injury or surgery. Fascia has a random unpredictable pattern to it, making it adaptable to many angles of movement (Guimberteau & Armstrong, 2015) When there is scar tissue, it is as if there is a seam sewn around the injury. That seam is more dense, more tightly woven, and less flexible than the tissue that was there. It may, like uncombed knots in one's hair, pull on other parts of the web. Like the wrinkles in a sheet, it can pull on and make uneven, the rest of our inner fabric. The density of the restrictions can be profoundly different—in a cadaver it looks and feels like packing tape with strings in it, as opposed to smooth and slippery in healthier or less dense tissue.

That's a lot of technical information, so here's an easier way to think about it.

Compare fascial restrictions to hair. When you don't comb your hair, it gets knotted up easily, and the more knotted it gets, the drier it gets and the more easily it knots. Trying to untangle the knots with a fine-tooth comb will only tear the fibres more. We want to use a soft brush to gently unwind the tangles. Conditioners, might be bodywork like myofascial release, ball work to rehydrate cells, softening the sticky gel of inflammation, rest, decreasing stress, good nutrition, frequent short bouts of exercise to lessen stiffness, moving the body in motions the opposite of what you spend your day doing (lengthening out arms, hands, back instead of facing phone or computer for example).

Learning how to sense and unwind your fascial fabric is one of the most important self-care things you can do, for your health and longevity. Small amounts of water often during the day is the most effective way to stay hydrated. Fascial tissues take about three months to grow and change in a significant way, so be patient with any change you make in training. During sleep, we grow new fascia; muscles and organs repair and replenish, so, get good rest.

There are so many wonderful dance, and somatic-informed methods to enhance technique, flexibility and stability: Rommett Floor-Barre and Progressing Ballet technique, as well as Pilates, Gyrotonics, Feldenkrais and Alexander technique for focused somatic work. For unwinding fascial restrictions, I use a massage ball and soft foam roller methods such as Suzanne Hintzmann's Melt method, and Barnes myofascial release. Body awareness meditation strengthens communication with our inner body. I found for my patients that moving gently progressing to more movement, within an easily available range of motion is a warmup, not stretching.

Conclusion

We are each unique in our makeup, and we are different at different stages in our lives. A human being doesn't stop growing at the end of puberty. We are in constant change. Every body develops so it has the best choice for the function we ask our body to do.

I am now 68 years old. I never got to be in a professional dance company. I have performed many times though. I am still dancing, performing and choreographing. I attribute my ability to still take professional level classes partly to getting bodywork on a regular basis, from colleagues, or working on myself.

To dance for as long as you want, know how your body works, and listen to what it needs. Honour how your body communicates with you and how it is unified. Honour the ways it is different, where it has restrictions and variations. Whatever way you fall, go with it. Whatever makes you special, follow that path. The way that you move is uniquely you and will always be. Taking care of yourself is finding your interoceptive sense and listening to your intuitive self.

I was improvising while dancing at a concert the other day. At the end, a friend remarked how I was on balance all the time. I laughed; said no I wasn't. I just let all the movement become part of the dance.

Notes

1. Fascia related dance and lecture videos by May Kesler, https://vimeo.com/showcase/7596813 https://vimeo.com/339984496.
2. Gerald de Jong, tensegrity models https://www.pretenst.com.
3. Flocking is an improvisational device where a group of dancers follow a lead dancer's movement.

References

Avison, J. S. (2021). *Yoga, fascia, anatomy, and movement* (2nd ed.). Handspring Publishing.

Barnes, J. (n.d.). What is myofascial release? Myofascial Release Treatment Centers & Seminars. Retrieved January 12, 2024 from https://www.myofascialrelease.com/about/definition.aspx

Benias, P. C., Wells, R. G., Sackey-Aboagye, B., Klavan, H., Reidy, J., Buonocore, D., Miranda, M., Kornacki, S., Wayne, M., Carr-Locke, D. L. & Theise, N. D. (2018). Structure and distribution of an unrecognized interstitium in human tissues. *Scientific Reports, 8*(1). https://doi.org/10.1038/s41598-018-23062-6

Biotensegrity Archive (2021) *About the biotensegrity archive.* (2021). Retrieved September 7, 2023, from https://www.biotensegrityarchive.org/about.html

Guimberteau, J. C., & Armstrong, C. (2015). *Architecture of human living fascia: The extracellular matrix and cells revealed through endoscopy.* Handspring Publishing.

Hedley, G. (2021) The seeming space. Retrieved January 12, 2024 from https://www.gilhedley.com/the_seeming_space

Lowel de Solórzano, S. C. (2021). *Everything moves: How biotensegrity informs human movement.* Handspring Publishing.

Oschman, J. L. (2016). *Fascia as a body-wide communication system.* Musculoskeletal key. Retrieved January 12, 2024 from https://musculoskeletalkey.com/fascia-as-a-body-wide-communication-system/

Scarr, G. (2014). *Biotensegrity: The structural basis of life.* Handspring Publishing.

Schleip, R., & Baker, A. (Eds.). (2015). *Fascia in sport and movement.* Handspring Publishing.

Sharkey, J. J. (2021). Should bone be considered fascia: Proposal for a change in taxonomy of bone – a clinical anatomist's view. *International Journal of Biological and Pharmaceutical Sciences Archive, 1*(1), 01–010. https://doi.org/10.30574/ijbpsa.2021.1.1.0001

Theise, N. D. (2023). *Notes on complexity: A scientific theory of connection, consciousness, and being.* Spiegel & Grau.

UKyOrtho. (2014, August 28). *Strolling under the skin* [Video]. YouTube. Retrieved January 12, 2024 from https://youtu.be/eW0lvOVKDxE?si=Vq6tpFT11vnrqGZv

Van der Wal, J. (2021, October 18). *Lessons from the embryo about growth by jaap van der wal 2017* [Video]. YouTube. Retrieved January 12, 2024 from https://www.youtube.com/watch?v=CE-1wwEZBH0&list=PL2ySrSp5igSH-34jy3XpN-3 1I9bSfc8CC&index=4&t=339s

12

FEMALETRACES

Helen Kindred and Sandra Sok

Sounds of environment, the sound of the agonised mind, of heavy footsteps in the snow... the summer breeze carrying children's voices in the air, the cacophonous sound of the motorcycle in the distance, the sound of the tireless fly, of water penetrating the pores of nature, the sound of silence, waiting ... these auditory cues open doors to self-discovery and evoke a deeper understanding of our existence; an eco-somatic journey of gracious movement research embracing connections of arms, pelvis, bodily patterns and breath. Our research has attuned our sensorial awareness connecting with visual and sound images, taking inspiration from spaces/places, colours, smells, living beings, water, roots and all the traces we share.

We have been working together in an eco-based embodied movement research project,[1] FEMALE*traces*, that has been nurtured through somatic dialogue, participatory workshops and performance, fuelled by a shared impulse to explore the Laban Bartenieff Movement System beyond the confines of a dance studio. Embracing the fluidity and constant change of the environments we inhabit, FEMALE*traces* has woven a tapestry of togetherness while being physically apart, transcending boundaries and time zones to live and document our somatic experiences in different corners of the world—Azerbaijan, Croatia, the UK and Thailand. Over this year-long research process we have deepened our awareness of our self, and each other, embracing and honouring traces of femininity, strength and vulnerability within us. Our experiences have taught us to appreciate the shifting landscapes of our surroundings, recognising *environment* through this research as inherently social, cultural, political, physical and ecological. By sharing daily, images, videos and our somatic awareness through feminist perspectives we have

DOI: 10.4324/9781003382874-15

come to know better our shared lived experiences across diverse cultural contexts.

In this chapter, we embrace a creative approach to sharing: breathing-through-writing. This method allows our embodied experiences to flow onto the page, departing from traditional academic writing. We see writing as an integral part of our research practice, intimately intertwined with our exploration, articulated and validated through our danced experience, rather than a detached academic abstraction. The words on these pages may flow in rapid currents, drift and meander in open spaces, nudge up against the edges of established terrain, or pause to encourage space for further thinking in movement (Sheets-Johnstone 2015). We invite you to approach this chapter with openness, much as you would a movement workshop—immersing yourself in sensorial moments, meditating on reflective notes, and playfully engaging with our word-based scores for your exploration beyond the page.

The essence of FEMALE*traces* lies not in a singular fixed model of perception but in a relational trans-model experience, exploring the interconnectedness between and through things (Alaimo, 2008; Manning, 2016). We have learnt to witness, listen and feel in motion, engaging in dances with the environments we inhabit, sharing through listening, patiently waiting for signs of female traces in the environments of our daily lives. Through FEMALE*traces* we have established ways of exploring—sensing from the inside—shifting landscapes, moving between inner connectivity and outer expressivity. In practice, we have walked, talked, wandered, wondered, noticed, noted and shared images from nature, sensations of our environments, as we experience moving in daily ritual.

Embracing an embodied feminist approach, we recognise the value of our lived experience in the relational spaces of our environments (Sullivan, 2001; Fraleigh, 2015) where sound-less does not mean silence, and where research is shared through processes which emerge from somatic experiences enabling us to be challenged, to confront and be confronted, and to grow as female artists. Central to our exploration is the work of Irmgard Bartenieff[2] and the Laban Bartenieff Movement System, which forms the framework for our movement explorations in natural environments. FEMALE*traces* through somatic dialogue, workshops and performance, makes visible some of the textures, imagination and improvisational nuances of Bartenieff's work within a philosophy of flow.[3]

Through our shared passion for exploring Bartenieff's work in nature we have developed a methodology for exploring and embodying key principles of the practice—*yielding-pushing, reaching-pulling, stability-instability, inner connectivity-outer expressivity*. These principles guide our movement allowing us to trace our bodies in ever-shifting environments. This engagement with Bartenieff's work invites us to understand further the established practice as an embodied research practice, gathering and analysing information from within the soma, within environments, fuelled by imagination and wonder. Our research centres our lived experiences as female-identifying dance-artists and scholars, living and dancing across diverse continents and cultures. Through the unfolding practice of witnessing and exploring we have committed to a rich storytelling process which has given us permission to explore our female identity and expressions of femininity by tracking changes, in-woman-in-nature. We have embraced the entangled web of relationships with everything around us, finding both joy and uncertainty in the process of daily living.

Embodying female | feminine | femininity

We embody the term 'female' as the identity that is (in)formed through our eco-somatic sensorial world. We discuss 'feminine' through a felt sense of relational experience rather than a set of behaviours attributed to 'being female', proposing that femininity encompasses the embodiment of both strength and fragility, action and contemplation, receptivity and proactivity within the somatic flow of environments. Rather than co-existing side-by-side, these traits integrate into a trans-corporeal experience of the world, where the somatic sensations arise from our openness to noticing, listening and actively responding to our body stories (Olsen, 2004). We question how society perceives our bodies: gendered as female, racialised as white, and how these perceptions both enable and suppress us in different contexts. We acknowledge externally imposed perceptions of female and move consciously through our encounters with resistance and resilience to our felt somatic experience.

> *Leaves letting go, falling and drifting to land on new terrain,*
> *the noticing of this as a point of departure for our dancing*

We view the world around us as a grand web of interconnectedness, where everything is contextualised. Harmony, as a part of this process, exists only as a function of diversity. We consider this a question of telling different stories from different angles and celebrate this through the language, movement, patterns, gestures, ceremony and ritual that emerge from the activity of FEMALE*traces*. As we traverse physical and emotional boundaries, our bodies become porous, and the potential for trans-corporeal experiences emerges. Through the process of exploring our questions of FEMALE*traces*— femininity in the flow of natural environments—through a feminist approach to Bartenieff Fundamentals, we have engaged with processes of heightened somatic awareness, shifting emotional states, and discerning experiential patterns of wholeness through intuitive, corporeal participation.

Scores that represent traces of our eco-somatic encounters are shared here, blending spirituality and dance within embodied spatial-temporal investigations. These scores, and we acknowledge here the myriad of approaches working with scores in Western contemporary dance practices that is discussed in other scholarship (Blades 2013; Irvine 2014; Millard 2015; Voris 2018) and therefore not the focus of this chapter, enable us to share our dancing together-apart and with others. The scores of FEMALE*traces* thus serve as portals to delve deeply into our inquiry around femininity, softness, strength, care, action, gathering, breathing, moving and grounding. In nature, we find support and grounding, connecting with ecological histories of place and experiencing extraordinary movement expressions with empathy and self-expression.

> *Gathering, scattering, scooping the sand*
> *with the hands...fallen leaves from the ground, snow from*
> *the garden, seeds, creating shapes with hands,*
> *fingers...seeing things around with fingertips ...dropping*
> *that sand, sugar, snow, throwing, launching, flipping,*
> *sending, projecting into the space or different body parts...*

> *What is revealed of our Self our soul, our spirit?*
> *What is felt of our physical, embodied histories in*
> *movement? What does shifting feel like?*
> *How might we shift boundaries of space to experience*
> *space harmony? What are the shifting qualities*
> *of femininity?*

In this body-space-environment-in-flow of FEMALE*traces* we are discovering ourselves as feminine; powerful vulnerable. We embody *Lilith*, the female demonic figure of Jewish folklore as a symbol of our experience of femininity.[4] Listening to her voice through her physical stance, preparing to pounce, cowering at the same time, dancing as Lilith, we undergo a metamorphosis, melding biological-histories and socially gendered identities. In this relational community of 'female' experience, we embody the essence of humanity—feeling, sensing, doing, enabling, with compassion, virtuosity and vulnerability.

By embodying Lilith, we highlight the tensions between body and society often reinforced through the uncritical preservation of gendered roles within social and philosophical discourse. Our research process embodies change, tracking shifts in-woman-in-nature, within the community of the environment. Through solo investigations and collaborative contemplation, we expand linear thinking, engaging critically with eco-somatic trans-corporeality, embracing the fluidity of our identities.

FGURE 12.1 Flesh and woven threads of nature. Copyright Helen Kindred

Breath, belly, pleasure in our bodies
Being with the quiet within, awakening the fire within.
Movements that invite softening and questioning of femininity

Water and rewilding: Somatic contemplation and nature's dance

During the process of our research, we respected the role of somatic contemplation and valued time for inspiration. This process resonates with the essence of Lilith, the dancing goddess, who gracefully roams springs, rivers, trees, oceans, seas, mountains, parks and grottoes, transforming stories through magical, ceremonial arm circles and pelvic shifting. Nature has long served as a sacred and expansive space, perfectly suited for ritual ceremonies and dance, a tradition dating back to prehistoric times (Yioutsos, 2013). The divine cult of dancing finds its expression in grottoes and places where water's presence is potent. The intertwining of the nymphs and the horned God's cults is evident in caves, where the wildness of the surroundings blends harmoniously with the freshness of water (Yioutsos, 2013, p. 47). These idyllic, picturesque settings, adorned with statues and flourishing plants, became ancient playgrounds for dance, worship, rituals and the expression of untamed passions. Visiting such places for us became a sanctuary, allowing us to attune to our embodied female identities, 'rewilding' in nature (Craigie, 2020).

FEMALE*traces* honours the time when dance served as a ceremonial act, extending legacies of women and igniting questions about human embodiment in motion—which bodies have access, feel, sense, move and are visible or invisible, abled or disabled (Cooper-Albright, 1997). 'Body' can be seen as a metaphor for one's whereabouts, for the limitlessness of the experience. The acceptance of diversity requires the recognition of some discoveries and differences beyond the corporeal, beyond the dancer, to a transactional interpretation of boundaries. This requires a recognition of physical, ecological boundaries with a view to shifting perspectives through metaphysical experiences of dancing.

Embracing the idea of multiple embodiments of diverse spaces stands in stark contrast to the notion of unity and stability (Foster, 1998). Our commitment to routinised actions allows our bodies to undergo transformative stages, perpetually leaving open the realm of extraordinary possibilities. These explorations lead us toward new traces of corporeal existence and resistance (see also Foster, 1998).

> *body is not just a container of negative things...*
> *body tells us a story about our spiritual condition,*
> *sends us information about how we are standing*
> *in this world,*
> *how we are grounding in the planet, country, street*
> *we live in, room where we are at the moment...*
> *the body is resonating its own noise*

In the process of listening and attending we experienced a realignment with our moving, revealing truths about who we feel we are, and questioning how we respond to the world through movement. In FEMALE*traces* we discover the powerful essence of water, rewilding ourselves in nature's embrace. The dance of Lilith within us resonates with ancient rituals, uniting our being with the rhythms of the earth.

The usual parameters no longer exist. There was a time when my arms stopped and the handlebars of my bike began, but not now. There was a time when the skin of my upturned face once prickled with the heat of the sun. Not now, now my face *is* the sun and behind what was skin there hisses and cracks enough energy to keep the world turning. My lungs and legs continue to move in and out up and down like the bellows and pistons of a steam train, only now they do so effortlessly because they are no longer inhibited by the pain and discomfort my mind used to tell them they were experiencing. The tussle with gravity and the elements has ceased. Everything is quiet and calm behind where my eyes used to be. I'm floating and free in this bubble of damp dirt and fresh sweat.

(Craigie, 2020, p. 65).

Lee Craigie describes the transformative potential of body and nature in the relational flow of cycling in the Scottish Highlands. For us in dancing, the tussle with gravity becomes intoxicating, visceral and undeniably central to our explorations. Through bodily patterns of pushing and yielding we embrace the humility of our human form in relation with gravity, yielding into the earth, pushing against the currents of the stream, encountering softness in the river beneath our feet, giving our weight to the smoothness of the rock, stabilising a sense of self in balance.

Our connection with the feet, pelvis and spine opens explorations of the imagery of the environment and personal experiences of three-dimensional movement as a metaphor of life; encompassing past, present and future, the entirety of existence.

> *breathing through the feet*
> *exploring the connection with earth with gravity into spinal activity*
> *more playful exploring with music and on a vertical axis,*
> *the space of the earth penetrating through the feet*
> *into the body, creating new rhythms, new gestures*
> *stepping, marking, respecting the earth*
> *pelvis and shoulders connection, playful patterns through the spine…resistance…vibrations*
> *3 dimensionality*

Being in the world: Dancing with nature's transformative flow

> *What is my motivation for moving forward, step to the side when is needed, cross the path, look up into a bright day and still turn my view into other dimensions and stay in realm of this life?*

The practice of Bartenieff Fundamentals has been a connecting passion for us, an undercurrent driving our shared motivation in movement research. Central to this is a deep focus on the breath as the primary movement through which the body is mapped in an on-going process. Mapping the body through a process of deepened listening and internal visualisation of the breath, allows for tuning and attending to the body's sensations on a micro level (self-scanning of the body) while establishing a sense of the connected whole on a macro-level (body in relationship with environment). Inner connectivity and outer expressivity, as described by Hackney (2002), forms a key aspect of human existence. For Bartenieff, an experiential understanding of inner and outer and the relational possibility between them is key to the pursuit of humans being in the world: functioning, expressive and efficient in movement (Bartenieff and Lewis, 1980).

Attending to internalised sensations of the body is common in other somatic practices (Eddy, 2016; Fraleigh, 2015) and practices of tuning are documented through Lisa Nelson's tuning scores (Nelson, 2006). Our approach to somatic tuning distinguishes itself through focus on ocular presence of our environment during our dancing. Unlike other somatic practices that often involve closing one's eyes to focus on internal bodily sensations, our research thrives on the beauty and multisensorial, eyes-open, engagement with natural surroundings. The 'tussle with gravity and the elements' Craigie gracefully surrenders to becomes our quest through dancing.

The articulated experience of body-space-environment-flow within FE-MALE*traces* follows an intuitive and sequential organisation based on developmental movement patterns. The six total body connectivity of Bartenieff Fundamentals are explored simultaneously: the *breath* on cellular level as essential for the movement, *core distal* connectivity of core support which allows limbs to move in and away from the centre of the body and refers to the continuum of the spine and movement range, *head-tail* connectivity important for connectivity with ourselves but also with the dimensions of movement (low, mid, high). Moving into *upper-lower* connectivity which connects upper and lower body and movement patterns such as yield and push and reach and pull which communicate our relation to the earth, *body-half* connectivity placing attention on stability and mobility and dynamic alignment between right and left side and *cross-lateral* connectivity developed by diagonal connections that cross the body's vertical line to establish rotation, deeper spirals and complex locomotion. These movement attitudes allow for the movement explorer to notice the nuances of many possibilities of an individual movement patterns (see also Hackney, 2002; Fernandez, 2015; Hughes, 2018).

> *hands sculpt the space around the body,*
> *arms connect them to their potential source,*
> *the pelvis is the source that anchors it all,*
> *arms give the hands life, life-force and meaning through*
> *the fingertips*
> *the pelvis connects all gestures to their original power*
> *source – the earth's core*
>
> *widening space and imagination,*
> *developing hand gestures,*
> *finding movement in the flow of weight,*

creating is conversation...
widening space from breath expansion
pelvis-chest-hands (fingertips)
shifting weight, shifting pelvis, shifting roots
moving from sensation and impulses
creating impulsive, spontaneous, emotional movement
stretch, reach out, let go
condense, bow, explode
accepting the rhythm and impulse of whatever comes
combined three-dimensional movement, three planes
of presence

negotiating with terms STOP
(freeze, park, still)
not to cease the movement,
[explore how we can stay still in movement and continue
with fluidly within the process

playing with the gravity,
try to collapse,
fail,
yet still we are gentle and soft to our body
changing dynamic, speed in a way it is anatomically and
kinaesthetically resonate

connecting with body parts and internal organs, connecting
within and beyond our skin

Embodied feminism and ritualistic practices

From an embodied feminist perspective, our research carves space for somatic practice that often linger on the periphery of academic discourse. By engaging with scholarship in the field of dance and somatic practice we gravitate towards the dominance of feminist phenomenological perspectives of the body (Sheets-Johnstone, 2015; Barbour, 2011; Fraleigh, 2018). Colin Wilson in Sondra Fraleigh's *Dance and the Lived Body*, argues that Merleau-Ponty points the way towards a new and purposeful existentialism, where intentional consciousness becomes the essence of understanding, ever-present and yet challenging to grasp (Wilson in Fraleigh, 1981). Our approach values simplicity, insight, delving deeply to look at what is there to be explored, accepted and seen. These realms may be mystical or sacred, of the lived melting-body with nature, or transcendent experiences practising ways of moving in harmony. We illuminate the distinctive values in dancing and the self, experienced and created through movement, steeped in compassion, love, acceptance and strength through intentionality. These approaches are made meaning-full as our ritualistic practice of bodies in nature unfolds. We move beyond a positioning of body being affected by the environment, to a place of relational flow where bodies exist in a dynamic relationship with their surroundings (Sullivan, 2001; Kindred, 2021).

In Ancient Greece 'dance served as a means of expressing mental conditions and as a sign of religious faith and devotion through rhythmic movement' (Papaioannou et al., 2011, p. 233). Rituals manifested as circle dances, ball games, or processions, considered sacred, a non-verbal mode of communication embracing spiritual, emotional and intellectual aspects of life. Rituals embodied gestures, hidden codes, expression of the body as a language of the soul, harmony within physical movement, emotional wellbeing, rhythmic exploration, and strong intra-action within community (Papaioannou et al., 2011; Yioutsos, 2017, 2021; Nowicka, 2016). Dance was treated with the greatest respect, enabling the communication of essential societal elements through human contact, infused with the power of natural forces. The dance of Pan and the nymphs was profoundly connected to music and sensual movements. Their rituals were performed inside caves bringing joy and fortune to many of these sanctuaries. In FEMALE*traces*, our rituals evoke a human power that fosters relations between individuals and their bodies within an ecosystem, shaping a global strategy that transforms reality (Burkitt, 1999; Mills, 2003). The human body is within these relations and its powers perceived accordingly. In these relations the identity of the individual emerges, along with all her experience, capacities and beliefs within the social, historical and biological dimensions of space and time, clearly inseparable and entwined (Burkitt, 1999).

Ritual, and the power of anima

In our participatory research we embraced a ritualistic approach, holding workshops for anyone interested in exploring concepts of traces through bodily-spatial encounters. The workshops were held on Zoom which presented new challenges for us as we explored and questioned what it was to open this intimate practice of research to others, and how to invite and honour their responses in virtual digital time-space. The beauty of using Zoom, of course meant that we were able to connect with movers in the USA, Mexico, Croatia, the UK, Azerbaijan, Poland. We approached the workshops with the same openness to sharing and honest exploration that we had enjoyed in our own process of somatic dialogue. We used words that we had drawn into scores within the process of the research, inspired by our reflections on our own embodied experiences. Through verbal guidance and physical participation in the process, we invited detail in gesture, rhythm, grounding and expansion through improvisation. Participants were generous in their sharing physically and in feedback after the workshops, commenting on feeling 'free', 'elated', 'calm, 'inspired'. Through this process of the research, we learnt more of the meaning of FEMALE*traces*, of the possibility of ritual with others: beginning always with the breath; tuning, listening, locating and moving from an embodiment of the spatial-temporal flow of the breath through our bodies drawing the flow theorist Csikszentmihaly rewarding experience of enjoyment (Beard, 2015).

The ritual of FEMALE*traces* has been kinaesthetic, embodied, deeply spiritual, weaving through our lives, strengthening our bond as collaborative partners, and fostering an understanding of female energy across time and space. The moments of giving and receiving images from nature have opened a new space to breathe. Each transaction, a shared pause in time-space, allows thinking to shift, energy to change, or simply a heightened awareness of the present moment. The ritual of sharing found itself anew through the workshops with others. The breath became our ritual of connectivity. Connecting with our own breath, the surfaces, spaces, tensions, hold and let go in our own bodily attending, while connecting as a community in this time together of sharing imagery and sound.

> *Breath—to begin, to open, to gather and to connect*
> *us all. Tentative beginnings held by the shared*
> *connection of breath and a welcome spiritual space*
> *which emerged.*

The workshops enabled us to explore storytelling as an expansion of breath support, delving into patterns of pushing, yielding, stability, mobility, grounding and expansion. Participants discovered their own 'body stories', unlocking a path to self-expression and exploration.

> *And when the music took over the world within, the magical forest became alive. This gentle, soft-legged bird freely opened her wings and started enjoying the forest, life, herself. The feelings of beauty and gratitude were overwhelming. Life is so beautiful, lush, green full of possibilities! Heart is open! So much to appreciate, love, be grateful for... Wow! And from these joyful thoughts the forest fairy has been born, sprinkling the forest with her gold-lit blessings. The creative, nurturing world within that has been buried under so much pain became alive and magical again and again. Lots of fresh, green, new energy. Rebirthing. Moving to the words...While listening to the guidance about the pelvic floor movement, the sensual, wise goddess started calling her energy back. Lots of soft orange. Connecting with the Earth, flowing like a soft sensual river, she started beaming her creative fire and love at the world surrounding her. (Female participant, Zagreb, Croatia)*

The workshops offered the possibility to be as we are, to dance as we are, to think as we are, to flow between fragility and strength, to understand the tensions of gravity and emotion, to find physical and spiritual alignment, to find ourselves out of comfort through storytelling, evoking through rich imagination, ancestral signs and perhaps reveal a sparkle of darkness in us. We delved into a safe space, a shielded cave where we explored our rejuvenation and growth, embracing our embodied shadows, fantasies, femininity and happiness. We accepted ourselves as we are and extended that invitation to others.

FEMALE*traces* emphasises the distinction between *animus* (which is very close to being a body) and *anima* (which is going to weigh down all spirituality), two interrelated developments that describe the mind and soul. The phenomenology of anima reveals feminine power. It has been felt in FEMALE*traces* and reminds us that anima resides in us and presents tranquillity and stillness within us, encompassing simplicity and the dream-like nature of the soul. Through FEMALE*traces* we are actively encouraging a philosophy of femininity. The anima is not a weakness. It has its own forces. It is the interior principle of our repose. It is soft, a harmonious substance which wishes to enjoy being on her own slowly. By possessing the anima, we are receiving the teachings of the natural calm of our own nature. The anima, the principle of our tranquillity is really the being of our still water, that nature within us, which is sufficient unto self, the tranquil feminine (Bachelard, 1960).

We have experienced through this research that we can shift, trace, score and transit our attention in order to reveal strength and persistence, all the time negotiating a feminine duality of strength and fragility. We have played with gravity, resistance and softness, questioned: what does it mean to be brave, to trust your body, suspend, or surrender into something new and unfamiliar? To learn how to get out of comfort zone and still being with(in) your own skin. Taking pleasure in being at home in the body takes bravery, curiosity, lightness, acknowledging the darkness, softening into this as much as seeking light. Concepts of pushing and yielding have become apparent in this constant work-in-progress of our lives. Still, we need to push: to yield, to exhale and receive nourishment from our surroundings, from each other; to know how to exhale lively from the gut or deep within the pelvis and find that fluid alignment in our body, central line, traces, trusting our femininity through simple complexities of ritualistic folded-unfolded movement.

Through this exploration, we challenged Western society's inscribed notions of female weakness (Weininger, 2006; Sutton et al., 2011) and questioned whether true strength lies in finding comfort in our own bodies, listening to our intuition and being true to ourselves. We navigated the complexities of femininity, embracing the fluidity of ritualistic movement as a means of empowerment. We questioned through this research if weakness equates to changing things or finding comfort in our own body. If weakness means listening to our own body in a way that society is telling us not to, am I weak if I do not listen to my body, or when I do listen? Am I weak and fragile if I do not push enough but still want to float, and remain curious? Am I weak if I think, see or feel differently? Am I weak if I become a masculine woman, or any other woman I want to be? FEMALE*traces* unravels the power of anima and challenges societal perceptions of femininity. Through ritualistic practices and participatory workshops, we explore the depths of self-expression and find strength in embracing our authentic selves.

Notes

1. We are understanding embodiment as an interweaving of physical experience, sensation and reflective thought, fundamentally denying a Cartesian separation of mind and body (Sheets-Johnstone, 2009, 2015; Fraleigh, 2018).
2. Irmgard Bartenieff (1900–1981) was a dance artist, educator and physical movement therapist. Her work in respect of Rudolf Laban's system of movement analysis developed the body aspect of his work and significantly contributed to the development of what is now known globally as the Laban Bartenieff Movement System (LBMS) https://labaninstitute.org.
3. The concept of flow by psychologist and longtime researcher of flow Mihaly Csikszentmihaly and what is exactly happening in the moments of deep involvement when the existential state of flow is experienced, when the physical body of oneself is inevitably intertwined with the world experience and how all that exists because of unifying of bodily action and awareness within the permanent form of nature here and now, through a clear set of goals, feedback, balance between challenge and skill, concentration, forgetting oneself, being in control, paying attention and joyful doing (mdx.kanopy.com/video/flow-psychology-FLOW: Psychology, Creativity and Optimal Experience with Mihaly Csikszentmihaly). Csikszentmihaly's research into flow thus outlines a decision-making approach to re-experiencing flow when faced with adversity, namely one should think one's way back into flow, for example make a decision and have the resolve that everything will be okay (Csikszentmihaly, 2015). 'Although the phenomenon of flow is best described as the merging of bodily action with awareness' (Lloyd, 2015, p. 25).
4. Lilith, female demonic figure of Jewish Folklore. Her name and personality are thought to be derived from the class of Mesopotamian demons called *lilû* (feminine: *lilītu*) https://www.britannica.com/topic/Lilith-Jewish-folklore.

References

Alaimo, S. (2008). Trans-corporeal feminisms and the ethical space of nature. In S. Alaimo & S. Hekman (Eds.), *Material feminisms* (pp. 237–264). Indiana University Press. http://www.jstor.org/stable/j.ctt16gzgqh.12

Bachelard, G. (1960). *The poetics of reverie: Childhood, language and the cosmos.* (Daniel Russell, Trans.) Beacon Press.

Barbour, K. (2011). *Dancing across the page: Narrative and embodied ways of knowing.* Intellect.

Bartenieff, I., & Lewis, D. (1980). *Body movement: Coping with the environment.* Routledge.

Beard, K. S. (2015). Theoretically speaking: An interview with Mihaly Csikszentmihalyi on flow theory development and its usefulness in addressing contemporary challenges in education. *Educational Psychology Review,* 27(2), 353–364. https://doi.org/10.1007/s10648-014-9291-1

Blades, H. (2013). Scoring dance. *Postgraduate Journal of Aesthetics*, 10 (2), 43–57.

Burkitt, I. (1999). Bodies of thought: Embodiment, identity and modernity. *Bodies of Thought*, 1–176.

Cooper-Albright, A. (1997). *Choreographing difference. The Body and Identity in Contemporary Dance*. Wesleyan University Press.

Craigie, L. (2018) ReWilding in H. Mort, C. Carter, H. Dawe & C. Barnard (Eds.). *Waymaking: An anthology of women's adventure writing, poetry and art*. (pp. 65–67). Vertebrate Publishing.

Csikszentmihaly, M. (2015). *The Humanistic Psychologist*, 43(26).

Eddy, M. (2016). *Mindful movement: The evolution of the somatic arts and conscious action*. Intellect Books.

Fernandez, C. (2015). *The moving researcher: Laban/Bartenieff movement analysis in performing arts education and creative arts therapies* (Cláudio Laerde, Trans.). Jessica Kingsley.

Foster, L. S. (1998). *Choreographies of gender*, Signs, 24(1), 1–33. http://www.jstor.org/stable/3175670

Fraleigh, S. H. (1987). *Dance and the lived body: A descriptive aesthetics*. University of Pittsburgh Press.

Fraleigh, S. H. (Ed.). (2015). *Moving consciously: Somatic transformations through dance, yoga, and touch*. University of Illinois Press, Chicago. http://dx.doi.org/10.5406/illinois/9780252039409.001.0001

Fraleigh, S. H. (Ed). (2018). *Back to the dance itself: Phenomenologies of the body in performance*. University of Illinois Press.

Hackney, P. (2002). *Making connections. Total body integration through Bartenieff fundamentals*. Routledge.

Hughes, V. (2018). Using dance/movement therapy and Laban movement analysis to build a better model of rehabilitation for chronic pain. *Dance/Movement Therapy Theses*, 42. Retrieved January 12, 2024 from https://digitalcommons.slc.edu/dmt_etd/42

Irvine, R. (2014). *Perception frames: choreographic scores for practice and performance*. Middlesex University.

Kindred, H. (2021). Dancing the in-between-ness: (Re)articulating Bartenieff fundamentals through improvised dance performance-making [Unpublished doctoral dissertation]. University of Middlesex.

Lloyd, R. J. (2015). From dys/function to flow: Inception, perception and dancing beyond life's constraints. *The Humanistic Psychologist*, 43(1), 24–39.

Manning, E. (2016). *The minor gesture*. Duke University Press.

Millard, O. (2015). What's the score? Using scores in dance improvisation. *Brolga: An Australian Journal about Dance*, 40, 45–56.

Mills, S. (2003). *Gender and politeness* (No. 17). Cambridge University Press.

Nelson, L. (2006). Composition, communication, and the sense of imagination: Lisa Nelson on her pre-technique of dance, the tuning scores. *Self-interview. Ballet Tanz. Critical Correspondence*, NYC, Movement Research.

Nowicka, E. (2016). Siberian circle dances: The new and old communitas. *Polish Sociological Review*, 194(2), 249–260.

Olsen, A. (2004). *Bodystories: A guide to experiential anatomy*. UPNE.

Papaioannou, C., Mouratidou, K., Mouratidis, G. & Doula, S. (2011). Association of dance with sacred rituals in ancient Greece: The case of Eleusinian mysteries, *Studies in Physical Culture and Tourism*, 18(3), 233–239.

Sheets-Johnstone, M. (2015). *The corporeal turn: An interdisciplinary reader*. Andrews UK.

Sullivan, S. (2001). *Living across and through skins: Transactional bodies, pragmatism, and feminism.* Indiana University Press.

Sutton, R. M., Robinson, B. & Farrall, S. D. (2011). Gender, fear of crime, and self-presentation: An experimental investigation. *Psychology, Crime & Law, 17*(5), 421–433.

Voris, A. (2018). *Forming, returning and deepening: Dance-making with the processual qualities of authentic movement* [Unpublished doctoral dissertation]. University of Chichester.

Yioutsos, N. P. (2013). Cave dancing in ancient Greece. In R. Poignault (Ed.), *Présence de la danse dans l'antiquite-présence de l'antiquité dans la danse.* Université Clermont Auvergne.

Yioutsos, N. P. (2017). Order in ancient Greek dance rituals: The dance of Pan and the Nymphs, *Revista do laboratório de dramaturgia (LADI), Ideas e Criticas, 5*(2), 212–234.

Yioutsos, N. P. (2021). Female ball-dance in ancient Greece. *Revista do Laboratório de Dramaturgia (LADI), Orchesis, 17*(6), 368–403.

Weininger, O. (2006). *Sex and character* (L. Marcus and D. Steuer, Eds., L, Löb, Trans.). G. P. Putnam's Sons. (Original work published 1906).

THE EMBODIED ARCHIVE OF THE SELF

Celia Shaw Morris

Where do you feel tender?
How do you need to be touched?

In most moments throughout most days,
I go about my life with an interior, sensorial experience of my body in relation to my surroundings,
and a mirrored but projected image of myself doing the thing that I am doing.

Inside out outside in.

I've lived inside this
splitting of awareness for a long time, I think since puberty started to morph me,
when the comments on what I wore, how I looked, moved, spoke, laughed, and ate changed in tone and frequency.
And until recently I thought everyone existed inside this.

Through researching embodied experience via texts, conversations with my community, and movement improvisation explorations, it's become clear that a large majority of individuals raised as 'female' experience this fracturing of their somatic selves.[1]
Only recently am I starting to see the snowball, the ricochet of how the outside too often takes precedence, the exhaustion of stepping away from yourself constantly. A drop-by-drop emptying.

DOI: 10.4324/9781003382874-16

how might we turn this fracturing into a superpower

six hands in the room,
four at a time kneading,
infusing muscle matter with care

to dance with your previous selves :
tossing a line out into the mist, trusting that you can carry what the boat of
your memory will drag back for you

I open into
where is tender, shifting my sense of self down, melting my brain down into
my pelvis.
Immediately, once I arrive, vomit crawls up my windpipe and a storm hits my
temples, collision into collision, kneading me.
I worry I might never return to solid earth, this current aches and twists for
destruction, I cower against it
moaning, curled,
rocking on haunches
simultaneous predator and prey
I know this place, it ruled my days for years, whipping me against myself, sucking me dry. I squashed it, shamed it, rejected it, tossed it. As too
much – too much too much too much. All aching need, bursting at the seams,
waving banners of singularity, reading

this has never been felt before.

I was afraid to do this today.
This is not a confession.

I haven't looked in this mirror recently, and now
I feel how much I buried here, how damp the air has become.
There is grief in exhuming yourself, excavating a landscape,
smelling the parts festering in stagnation,
swampy pits.

how do you feel tender
where do you want to be touched

Desire is a word streaked across lips

that threatens careless.

how do you want to experience your body,
your inherent enoughness

The breathless clarity of knowing you are no longer ashamed of the size of
your own shadow anymore.

With this pumping chorus of a body, we offer movement for what was previously stuck, or we caress that stuckness with the reminder that we're not there anymore. We kiss the younger selves that were raw and aching for softness, we scream for the ones that didn't find the voice, we breathe for the ones that were closed in too tightly for air, we laugh with the fullness of their joy. We make space for all of them, and we repair not as a mechanism of fixing but to celebrate and honor and forgive. We create an archive of an archive, breathe life back inside what was already lived.

There's something akin to freedom here, the possibility of it glinting like mica in the sun.
Fractured light tasted
on skin, warm to the touch.

Note

1 Lexie Kite and Lindsay Kite, "More Than A Body" (Houghton Mifflin Harcourt, 2020).

PART III
Taking up space

13

SUSTAINING A DANCE CAREER AS A PARENT

Lucy McCrudden and Angela Pickard

Introduction

Over the last 15–16 years, there has been a growing interest and a body of literature in the UK and beyond, that examines the intersections of the dancing body, caring responsibilities and managing a career in dance (Sanders, 2008; Vincent Dance Theatre, 2009; Duffy, 2018; Musil et al., 2022; Pickard and Ehnold-Danailov, 2022). Such research provides evidence of the challenges and barriers navigated by dancers who are parents, as they to try to balance parenting with a dance career:

> Parents who have chosen to make dance a career suggest multifarious and layered experiences, challenges, and emotions that arise for most dancers who parent. The balancing act of negotiating both parenthood and a career in dance requires the navigation of uncertainty and ambiguity.
>
> *(Musil et al., 2022, p. 129)*

Barriers include expectations that dance work will often happen outside regular 'business' hours. Such work is often intensive, project based and can be inflexible, with long hours in the studio for rehearsals and/or evening performances. There are examples of enabling working conditions and supportive structures for dancers that are parents, and these learnings demonstrate that it is possible to continue with a career in dance, while also being a parent. Such strategies are useful for employers, (ranging from independent choreographers to companies) as ways of knowing what is possible across the sector.

In 2007, Dance UK (now known as One Dance UK), the national body for dance in the UK, produced an information sheet entitled 'Pregnancy and the

DOI: 10.4324/9781003382874-18

dancer' that provided some detailed information about dancing during and post-pregnancy. Also, in 2007, Dance UK held a symposium in partnership with Dance Umbrella, that focused on recruitment and retention of mature professional dance artists and the impact that parenthood had on attrition in the sector. Further, in 2009, Dance UK and Dance Umbrella hosted a debate around the lack of high-profile female choreographers working in the UK. The challenge of affordable childcare and balancing parenting with dance was discussed as a barrier (see Baum, 2002 for similar findings). In addition, Charlotte Vincent of Vincent Dance Theatre, in partnership with Dance UK and Creative and Cultural Skills undertook a research project in 2008–2009, that explored issues and challenges around dance, pregnancy and parenthood. The project concluded that there is a lack of dance-specific advice and information for dance companies and organisations, with some best practice approaches highlighted, including:

- employers understanding the need for agreeing and committing to rehearsal and performance schedules in advance to enable childcare arrangements.
- provision of an understudy in case/if a child is ill.
- providing physiotherapy, Pilates, rehabilitation and fitness work as part of rehearsal/company working.
- enabling the potential to tour with children.

(Vincent Dance Theatre, 2009)

The 2009 report advocated that there should be better access to information about government policy and practical issues such as maternity pay and tax credits, and that there should be a supportive network of dancing parents developed.

Five years later, in 2014 Dance Mama was founded by Lucy McCrudden. This non-profit organisation started out as a website (www.dancemama.org) housing a collection of case studies of parents working in the dance industry. The site now has over 70 stories (including in podcast format), and the organisation provides a variety of supportive resources and is host to the Parenting and Dance Network UK and Northern Ireland and ARHC-funded International Parenting and Dance Network project. In 2015, Parents and Carers in Performing Arts (PiPA) was created by Anna Ehnold-Danailov and Cassie Raine and works in partnership with national performing arts organisations and academics (e.g. Pickard), to build an evidence base of challenges and barriers impacting on the workforce. PiPA promotes a flexible workforce inclusive of parents and carers. Many arts organisations have integrated PiPA's action research, resources and best practice charter into new workplace structures and approaches, reflecting an increasing appetite for representation and change.

Ways of sustaining a career in dance as a parent is an area that is gaining momentum in research and working practices in the UK. Although there is existing research and practice to support parents in dance in Canada, the USA and beyond, this chapter is focused predominantly on a UK context. The chapter is useful for all dancers, whether in training, working with one dance company long-term with an infrastructure of support, and/or dancers working professionally as freelance dance artists. It will offer some guidance and support for dancers who are thinking of becoming a parent or those that are parents, from post birth to raising children (with an emphasis on but not exclusive to, biological parents). In addition, this chapter will explore physiological (biomechanical) and psychological considerations, resources, support and strategies, for managing a dance career alongside parenting.

Key terms

It is important to note that several key terms are used during pregnancy and after giving birth, such as:

- 'Perinatal' meaning the time from the start of pregnancy up to roughly one year after giving birth ('peri' meaning 'around' and 'natal' meaning 'birth').
- 'Antenatal' or 'prenatal' meaning 'before birth'. This refers to the time in pregnancy.
- 'Postnatal' or 'postpartum' meaning 'after birth,' usually referring to the first year after giving birth.

The dancer-mother

The postpartum period is a significant time in a woman's life with physiological, psychological and social impacts. Every birth experience and recovery is highly individualised. The first three months after giving birth are often referred to as the contradictory '4th Trimester', as this relates to the next three-month phase of a baby's development and mother's recovery. During this period a baby is heavily dependent on their parent(s) and is acclimatising to the outside world. While research into the physiological and psychological changes in postnatal dancers specifically is emerging, it is important to understand that this can be a time when dancers are vulnerable because physiological and psychological changes are connected and embodied, and therefore a dancer's identity is often disrupted:

> A professional dancer's sense of self and their life as a dancer are inextricably intertwined through years of socialisation in training, often from a young age, and in the profession, so identity is deeply embedded within the dancers' body and embodied sense of self…[it] is not just what dancers do, it is who and what they become.
>
> *(Pickard and Ehnold-Danailov, 2022, p. 5)*

The evolution of identity to dancer-parent is a period of transition. Postnatal women in the UK are usually invited to an appointment with their midwife or health visitor six weeks after giving birth to check their physical and mental health, as well as that of their baby. However, according to 2021 National Institute for Health and Care Excellence (NICE) guidance (NICE, 2021), only 1 in 10 women are being checked. This may be because they are not invited for an appointment or are not engaging. It is important that the parent-dancer population proactively seek checks through programmes such as the Mummy MOT, with pelvic health specialists, as well as raising awareness of signs that additional mental health support at this time may be required.

Psychological impacts for postpartum dancers

It is not uncommon for new mothers to experience loneliness, anxiety and stress. For those who dance, the disruption of dancer identity, fear of the unknown and a new identity as a parent can be challenging (Pickard and Ehnold-Danailov, 2022). Professional dancers have increased vulnerability to perfectionism (Nordin-Bates et al., 2021) and disordered eating, with three times higher risk than non-dancers (Gorrell et al., 2021). Nutrition for parent and child is important during the postnatal phase. Nutritional choices can be influenced by a desire to lose weight gained to support pregnancy, hormonal changes, sleep deprivation, physical and mental recovery from birth, as well as the logistics of physically gaining/bringing food into the house. However, a balanced diet consisting of complex carbohydrates, fats, proteins, fruits and vegetables, vitamins and minerals as well as hydration, are essential to support physical and mental recovery, rest and longer-term health. While further research specifically with dancer-mothers is emerging in this area, it may be useful for parent dancers to seek individualised support from a registered dietitian or nutritionist during this period if they are able.

Cultural pressures to outwardly show happiness as a new mother/parent can also present a further challenge. Hormones oestrogen and progesterone also drop in this period and can result in low mood, or anxiety and/or depression. The National Institute for Health and Care Excellence (NICE, 2020) guidelines state that 12% of women experience depression and 13% experience anxiety at some point during pregnancy; and many women will experience both. Depression and anxiety also affect 15–20% of women in the first year after childbirth. Therefore, the parent-dancer may need particular attention, communication, conversation and care during this time as well as signposting to support groups/networks of other dancing parents for example.

Managing body changes post-partum

UK Sport's Pregnancy Guidance (2021) was produced shortly after the UK Chief Medical Officer Guidelines for pre and postnatal activity (2019). This is a resource developed by UK Sport for athletes and governing bodies. The guidance advises how to best support an athlete's pregnancy, providing recommendations for support during pregnancy, and for when an athlete returns to training and competition postnatal. Although written with a focus on sport, this is also a useful resource for dancers.

Generally, new mothers may experience some physical discomfort, pain, swelling, constipation, or incontinence and feeling that one's body may not feel immediately like their own (Pickard and Ehnold-Danailov, 2022). Dancer-mothers may also experience challenges with realignment of neutral posture through increases in lordosis (arched lumbar spine), and/or kyphosis (sometimes accompanied by forward head) that can be further exacerbated from feeding, carrying, extended periods of sitting, and tasks requiring asymmetrical positions such as strapping baby in a car seat, constructing prams, changing and bathing children (DiFore, 1998, cited in Quin et al., 2015). Some of these actions are often performed with one hand and can have musculoskeletal implications if performed repetitively. General postnatal physiological changes that will improve with a gradual return to activity are cardio-vascular fitness, abdominal strength and related mood improvement (UK Sport, n.d.). However, the condition diastasis recti (DRA) which Brockwell (2021, p. 194) defines as 'a separation of the abdominal muscles at the linea alba' (or central line) has implications for dancers, as often there is a functional expectation in dance to have a strong abdominal core. While most people heal this gap relatively quickly after birth, approximately 30% of females will continue to have this condition one year after giving birth (Cavalli et al., 2021) which presents a challenge for return to work in the dancing parent population.

In addition, the relationship between a strong core, pelvic floor function and stability, is essential for harmonious movement function, particularly in regard to the pelvic floor's connection to the obturator internus, a deep rotational muscle in the hip used in turnout (Hampson et al., 2020). Dancers do need to be aware of any signs and symptoms of pelvic floor dysfunction and seek immediate support if found (Brockwell, 2021). They also need to be aware of the differences in recovery procedures for any medically assisted births, such as C-sections and episiotomies. Both methods come with scars which need attention in their healing and can involve massaging scar tissue to aid recovery (see Brockwell, 2022).

Relaxin (a hormone that loosens joints during pregnancy) decreases after birth but remains at a low level for several months (Dehghan et al., 2014). Dancers need to be aware to not over-extend their range of movement while relaxin levels are higher to protect their joints. The complex fluctuation of oestrogen post birth, and during post-breast feeding (Keay, 2022) has an impact on a mother's physicality in terms of the ability to produce milk, range of movement, energy levels and journey towards positive body image. Some of the more negative impacts of these changes to mental and physical health can be mitigated against by staying active through the perinatal period as stated in the UK Chief Medical Officer (CMO) Guidelines for pre and post-natal activity (Department of Health and Social Care, 2019). This guidance (concluded from high-quality evidence that meets the CMO's stringent inclusion criteria and in-step with other countries' guidance on this issue, including Canada, Australia and America), advises a gradual return to moderate intensity activity in the postnatal period, if a mother has been moderately active before. This can aid dancers to advocate for and plan their return to physical work safely, as well as validating the choice of working practically because of the psychological and physiological benefits. While evidence-based advice in relation to return to more vigorous activity is being developed by researchers, it is possible for dancers to recover and rehabilitate postnatally with appropriate advice and support from health care practitioners such as a pelvic health physiotherapist, an osteopath (or other physical therapists) and/ or counsellors, in addition to patience and self-care.

Sleep deprivation is a common challenge for most new parents as they experience limited sleep with multiple interruptions for feeding, changing and reassuring their baby, which can continue into toddler phase and in the early years. It is an area that is under-researched in terms of the postnatal dance population but has gained some momentum in sport (Leger et al., 2005; Postolache et al., 2005). Sleep is key in maintaining healthy hormone function (Keay, 2022, p. 247), and for effective physical and mental recovery during the postpartum phase. Sleep deprivation affects brain function too that can impact on decision making, outlook and ability to recover and rest (Brockwell, 2022, p. 224). Having a support network of family or friends (also referred to as social networks or support) can reduce impacts of challenges of caring responsibilities. Limited social networks or support can make for a more arduous parental experience. Sustaining energy for basic levels of self-efficacy while caring without frequent support, can leave very little energy to invest towards maintaining a career. Therefore, support is of paramount importance in ensuring rest and time to recover, and crucially for dancers as artists, to have time and space to be creative.

Navigating maternity leave

As well as manging physical and psychological changes in the body, dancers, (especially freelancers) will need to be mindful of how they will manage socially and economically. Globally, parental rights are diverse with approaches such as shared parental leave still a relatively new concept in the UK. It is important that all dancer-parents know about government policy for the country they currently reside in and practical issues (e.g. maternity pay and tax credits). Being informed on the legal framework, knowing what statutory support there is and employment rights is empowering for the prospective parent in dance. It is useful for communicating and negotiating with employers in dance companies or organisations. For those working on a freelance basis and managing oneself, it offers an understanding of what support is and is not available and this can help to inform choices in managing issues such as maternity leave. Maternity leave is highly individualised and idiosyncratic needs are central to considerations and to navigating this complex period. Flexible planning for this moment creates better conditions to enable a successful re-entry to the workspace (if desired), with important time and space for family bonding and to adjust to the new parental role. However, due to the physical, economic and social demands on dancers, maternity leave for this population does not tend to follow a similar pattern to other more mainstream sectors.

Distinctive factors that impact maternity leave include the pressure to recover physically and return to dance for occupational/career progression reasons, to rekindle social networks that tend to be within dance and general employment or financial status. On a practical level, physical and psychological recovery needs time, childcare support and sometimes expertise to render effective recovery. Opportunity and access to physical postnatal recovery is dependent on a parent's employment status and working circumstances. Some long-term contracted company dancers may have an infrastructure of support where they may have a range of therapies and expertise to support them, as well as options around maternity leave periods and re-entry mechanisms.

Freelance professional dancer-parents tend to have to be self-reliant, building their own support package and learning which may include drawing on organisations like Dance Mama and PiPA. The parenthood journey may impact working arrangements and finances so costs for any physical or psychological activities/therapy(ies) may need to be carefully considered and planned. Online support and classes as well as low-cost gyms, yoga and Pilates can be more economic options.

Many dancers work in a freelance capacity and therefore have fewer maternity benefits than their counterparts in longer-term employed situations (Pregnant Then Screwed, 2023a) and this can be a precarious landscape to navigate. Financial and opportunistic pressures (such as auditions) are compounding factors. While freelancers have more control over their time to juggle competing priorities in comparison to longer-term employed dancers, they may not benefit from supportive employment structures and legal frameworks/policies. Maternity leave or paying someone to cover the freelancer's work (such as teaching classes) can be a financial burden that freelancers cannot often afford. This can influence decisions in relation to if/when to have children and when they return to work.

There are a few, limited options in regard to parental leave in the UK. Compared to Finland, Germany, Iceland and Norway for example (Global

Strategists, 2021), the UK has expensive, challenging and varying options, laws and policies. Standard paternity leave in the UK is just two weeks but in recent years, shared parental leave has become part of leave options for parents in the UK, and many companies have increased their paid paternal leave, but this differs from company to company. The minimal time a father can take leave in the UK demonstrates how the structure of the UK's parental leave framework can often result in mothers taking greater responsibility for childcare (Pregnant Then Screwed, 2023b). This can lead to isolating situations and restrictive career decision for dancing-mothers who wish to work.

At the time of writing, UK Statutory maternity leave (if you are in a long-term employed role) is 52 weeks and is split into two equal halves of 26 weeks (Department for Work and Pensions, 2023a). The first half is called 'Ordinary' the latter called 'Additional'. It is interesting that the British government advises that mothers 'must take 2 weeks' leave after your baby is born (or 4 weeks if you work in a factory)', which must account for the higher physical load a factory worker may experience but is not prescriptive about other careers with high physical load such as dance. Dancers have financial challenges in pursuing parenthood due to many having to rely on disproportionate state maternity support to cover high living and childcare costs. Some may have access to additional financial support through other streams, such as other areas of work, a partner's income (if they are not a single parent) or family, but not all have such access.

Statutory maternity pay is available for eligible employees and can be paid for up to 39 weeks. The first six weeks are 90% of average weekly earnings before tax, and the remaining 33 weeks is £172.48 or 90% of average weekly earnings, 'whichever is lower' (Department for Work and Pensions, 2023b). Maternity Allowance is available for self-employed, who are dependent on Class 2 National Insurance contributions and varies between £27 and £156.66 per week for up to 39 weeks (National Childbirth Trust, 2022). These figures are below the average spend of an adult in the UK at £585.60 per week according to the Office for National Statistics (ONS, 2022).

There are a variety of legal rights that are in place on returning to work, when employed on a contract, such as: up to ten 'keeping in touch days', known as 'KIT days' which do not disrupt pay or leave while on maternity leave, support to facilitate breastfeeding, childcare support and reasonable time off to support a dependant. The latter of which the employer is not legally obliged to pay (sometimes called 'unpaid childcare leave'). This all presents challenges for the dance sector as so many of the workforce are freelance and are either having to negotiate support or find ways to support themselves. With limited social networks, effective time-management becomes an important tool during this period. Many freelancers work in condensed pockets of time (for example when their child is asleep if their child sleeps for longer periods of time). Balancing work with rest and recovery should also be prioritised during the postpartum period as much as possible. Dancer-parents have often been socialised through years of training to push through bodily discomfort and tiredness, but this is not appropriate for the postpartum dancer as this can lead to fatigue, and consequently, can slow-down physical and mental recovery.

Childcare

Formal childcare enables some structure for dancer-parents to have child-free time to work. Childcare and education through nursery or pre-school settings is a common option in the UK but has to be financed by the parent until the child is aged three years old. When a child is three years old, families can access 15–30 hours free childcare with an approved childcare provider via the government. However, even with a three-year wait, this childcare is not always in synchronicity with dance work, which tends to be unstructured and during 'unsociable hours'. Childcare via nurseries or pre-schools is usually set at fixed times during the daytime and sometimes during school term times. Consequently, career decisions may be planned based on synchronising with nursery and pre-school scheduling. This point alone impacts career trajectories of parent dancers as their choices may be defined by this context. Childcare in the UK is also one of the most expensive in the world. Pregnant Then Screwed (2023c) released a report that found:

– 1 in 4 parents (26%) who use formal childcare, say that the cost is now more than 75% of their take-home pay.
– 1 in 3 (32%) parents who use formal childcare say they had to rely on some form of debt to cover childcare costs.

Without comparative research into parents in the dance sector, these figures can only be related to those in the general population who took part in the Pregnant Then Screwed research. Further, PiPA's (2021) report, that was undertaken during the Covid-19 pandemic found that 72% of parents with careers in music, theatre and dance were considering leaving the profession due to financial pressures.

Working arrangements that can support dancer parents

Some dance companies and choreographers have begun to action supportive working practices for dancer-parents in the UK such as flexible working, job shares, shorter working days and co-scheduling rehearsals. Continuous dialogue between employee and employer (whether self-employed or longer-term contractually employed) is imperative throughout the career of a professional dancer, and especially in navigating the landscape of issues such as maternity rights, pregnancy and return to work. This can be challenging for dancers where an institutionalised hierarchy is often endemic. This can render the dancer-parent to feel powerless in speaking up for themselves and can be further amplified by dancer-parents fearing consequences of expressing their parental needs as resulting in less work/roles.

Nevertheless, there are examples of companies and choreographers in the UK supporting flexible working, advance scheduling and shorter working days. Such approaches give more opportunities to balance a dance career with parenting. Self-management (and that of organising childcare) can sometimes be stressful and administratively taxing if information is not provided well enough in advance. Some companies have been able to work more inclusively to enable a higher percentage of parents to continue their work such as Vincent Dance Theatre, who set an example that is beneficial for other companies to follow through their family-friendly policy (Vincent Dance Theatre, 2009). This includes flexible working, shorter working days and arrangements for children on tour for example. This is deepened by the subsequent work of PiPA who have established best practice charters for organisations across dance, music and theatre and continue to research in these areas.

Legal firm, Gorvins Associates, worked closely with Pregnant Then Screwed and outlined flexible working rights as 'Almost all employees with at least 26 weeks' service have the right to ask for flexible working' (Gorvins, 2023). While this is something that may be achievable for non-performance roles, this can be a challenge for dancers in companies that traditionally have heavy performance schedules, traditionally starting in theatres from 7.30pm (call at 6.00pm). Approaches to recognise and provide flexibility to dancing parents include job shares/sharing roles where a pool of dancers within a company is larger so there is potential to support this way of working (as has been instigated at Matthew Bourne's New Adventures and The Royal Ballet). The London West End production of *42nd Street* did this very successfully with Charlene Ford in 2017 through her appearing in three out of eight shows per week with her counterpart, Jenny Legg, performing the other five (Malvern, 2018). The Royal Ballet has also supported many dancer-parents thanks to their established infrastructure.

In addition, Pregnant Then Screwed (2023d) outline that legally in the workplace, 'Employers are obliged to provide you with somewhere to rest, including to lie down if you need to.' While this is not a legal requirement it is considered best practice, as is providing a hygienic, private area for those breastfeeding so that milk can be expressed if desired, as well as stored (e.g. providing a fridge). However, an employer does not have to allow additional breaks to facilitate this, but a legal challenge could be made by the working parent if the company are unable to prove that 'allowing a break for this reason would have an unacceptable impact on their business' (Pregnant Then Screwed, 2023d). Without specific research in the dance sector on this issue, it is important to encourage this topic within discussions as part of return-to-work plans with employers as early as possible. This will enable the best possible chance for needs to be facilitated to the best of an organisation's ability.

Community and support

Dancing parents can feel excluded at the notion of going to a dance class or workshop pregnant, postnatal, with or without their baby, as this is not yet normalised in most dance communities in the UK. Greater visibility of role models is needed as well as a supportive community of parents who also work in dance. For example, Dance Mama provides in-person and online professional development sessions with national dance organisations and experts from other sectors such as sport and health. These webinars, workshops and classes are specifically for parents across the perinatal period with adaptations to the physical changes discussed here, integral in their design. A participant stated;

> If it were not for Dance Mama Live, I would not be dancing right now. I feel I have started to rediscover who I am and who I have become now I am a mum.
>
> (Shelley Watson, Participant—Dance Mama, 2022)

FIGURE 13.1 Shelley (third from the right) at Dance Mama Live: Back on the road, at One Dance UK, Birmingham. Copyright Dance Mama, One Dance UK and Anthony Shintai 2023

In addition, Parents and Carers in Performing Arts (PiPA), collaborate with parents, carers, companies, performing arts and national sector organisations and universities to research, advocate and support inclusive working practices through their best practice charter programme. The charter programme is a tried and tested framework which provides organisations with tools, resources and policies to support the implementation of family-friendly working practices.

Although this chapter has outlined challenges associated with sustaining a dance career as a parent, it is worthwhile noting that becoming a parent can be a joy and the responsibility is life changing. It brings a new identity from dancer to dancer-mother-parent. It is possible to navigate and balance maternity leave, financial implications and safe return to work in dance. The dancer-parent is gaining interest as an evolving research area and there are an increasing number of dance companies, organisations and choreographers investing in family-friendly, inclusive working practices. Therefore, support for dancing parents to return to work safely and maintain a career is growing in the UK.

It may be useful for dancers to consider parenting as a broad and deep improvisation exercise rather than a 'set barre'. Dancers tend to have an understanding of self-management, discipline and preparedness through dance training, often from a young age. Such skills can be applied to returning to work after having a baby and can support dancers through the rigours of balancing parenting and a dance career. Importantly, awareness and care of postpartum recovery of the dancer-parent-self is crucial, in order to actively support both family and a creative life.

Key points

- Each postnatal journey is highly individual and should be respected and treated as such in terms of approach, decision making and support.
- Being aware holistically of physical and psychological postnatal changes, the benefits of being active, and planning a gradual return to activity with support from professionals along the way (if available and affordable) enables dancers who are parents the best long-term trajectory to balance family and career.
- Researching maternity rights and entitlement informs conversations with employers regarding leave and finances, as well as return to work.
- Self-employed workers need to consider multiple plans and what the financial implications might be when returning to work.
- Dancers may wish to consider investing in a health insurance policy, if possible.
- Support from a network of other parents in dance is highly valuable to help parents navigate this parenthood and dance.

- Health, wellbeing and safe practice for the dancer-parent is vital to support themselves, their family and their career.
- There are resources and support for dancers who are parents and organisations to implement family-friendly working practices.

References

Baum, C. (2002). A dynamic analysis of the effect of childcare costs on the work decisions of low-income mothers with infants. *Demography, 39*, 139–164. http://dx.doi.org/10.1353/dem.2002.0002

Brockwell, E. (2021). *Why did no one tell me?: How to protect heal and nurture your body through motherhood*. Random House.

Cavalli, M., Aiolfi, A. & Bruni, P. G. et al. (2021). Prevalence and risk factors for diastasis recti abdominis: A review and proposal of a new anatomical variation. *Hernia, 25*, 883–890. http://dx.doi.org/10.1007/s10029-021-02468-8

Dance Mama (2022) *Dance Mama Live 2021/2022 impact report*. Retrieved January 14, 2024 from https://www.dancemama.org/_files/ugd/303503_cb2f4565b6e94f-70957926c7f9bae34b.pdf

Dehghan, F., Haerian, B. S., Muniandy, S., Yusof, A., Dragoo, J. L. & Salleh, N. (2014). The effect of relaxin on the musculoskeletal system. *Scandinavian Journal of Medicine & Science in Sports, 24*(4), 220–229. http://dx.doi.org/10.1111/sms.12149

Department of Health and Social Care (2019). Physical activity guidelines: Pregnancy and after childbirth. Retrieved June 1, 2023 from https://www.gov.uk/government/publications/physical-activity-guidelines-pregnancy-and-after-childbirth/physical-activity-for-pregnant-women-text-of-the-infographic

Department of Work and Pensions (2023a). *Maternity pay and leave*. Retrieved January 24, 2024. https://www.gov.uk/maternity-pay-leave/leave

Department of Work and Pensions (2023b). *Statuatory maternity pay and leave: Pay*. Retrieved January 24, 2024 from https://www.gov.uk/maternity-pay-leave/pay

Duffy, A. (2018). A delicate balance: How postsecondary education dance faculty in the United States perceive themselves negotiating responsibilities expected for tenure. *Research in Dance Education, 20*(1), 73–84. http://dx.doi.org/10.1080/14647893.2018.1523382

Global Strategists (2021). *Four countries with the best parental leave laws*. Retrieved June 1, 2023 from https://www.globalpeoplestrategist.com/4-countries-with-the-best-parental-leave-laws/

Gorrell, S., Schaumberg, K., Boswell, J. F., Hormes, J. M. & Anderson, D. A. (2021). Female athlete body project intervention with professional dancers: A pilot trial. *Eating Disorders, 29*(1), 56–73. http://dx.doi.org/10.1080/10640266.2019.1632592

Gorvins Solicitors (2023). Flexible working rights, regulation and law. Retrieved June 1, 2023 from https://www.gorvins.com/services-for-business/employment-law-advice-for-employers/flexible-working/

Hampson, D., Winder, B. & Dolquist, N. (2020). *One dance UK: The pelvic floor in dancers,* Retrieved January 24, 2024 from https://www.onedanceuk.org/resource/pelvic-floor-dancers/

Keay, N. (2022). *Hormones, health and human potential*. Sequoia Books.

Leger, D., Metlaine, A. & Choudat, D. (2005). Insomnia and sleep disruption: Relevance for athletic performance. *Clinics in Sports Medicine, 24*(2), 269–285. http://dx.doi.org/10.1016/j.csm.2004.12.011

Malvern, J (2018). Mother stars in first West End job share. The Times and Sunday Times Newspapers. Retrieved January 14, 2024 from https://www.thetimes.co.uk/article/mother-stars-in-first-westend-job-share-q85mzsg5z

Musil, P., Schupp, K. & Risner, D. (2022). Parenting while dancing while parenting. In P. Musil, D. Risner & K. Schupp (Eds.), *Dancing across the lifespan* (pp. 129–147). Palgrave Macmillan.

National Childbirth Trust (2022). *Maternity pay explained.* Retrieved June 1, 2023 from https://www.nct.org.uk/pregnancy/pregnancy-work/maternity-pay-explained

National Institute for Health and Care Excellence (2014). Antenatal and postnatal mental health: Clinical management and service guidance, NICE Clinical guidelines. Retrieved January 14, 2024 from www.nice.org.uk/guidance/cg192/chapter/introduction

National Institute for Health and Care Excellence (2021). *Postnatal care.* NICE.

National Institute for Health and Care Excellence, Royal College of Obstetricians and Gynaecologists.(2020). *Antenatal and postnatal mental health: Clinical management and service guidance.* NICE.

Nordin-Bates, S. M., & Kuylser. S. (2021). High striving, high costs? A qualitative examination of perfectionism in high-level dance, *Journal of Dance Education, 21*(4), 212–223. http://dx.doi.org/10.1080/15290824.2019.1709194

Office of National Statistics (2022). *Family spending in the UK: April 2022 to March 2022.* Retrieved July 1, 2023 from https://www.ons.gov.uk/peoplepopulationandcommunity/personalandhouseholdfinances/expenditure/bulletins/familyspendingintheuk/april2021tomarch2022#toc

Parents and Carers in Performing Arts (PiPA). (2021). *PiPA COVID report.* Parents and Carers in Performing Arts. https://pipacampaign.org/research/covidreport

Pickard, A., & Ehnold-Danailov, A. (2022). Professional contemporary dancers becoming mothers: Navigating disrupted habitus and identity loss/evolution in a UK context, *Research in Dance Education, 24*(1), 5–19. http://dx.doi.org/10.1080/14647893.2023.2167973

Postolache, T. T., Hung, T. M., Rosenthal, R. H., Soriano, J. J., Montes, F. & Stiller, J. W. (2005). Sports chronobiology consultation: From the lab to the arena. *Clinical Sports Medicine, 24,* 415–456. http://dx.doi.org/10.1016/j.csm.2005.01.001

Pregnant Then Screwed (2023a). *Pregnancy rights when you're self-employed,* UK. Retrieved January 14, 2024 from https://pregnantthenscrewed.com/pregnancy-rights-when-youre-self-employed/

Pregnant Then Screwed (2023b). *Boosting paternity leave has economic eenefits,* UK. Retrieved January 14, 2024 from https://pregnantthenscrewed.com/boosting-paternity-leave-has-economic-benefits/

Pregnant Then Screwed (2023c). *Three quarters of mothers who pay for childcare say that it does not make financial sense for them to work,* UK. Retrieved January 14, 2024 from https://pregnantthenscrewed.com/three-quarters-of-mothers-who-pay-for-childcare-say-that-it-does-not-make-financial-sense-for-them-to-work/

Pregnant Then Screwed (2023d). *Your rights for returning to work,* UK. Retrieved January 14, 2024 from https://pregnantthenscrewed.com/your-rights-for-returning-to-work/

Quin, E., Rafferty, S. & Tomlinson, C. (2015). Adaptations for specific populations In E. Quin, S. Rafferty & C.Tomlinson (Eds.), *Safe dance practice*. Human Kinetics, 197–234.

Sanders, S. (2008). Dancing through pregnancy: Activity guidelines for professional and recreational dancers. *Journal of Dance Medicine and Science, 12*(1), 17–22. http://dx.doi.org/10.1177/1089313x0801200103

UK Sport (2021). *Pregnancy guidance and support for UK funded athletes*. Retrieved June 1, 2023 from https://www.uksport.gov.uk/resources/pregnancy-guidance,

Vincent Dance Theatre. (2009). *Pregnancy and parenthood: The dancer's perspective*. Vincent Dance Theatre, Dance UK, and Creative and Cultural Skills. Retrieved January 14, 2024 from https://www.vincentdt.com/wpcontent/uploads/2008/12/PregnancyReport.pdf

14

DANCER (NOUN)—MOTHER, DAUGHTER, SISTER, COLLEAGUE, PARTNER, WARRIOR, SORCERESS, FRIEND

Erica Stanton

The tone of the writing is nostalgic and to anchor these reflections as temporal phenomena, I use T. S. Eliot's *Four Quartets* as a framing text which holds the writing in time. Quotations from the poems are present to create a sense of circularity and to attempt to emulate Eliot's desire for his work to transcend personal experience.[1] Dylan Thomas's *Under Milk Wood* is also present for a similar purpose—as a Welsh woman I have DNA which resonates with music and with melancholy (hiraeth) which contribute to the nostalgia of the text. As the writing is essentially retrospective, its basis is a body of work in teaching dance which sits both inside and outside my body and is known, or more accurately now, has been known, mostly through dancing—doing dancing. As the writing looks back and relies on recall and somatic memory, it should be approached with caution as it has both the benefit of hindsight and the slipperiness of memory. After many years of planning classes, working out curricula and dancing with students and colleagues, I am trying to reflect on what happens between dancers during a (my) dance class, what lies dormant waiting to be un/dis/covered during the practice of becoming yourself dancing. What are the particularities and peculiarities of doing this together and alongside others who are similarly engrossed.

Time present and time past
Are both perhaps present in time future,
And time future contained in time past.

T. S. Eliot—'Burnt Norton'

When a noun is identified in a dictionary, the most common usage is put first. The most commonly spoken abstract noun in conversational English

DOI: 10.4324/9781003382874-19

is 'time'. It is also the second most common noun of any type, behind only 'people' (Love, 2020). This reflection on dance experience sits firmly in this commonality of time; time which was spent in the company of women dancing. There is a deliberate omission from the roles that I list in the title, and that is 'teacher'. Teaching is a central part of the working/dancing lives of women; the teaching workforce across the UK is consistently predominantly female—74% in 2021/22 (Gov.UK, 2022). In this writing I am not complaining about the lack of visibility of women in a fit of feminist pique, but rather proposing a helpful *invisibility* in the role of the female teacher. What are the qualities that reside in the female dancer that enable the stealthy strategies, embodied gaze and ghostly presence of this somatic whisperer, deep listener? (Oliveros, 2005). Who is this someone who can help you navigate the in-between of the visibility of dance skill acquisition and the gloriously autonomous inner dancer who affirms the certainty of you dancing you.

The interplay between the exterior world of being a dancer with all the itinerant hopes, aspirations, doubts and frustrations that go with that, and the inner joy of purposeful or purposeless dancing is complex and delicate. One ill-placed word, a badly chosen movement or a careless oversight can so quickly sour the alchemy of a nourishing class or break the thread of the intangible learner's concentration or commitment. In this opaque territory of another's dancing process where curiosity, play and discovery seem to be key elements, how does the time and place for wondering and wandering allow us to shed the limitations of a discipline and to see what we can find out through dancing? Practitioners are 'wanderers, wayfarers, whose skill lies in their ability to find the grain of the world's becoming and to follow its course while bending it to their evolving purpose'. (Ingold, 2011, p. 211). In a material world which values production, how might we give dancing its time and place where the emphasis is on discovery rather than acquisition? This presents a necessity to slow down so that the emergent experience of the present moment can be fully investigated. That is not straightforward, it 'involves a difficult, awkward, ambiguous encounter between two differently shaped bodies that are themselves ambiguous—and this meeting, this sensing requires and takes place in time' (Odell, 2019, p. 24).

There they were, dignified, invisible,
Moving without pressure, over the dead leaves,
In the autumn heat, through the vibrant air.

                                        T. S. Eliot—'Burnt Norton'

If I observe the roots of my desire to dance and preferably to be dancing with others, I can pinpoint the solitude of being an only child. I was unruly, running outside without shoes, climbing trees, falling in streams, forever grubby with grazed knees. A tomboy. Why walk when you can run? Who says a boy can run faster, climb higher, throw a ball further than I can? I was a strong, muscular, fidgety, restless girl and in 'those days', this was not quite seemly. I did not 'play like a girl'. My parents channelled this energy into physical education (where they were experts) and whilst I loved to win at sport, I was clear that my interest was captured not by moving with the purpose of getting there first, or making sure that opponents did not get there first, but in paying attention to the movement itself in the place that it was happening. It was captivating. Swimming and feeling the rippling flow of water on skin as I negotiated the power in my limbs and relished the familiar rhythms of swimming strokes, playing team sports where there was the exhilaration of elevation as well as the objective of being higher than an opponent to trap a ball, and the pleasure of the pendular swing of a tennis racket with its satisfying sound of a ball well struck. All of these held more compelling reasons to be moving than learning the codes and strategies for winning. The production of a faster, stronger me bound by the codes and rules of sport was not appealing, but once I was free of the burdens to be goal driven in sport-based movement, there was time to explore this complex world of dancing—moving without pressure. This connection to another world is so compelling that I still want to discover more about it 50 years later and to be able to share this mystery through the teaching of dance.

Mostly through doing, no particular day

> *Only you can hear and see, behind the eyes of the sleepers, the movements and countries and mazes and colours and dismays and rainbows and tunes and wishes and flight and fall and despairs and big seas of their dreams.*
> Dylan Thomas—Under Milk Wood

We are working through the materials of class. There are questions; there are frustrations; there is laughter. *We* are doing this. Making decisions, making bad decisions, going with something just because ... you are finding dreams, confirming/disrupting beliefs, pushing at boundaries. I am listening. Wondering where/if you need a hand, a word of encouragement, a provocation? Watching your dreams unfold and searching for the words that will bring them to life in a kind of creative midwifery. Working with metaphors, we are all casting about to find words which will fit what is happening.

> The ability to think metaphorically is not the outcome of a single occasion; it requires repeated opportunities to explore the poetic use of language, a use of language that generates meaning through indirection, allusion, and innuendo.
> *(Eisner, 2002, p. 12)*

Five years ago, a group of students attributed the moniker 'dancing mother' to me. It was a funny and playful moment but one which made me pause for thought. What did this mean? This metaphor they had conjured up in description of our encounters raised questions about the role of mother as a pedagogic approach. I looked back at my own dancing mothers. What was it that connected me to these dancers who had provided me with the right knowledge at the right time? I reflected on the concept of maternal pedagogy and was deeply moved by Adwoa Ntozake Onuora's writing on storytelling, mothering and teaching.

> my political project is to reclaim and use our stories to transform ideas about what is considered valid knowledge. Telling multiple stories about African women who use mothering as a site of empowerment, resistance, reclamation, teaching and survival.
>
> *(Onuora, 2015, p.xxii)*

Somehow the stakes were higher as I reflected on the care, nourishment and responsibility of this 'motherhood'. Have I been performing a gender norm in my teaching practice? Where was the template for this role? I was reluctant to theorise 'maternity' as a teacher and lecturer; I understood that this was a necessity, but the gate had opened to waves of possibilities, problems and responsibilities. I am a mum, so I have experience. Was this enough? This was an opportunity to transform and to find greater authenticity in my teaching, so stories of motherhood occupied my 'dreaming' of class. These were further complicated by the arrival of the pandemic and with it, 'pandemic pedagogy'. What would a place of care and nourishment look like online, how would we connect? Would our pursuit of creativity enable us to find empathy in spite of our physical separation (Tempest, 2020).

And so each venture
Is a new beginning, a raid on the inarticulate
With shabby equipment always deteriorating
In the general mess of imprecision of feeling,
Undisciplined squads of emotion.

T. S. Eliot—'East Coker'

As I look back at the time, effort, energy and striving in making and inhabiting dance experiences in the warp and weft of the material world of dance, I am aware that the fabric of this work is currently extremely fragile. Post-pandemic pessimism, global unrest, the continuing arts funding crisis and the closures and reductions of dance departments in the HE sector in the UK make us want to connect and to draw our allies close to us. Ecofeminist Vandana Shiva observed that the coronavirus pandemic and lockdown in particular, revealed even more clearly how we are being reduced to objects to be controlled. Our bodies and minds as new colonies ripe for invasion (Shiva 2020). In the challenge of dancing during the pandemic, we improvised frantically to find the necessary toolkits for resistance and resilience in our dancing. It was even more important to relish in the power and capacities of our own moving bodies and to see how these transfer to our health and to the physical and mental challenges of daily life. My colleague Andrew Sanger repeatedly reminded his students that 'outside was not cancelled' and he inspired us all to embrace the possibilities of outside. Andrew's own writing reminded me that, 'artistic and somatic practices may offer avenues for altering our perception of a disconnected modern world, generating a sense of kinship and belonging through eco-somatic enchantment' (Sanger, 2022, p. 265). I sense here a spiritual pedagogy at work which brings nuance to the processes between thought and action, and self and community.

In the hiatus of the pandemic, the survival pedagogy of teaching online required the skills of motherhood, magic, enchantment and gossip. Gossip is largely attributed as a female phenomenon, but this was a decision made by a predominantly female team of teachers to position gossip as a survival tool. We made the plan to gather regularly as small groups of students and teachers and to gossip.[2] They were gatherings for decompression and were one of our attempts to develop collective resistance to the dis-ease of lockdown.

Here is a place of disaffection
Time before and time after
In a dim light:

T. S. Eliot—'Burnt Norton'

As I look back at my 'landscape of doing', it stretches wide and its edges are hazy; do I really remember that lightbulb moment, those words that seemed important, that dancing that seemed to spontaneously combust into surging empowering joyful passages of moving? Moving with no purpose other than movement itself, dancing with others who are also caught in the flow, moments where stillness and exhilaration sit side-by-side before, during and after urgent urges to dance—the pursuit of dancing as if nobody's watching and everyone's watching at the same time. Can I avoid self-indulgence in the nostalgia of reimagining this 'time before'?

I am a teacher of Limón technique and there are particular limitations and possibilities as to what this means. I have a relationship with the past and teach the technique as an historically informed practice, teaching from memory, recalling movements from the past, communicating inspirational content from dead people, and I am beleaguered by all the problems of silent narratives that reside there. Whose voices are stored in my memory, why these and not others? The complex forces that contribute to the reiterative materials of teaching as a continually evolving 'intra-active entanglement' (Barad in Juelskjaer & Schwennesen 2012) sometimes render me inert, but I need to get myself out of the way—this work is not about me. My pedagogic practice is also a feat of memory. I was trained not to teach with notes. This is not to say that class notes don't exist. They just don't accompany me into the studio. The plan for class was prepared and retained bodily. In my early days of teaching this was very stressful, but this preparation allows the flow of class and the engagement of participants to have my full attention; no props and no notes creates an interesting state of 'nakedness'. The class has my full attention and I am alert to possibilities as the 'plan' is porous and mutable. I am ready (eager) to veer off into side roads according to the interests and curiosity of the class. The daily practice of working positively with uncertainty involves surrendering to it, 'that thing the nature of which is totally unknown to you is usually what you need to find, and finding it is a matter of getting lost' (Solnit, 2005, p. 6), and being receptive to capture the cunning of uncertainty. 'The arrow of time continues to advance the tenuous balance between the punctuated, incomplete and biased knowledge of the past and the uncertainty of what the future may bring' (Nowotny, 2016, p. vi).

Latency and opposition

Opposition is a playful phenomenon in the Limón technique—'this' but also 'that'. Going somewhere *and* staying anchored. The real-time decision-making or instant problem solving of deciding to commit to 'this' or 'that', or find the middle ground, is absorbing and is compelling to watch. Do I fall or stay still? Do I stand firm or yield? Do I hover in an attempt to suspend time and motion? It is not hard to see how these movement transactions are metaphors for life and how the physical experience of opposition is not straightforward. Dance and life are both complicated.

Dancing is a way of being in the world: being in the world is a way of dancing. The dancing mother teaches from the perspective of her lived experience, from her female body. Her embodied gaze is informed by years of conscious and unconscious bias and the practice and preferences both hidden and visible in 'this' body pay attention to what is and isn't there in 'those' bodies. Who is included and why? Why are these choices pursued today? How might we know each other better? 'The closer attention I pay to my 'particular', the better chance I have of reaching you in yours' (Tempest, 2020, p. 7).

Who are you? I can learn your names and become aware of your somatic disposition. We can work in this 'dance technique' where female exponents have drawn Feldenkrais, Body Mind Centering®, experiential anatomy and yoga into their versions of it. We can engage in lab tasks for postural and movement patterning and decentralise the role of the teacher, but alongside this development of our perceptual, kinaesthetic and proprioceptive awareness in doing dancing, we are also engaged in the important matters of practising hope, practising presence (Gutierrez, n.d.) and practising empathy (Tempest, 2020).

Dancing and corresponding

In dancing—where this takes place in a context where we are finding something out, transferring skills or generating knowledge—I may not fully articulate the inner somatic world that informs my capacity to perform this dancing, or the purpose of this danced idea, to communicate *this* exactly. In this inexact kinaesthetic correspondence, it does not necessarily follow that, 'these acts of communication fail to be intentional, nor does it demonstrate that understanding these mechanisms is irrelevant to explaining this form of communication' (Carrol & Seeley, 2013, p. 182). In engaging with the process of correspondence (kinaesthetic empathy), a meaningful trialogue occurs under the auspices of a 'knowledge creation metaphor' (Paavola & Hakkarainen, 2005, p. 538) where common areas of interest arise out of collaborative activities. They can arrive uncertainly, cunningly, without planning and without an impulse towards a goal. Engaging with trialogue when we are dancing while emphasising the sensations of movement necessitates paying attention and requires us to have time to ruminate (Claxton, 2000, p. 40).

There are many valuable techniques which work through tasks to tune the body and to create a space where my dancing attention becomes your watching attention. But I am trying to land on something specific about the female qualities of dancing and watching. For example, when a mother watches her toddler take their first unsteady steps and reaches out with hands that stabilise and encourage, does she allow an interest to be followed to the brink of falling over or failing? What do you need? How may I help? I realise I am comfortable with the ambiguous notion of 'female intuition' and waiting to see the 'right fit' but as Guy Claxton observes, 'Have the more gentle, slow, ruminative or solitary forms of reflective intuition been neglected by an education establishment that is in thrall to the explicit?' (Claxton, 2000, p. 40).

There is only the fight to recover what has been lost
And found and lost again and again: and now, under conditions
That seem unpropitious. But perhaps neither gain nor loss.
For us, there is only the trying. The rest is not our business.
T. S. Eliot—'East Coker'

As I write this, it is Mental Health Awareness week in the UK and I am fresh from a Yin yoga class. I find the stillness of this practice difficult, but my teacher is a magician. She describes processes as they happen. How does she know *when* to say *what* she says? Connection, breath, resistance, tension, recovery ... her words appear at just the right moment, and I can make an informed choice—stay, go on, or go back. Dance is not a language, but words matter in its coming to life. The use of language is helpful in stirring images into being for coaxing the dancing body into unfamiliar textures and into what Sonia Rafferty calls 'dusty corners and empty sectors' (Hiscoke, 2018) and regardless of the words which we use to describe the movements and sequences of a particular code, style, genre, form of dance, the idiosyncratic dancer reveals herself through her sensation of discovery; she follows impulses to move as they arise without being encumbered about what to call it other than dancing.

Dance may function as a communicative medium, but the expectation that it operates as a language, that we can translate dance into language in order to convey ideas is a superficial one. It is a matter of convenience since words dominate our everyday existence, but they also get in the way. In striving to find the words that will fit our experiences of dancing we miss the point. By paying attention to the '"what it is like" of experience' (Pakes, 2011, p. 42), our dancing becomes a deeper and more satisfying endeavour and allows us to understand ourselves and our spaces in more intuitive and imaginative ways. What is it like for the female dancer to define her own dancing? It is more important than ever to create opportunities in the dance studio for her to choose this for herself; free of cultural expectations and constraints and outside the currently fractious discourse of gender identity.

Conjuring, magic and the ghosts of the past

On the edge of a grimpen, where there is no secure foothold,
And menaced by monsters, fancy lights,
Risking enchantment

T. S. Eliot—'East Coker'

I watch from the side-lines of our field, and I see that dance artists are very comfortable with disrupting models of teaching and banishing the 'sacred cows' of pedagogies which have belonged to our discipline. They are not afraid to pronounce that 'learning outcomes are corrosive' (Furedi, 2013, p. 1) and to rid themselves of models of content, delivery and assessment which are constrained by the limits of their own knowledge or comply to institutional norms. Who would want a compliant life? One which is lived meeting the expectations of others, 'an endless procession of duties to serve'. In dancing we have the opportunity not to fear the limits of our capacities, but to spend our time in a more fulfilling way consulting the 'spirit of the depths' (Tempest, 2020, p. 112).

Research interests in spirituality, witchcraft and enchantment find their way into dance practice and dance pedagogy and they work their magic.

Charlie Ashwell proposes witchcraft as a place where multiple truths can coexist and performs a lecture 'Becoming Witch' which proposes a radical rethinking of how dance is made and who is making it. Out of the ashes of a burnt-out public discourse around female choreographers, 'Becoming Witch riffs off the question "Where are the women?", unearthing the nomadic, coven-like ways that dance artists produce, create and survive together' (Ashwell, 2023). These possibilities give an insight into a genuinely pluralist dance culture where dance content is taught in a way that engages with issues that are integral to idiosyncratic viewpoints and which pre-suppose the divergent interest of our students.

I observe a connection to aspects of my own training and the focus in Nikolais classes to develop individuality *and* to decentralise *and* embody a totality of mind, body and spirit. (If I could, I would insert the head on fire emoji or the crying emoji here as I still haven't reconciled these ideas.) I attempt to remember these embodied struggles and I reach for my choreography notebook from the 1980s. I was fortunate to have a choreography class with the iconoclastic Phyllis Lamhut who would regularly exhort us to 'write this down'.

> *God's gift to humanity is mediocrity.*
>   *Am I going to indulge myself or am I going to dig deeply?*
>   *What does identity mean?*
>   *a) myself?*
>   *b) the dance?*
>   *c) combination of a) and b)?*
>   *d) new entity to deal with?*
>   *Think creatively—be a filter of life. Don't separate the mind from the body. Develop individuality. Do not succumb to peer pressure.*
>
>   *(7.09.84)*

As dancing leaves so little that is tangible, I am reassured that the notebook has survived the long journey and I remember that Phyllis gave an interview to *Dance Magazine* in 1975 describing herself as a witch. It was revisited in a 'TBT' article for the magazine,

> That's why I'm a witch. I like magic, levitation, illusion—above all, illusion. I'd like to evaporate during a dance. I'd like to do big, wild, wacky, crazy numbers. But I also feel like doing tiny dances to Mozart.
>
>   *(Escoyne, 2022)*

The learning I received from these classes was transformative and the choreographic tasks I pursued did feel like spells at times. I look at phrases learnt from Phyllis such as, 'learn to be a little more at home in your body' and 'your surface must be shaken; this is unfamiliar and uncomfortable' knowing that she herself has located these ideas from her past connections with Hanya Holm. I realise that I too have kept hold of this information, felt it, questioned it and passed it on in my teaching.

The dancers are all gone under the hill.

                                        T. S. Eliot—'East Coker'

'Because I am dreaming of you now as I plan it, so it's already begun'

(Gutierrez, n.d.)

The dreaming before a class seems to combine expectancy and desire. I wonder where we will go. Who will show up today? How are they feeling? Is she still injured? Will she find that quicksilver quality that transformed her yesterday? What about the before of your class? The commuting, taking children to school, visiting of a frail relative, putting in an early shift—all the care and all the things that need to be taken care of before you can give this gift of time to yourself to take your class. Now—and only *now*—there is this precious and important opportunity to 'dream myself anew' (Barbour, 2011, p. 69) and not only 'myself' but 'ourselves' as we practise empathy. Who and what do we want to become today? How can we manifest things differently, collectively?

There you are, quietly following your interest. You make a phrase that seems to last forever, capturing your momentum between standing and falling. Like mercury, you are seemingly neither solid nor liquid. I am transfixed, concentrating on how you are moving. Travelling with your movement journey as you weave threads of motional complexity into something whole, something in which you are totally immersed. You are in your moment.

I'm aware that other dancers in the class are watching you; we catch each other's eyes and smile. Your eyes are occupied, following hands arcing in space, seeing space around your movement, occasionally drawing your interest softly into your body—never stuck, not 'projecting', staying with the possibilities of your dancing. And suddenly, you are aware that you are being watched. You pause and look up as if waking from a dream. You smile at us. 'What?' your gesture seems to say. One of your friends has tears in their eyes. Another comes to hug you. 'What?' You are not conscious of the gift of your dancing to us; its resonant metakinetic potency. I know that your prior training has encouraged humility as a deep-seated value, but today your guileless exposition of you dancing you is transcendent. Can you do it again? Of course, you can.

There you are, a smile of mischief passes your lips, a little lift of your centre and you're off, racing through the space, tumbling, flailing, breathlessly trying to keep up with yourself. Your appetite for motion is huge, your deployment of your physicality is rampant. I enjoy that I'm a bit scared of you. You're a catalyst and you lift the energy in the room, suddenly everyone is galvanised into motion. The air in the studio ebbs and flows; there is laughter and sweating and a lot of falling over. Giddiness and play at work in this strange mysterious experiment of dancing together.

Time passes. Listen. Time passes.
Come closer now.

Dylan Thomas—'Under Milk Wood'

I am still dreaming a long time afterwards as I look back and reflect on the gobbledygook of once-upon-a-time imagery that changed a moment, shifted the quality, made us attend, or enriched the texture of you dancing you, or just distracted you and made you laugh. Something that surfaced at that time but has stayed with you. Or so you tell me.

Spock ears.
Teletubby antennae.
Kite wings.
Dinosaur, dragon, lizard and lemur tails.
Feet in warm sand.
Monty Python hands.
Rolls Royce shock absorbers.
Juicy hips.
Puppies off the lead.
Shape no shape.
Surfing on the floor.
Seeing the horizon without an opinion.

That was a way of putting it—not very satisfactory:
A periphrastic study in a worn-out poetical fashion,
Leaving one still with the intolerable wrestle
With words and meanings.

T. S. Eliot—'East Coker'

Where are you now? Feeling the exhilaration in your dancing and finding catharsis? Or deploying these sensations in your own way? I see you dancer/warrior women ultra-running, rock climbing and wild water swimming. Moving for yourselves, making choices and finding ways to move together with others. Being alive. Yet some warriors don't make it. The battle was too hard for you despite our best efforts. I am indebted to my friend, and independent dance artist Elaine Thomas who found the words for this moment when I could not.

For G
You are beautiful.
Your fingernails are bitten, your hands worked and battered from the
nurture of others,
Rolling cigarettes, tending plants.
Your arms and torso are strong,
Right, perfect in form.
Extraordinary, luminous, a grafter, solid grit, truth, intensity, love.
The lifter of spirits, the one with the right words to say, the collector of
exquisite things.
You are exquisite.

Measured, considered, over-considered, desire, passion, absolute dedication.
Never let go.
Fragile, frail, too good for many ordinary things, talented, honest.
Daft, always with the in-joke, hysterical laughter, witty and wise.
Raising eyebrows, that look, a listener, a giver to all,
Again and again.

There are little scars on your arms; you have inimitable style,
Curated.
You create joy, energy, drive in others.
People rightly want to please you.
You don't suffer fools.

Generous to the point of poverty, kind, insightful, cook, plant whisperer.
A chivvier, nurturer, magnet,
Seeking those who might need you,
Delicate, gentle, hard as nails, carefree,
Dangerous for all the right reasons.
Hurt, joyous in everyday things, sausage and mash, tea in a china cup.

A flame burning bright, singer, lover.
Dancer in every inch and aspect of your being.

(Thomas, 2020)

Letting go

In March 2014 I visited Aotearoa/New Zealand. The day after I arrived in a delirious state of jetlag, I visited the Auckland War Memorial Museum which was hosting an exhibition entitled 'Space Between'. Its focus was the child-led play space between home and school in Colonial New Zealand. The children depicted in the exhibition had unrestricted access to the outdoors without supervision. There was freedom, much more freedom than children in the UK encounter today. Their childhood involved, 'a vigorous autonomy, a passionate excitement and a furtive rebelliousness all at the same time'. I recall my own unruly childhood, especially the years that I spent in rural Wales, and I observe my still strong desire to perpetuate these themes by connecting through dancing with 'Everyone. All the time. No matter what' (Tempest, 2020, p. 9) in 'the communal rapture of the dance floor' (Maconie, 2023).

And the end of all our exploring
Will be to arrive where we started
And know the place for the first time.

T. S. Eliot—'Little Gidding'

Notes

1. 'Eliot's well-known statement that the poet concentrates on an external task, "a task in the same sense as the making of an efficient engine or the turning of a jug or a table-leg" (Eliot 1950, p. 96), expresses Eliot's idea of the poet's strategy in escaping his personality, in utilizing the creative process as a distraction from self' (Austin, 1966, p. 303).
2. It does not escape my attention that 'gossip' features in the Dasarts methodology for feedback for artistic processes (see Faber, 2013).

References

Ashwell, C. (2023). *Becoming witch*. Retrieved January 14, 2024 from https://www.charlieashwell.com/becoming-witch

Austin, A. (1966). T. S. Eliot's theory of personal expression. *PMLA, 81*(3), 303–307. https://doi.org/10.2307/460816

Claxton, G. (2000). The anatomy of intuition. In Atkinson, T. & Claxton G. (Eds.), *The Intuitive practitioner. On the value of not always knowing what one is doing.* Open University Press.

Barbour, K. (2011). *Dancing across the page*. Intellect Ltd.

Carroll, N., & Seeley, W.P. (2013). Kinesthetic understanding and appreciation in dance. *The Journal of Aesthetics and Art Criticism, 71*(2), 177–186. https://doi.org/10.1111/jaac.12007

Eisner, E. (2002). *The arts and the creation of mind*. Yale University Press.

Eliot, T. S. (1944). *Four quartets*. Faber and Faber.

Eliot, T. S. (1950) *Selected essays*. Harcourt, Brace & Co.

Escoyne, C. (2022). TBT: Why Phyllis Lamhut described herself as a 'witch' in 1975 in *Dance Magazine*. Retrieved January 14, 2024 from https://www.dancemagazine.com/phyllis-lamhut-tbt/

Faber, J. (2013). A film about feedback. DAS Graduate School. Retrieved January 14, 2024 from https://vimeo.com/97319636

Furedi, F. (2013) Learning outcomes are corrosive. *CAUT/ACPPU Bulletin Online,* Retrieved January 24, 2024 from https://bulletin-archives.caut.ca/bulletin/articles/2013/01/learning-outcomes-are-corrosive

Gov. UK. (2022, June 9). Teacher characteristics. *School Workforce in England 2021.* Retrieved January 14, 2024 from https://explore-education-statistics.service.gov.uk/find-statistics/school-workforce-in-england

Gutierrez, M. (n.d.). *This is why I teach class.* Retrieved January 14, 2024 from https://www.miguelgutierrez.org/teaching

Hiscoke, A. (Producer and Editor). (2018). Teachers' wisdom interview with Sonia Rafferty. [Video recording]. University of Roehampton

Ingold, T. (2011). *Being alive. Essays on movement, knowledge and description.* Routledge.

Juelskjaer, M., & Schwennesen, N (2012). Intra-active entanglements. An interview with Karen Barad. *Feminist Materialisms, 1–2.* http://dx.doi.org/10.7146/kkf.v0i1-2.28068

Love, R. (2020, March 18). *It's about time: Talking about time in everyday English.* Retrieved January 14, 2014 from https://www.cambridge.org/elt/blog/2020/03/18/its-about-time-talking-about-time-in-everyday-english/

Maconie, S. (2023, July 21). Northern soul prom. *Front Row.* Retrieved January 14, 2024 from https://www.bbc.co.uk/programmes/m001npdh

Odell, J. (2019). *How to do nothing. Resisting the attention economy.* Melville House Printing.

Oliveros, P. (2005). *Deep listening.* iUniverse, Inc.

Onuora, A. N. (2015). *Anansesem: Telling stories and storytelling African maternal pedagogies.* Demeter Press.

Nowotny, H. (2016). *The cunning of uncertainty.* Polity.

Paavola, S., & Hakkarainen, K. (2005). The knowledge creation metaphor. An emergent epistemological approach to learning. *Science and Education, 14,* 535–557. http://dx.doi.org/10.1007/s11191-004-5157-0

Pakes, A. (2011). Phenomenology and dance: Husserlian meditations. *Dance Research Journal.* 43 (2) 33–49. http://dx.doi.org/10.1017/s0149767711000040

Sanger, A. (2022). Gaga and naming as eco-somatic practices of enchantment. *Journal of Dance & Somatic Practices* 14(2) 263–275. https://doi-org.roe.idm.oclc.org/10.1386/jdsp_00086_1

Shiva, V. (2020). *Oneness vs the 1%: shattering illusions, seeding freedom.* Chelsea Green Publishing.

Solnit, R. (2006). *A field guide to getting lost.* Canongate.

Tempest, K. (2020). *On connection.* Faber and Faber.

Thomas, D. (1962). *Under milk wood.* J. M. Dent & Sons.

Thomas, E (2020, February 20). For G.(Gemma Donohue). Facebook post. Retrieved January 14, 2024 from https://www.facebook.com/671675655/posts/pfbid0sR3DCNsLtfQvYFs1qJQ3eeZBUV2ouBhu2dcSnAFZ8LYTCyxTjtyaqnoT5y5rB2KHl/

15

ARE YOU A LEADER? THE L-WORD THAT WOMEN IN DANCE FEAR

Avatâra Ayuso

Introduction

Leadership, women and *dance*. What comes to your mind when you think of these three terms juxtaposing each other, and in relation to your practice? Women that have been asked this question in the UK dance sector used words like problematic, uncomfortable, unseen, rare, hope, women of the past, conflictive and patriarchy. These words reflect a sad story in our dance sector that reflects an issue that affects wider society: women seem not to empathise with the current understanding of what leadership is. They might already be leaders (even though they will not use that word in reference to themselves), but they are invisible to the public eye, or left on the margins of the sector, more often than not receiving fewer and less significant opportunities than men in similar positions.

Over the following pages, I will approach this matter from an experiential point of view, telling my story as choreographer and leader of the charity AWA DANCE, which is dedicated to the leadership development of women and girls through dance. I will share some data to illuminate the issue and some of my approaches to help make the dance sector better not only for women, but for anyone that wants to work in a healthy, supportive and encouraging environment.

A leadership journey

I have always felt I had leadership capabilities that I have been practising since I was a child, but it was not until my mid-twenties when I realised I was definitely a leader: I was in charge of a group of people that were there

DOI: 10.4324/9781003382874-20

to follow my vision, and help me achieve an artistic dream I could not realise without them. I remember the first time I recognised publicly I was a leader, using explicitly the L-word. I was in Germany, leading a full-length production for 16 dancers. We had an issue with one of the major set structures and in a moment of conflict, panic and anger, someone asked, 'Who is in charge of this? I need to speak to *him* immediately!' and without any doubt I stepped forward and said 'That's me, I'm the leader of this project, the one in charge. Sorry to disappoint you, but I'm a *she*'. That was a life, and professional, turning point. The L-word would never leave me after that, and since then I used it with pride, responsibility and humility.

Before associating myself with the word *leader,* I defined myself (and still do) in other terms. One of the most liberating moments, early on in my career, came from the English language. By working in the UK, I found that one doesn't need to be just a dancer, just a teacher or just a choreographer; one can actually be all of those things at once, and even more: you can be a 'dance artist'. This concept made me realise that I did not have to choose between all my dance passions: performing, choreographing, teaching, researching, photography, writing articles, studying new forms, enjoying dance—they all could be part of who I am, and I could make a living out of all those different passions combined. I decided to define myself as a 'contemporary dance artist' whose aim was to interact with artists from around the world in order to grow, learn, be inspired and inspire others. I also made the decision not to be dependent on any large organisation as a full-time worker, I wanted to develop my own projects with my own vision and collaborate with institutions around the world that align with my values and would challenge both my practice and inherited Eurocentric perspective.

I officially categorised myself as a 'freelance contemporary dance artist', soon after becoming leader of AVA DANCE COMPANY, working in contemporary dance, a relatively free form that allows me to filter many different experiences and ideas into the creative process. *Contemporary* is, for me, simply what happens now: to me, to others, to society. For me, being contemporary is unavoidable. My praxis is then a reflection on where I am and who I am with, at a specific moment in time.

As a contemporary artist, aware of our sociopolitical and economic world issues, and as a woman in that world, I could not help feeling deeply affected by what women go through on a daily basis, in the UK, in Europe and around the world, from physical and sexual violence to more sophisticated ways of silencing our views and perspectives.

With this in mind, I founded the charity AWA DANCE (Advancing Women's Aspirations with Dance), a charity whose mission is to develop leadership skills in girls and women in the dance sector. It was born out of my personal frustration with the inequalities of our societies, and at the same time my fascination with and admiration for the incredible women and girls I met through my work as a choreographer across the world. Despite all of the leadership and artistic talent and commitment to make things better, women and girls were not at the forefront. They were not being listened to, or supported, in the same way as their male counterparts. Why? What is stopping them from developing their full potential as leaders? My answer was to create a platform to offer a brave and safe space for change to happen, using dance as the catalyst to understand leadership differently.

Working with women

As a woman working in the UK and European dance sectors (being aware that the situation can be very different in other continents, as well as between the UK and Europe), I have experienced some of the issues that affect, I would dare to say, all of us (women in dance): from unwanted and disrespectful comments about my body in the dance studio to advice on losing weight in order to be considered for a role; hard competition and unfairness in selection processes like auditions; suggestions such as 'don't get pregnant now that your career is going to kick off'; talent dismissal because 'you are a super woman, you don't really need support like others'. All of these behaviours and comments came to me both from women and men that supposedly cared about me. Unconsciously, they were reproducing sexist and unhealthy patterns that could knock my confidence. However, I was also lucky enough to have others that were brave enough to support my talent when nobody else did, and gave me life-changing opportunities which helped make me the artist I am today. Some other women also have the weight of juggling motherhood with a professional career and the lack of opportunities to develop professionally their artistic practice.

These experiences might trigger two, or more, psychological responses: they damage your confidence, patience and self-esteem; or they make you so angry that this anger becomes a driving force for change, pushing you to achieve your artistic dreams to your (sometimes unhealthy) limits. In my case, rage became my motivation to create opportunities for myself and other women.

In the projects for my independent dance company, I work mainly with women on stage, a body-political-performative and very conscious decision, in order to give space to women to develop their artistic and physical voice, all in a respectful, supportive and encouraging environment.

From the early stages of my ballet training, I realised that in the European dance tradition women were either portrayed as symbols of purity and innocence, 'sweet and girly', or over sexualised, and physically dependent on the men, in particular in the field of ballet, and in some contemporary practices. In general, their stories have been told my men, filtered by a patriarchal gaze that reproduced and consolidated clichés, and the women choreographers that existed and told 'other stories', were marginalised from that history and therefore hardly known to subsequent generations. As an artist, I did not identify with any of these, so I had to find my own way to represent the woman I was, and the women that lived around me. The key for me was to develop a *physical voice* that accepted and nurtured who I was.

To get there, I need the dancers (both women and men) to tell a *physical truth*. By this I mean, to be honest and get to a deep understanding of the potential of their body, to feel comfortable with it, in such a way that all the textures you achieve (subtlety, viscerality, delicacy, sharpness, sensuality, roughness) are fully embodied. It is not easy to move away from the many restrictions, constrictions and fears society has imposed onto our relationship with our own bodies, but when one gets to that point of physical understanding, both you and the audience realise that the body doesn't lie—pushed to its limits of honesty, it will always tell the truth. And for the body not to lie, it is important to me to make sure I work with dancers that come from diverse cultural backgrounds where they are confident about their roots and heritage, and that they are allowed to share who they are. Being honest on an emotional, intellectual and physical level, I consider an act of leadership.

This is one of the ways I give artistic and leadership space to women in dance, but how can we share that sense of honesty and self-worth with those that are not part of the dance sector? The first project which taught me how to approach this was The HAMS ('whisperer' in the Arabic language)—a multicultural community project with refugee women from ten countries, part of the Refugee Art Centre at the European Centre for the Arts in Hellerau (Dresden). The project brought together three concepts: women, dance and empowerment. We worked with a total of 50 refugee women, most of them fleeing from war. This is one of the social groups who are most isolated, least confident, least likely to get a job and therefore least integrated in society. We wanted to provide a safe environment where they could relax, develop new friendships, explore physical experiences through dance and feel free to be who they want to be, leaving aside the traumatic experiences they all went through. We met every three months in long sessions where we danced, ate and got to interact with fascinating women from different cultures. Men were not allowed to join the group in order to respect their different faiths, and babysitters were provided so they could bring their children with them. It was a space for exchange, for women, with women. We became an international family, where we trusted each other, where we could share our real selves without fear, with courage, where we could develop our creativity through dance.

Working in spaces for, and with, women has offered me the possibility to explore a type of leadership that does not fit into the traditional hierarchical Western canon. Projects like *The HAMS*, allowed me to understand how important creative, empathetic and adaptive leadership is when working in a truly multicultural project, where different cultures, faiths and personal realities come together in the same space.

FIGURE 15.1   Avatâra Ayuso in HAMS Project for Refugee Women in Dresden

What the data says

Women and girls are half of the worlds' population; nevertheless data from United Nations regarding their sustainable development goal (SDG) number 5 (UN Women, 2022) on the empowerment of women and girls shows that the world is not on track to achieve gender equality by 2030. Somehow it is not surprising to know the goal will not be met, but it is sad and extremely disappointing to know that organisations and countries around the world are not truly committed to make use of the intelligence, creativity and problem-solving skills of half of its workforce to solve the problems the world currently faces.

The Western dance sector (European and North American traditions) predominantly consists of women and girls taking part in dance activities in a professional or amateur capacity. I am not aware of any research that has precisely tracked the statistics of the sector's demographics, while there have been attempts by Arts Council England in respect of gender representation on permanent, contractual and voluntary staff of the organisations it funds, showing that there is a majority of women in all categories (Arts Council England, 2022).

The day-to-day experience of anyone involved in the sector shows that one only needs to step into a dance class or an audition to see the disproportionate numbers, in favour of women and girls. This, however, has not guaranteed that women's and girls' voices are heard and valued as much as men's, nor that their personal physical space is respected, or that specific policies and regulations are put into place to tackle specific issues relating to women. This paradox also seems to translate to leadership positions. When rising to the higher levels of power, women seem to dissolve from the public eye, and/ or have less visibility than their male counterparts in leadership positions.

There is one organisation that is at the forefront of research on women in leadership positions in the US dance sector—the Dance Data Project. Their aim is to raise awareness on issues relating to gender equality in ballet companies. Founded in 2015 by Elizabeth Yntema, it has now expanded globally and has even established a *Gender Equity Index* to assess how dance companies measure up in terms of commissioning choreographers, the proportion of women in leadership positions and transparency and accountability practices. At the moment, progress in the US seems very slow, but this organisation is no doubt creating change in the US dance sector and should be kept on our collective radars to inspire future actions in the UK.

To tackle the lack of data specifically related to the UK dance sector— what the United Nations would call 'invisible data' (UN Women, 2022)— the charity AWA DANCE has, alongside C-DaRE (Coventry University), recently published a report on leadership gender balance in the UK dance sector (Ayuso et al., 2023) to better understand the current situation and provide data that would support changes towards equity in dance. The data gathered was of two types: statistical data concerning the gender of top leadership positions in a select group of dance organisations; and qualitative data capturing the lived experience of women working in the UK dance sector, focused on their experiences of gender and leadership. Below is an extract of the report and its key findings:

Leadership gender balance in the UK dance sector

Key findings

1) The data gathered on the leadership landscape of nationally funded dance organisations in the UK show that there are more women in leadership positions than men (for the financial year 2021–2022). This information is in direct contrast to the perceptions of leadership that women in the UK dance sector have. These are the results in the combined UK data (England, Scotland and Wales);

Artistic director positions: 56.2% women – 43.8% men
Executive director positions: 68.5% women – 31.5% men
Board member positions: 61.1% women – 38.6% men

2) When looking further into funding bands, the data show that organisations receiving greater funding are more often led by men than women, in

both artistic and executive director positions. The majority of financially powerful organisations (those assumed to be able to create a greater impact on the sector) are led by men, with the majority of organisations receiving less funding from national funding programmes led by women.

3) The data on lived experiences show that 79.7% women in the UK dance sector perceive an imbalance in leadership (16.4% are not sure, and 4% say they don't believe there is an imbalance) and the main reasons they identify for this imbalance are:

- Patriarchal set up of UK society
- Maternity and motherhood
- Lack of supported infrastructures within organisations

One of the most revealing aspects of this research relates to the language used by participants to express their experiences of leadership in the dance sector. Words and expressions like 'disposable commodity', 'overlooked', 'greater criticism', 'motherhood', 'undermining', 'not taken seriously' or 'perceived as less reliable' send a clear message to the wider sector of disappointment, pain, struggle and exhaustion.

How, then, can women feel that the word *leader* relates to them, if their day-to-day experiences appear to value a type of leadership that seems to exclude them, and does not adapt to the specific issues that affect their professional practice: from motherhood, period pain or infertility to body shame, racism, being overlooked, shut down, or not promoted despite the experience they have accumulated.

Despite the data showing there is relative balance in leadership positions in the UK dance sector (Ayuso et al., 2023) (although the organisations with more funding are still predominantly led by men), women's experiences shed light on the type of leadership that the sector seems to practise at large. It is clear that a paradigm shift is needed if we want women to identify with, and put into practice, the type of leadership that includes them and allows them to thrive, becoming the change makers they deserve to be.

What can dance teach us about leadership?

I understand leadership as a way to take ownership of your own life, to be proud of who you are, and impact the lives of others. However, for that impact to be meaningful to our dance sector, we need a new understanding of what leadership is, which is more relevant to our 21st-century reality. Old patterns and behaviours seem not to be adaptable and inclusive enough. If we want to empower current and future generations, embrace diversity of perspectives, and make people feel safe both psychologically and physically, we urgently need a leadership that is transformational, empathetic, inclusive, collaborative, intersectional, creative, resilient and resourceful. The good news about moving towards this paradigm shift is that those working in the dance sector already have many of the tools needed to put this into practice.

Dance and leadership make an excellent partnership to prepare us for the creative and social challenges our societies and sector are experiencing. Dance encourages respect towards your body, mind and soul. It promotes physical and mental wellbeing, confidence, self-expression, communication skills, teamwork and adaptability. It boosts problem-solving abilities, resilience, trust and creative thinking. There is one specific trait that both dance and leadership need to be successful: the power of *empathy*. Empathy (from the Ancient Greek *epathos, feeling, emotion,* and the prefix *en* meaning inside), is what brings people together, what makes you value the other person. Dance is all about this: to value yourself, so you can value others, and transcend social, political and cultural boundaries in order to connect with each other.

There are specific challenges that women and girls face—the lack of body confidence, and the pressure imposed by society to make us believe our voice does not matter—and dance can be the perfect tool to confront those issues:

- Dance can be physically very empowering. It allows you to connect deeply with your body, your heart, your soul, it allows you to trust yourself, to accept yourself.
- Dance is also a way to channel your passions. It fosters self-expression. We need women and girls that are not afraid of sharing their ideas and passions, and dance can be the way for them to do this.
- Dance has the potential to create spaces of inclusion, intersectionality, democracy and cultural appreciation, which can be called feminist leadership—a way of understanding the world where traditional power structures are challenged and the voice of the most marginalised is nurtured and supported.

Building safe and brave spaces in dance

Most women and girls in the dance sector experience invisible sexism on a daily basis, despite being the predominant gender in our sector, and there are specific issues that affect them that for a long time have been ignored or set aside as non-priority. Being a leader comes with responsibility, but also requires the strength to know you are going to be heard and that you will fight for your vision no matter what. A true leader needs to be confident in their abilities, and aware of any gaps in skills in order to bring together the right team to realise that vision. That confidence does not come out of nowhere. It comes from the experience of being in spaces that allow you to reflect, be yourself and express your views.

For too long women and girls have not had these spaces—quite the opposite. How can we start building these into our daily practices as teachers, choreographers, directors, rehearsal directors and administrators, to boost the confidence of women and girls? How might the dance sector do this for them to feel their voice matters, therefore, seeing their potential as leaders, as changemakers that can make our dance sector a better place for all?

Below I share a series of practices that I have developed, or experienced, in working with a wide variety of organisations and people from many different cultures. From my personal experience, I have been able to see how these approaches to creating welcoming and designated spaces for women and girls not only to work, but also create change in the communities they live in.

This below is my personal checklist to build safe and brave spaces in dance not only for women and girls, but also for anyone present in the space. These are a series of questions that aim to stimulate a reflection where answers and solutions should be found according to the context and financial means of those willing to build those spaces. When I say 'you' it can refer both to an individual or an organisation. Let's dare to ask:

1) Women and girls in company rehearsals

Do you have childcare support in your budget? Recognising this is not exclusive to women but a consideration for any parent, with women being the primary caregiver.

Does your building or the space you work in offer access to period products?

Do you allow them to speak their mind without psychologically punishing them if they disagree?

Do you give them opportunities to develop their choreographic practice?

Do you have reporting mechanisms in place to ensure that incidents are taken seriously and addressed promptly?

2) Women and girls in workshops

Do you encourage debate and open communication?

What kind of dancewear do you ask them to wear?

If uniform, does it reflect their ethnicity?

Are they allowed to talk about their period if that is what stops them from performing at their best?

3) Women and girls on stage

Are you allowing women on stage to be rough, sexy, sharp?

Are you biased in the way you use movement? Feminine vs masculine?

Are you oversexualising girls in their movements?

Are you infantilising women's roles in the stories you tell?

Who tells the stories about women?

Do you invite women to choreograph mid- and large-scale productions?

4) Women and girls in application processes

How many women have applied? If not many, why?

Have you considered pausing the process until you approach more possible candidates?

Did the call out consider flexible work arrangements if needed?

What vocabulary is used in the call out? Did it use inclusive language to avoid gendered stereotypes?

Are you aware of any unconscious biases and stereotypes than can affect the evaluation of women's applications?

5) Women and girls and safeguarding

Do you have clear policies and procedures in place to address and prevent harassment, discrimination and any form of misconduct?

Are your women and girls aware of what consent looks like?

Have you identified and taken measures to stop bullying behaviours?

Do you have a wellbeing policy or training to support your participants?

6) Women and girls and language

Are you using inclusive language to refer to the group like 'dancers or team' rather than guys, boys or girls?

Do you know the chosen pronouns of the people you work with?

Are you aware of any infantilisation of professional women like calling them girls or using patronising language?

Do you offer a platform for open communication and feedback to ensure they feel heard and valued?

7) Intersectionality

Do you have a good understanding of what intersectionality is and what it looks like in your workplace?

Have you identified your biases and are you willing to challenge them?

Do you have an inclusion policy and practices that are reviewed annually?

Do you engage your women in any empowerment programme or initiatives that focus on building self-esteem, confidence and leadership skills?

Are you openly advocating for equal rights and opportunities for all women?

Do you give space for the most marginalised to express their worries, concerns and aspirations?

Creating safe spaces for women and girls requires a collective effort from dance studios, organisations, teachers and the dance community as a whole. By prioritising inclusivity, respect and support, we can definitively cultivate environments that empower women and girls to thrive and contribute to building a leadership landscape where more diverse voices are nurtured and valued.

Final reflections

Change is possible if the will is there. If we want women to feel they can be leaders and dare to say the L-word, we need to stop unhealthy practices in our society, and therefore in our dance sector too. Taking action to empower women is not about isolated measures that cover up hidden issues. It is a long-term commitment to equity, with a 360-degree approach, that affects every area of an organisation in order to produce much-needed change to help the sector thrive, as much as it deserves to.

Change, nevertheless, can seem like a big task, and it can certainly be frightening, but if we think of *change* simply as *movement towards* something else, we will realise that in the dance sector we know a lot about that. My suggestion is to simply start moving towards changing mindsets: let's start small, by asking questions that challenge us and the places we live and work in; then let's create the right environment for women and girls to envision themselves as changemakers rather than second-class citizens; and last but not least, let's develop practices, policies and a work culture that promote an inclusive, intersectional and empathetic leadership, where there is respect and support for each other, in order to make the world a better place for all.

References

Arts Council England. (2022). Equality, diversity and inclusion – a Data Report 2020–21. Arts Council England. Retrieved January 14, 2024 from https://www.artscouncil.org.uk/equality-diversity-and-inclusion-data-report-2020-2021

Ayuso, A., Cisneros, R., Shire, G., Stamp, K. & Whitehead Smith, M. (2023). Leadership gender balance in the UK dance sector, AWA DANCE. https://awadance.org/research/

UN Women. (2022). In focus: Sustainable development Goal 5: Achieving gender equality and empowering women and girls. Retrieved January 14, 2024 from https://www.unwomen.org/en/news-stories/in-focus/2022/08/in-focus-sustainable-development-goal-5

16

COMING OUT IS A PROTEST

A score for ritual queer emergence

Kars Dodds

Introduction

After completing both sides of the combination, we'd turn to face the centre of the studio to find *Her* fixated on Her image in the mirror. She'd pull at the skin on Her face to make Her wrinkles disappear and press on Her waist to look thinner. Sometimes, after such an indulgence, she'd turn to us and remark about Her new diet before administering corrections or introducing the next barre combination. I adopted many such fears from Her. Not her, but Her with a capital 'H'. I adopted a collective expectation of femininity assigned to my body from conception. I was intended to mother this precious pronoun. Rear Her into myself, into my body.

Before I edged towards the transness and fluidity that inhabit my body now, I held Her closely. I impersonated Her to an indistinguishable resemblance. For those who do not recognise such an experience, I describe a ballet teacher and the imposition of feminine beauty standards I witnessed and internalised as a pubescent 'female' ballet student.

The pronouns she/her/hers are assigned to females at birth. 'Female' is the biological category for someone born with two X chromosomes, a vulva and/ or a womb. Yet none of these biological attributes can correlate directly to womanhood or even girlhood. Trans men, non-binary, gender fluid, gender non-conforming, and intersex individuals have all been told to exist under the label female with the obligation of being a girl/woman. Girlhood, womanhood and femininity are words and elements of identity that inform the gender construction many individuals walk through the world with. Also, note that not all women are assigned female at birth (AFAB). I am writing

DOI: 10.4324/9781003382874-21

from my AFAB perspective as a non-binary, trans-masculine person who grew up under the title 'female dancer'.

Transness demonstrates freedom from assigned gender roles. In *The Second Sex,* the French feminist theorist and philosopher Simone de Beauvoir (she/her) writes, 'One is not born a woman, but rather becomes one' (1989). She suggests that womanhood is a socially learnt behaviour and calls attention to the underwritten obligation of the female sex to become a woman. Judith Butler (they/she), an American queer theorist, is famously quoted saying they are 'never at home' being AFAB. This sentiment becomes the critical lens through which they write *Gender Trouble,* explaining that individuals are subject to worldly gendered expectations that limit their power (1999). Trans and gender non-conforming (TGNC) people deny the prescription of identity. TGNC existence embodies protest of binary gender expectations and reclaims freedom of expressive power and desire. By considering embodiment as 'the experience of living in, perceiving, and experiencing the world from the physical and material place of our bodies', we recognise that the body takes on context and messaging from the social environments (i.e. school, family, church) (Fahs and Swank, 2015, p. 150). In other words, the body is subjected to social contexts to learn and orient itself. This describes the nature of embodiment and the nature of being queer in the world.

Social convention presents a challenge to queer individuals, where they must value themselves, their desires and their (LGBTQIA+) community over social conventions that would otherwise consume their bodies. Here the concept of 'queering' or 'to queer' becomes relevant. By queering the concept and embodiment of gender, TGNC individuals benefit themselves and the world than would otherwise be possible. The joys of drag would not exist without TGNC people defying convention for their desires. Jack (or Judith) Halberstam (he/she), a gender and queer theorist, calls this notion 'queer failure', where queers fail at fitting into binary categories of gender. To queer something, all you have to do is protest against traditional social contexts. He implies that social conventions fail to hold TGNC and queer people because they cannot be contained by such rigid expectations (2011). To offer an example, ballet training, its standards and conventions, took precedence over my wellbeing. Coming to terms with the trauma and abuse of the ballet world allowed my queerness to emerge and flourish when, outwardly, it looked like I failed.

'Coming out' is something we do to be seen, heard and respected. Queer folks are queer whether or not they share their queerness with everyone or anyone at all.

The term 'coming out' is identifiable and widely accepted despite its flaws.

Throughout this chapter, I draw attention to the ritualistic nature through which TGNC people come out by providing my learnt and embodied perspective as an AFAB mover/dancer/performer. My experience does not speak for all LGBTQIA+ people. Everyone's coming out experience is uniquely nuanced and intersectional. This chapter cannot hold the intersectional abundance of everyone within the LGBTQIA+ community or what it means to be queer.

A movement score of prompts and spatial inquiry is provided for processing of self-exploration and embodiment of some of the topics of protest and queer emergence discussed in this chapter. As you read on, I invite you to protest as you wish. My words are not empirical, and there is no single pathway through protest or into emergence. I encourage you to be mindful of my words' impact on your preconceived notions of gender and identity, emotional constitution and bodily sensations.

On coming out

There was NO organisation, only frustrated heat rising through my body and out of my ears. I did not just open the door and come out. I oozed out. Slowly and thick like molasses that has baked in the humid heat of South Carolina. Then I started to drizzle. Then, a trickle, bit by bit, as I slowly began to understand myself in the sticky mess of gender identity.

Queer people come out again and again. It's exhausting, constantly being reminded of our otherness. Coming out is a continuous process, not something that happens once in a lifetime. 'Coming out' refers to a common LGBTQIA+ experience where an individual communicates their romantic orientation, sexual orientation and/or gender identity. It is frequently used to describe a single moment of coming out, for example, coming out to your parents. I find this association with the term is dishonest to the reality that faces LGBTQIA+ people. It assumes a singularity of the effort and minimises the labour a queer individual goes through to be 'out'. It is a ceremonial happening that verbally protests against perceived notions of identity. Certainly, repetition can take a toll. It is not easy or fun to repeat ourselves. I would argue that it informs an individual's queer embodiment. Coming out is a statement that starts from within the body to the self and then finds its way into how you carry yourself, your interests and embodiment. To be externally known as queer, we rely on repeating ourselves. Cyclical processes heal and comfort the body, just as repetition and order do. Such a cycle, or circle of existence, starts to hold the Self so that it finds a home in the body.

By referencing coming out as a ritual, I draw inspiration from Daria Shamina (she/her), an integrative bodywork and movement therapist, and her discussion of the circle as a healing container for movement and fluidity (2022), considering this as a ritualistic practice. She uses the psychoanalytic concept of a 'holding environment', frequently called 'holding space' in dance practice. A 'holding environment' describes a relational environment where one person is focused on the safety and needs of another to support their healing, growth and exploration. The concept was initially used to describe a mother's support to an infant (Finlay, 2015). The infant cannot understand and answer its own needs. When applied to coming out, I view the queer part of the self as the infant. The role of the mother then becomes the responsibility of one's Self and those the individual is coming out to. With ourselves, we support our queerness to emerge. With others, they contain the attention and energetics that offer supportive coming out.

TGNC safety only comes into question when the innate protest of queer visibility threatens another individual's social context and reality. A queer person threatens conventional gender roles that another finds safety and anonymity within. Neither party is held in this scenario, and there is less room for mutual understanding and growth.

There is violence in reaction to the protest queer individuals represent. And yet coming out is not exclusive to queer folk. The process and feeling of 'coming out' is mirrored by many other words. While building the score shared in this chapter, I played with several similar words, actions and statements: 'emergence', 'display', 'I am' and 'I become'. I resonated particularly with the term 'emergence' as it speaks to the queer resilience innate to the coming out experience.

We all experience moments of emergence, where we come into ourselves or arrive as ourselves, similar to coming out. There are stereotypes and stigmas for each individual walking the planet. The individual is always so much more than the stigma, the socially constructed and perceived view of an individual. Sarah E. Frank (Frankie), a queer activist and researcher, uses Goffman's concept of stigma to describe queer identities' experience of silencing through avoidance and shame, specifically in relation to TGNC menstruation (Frank, 2020). Stigma, avoidance and shame minimise the feeling of being held with many of the experiences bodies have. The gross, freaky and kinky become shameful and lonely. In protest, our score aims to encourage you to bring these messy questions to the surface of your attention, to be felt and held.

Further, the term coming out assumes that all queer people want to be seen from the perspective of their sexuality and/or gender identity. While this may be true for many of us, it highlights marginalised aspects of our identities as the most exciting thing about us. And let me assure you, not one of us is that boring.

Identity is personal, fluid and evolving, whether it is queer or not (Butler, 1999). In this sense, Butler suggests that everyone must come out occasionally. The nuance of being is informed by the social scenarios we find ourselves in. Each scenario will ask something different of the individual and their identity (Goffman, 1956). Queer folks use emergence, or 'coming out', as a tool for when they require a reckoning between themselves, another person (or persons), and the performative aspects of their identities. By coming out, the individual reclaims their identity in a way they feel safest and comfortable.

Protest is typically used to express a political belief or resistance to a dominant power or decision-maker. On a more individual level, 'protest' is felt.

Travis Alabanza (they/them), British performance artist, writer and theatre-maker, states, 'When a part of you is so heavily scrutinised and interrogated, to protect yourself, you have to present it as immutable' (2022, p. 20). An emphatic desire to express and be heard. This is the essence of queerness. LGBTQIA+, or queer folks, innately need to express and manifest their inner truth. Queerness within is contrary to the social norm, so exhibiting queerness protests false pretences of normality. Trans and queer people are categorically unable to fit in the boxes of normality, and frequently we become dart boards for other people's confusion. We threaten anyone who has constructed themselves according to the assumptions of binary, cisgender, heterosexual life. Therefore, queer existence is a protest. Transness is a protest.

Memory

This practice and the memories that may surface are for you in the present moment, as you are now. I say this because we cannot know the truth of our memories, nor should we hold ourselves accountable for the whole truth of remembering.

Misremembering in this creative, messy, playful space is encouraged, as it can assist you in opening up the layers from which you are to emerge as you emerge in the present moment. We can only hope to emerge or come out as who we are in the present moment. Change and fluidity are imminent in how we experience memory, identity, gender and sexuality. For now, the score will exist as a solo improvisation practice. Within the score, the body-mind connection is the intended processing vehicle.

First, our experiences are lived and felt within the body. This is in part the position Maurice Merleau-Ponty (he/him), takes in *The Phenomenology of Perception* (1962). Only post-experientially does the mind contextualise our memories for us. For many queer people, it is only later, once memories, experiences and social expectations have been processed, that we can see our past selves as queer. Susan Kozel (she/her), performer and dance researcher, discusses memory and false remembering as potentially revealing elements of our present selves. She writes:

> The pre-reflective is considered through: first, language and gesture; next, a spatial understanding of regions similar to a topographical mapping of external landscapes; and, last, an internal mapping of the regions of the body as if moving from topography to tomography.
>
> *(Kozel, 2007, pp. 17–18)*

Before we can put language to our experience and judge ourselves, our movement and our behaviours, we must first consider our bodies. Instinctual gesture and understanding of our internal landscape, what I would liken to the impacts of trauma, genetics and upbringing on our nervous systems and, therefore, our lived experiences, are what will naturally come first, even before the information can make it up your vagus nerve and into your brain stem. These considerations are helpful in how you may approach coming out or the score. The internal map in communication with the external environment will be a gesture before reflection.

My primary source material is my landmark memories to suggest an internal mapping of your experiences and propose this map as a route for further participant emergence. A landmark memory draws on the psychology of topographical memory and emotional landmarks the brain uses to navigate. Sarah Ahmed (she/her), British-Australian queer theorist, demonstrates that a queer phenomenology would pose this as a way that we 'orient' ourselves within the world. An individual's orientation can be likened to their perspective, as informed by their lived experiences (2006). Simply put, a trans-masculine/non-binary/AFAB person would read this chapter differently from a cis/AMAB individual and that one cis/AMAB person would read it differently from another. This suggests that our identities are central to navigating the physical world and our experiences or memories. This is one way of examining the process of coming out.

Additionally, it's justified that we must have familiarity with the potential possibilities for queer expression when we orient ourselves among the array of ways to be LGBTQIA+. We learn who we are through exposure to new ways of living. You cannot become it if you cannot see it.

Scoring a pathway

My chosen style of developing this score is primarily inspired by Deborah Hay (she/her), founding member of Judson Church and postmodern minimalist. Ros Warby (she/her), a dancer/choreographer and collaborator of Hay, described the scoring style as 'articulated by a series of instructions and spatial pathways. Often these instructions are nonsensical and apparently impossible to execute.' Warby offers examples, such as 'take six steps into the light without taking a step' (Warby as cited in Dempster & Gardner, 2007, p. 77). Hay's purpose in working this way was to reveal a moment of complex decision-making and negotiation to the audience who are witness to the performer's experience and perception of the task at hand (Millard, 2015). Drawing on Hay's notion of an impossible task, I can hardly help but relate this to the puzzling and unpuzzling of binary gender identity and transness, and while drawing on image and memories of protest.

When thinking about protest, two images come to my mind: 1) groups marching and moving forward and 2) placards and signs that make statements of need and desire. The score I've provided is to aid the digestion and action of protest as an embodied concept for personal emergence and development. It is queer and designed with queerness in mind but is entirely inclusive and can be used by all. It is intended to be an open score, to provide you with as much freedom and permission as you desire.

Frequently, this practice challenges me to remember and reconstruct landmark memories in the hopes of pleasure and self-discovery. Delving into memory can be dangerous and painful for many of us. It can also be a helpful resource when coming out or emerging. Remembering yourself and your feelings, alongside events of the distant and near past, gives the individual the power to take control of the story and their life. This is a challenging undertaking. Coming out can be challenging. It takes practice. In offering my practice and memories as a written example, this practice will develop to become a resource for self-discovery and embodiment.

I am proposing this score and anything this score may inspire as an act of protest. Suppose we, as a community and individuals, allow ourselves to practise, ritualise and embody the coming out process. In that case, we allow ourselves to become increasingly comfortable and powerful. Practice and grappling with the subject matter mentally prepare us and our nervous systems to expect truth, expression and queer embodiment.

There are three primary tasks within the score. These tasks can be followed linearly or as desired to choose your adventure. The first task is to ground. I've written a follow-along guide for grounding when initially entering the score and going through parts one and two cyclically. I've chosen to start here and offer it as a place to return to when thoughts become too much to hold, when you need to slow down when the body requires rest, and so on.

Second, I've provided many protesting/expression prompts. Multiple sources inspire these prompts. I've taken synonyms of 'coming out' and formatted them to offer statements and actions for the mover to use. For these, fill-in-the-blank prompts are additionally provided for the mover/explorer to utilise. Lastly, I've provided protest slogans I heard, read and chanted from London Trans Pride 2023. They can be used for reflection, as movement prompts, to inspire further discussion, and so on. Some are inspired by my coming out story of ups and downs and personal landmarks.

THE SCORE: COMING OUT IS A PROTEST

GETTING STARTED/INITIAL GROUNDING

Start by taking three deep cleansing breaths. Breathe in through your nose, allowing your belly to expand with air lightly, and exhale out your mouth with a sigh. Repeat until you feel grounded within yourself.

Ground/return to self

Return to your natural breathing pattern. As you continue to breathe, notice your body's small movements when inhaling and exhaling. In tandem with the rhythm of your breath, follow the intuitive cues of your body to ebb and flow with seaweed-like movement, similar to a 'rocking' sensation. If you find this soothing, continue until you feel ready to move on to another prompt or exit the score with grounding.

Protest/express

- Trace long lines with your limbs. Colour within the lines until the lines no longer serve you.
- Welcome weightlessness and effortlessness into your flesh, muscles and bones. Then, drop everything. Refuse to hold on.
- Now show yourself. Put yourself on display. Sell yourself in a store window. Attract only people who genuinely love you.
- Clench, whether empty or full.
- Play dress up within your skin, within your movement. Dress up as yourself.
- Chant: 'Whose rights? Trans rights.'
- Ask yourself, then recite to yourself: 'What do we want? (Fill in desire here) When do we want them? Now.'
- Walk/Run and connect to the soothing rhythm and vibration of your feet against the ground.
- Shake and bounce your body. Get your flesh to vibrate.
- My existence is resistance.
- I am me. I am (fill in).
- What constitutes childhood?
- Quantify your desires.
- Find a place of rest and contemplation.
- Remind yourself of who you are. Repeat yourself as needed.

As TGNC and queer people continue to emerge, come out and make themselves visible, there is growing political fire against us. This score is raw and young. The score's publication can only represent a seed of the vast potential queer freedom can offer the world. Only with the queer community and its grit will it grow.

References

Alabanza, T. (2022). *None of the above: Reflections on life beyond the binary.* Canongate Books.

Ahmed, S. (2006). Queer phenomenology: Orientations, objects, others. *Queer phenomenology.* Duke University Press.

Butler, J. (1999). *Gender trouble: Feminism and the subversion of identity.* Routledge.

De Beauvoir, S. (1989). *The second sex.* Vintage Books.

Fahs, B., & Swank, E. (2015). Unpacking sexual embodiment and embodied resistance. In J. DeLamater & R. F. Plante (Eds.), *Handbook of the sociology of sexualities* (pp. 149–167). Springer International Publishing. https://doi.org/10.1007/978-3-319-17341-2_9

Finlay, L. (Ed.). (2015). *Relational integrative psychotherapy: Engaging process and theory in practice* (1st ed.). Wiley-Blackwell. https://doi.org/10.1002/9781119141518

Frank, S. E. (2020). Queering menstruation: Trans and non-binary identity and body politics. *Sociological Inquiry, 90*(2), 371–404. https://doi.org/10.1111/soin.12355

Dempster, E, & Gardner, S. (2008). Ros Warby: Framing practice (an interview with Ros Warby and Sally Gardner). *Writings on Dance, 24,* 77–93.

Goffman, E. (1956). *The presentation of self in everyday life.*

Halberstam, J. (2011). *The queer art of failure* (Online-ausg). Duke University Press.

Merleau-Ponty, M. (2002). *Phenomenology of perception: An introduction.* Routledge.

Millard, O. (2015). What's the score? Using scores in dance improvisation. *Brolga: An Australian Journal about Dance, 40,* 45–56.

Shamina, D. (2022). Circle: The nature of containment. In L. Hartley (Ed.), *The fluid nature of being: Embodied practices for healing and wholeness.* Handspring Publishing.

17

GEOMETRY OF GENDER

Analysing the anatomical specifications of the Bharatanatyam dancer

Shreya Srivastava and Shilpa Darivemula

'Sit. Knees out. Arms up. Lean forward. Back straight. Smiling, bright eyes.' My Bharatanatyam teacher repeated these instructions to the students before every movement. Now conditioned to these orders, the students instinctively aligned their bodies to satisfy my teacher's request. She scanned the room of nearly three dozen students, analysing the structure and stability of each individual dancer. A slight drop in the arms or unsatisfactory angle of the knees received prompt and stern verbal correction. Precise posture is the core of Bharatanatyam. It satisfies the underlying philosophy and technique that has built the ancient dance form. Only after my teacher determined that all our postures were acceptable were we then allowed to dance.

Bharatanatyam is a widely performed, popular classical dance form. Originating in the South Indian state of Tamil Nadu roughly two millennia ago, it has transformed drastically since its conception to become one of the most performed classical dance forms in the world (Bergeron, 1997). Despite growing up in a small, predominantly White town in the suburban Midwest of the United States, I had no trouble finding a Bharatanatyam teacher. Community interest and excitement towards learning Bharatanatyam was visibly apparent—classes were always full of students, many belonging to Indian-American families who had recently moved to the area and were in search of cultural activities their children could participate in. For many, Bharatanatyam class was not only a lesson in dance, but a means of connecting with Indian culture, religion and history.

The posture that Bharatanatyam dancers begin most movement in is called the *ardhamandala*, or *araimandi*. The araimandi is the fundamental posture of Bharatanatyam (Vatsyayan, 1992). It is based on a complex alignment of geometric shapes, one stacked upon another, that then develops a standard

DOI: 10.4324/9781003382874-22

Bharatanatyam dancer, Monica Shah, completing a Namaskaram (prayer) in ariamandi. Credit Erik Zennstrom

position from where most movement originates and ends. Indian performing arts scholar, Vatsyayan, describes the araimandi as such:

> The triangle is formed with the line joining the two knees (flexed and out-stretched as in the demi plie in the first position of the classical ballet) as the base, and with its apex at the heels (where the feet are outturned as in the first position of the ballet). Another triangle is formed with the waist as the apex and the line joining the knees as the base. A third triangle is conceived with the waist as the apex and the line joining the shoulder as its base. This is further emphasized by the outstretched arms, which make yet another triangle in space on either side of the vertical median.
>
> *(Vatsyayan, 1977, p. 336)*

Another fundamental posture we learnt in Bharatanatyam class was *Soushta-vam*. Our classes always began with us reciting the following poem together: '*Kati Karna Samaayatra Koorparamsa Sirastadha, Samunnata-muraschiva, Soushtavam Naamatadbhaveth*' (Bharatamuni, 1950). The phrase is from the *Natya Shastra*, the ancient text outlining the specifications of the Indian classical performing arts (Vatsyayan, 1977; Bharatamuni, 1950). Written by scholar and theatrician Bharatamuni between the 2nd century BC and the 2nd century AD, the Natya Shastra is one of the oldest texts that theorises the performing arts (Vatsyayan, 1992). It details everything from the anatomical requirements of performers, such as height and body shape, to categories of emotions that must be conveyed in dance. The phrase recited by the students dictates the requirements that must be satisfied to embody the 'Soushtavam' posture of Bharatanatyam: first, the dancer must align their hips to be directly underneath both of their ears—that is, they must stand vertically straight, without any tilting of the head or pelvis. Second, they must lift their arms so that the elbows are in alignment with the neck. Third, they must stand tall and raise their chest, displaying strength and stability (Tarlekar, 1999). Such recitation of the Natya Shastra provided a fascinating display of the migration and preservation of Bharatanatyam, geographically and chronologically. Students far from Bharatanatyam's original intended audience were practising Sanskrit verses and embodying ancient descriptions of human body positions.

Posture, therefore, acts as the foundational unit of Bharatanatyam, a technical element of the dance form that also facilitates a direct association between tradition and modernity. With the study of posture comes the study of Indian philosophy, language, religion and history.

Performance of sculpture

The importance of posture in Bharatanatyam finds its roots in the Indian art of sculpting (Vatsyayan, 1977, 1992). Sculpting in India holds great significance, as it not only acts as a means of visual art development, but also as a skill that permits the production of Hindu idols and the subsequent establishment of Hindu temples. Due to the necessity of sculpting a wide array of divine figures mentioned in Hindu texts, from gods and goddesses to dwarfs and demons, the art of ancient Indian sculpting depends on a calculated system of anatomical proportions (Vatsyayan, 1977). These sculptures exist not only within temples, but also among various displays of art and architecture throughout Indian society, such as in the caves of the Ajanta Allora and the exterior surface of the Chidambaram temple (Duran, 1998).

Sculptures provide an akinetic model of posture. Ancient Indian sculptures distribute great information about societal roles, gender, sensuality and their ongoing, widespread display throughout Indian society suggests their continued role in visual messaging. They present the body as a snapshot of time, a particular point in a story that is narrated through an artistic alignment and manipulation of human stance (Vatsyayan, 1967). The anatomical structure depicted by a sculptor conveys ideas of how the Indian aesthetic perceives perfect posture and how far that ideal is from biologically informed human anatomy. This raises the question of whether these ancient displays of posture can even be embodied—and if so, who is able to embody them?

The role of performing sculpturesque postures belongs to the Indian classical dancer (Vatsyayan, 1967, 1977). The emphasis on geometrically exact postures in Bharatanatyam is based on the idea that an Indian dancer is adding life to the sculpture—a deity, a demon, a dwarf, or a mortal human being—all must be enacted by the dancer. Vatsyayan describes this phenomenon by saying:

> The poses which the dancer utilizes for this purpose are identical with those of Indian sculpture, and very often the one is a visual representation in movement of the static pose of another [...] Even though the Indian dancer can use space more freely than the Indian sculptor, the emphasis is always on the pose which the dancer attains through a series of movements.
>
> *(Vatsyayan, 1977, p. 19)*

Therefore, the accurate postural alignment of a dancer is of utmost importance. It not only satisfies an image in a story that communicates a specific identity and character to the audience, but it also provides a sense of stillness and stability, conveying order and structure within chaos.

Gendered posture in America

Compared to the visual depictions of posture in India, which are publicly displayed through ancient Indian art, the perceptions of perfect posture in the United States are less obvious. Unlike India, the Midwestern United States possesses little public artwork and accessible architecture that broadly displays ideas of the human body and anatomical alignment.

The one area of American society in which posture is most extensively utilised, distributed and consumed is the commercial market. Advertisements of products in the United States serve important roles in subliminal messaging and social influence (Paulson & O'Guinn, 2017). The success of an advertisement depends on a viewer's ability to identify with a presented image, so much so that they accept the image's commentary and act in support of the associated product. In 1979, American sociologist Erving Goffman famously described the phenomenon of depictions of posture within advertisements in the United States. He discussed the utility of still imagery as effective communication within complex surrounding environments:

> still photography can [...] condense, omitting temporal sequence and everything else except static visual arrays. And what is caught is fixed into permanent accessibility, becoming something that can be attended anywhere, for any length of time, and at moments of one's own choosing.
>
> *(Goffman, 1979, p. 10)*

Like a sculpture, a still advertisement depicts a timeless presentation of a posture that communicates an idea of structure to the audience. For example, an advertisement of a prescription medication for joint pain may present the human structure as healthy, active and strong, while an image for a perfume brand may alter the posture to satisfy one of sensuality. But while Indian sculptors rely on character type (deity, demon, mortal) to influence their work, American advertisements rely heavily on gender. Gender acts not only as a tool that advertisements use to appeal to certain target audiences, but also as a label that is associated with distinct types of postures.

According to Goffman, the male and female structure differed in visual advertisements in the country (Goffman, 1979). Goffman stated that when women were presented in still advertisements, they had a specific alignment to them—they were slightly off centre, leaning towards one side, head tilted, looking towards the corners. Men however, stood straight and looked consumers directly in the eyes. The female, therefore, is made to appear more suggestive, subversive and uncertain, while the male is confident and steady (Goffman, 1979).

While Goffman's theories have since been diversified and evolved by scholars, many argue that such gendered postures continue throughout advertisements today with commercial images that reinforce societal gender norms through visual cues (Kang, 1997; Altman, 2021). As gender stereotypes remain significant players in the US economic market, the association between gender and posture seems permanent. However, as the USA adopts new ideas of human stance through global cultural exchange, the predetermined relationship between gender and posture that is so visible in American society may be challenged.

Deconstructing gendered posture

The use of posture in US advertisements serves to create gendered images of human structure that are then broadly consumed throughout American society. While these images may fulfil essential roles in American capitalism, they present a restricted, singular equation of posture and gender. That is, instability in posture correlates with the female gender, and stability correlates with the male gender.

Bharatanatyam, however, does not associate stability with gender. Rather, the goal of achieving stability is rooted in the idea of finding composure within disruptive, abstract environments. The process of aligning the body first begins with embodying instability—whether it is the complex triangular arrangement of the araimandi, or the angular specifications of the Soushtavam, Bharatanatyam postures follow defined geometric planes that disrupt our understanding of human structure. Adopting these postures is a challenge. But as the process continues, stability is eventually reached.

It takes years of training before a dancer feels even a slight essence of steadiness and composure when the body is positioned in such unfamiliar, angular organisations of human anatomy. This discomfort is intentional—when a dancer spends decades training the body to adapt to such complexity, they develop strength and confidence. This phenomenon stems from the philosophy of the Indian aesthetic, which incorporates the idea that beauty, harmony and resolution are results of the journey of finding unity within the abstract environment (Vatsyayan, 1977). The multiple angular specifications and precarious structural demands of Bharatanatyam postures add significant disruption to the human structure—however, as Vatsyayan suggests, the Indian aesthetic would support this as an opportunity for the dancer:

> the fascinating and overpowering quality of the most completely conceived technique is a distinctive feature of all forms of classical Indian art, where the smallest mathematical fractions and complex combinations of measurements all combine to suggest a unified experience on the psychical plane.
>
> *(Vatsyayan, 1977, p. 16)*

Therefore, when a dancer works tirelessly to embody the demanding postures, they work to overcome uncertainties of physical capabilities and consequently grow into stronger and more stable individuals.

Today, Bharatanatyam exists in American society as a popular and widespread classical dance form (O'Shea, 2007). Its growth has been monumental—I have seen firsthand how it has enhanced diversity and facilitated discussions of inclusivity in a relatively homogenous, Midwestern American town. Yet America is not an environment in which one would have expected Bharatanatyam to thrive. Limited performance spaces due to lack of appropriate religious settings or Hindu temples, few accessible options for traditional costume and jewellery purchasing, and lack of social structure allowing children and adults to practise multiple hours a day all interfere with Bharatanatyam's growth. But most importantly, the USA does not facilitate the same visual displays of Bharatnatyam dance, posture and history throughout modern society as India does—an everyday reminder to the Indian classical dancer of their presence in time and their contribution to culture.

Within this new setting, Bharatanatyam has evolved. As is the case with many forms of classical art, Bharatanatyam is not static—it continues to shape itself according to changes in its surroundings. With the increased diversity of today's Bharatanatyam dancers and the influences of global dance trends, Bharatanatyam has changed in many aspects including technique, emotion and storytelling. It would be inaccurate to define today's Bharatanatyam as having a specific, standardised performative form. But despite these alterations, Bharatanatyam continues to fulfil outlined specifications of the Natya Shastra, albeit in a contemporary manner.

Now, in the USA, a modified version of Bharatanatyam exists—one that may be malleable to the structure of American society but firm in its ancient requirements. It is in this new setting that Bharatanatyam can hold a unique and important position in gender-specific portrayals of posture. Rather than continuing to convey the same gendered anatomical structures that define modern society, commercialism and gendered norms, Bharatanatyam creates an opportunity for gendered deconstruction of human stance. Informed by the philosophy of Indian aesthetics, Bharatanatyam eliminates the association between stability and gender by correlating the achievement of stability with the attainment of absolute form. Furthermore, this attainment is never conclusive. Indian aesthetics scholar, Chakrabarti, states that:

> It would be absurd to posit an unchanging continuity in 'Indian aesthetics' and to claim its 'essential quality' when, in every instance, a fresh equilibrium has to be arrived at.
>
> *(Chakrabarti, 2016, p. 252)*

This journey of exploration of centred structure within unstable settings is ongoing for dancers, as each new posture presents with a varied geometric alignment of human structure that then requires new adjustment and further training to establish. Hence, the search for stability remains eternal. It is a reflective, spiritual and physical pursuit, one that arises from within the individual dancer, allowing the process to initiate regardless of the surrounding community, culture, or environment. Stability, therefore, cannot be communicated through a static, visual presentation of posture. While viewers may appreciate a symmetric and centred human structure to represent stability, this is only a superficial image of stability, one that fails to present any indication of the emotional and physical journey required to demonstrate internalised alignment. While a Bharatanatyam dancer experiences stability through direct embodiment, the American consumer simply views the outline of stability that is manufactured on the principles of gendered societal norms.

Diversity of gender

While the connection between stability and gender presented in US markets implies that gender is binary, the foundational texts of Bharatanatyam support the actuality of gender as a nuanced, diverse concept. Bharatanatyam dancers adopt various genders through technique that allows for roleplaying and storytelling. In the narrative component of Bharatanatyam, the *abhinaya* (facial expressions) and the *bhava* (emotion of mental state) combine to tell stories extracted from the Hindu canon (Vatsyayan, 1992). Dancers alternate from one character to another, employing abhinaya and bhava to embody several states of being, including varied gendered experiences.

One story of Hinduism that demonstrates exploration of gender is the story of *Amba-Shikhandi* (Singh, 2013). Amba was a princess of the city of

Kashi who was in love with another man, but was kidnapped by the Kuru Chief, Bheeshma, to serve as a wife for Bheesma's brother. Enraged, Amba tells Bheeshma he must marry her now since he was the one who stole her away. Bheesma declines due to his vow never to marry, and Amba begins severe penance to Lord Shiva, god of creation and destruction of the universe, who grants her wish-that she would be the one to kill Bheeshma in her next life. She is reborn as Shikhandini. However, because Bheesma refused to attack someone who identified as a woman, Shikhandini exchanged her sex with that of a male sage and became biologically male. Now referred to as Shikhandi, he then rides into battle and shoots the arrow that pierces Bheesma's heart (Singh, 2013). This story is celebrated as the great epic *Mahabharata's* transmasculine warrior.

Many other examples of gendered experiences exist throughout Hindu text, including the story of the Lord Krishna who became a woman for one day to marry a man fated to die after his wedding, or the story of Chudala, who became a man so her husband would stop ignoring her views. Or the well celebrated danced power of Ardhanareeshwara, the blend of both the male god Shiva and his female consort goddess Parvati, into one dancing body (Raveesh, 2013). A half male, half female, but independent gendered state that performs a classical dance of universal destruction—an essential process for the creation of new life.

Gendered performance permeates throughout Bharatanatyam. These stories reveal not only the existing gender fluidity in classical Indian dance and Hindu mythologies, but also the gender norms and boundaries that danced stories attempt to challenge.

In the USA, Bharatanatyam's presentation of gender as non-binary further questions the relationship between posture and gender. Stability, therefore, cannot exist in a binary form where stable is male and unstable is female. Bias is present within Bharatanatyam as well, with choreography that often implies how males cannot be delicate, or women cannot be fierce in their own gendered roles. These biases require further investigation by critical artists, with evaluation of the importance of gendered roles in Hindu mythology and how that translates to barriers in gendered expressions in current Indian society.

Within the environment in which I experienced Bharatanatyam, I quickly learnt that this dance form was sensitive to its surroundings. It provided dancers with tools to explore complex ideas of society, religion and gender. Throughout the years, I began to experience the journey towards stability, from which I understood that the gendered visual cues I encountered in popular media were flawed. While conventional society continues to associate gender with posture, Bharatanatyam allows us to escape these societal limitations and not just question the stereotyped perception of structure, but also deconstruct gendered posture through performance.

References

Altman, M. (2021). Yes, marketing is still sexist. *The New York Times.*

Bergeron, A. (1997). *Jammin' with Shiva: Tradition and transformation of the dance in India.* Educational Resources Information Center, USDE.

Bharatamuni. (1950). *The Natyashastra of Bharatamuni,with an introduction and various readings with translations* (Manomohan Ghosh, Ed., Vols. I–n). Calcutta.

Chakrabarti, A. (2016). *The Bloomsbury research handbook of Indian aesthetics and the philosophy of art.* Bloomsbury.

Duran, J. (1998). Ajanta and Ellora: The aesthetics of the cave. *Philosophical Inquiry. 20*(3), 64–70. https://doi.org/10.5840/philinquiry1998203/416

Goffman, E. (1979). *Gendered advertisements.* Red Globe.

Kang, M. (1997). The portrayal of women's images in magazine advertisements: Goffman's gender analysis revisited. *Sex Roles, 37,* 979–996. https://doi.org/10.1007/BF02936350

O'Shea, J. (2007). *At home in the world: Bharata Natyam on the global stage.* Wesleyan University Press.

Paulson, E., & O'Guinn, T. (2017). Marketing social class and ideology in post-World-War-Two American print advertising. *Journal of Macromarketing, 38*(1). 7–28. https://doi.org/10.1177/0276146717733788

Raveesh, B. N. (2013). Ardhanareeshwara concept: Brain and psychiatry. *Indian Journal of Psychiatry, 55*(Suppl 2), S263–S267. https://doi.org/10.4103/0019-5545.105548

Singh, A. (2013). An interview with Mangai. *Asian Theatre Journal, 30*(2), 486–505. https://doi.org/10.1353/atj.2013.0044

Tarlekar, G. H. (1999). *Studies in the Natyasastra: With special reference to the Sanskrit drama.* Motilal Banarsidaas Publishers.

Vatsyayan, K. (1967). The theory and technique of classical Indian dancing. *Artibus Asiae, 29*(2/3), 229–238. https://doi.org/10.2307/3250274

Vatsyayan, K. (1977). *Classical Indian dance in the literature and the arts.* Sangeet Natak Academy.

Vatsyayan, K. (1992). *Indian classical dance.* Publications Division, Ministry of Information and Broadcasting, Government of India.

PART IV

Embodied wisdom

18

FOREGROUNDING (THE) SELF IN DANCE PRACTICE

Gemma Harman and Jayne McKee

Introduction

As colleagues at the University of Chichester, located in West Sussex (United Kingdom), we have spent time sharing a wealth of combined experiences in dance and performance across a variety of contexts and settings. As a lecturer in HE with nearly 20 years of experience, Gemma continues to work across several universities and conservatoires within the sector. Jayne has worked as an independent dance artist, performing in the UK, America, Europe and Japan alongside teaching at Trinity Laban Conservatoire of Music and Dance, before relocating to West Sussex. We are both senior lecturers in the Dance Department at the University of Chichester, where we deliver a variety of practice-based and theoretical discourse across the undergraduate and postgraduate programmes.

In recent years, our teaching collaborations have brought to fruition a shared pursuit of better understanding our own voices within our respective practices. Further, we have a shared desire to acknowledge and celebrate the self in our own lives, as women and parents, working within HE where we continue to manage roles and responsibilities. Through conversations together, we acknowledge that as a result of managing these varied roles and the expectations that come with them, we often shelve 'the self' in our daily lives and wider practice. We acknowledge that emphasis of the self is continually prevalent within discourse where 'the focus on the self as the centre both of lived experience and of discernible meaning has become one of the—if not *the*-defining issues of modern and postmodern cultures' (Mansfield, 2000, p. 1).

In this chapter, we explore some of the thinking and theoretical frameworks that provide context for our exploration of practice and the role of

DOI: 10.4324/9781003382874-24

subjective approaches as a valid methodological approach in contributing to wider discourse. Ideas throughout the chapter are interwoven with the sharing of personal reflections and considerations as educators, researchers and practitioners on the role of individual experience in dance and how we have employed the first-person perspective in our own journeys.

Jayne draws on her experience as an independent dance artist to explore the subjective perspective of the dancer in relation to her own dance practice, through exploring the possibilities, interruptions and challenges of placing the dancer voice at the foreground. Explorations and provocations are framed with attention to the moment of dancing, dance training and performance, navigating a career in dance, and dance research. Gemma, as an educator and researcher, shares insights into her experiences, considering her own subjective positionality as a researcher, facilitating students' curiosity in dance practice through her teaching, and her thoughts on capturing the subjective experience of others in a research setting. Although the foregrounding of the first-person perspective has resonance in dance, our combined experience as professional women is supported in the field of cognitive science and education by Terry Atkinson and Guy Claxton (2000) who comment that within the professional field 'intuitive forms of knowledge and ways of knowing have tended to be ignored and under-theorised' (p. 2). We would like to start by introducing our stories in dance.

Gemma's story

My areas of interest are inspired by a personal quest to uncover what lies beneath artistic practice. My teaching and research practices fall predominantly within the fields of dance and dance medicine and science but also extends to the disciplines of music and theatre. By emphasising the subjective lens through my research and teaching practices, I celebrate the first-person voice, including those of my colleagues, students, artists and individuals. This approach allows their perspectives and experiences to inform their own practice and aligns with the perspective of Celeste Snowber (2012), who views dance as 'a place of inquiry and its generative possibilities for deeper understanding' (p. 54).

A curiosity to examine the subjective considerations of practice began during my undergraduate studies in performing arts (majoring in dance) at Middlesex University (London, UK). I had sights on wanting to pursue a career in professional dance practice, but a chronic knee injury limited such opportunities. Having then spent time employed working in various professional arts organisations and settings in a multitude of roles, I came to postgraduate study through an MSc in dance science at Trinity Laban Conservatoires of Music and Dance (London, UK). Soon after commencing my studies, I became increasingly aware of a growing desire, among educators and researchers, to seek to enhance the training practices and performance of artists. Upon further investigation into the phenomenon of performance, I noted a shared commonality across research studies that were directed towards examining specific facets of performance. Even though there is an acknowledgement that artists are fundamental to performance and that the significance of a performer's own experiences of dance performance suggests that their professional identities and activities are linked inextricably to their performances (Dunn, 1998; Hays, 2002), there is a lack of understanding concerning the performer's experiences from the performers themselves. As a result, such attention has precluded a deepened understanding of how these elements form the experience of the individual in a holistic sense.

The fields of dance and dance studies have a history of using qualitative modes of inquiry. Researchers such as Fraleigh (1991, 2004), Hanstein (1999) and Snowber (2012), among others, have contributed to the development of qualitative inquiry within these disciplines. Further, the Western body of literature in dance denotes it as having an inherently qualitative nature, predisposing it for qualitative research that focuses on individual experiences (Eisner, 1998). Attention has thus been given to the study of a dance in relation to gaining the essence of experience and as a 'unique window on human knowledge and experience' (Warbuton, 2011, p. 65).

In dance research, there is an interest in exploring the subjective experiences of individuals within the qualitative research domain. This approach has been used to investigate various aspects, including reflecting upon the processes and outcomes of phenomena; gathering the subjective narratives of dancers' experiences as a means of investigating perspectives on the 'body' (Reeve, 2011); exploring choreographic practices (Bacon & Midgelow, 2014) and the dancer's creative role in performance (Newman, 2004). In the field of dance medicine and science, research has similarly encompassed the qualitative research paradigm (Fortin, 2005). However, research within the field has largely privileged a positivist research position, which emphasises measurable outcomes and robustness of findings over subjective experiences and insights.

As a researcher, I advocate a qualitative approach to be fruitful in the understanding of practice from the viewpoint of the individual. This is echoed by Gough and Madill (2012), who note that within the research process, subjectivity offers a valuable means of illuminating the phenomenon of focus and the practicalities of the research in question. The stance of 'methodological plurality' is adopted throughout my research interests, where I have remained open to all methodological approaches and methods, without assuming that any one is more important or more valuable than the others (Chaffin & Crawford, 2007). This was evidenced in my doctoral research, concerned with investigating the phenomenon of dance and music performance through the experience of the performer. The research was informed by the ideas of Warburton, (2011) who believes that to know what dancing is requires asking dancers what they experience in terms of what is felt or thought, and how it is known, as a means of distinguishing between experiences. I sought to bridge the gap by employing a range of research methodologies as a means of acquiring a multidimensional insight into the experience of the performer.

The role of the self in subjective practice

During my undergraduate studies, I found myself intrigued by the role of the self and self-motivation in my own practice and artistic practice, more generally. This continued throughout my postgraduate and doctoral studies, where I became interested in why performances that draw on the 'self' are often the most effective, irrespective of general competence. What unfolded from the three studies which made up my doctoral research was that professional performers view themselves as embodied entities, evincing a strong sense of individuality. The idea that it is the 'individual' who is central to performance and not the 'performer', as ordinarily conceived in the literature, was a finding of particular interest and significance. This sense of 'individual' was central in the narratives of participants studied, suggesting that the embodied experience of a performance is very much dependent on the performer's ability to self-reference it in relation to themselves. It could therefore be construed that the notion of *being* a performer in relation to who they are impacts greatly upon the performers' sense of self.

My various teaching roles have prompted me to recognise the need for a clearer understanding of 'subjectivity' and 'the subjective'. Mansfield (2000) states that subjectivity refers 'to an abstract or general principle that defies our separation into distinct selves' (p. 3). His view is that the concept of the 'subject', is always linked to an idea or principle outside of itself. This perspective implies that the self is not an isolated entity, but it is connected to external influences: 'One is always subject *to* or *of* something' (Mansfield, 2000, p. 3). I reflect on the choice of the word 'self' instead of 'subjective' and that the 'self' might encapsulate a greater sense of being on the part of the individual.

The importance placed on the 'self' has also continued throughout my research, where I adopt the ontological stance of 'self as instrument' (Ely et al., 1991, p. 86). I further acknowledge my own subjective experience as an educator with a performing background, to be of value in my research, as with other researchers in dance (Chappell, 2006; Fortin, 2005). My research approach aligns with an interpretivist approach, which holds that the best way to understand a phenomenon is through the involvement with a human researcher. In research, I engage in a continuous process of reflection concerning my roles as researcher and my own assumptions and motives for conducting the research (Chaffin & Crawford, 2007). I reflect on how my position and interests influence the research process and how my impressions and feelings contribute to the interpretation and co-construction of knowledge (Finlay, 2002).

The qualitative paradigm is thus central to my teaching and research practices, where I aim to capture the subtleties and complexities of individual human behaviour (Robson, 1993). These approaches further allow me to place importance on studying the whole, subjective experience, and the ways in which individuals perceive, create and interpret their world. I further echo McFee's (1999) perspective on subjectivity, which can encompass a range of meanings. As noted by McFee: 'subjective might mean private or inner; it might mean idiosyncratic; it might mean biased or prejudiced; or it simply might mean personal, based on feelings or personal involvement' (p. 22). With this in mind, my research interests are centred on exploring what dancers feel, think and know about their experiences and on delving into the inner and personal aspects of dancers' subjective experiences.

Jayne's story

Attention to the moment of dancing has been at the forefront of my experience as a dancer, teacher and researcher for as long as I can recall. I remember my first dance experience, in the school hall, aged five or six, dancing to *Music and Movement*, part of BBC Radio's primary school series. I remember the moment as a very happy and fulfilling one and, on reflection, as a moment of feeling truly connected to self, and fully immersed in the activity. The experience itself, the act of moving creatively, and my individual response was at the foreground. This singular moment at such a formative age, triggered a passion for moving to music that propelled me towards dance at every opportunity: ballroom dancing lessons; after school dance clubs; 'O' and 'A' Level dance studies; a degree in dance; and finally, pursuing it as a career.

I have managed to recapture this experience on a few occasions. It is an experience that always resonates deeply with me as an individual, whether it be in a performance, educational, community or social dance context. In these captured moments I have felt at one with the experience, the dance, with others and myself. On each occasion this experience has generated an increased awareness of self that author Kae Tempest considers to be an outcome of being fully engaged in creative activity (Tempest, 2020). These 'moments' are often fleeting, and are characterised by a synthesis of movement, physical skill and artistic expression, with the dancer at the centre. This experience aligns to the notion that the foregrounding of the first-person perspective, the qualitative experience, has prevalence in dance, wherein thought, action, body and mind are interrelated in the exchange between thinking and moving (Fraleigh, 2004).

In the practice of dancing, the subjective voice is continually interrupted in the discipline of dance. Here, the act of doing and the dance experience, the meeting of body-mind and the movement itself, is not always easy or fluid. Historically, the quest for control, strength, flexibility and skill acquisition promotes a power ratio of mind over matter, a tendency towards didactic methods (teacher says, dancer does). Dance training requires the dancer to bring self to meet, assimilate and interpret given material or guided instruction offered by the teacher, in a drawing together of the internal dancer body-mind and externally imposed movement content. In the context of the dance technique class, the dialogue between these two elements, the subject/dancer and the object/dance, begins in the exchange between teacher (source of the material) and student (recipient of the material) and ends in an internal body-mind dialogue as the dancer digests and interprets within their own dancing body. In my own dance training, this dialogue has most notably been one sided, in the bid to achieve mastery of movement. An overwhelming desire to 'get it right' has been the dominant presence in this pedagogical process. While the self was always actively present in my dancing body, felt in the body-mind dialogue and focused attention to the act of dancing, it was often at service to the technical phrase or choreographed work, the material offered by teacher to student, choreographer to dancer.

The dancer's ability to commit to object (shaping the material body into the required movement), over subject (an interwoven experience of body-mind-self), is seen as paramount to becoming a good dancer, where the drive to take control over the body has hierarchy over connecting with the body (Jameson, 2016). In a widening field where training practices no longer align to individual choreographic styles, the demand for versatility in the dancer has prompted a desire to develop the 'dancer-self' (Bales & Nettl-Fiol, 2008, p. x.), with an increased focus on nurturing individuality. This view considers dance as a journey of discovery, where the performer's experience is regarded over the interaction with (or presentation for) an audience. This experience is concerned with the dancer drawing upon their inherent ability to create the 'dancer-self' and where the dancer is at the centre of their own artistic practice. And in recent years, professional contemporary dancers have increasingly incorporated somatic movement methods into dance training practices in a bid to connect more deeply with their own dancing body (Bales, 2008).

Following undergraduate dance study at The Laban Centre for Movement and Dance (1987–1991), I pursued a career as a dancer, performing in small- to middle-scale contemporary and commercial dance work, and in opera. This did not always go smoothly, and it was often challenging, but I enjoyed performing and the desire to perform propelled me on. This career pathway required continual self-reflection, self-analysis and self-judgement in the bid to be better: stronger, more flexible, creative and expressive in audition and performance contexts.

The influence of the first-person perspective on an individual's own dance journey (Fortin et al., 2002), highlights the wider subjective lens the dancer navigates in terms of creating and steering a career. The challenge of sustaining a career in dance is fraught with difficulty where work opportunities are limited, contracts short and dancers many. The emergence of the portfolio career has allowed dancers to engage in the field in a wider sense, beyond the parameters of work as a performer. For me, this resulted in opportunities to teach in HE that continue to be a large part of my working life. The different facets of my dancer/performer/teacher-self have been co-created on this work-life journey, entwined with the shifting sense of myself as a female, dancer and mother. This has also required a continual process of self-reflection and this journey continues to prompt questions surrounding the challenge of trusting and foregrounding individual experience, even prior to understanding and articulating it.

Research undertaken while working in HE has enabled time and space to explore new and growing interests in the dancing body, experiential anatomy and dance training. Explorations into the material body and the fascia, part of the body's connective tissue system, have prompted a willingness to further understand and articulate my dance experience, foregrounding the tacit knowledge that I may know innately, but struggle to unravel in my own mind and to convey in words. In my current practice, research into fascia offers avenues of exploration into the materiality of the body and its ability to sense, feel and shape, accumulating our physical history and experiences into corporeality. I began, and I continue this research journey with many questions about my own dance practice, most notably a desire to understand, rediscover and expand it.

With a movement focus that is no longer performative in outcome, my stance as a dancer researcher moves to one of foregrounding my subjective experience with a view to understanding and articulating my own dance practice. In this sense, I find myself returning to 'the moment', navigating a relationship with dance that has taken me full circle, with time spent in studio-based explorations that have allowed for embodied reflection. In the search for my dancer voice, I have been drawn to other dancer voices in the literature, both poetic and philosophical (Bales, 2008; Fraleigh 1987, 2004; Laban, 1984; Wigman, 1975), and to phenomenological fields of inquiry in a bid to explore and embrace first-person perspective and the lived experience (Merleau-Ponty, 2002; Fraleigh, 1987, 2004). For MA research conducted in my mid-forties, the process of engaging in individual practice-based research for the first time was a challenging one. The Creative Articulations Process (CAP) (Bacon & Midgelow, 2014) resonated with me and became a valuable resource as a way of illuminating, guiding and documenting this process.

The means by which I validate my dance practice and experience is in my body. Drawing and relying on bodily knowledge, knowing/not knowing and articulating in/through my body feels achievable. When trying to articulate my dance experience in language, as in my recent research, it becomes an issue, and I am often lost for words. Erica Stanton highlights the special place of dance (and the arts) in articulating what cannot be expressed in words, observing that in the context of the dance technique class, '...this physical work is a journey which is accompanied by connections with thoughts, sensations and questions which are not easily labelled, or indeed receptive to articulation in language' (Rafferty & Stanton, 2017. p. 8), thus questioning the need to refer to language to authenticate the dance experience at all. Conversely, choreographer Efva Lilja considers the value of pursuing the inner movement/language discourse, creating a collaborative exchange that is mutually co-existent:

> Maybe it is futile to waste time on hypothetical questions. But somehow it helps me value words and movement I actually need and reduce the use of those that are unnecessary. Maybe it helps me rephrase the practice of thinking, talking and doing, in a process of peeling away the body's protective barriers, so that I, [...] can expose something else with dance.
>
> *(Lilja in Brown & Longley, 2018, p. 20)*

Questions surrounding the role of self within my own practice remains a focus of my research as I continue to explore ways of reflecting, documenting and articulating my experience. On this journey I continue to adopt a creative approach in the use of movement, written word, drawing and theoretical frameworks as a way of researching and documenting. This continues to be a process of experimentation, an interweaving of the methods and philosophies of others to inform, steer and frame my own explorations. In this way the work of others provides a frame of reference to stimulate, limit and guide creative explorations and illuminate findings, helping me document and articulate my experience. With the absence of the performative in my current practice, and with a focus on dance-for-self rather than dance-for-other, issues of falling self-confidence that have been observed in midlife female dancers (Lovatt, 2011) are diminished.

I remain curious about how my relationship with dance and the many facets of my dancer/teacher/researcher-self continues to shape, and be shaped by, the person that I am today. Transitioning the relationship between dancer-self from one of judging and assessing, to accepting and listening (Fraleigh, 2004) is a key feature of the changing shape of my own dance practice, a shift in perception that is supported by the phenomenological concept that 'I am my body' (Merleau-Ponty, 2002), foregrounding the first-person perspective. There may be potential then for the fields of dance, dance studies and dance medicine and science to further critical thinking in aspects relating to other ways of knowing, to the role of tacit knowledge and practitioner intuition.

Concluding thoughts

In this chapter, we have described some of the theoretical frameworks and concepts that provide a context for our own explorations of dance practice and its relationship to individual experience. We have further shared our personal journeys as educators, researchers and practitioners in the field of dance and dance medicine and science and in understanding how individual experiences play a role in them. Such reflections have further contributed to our shared desire to acknowledge the value of our identity and experiences beyond just our professional roles. Namely, it has involved acknowledging the intersection of our roles as women, parents and professionals in HE.

United in our pursuit of better understanding our own voices in our practices, we continue to be curious about how our subjective experiences can inform our teaching and research. This reflection has led us to realise the importance of accepting our voices in practice and being open to acknowledging and questioning the 'self'. These conversations share the sentiments of Warburton (2011) who believes that dancing can bring individuals into the present moment, emphasising the importance of being fully engaged in the here and now. An emphasis on the role and value of intuition and ways of knowing foregrounds intuition within decision-making and understanding in a variety of domains. Further recognising and valuing tacit knowledge may therefore be essential in the context of dance and related disciplines and there is potential for the fields of dance, dance studies and dance medicine and science to encourage critical thinking beyond the first-person perspective.

Through documenting our personal experiences in dance, we have collectively gained a deeper understanding of what constitutes our own experiences and how exploring personal perspectives has been valuable for our self-awareness and self-discovery. Our reflections have further emphasised the significance of personal embodied experiences over attributes specific to individuals' roles (for example, dancer, performer, educator, researcher). Further, we advocate that value should be placed on a personal embodied experience over solely physical attributes possessed by the individual, as a means of informing experience. We propose it is essential to view individuals as separate entities from the contexts in which they find themselves, recognising their unique experiences and perspectives, independent of external factors. This will, in turn, help individuals gain a deeper understanding of themselves and their experiences, both in the context of dance and in their personal lives. By offering the opportunity to speak openly of what is of importance to the individual, researchers and educators might productively address the components that exist within experience. This may prove particularly useful in both training and research settings, where individuals are often left feeling unempowered. Moreover, this highlights the potential benefits of this approach for personal growth, empowerment and a deeper understanding of experiences.

In this chapter, we have evidenced the ways embracing a first-person perspective can allow individuals to share their personal experiences and insights, contributing to a deeper understanding of the field. From our personal experiences within dance, we recognise a similar feeling of needing to validate our own experiences as a way of qualifying our self-worth and trying to make our experiences 'count'. With this in mind, we want to add our voices to further celebrate the role of subjective approaches as a valid methodological approach in contributing to wider discourse and in facilitating a curiosity of practice. By emphasising the value of personal experience and subjective approaches, we believe these perspectives can enrich and expand the conversation about dance, hopefully leading to a richer and more holistic understanding of the art forms.

This chapter has brought to fruition the possibilities and challenges of highlighting the subjective aspects of dance practice. We have sought to provide an initial framework for considering the self and understanding the various facets that contribute to existing dance practice. By sharing our own experiences and the challenges we have faced, we hope to encourage other practitioners to foreground their personal perspective. Moving forward, we are committed to continue this provocation through our teaching and research practices and to advocate for the recognition of personal experiences in dance and wider artistic practice.

References

Atkinson, T., & Claxton, G. (2002). *The intuitive practitioner: On the value of not always knowing what one Is doing.* Open University Press.

Bales, M., & Nettl-Fiol, R. (2008). *The body eclectic: Evolving practices in dance training.* University of Illinois Press.

Bacon, J. M., & Midgelow, V. L. (2014). Creative articulation process (CAP). *Choreographic Practices, 1,* 7–31. http://dx.doi.org/10.1386/chor.5.1.7_1

Brown, C., & Longley, A. (2018). *Undisciplining dance in nine movements and eight stumbles.* Cambridge Scholars Publishing.

Chaffin R., & Crawford, M. (2007). *Unresolved dissonance? Subjectivity in music research.* In A. Williamon, D. Edwards & L. Bartel (Eds.), *Proceedings of the International Symposium on Performance Science, 2007* (155–160.) European Association of Conservatoires. (AEC).

Chappell, K. (2006). *Creativity within late primary age dance education: Unlocking expert specialist dance teachers' conceptions and approaches* [Unpublished doctoral dissertation]. Trinity Laban Conservatoire of Music and Dance.

Dunn, R. (1998). We don't talk about it. We engage in it. In J. Morrison Brown, N. Mindlin & C. H. Woodford (Eds.), *The vision of modern dance* (2nd ed). Dance Books.

Eisner, E. W. (1998). *The enlightened eye: Qualitative inquiry and the enhancement of educational practice.* Merrill Prentice Hall.

Ely, M., Anzul, M., Friedman, T., Garner, D. & McCormack Steinmetz, A. (1991). *Doing qualitative research: Circles within circles.* Routledge.

Finlay, L. (2002). Negotiating the swamp: The opportunity and challenge of reflexivity in research practice. *Qualitative Research, 2,* 209–230.

Fortin, S. (2005). Measurable? Immeasurable? What are we looking for? In M. Hargreaves and T. Shaw (Eds) Immeasurable? The dance in dance science, *Papers from the Laban Research Conference* (pp.3–14). Trinity Laban

Fortin, S., Long, W. & Lord, M. (2002). Three voices: Researching how somatic education informs contemporary dance technique classes. *Research in Dance Education, 3*(2),155–179. https://doi.org/10.1080/1464789022000034712

Fraleigh, S. (1987). *Dance and the lived body: A descriptive aesthetics.* University of Pittsburgh Press.

Fraleigh, S. (1991). A vulnerable glance: Seeing dance through phenomenology. *Dance Research Journal, 23,* 11–16. http://dx.doi.org/10.2307/1478693

Fraleigh, S. (2004). *Dancing identity: Metaphysics in motion.* University of Pittsburgh Press.

Gough, B., & Madill, A (2012). *Subjectivity in psychological science: From problem to prospect. Psychological Methods, 17*(3). 374–384. https://doi.org/10.1037/a0029313

Hanstein, P. (1999). Introduction. In S. Horton Fraleigh and P. Hanstein (Eds.), *Researching dance: Evolving modes of inquiry.* University of Pittsburgh Press.

Hays, K. F. (2002). The enhancement of performance excellence among performing Artists. *Journal of Applied Sport Psychology, 14,* 299–312. https://doi.org/10.1080/10413200290103572

Jameson, K. M. (2016). *To be connected / To stay connected.* In J. Coogan (Ed.), *Practicing dance: A somatic orientation.* Logos Verlag Berlin.

Laban, R. (1984). A *vision of dynamic space.* Falmer.

Lilja, E. (2018). *Artists as facilitators of change.* In C. Brown & A. Longley (Eds.), *Undisciplining dance in nine movements and eight stumbles.* Cambridge Scholars Publishing.

Lovatt, P. (2001). Dance confidence, age and gender. *Science Direct: Personality and Individual Differences, 50,* 5, 668–672. http://dx.doi.org/10.1016/j.paid.2010.12.014

Mansfield, N. (2000). *Subjectivity. Theories of the self from Freud to Haraway.* New York University Press.

McFee. G. (1999). *Understanding dance.* Routledge.

Merleau-Ponty, M. (2002). *Phenomenology of perception.* Routledge.

Newman, B. (2004). *Striking a balance: Dancers talk about dancing.* Limelight Editions.

Rafferty, S., & Stanton, E. (2017). I am a teacher, and I will do what I can: Some speculations on the future of the dance technique class and its possible transformation. *Research in Dance Education,18*(2), 190–204. http://dx.doi.org/10.1080/14647893.2017.1354841

Reeve, S. (2011). *Nine ways of seeing a body.* Triarchy Press.

Robson, C. (1993). *Real world research: A resource for social scientists and practitioner researchers.* Blackwell.

Snowber, C. (2012). Dance as a way of knowing. *New Directions for Adult and Continuing Education, 134*, 53–59. http://dx.doi.org/10.1002/ace.20017

Tempest, K. (2020). *On connection.* Faber & Faber.

Warburton, E. C. (2011). Of meanings and movements: Re-languaging embodiment in dance phenomenology and cognition. *Congress on Research in Dance, Winter*, 65–83. http://dx.doi.org/10.1017/s0149767711000064

Wigman, M. (1975). The dancer. In W. Sorrell (Ed. and Trans.), *The Mary Wigman book*. Wesleyan University Press.

19

THERE'S WISDOM IN THEM BONES—MOVING BEYOND THE SHAPE

Janine Cappello

Technique and artistry

There is a depth of movement and qualitative nuance of the body that develops over time that powerful movement artists well over the age of 30 are capable of bringing to roles. These artists prove that the stereotypes and culturally motivated timelines are arbitrary and that dancers who choose to continue to perform well beyond the 'accepted' timeline of Western European dance not only bust through the ageing stereotypes but can in fact show us what is possible versus what is predicted. The type of movement quality they bring simply cannot be taught, but is earned over time in a body that has experienced pain, limitation, grief, joy, small deaths of abilities that become tiny births for a new awareness and formulation of new approaches born out of the necessity to keep going—to find a way. The wisdom in these bodies is undeniable and, if we are lucky, gives us the opportunity to watch them transform before our eyes into seasoned performers who have figured out their body's own personal longevity formulas or codes. These bodies enable audiences to experience the human body in dance in ways that are not only beautifully relatable for an older audience, but that provide a roadmap and inspiration for younger dancers themselves to keep going.

Many dance genres are rooted in cultural heritage and are passed down from dancer to dancer. For instance, Japanese Butoh or Spanish Flamenco dance artists are celebrated and considered innovators who are given recognition for being central in their genre's development.

When Ohno performed in the Stadsschouwburg, the audience was enthusiastic and treated him with respect and admiration The audience's response

DOI: 10.4324/9781003382874-25

contrasted with the way that western society usually sees and treats old people, and more specifically the way western society treats older professional dancers. In fact, in Norway where we live and work, we cannot remember having witnessed any performance with a professional 83-year old Norwegian dancer in it.

(Rustad & Engelsrud, 2022, p. 6)

There are stark contrasts to the European understanding of age and dance, especially as it is manifested in the world of ballet. 'In Japan, dancers are not excluded from performing due to old age' (Rustad & Engelsrud, 2022, p. 6). It is often the older dancers of a specific culture or company who possess the knowledge about traditions, having carried them down from their own teachers. By continuing to perform, even as they age, these dancers contribute to and continue to help preserve their own heritage. These seasoned powerhouses challenge societal norms of ageing, beauty and capability, offering more diverse and inclusive perspectives on performance.

Often after years of trial and error, older dancers have figured out how to tap into the resources of their own bodies via a specific daily practice, individual nutrition and effective, personalised warm-up routines, patiently developed over time. Many older dancers across the world are setting a new standard in dance, and are creating avenues of acceptance boldly fought for, and firmly held, thus paving the way for a new generation of dancers to come, who might enjoy longer careers, and perhaps not become an afterthought once a certain birthday milestone is achieved.

Age and ageing

There are many definitions of the term 'ageing' available that include defining a life stage, a time in history or a process of slow and steady decline. For the purposes of this chapter, the following working definition of ageing will be utilised: the process of becoming older, a process that is genetically determined and environmentally modulated (Hamerman, 1997). The following terms will also be used: dancer, dancer-athlete (Koutedakis, 2004), collagen (Zioupos, et.al. 1999), younger (under the age of 35), older (over the age of 35), considering hormonal changes documented in the literature. The terms dancer and dancer-athlete will be used interchangeably and unless otherwise stated, in relation to Western European dance forms.

The dancer-athlete is susceptible to similar wear and tear on the body as an athlete who participates in sport and dancers, potentially suffering from repetitive motion strains, sprains, ruptures and even concussions (Koutedakis, 2004). Perhaps the greatest threat to both dancers and athletes, is the impact that the process of ageing has on both hard and soft tissues of the human body. Ageing affects ligaments, tendons and bones in specific ways that are parallel but independent (Held, 2002). Dancers know their bodies and often intuit what is happening to them and dancer-athletes are actively seeking out new technologies and fitness/conditioning techniques that may help delay, or at least sufficiently cope with the ageing process. Often, it's the older dancer who can provide the most insightful information on this process through sufficiently lived experience.

The required aesthetic of each individual genre presents specific challenges for dancers existing within that genre. When looking at the different body regions that dancers rely on to maintain the required aesthetic in their various genres, the literature on ageing, as referenced throughout this chapter, points specifically to: articular cartilage, ageing and flexibility/range of motion (ROM), the ageing of specific spinal regions (cervical, thoracic, lumbar), special considerations of the ageing athlete, ageing and osteoarthritis, ageing and muscle strength, bone and ageing, and the role of collagen in ageing and ROM. Collagenous structural changes, regardless of type, cause degenerative effects in the mechanical properties of bone, tendons, ligaments and cartilage (Held, 2002). The process of glycation on collagen can be particularly damaging and will be discussed later in the chapter (Zioupos et al.,1999). Dancer-athletes may experience these age-related changes in various ways depending on age, activity level and genetic disposition with the major commonality being compromised biomechanics and loss of range of motion to some degree (Koutedakis, 2004).

Challenging social, cultural and industry expectations

Dancers work in a community permeated by a culture of 'youthful ageing', which can be more pervasive in some cultures while not so in others. In the world of dance, as in many athletic sports, a 30-year old may be perceived as 'old', and ageism continues to exist in the field to varying degrees. Even young dancers who experience injuries may feel threatened that they are losing precious time out of their short careers (Wainwright & Turner, 2006). It is also not uncommon for dancers to hide an injury or downplay body pain in order to retain a role, or continued status in a dance company. This selective downgrading of an injury out of fear of losing roles and therefore income or being perceived as injury prone, can delay a dancer's progression up to soloist status and perpetuates the idea that dancers need to be indestructible. It creates a culture of fear and, as a dancer grows up in this culture, normalises unsafe practices that delegitimise the very essence of why a dancing body is so beautiful—it reflects humanity. Seasoned dancers know this game all too well and have existed within this structure, carrying with them ways of knowing and ways of coping that could be considered, over time and practice, like mined gold. Speaking from personal experience of observing and speaking with colleagues of many ages, over many years, what can also be said for more seasoned dancers is that they possess a body knowledge that is enviable to younger dancers. Seasoned dancers possess a deep understanding and connection to their own physiology that takes years, often decades, to develop.

Whether the ritual of the dance class begins at the ballet barre or standing or sitting in the centre of the studio, the dancer-athlete subjects their body to countless hours of classes repeating over and over the basic movements that are the foundation of every ballet dancer's training. The repetition ultimately creates a strong artist and athlete who performs effortlessly on stage, leaving audiences stunned at the height of jumps, the incredible control of a single *relevé* or the seemingly inhuman degree of range of motion of a *penché* which moves effortlessly to a position that dancers call 'six o'clock', or a full 180-degree extension of the gesture leg (Quin et al., 2015).

Dancers connect deeply with the instruments that are their bodies and, over time, this body knowledge becomes layered and nuanced, as each individual overcomes specific limitations, learns to highlight individual gifts and competencies, and draws upon year after year of invaluable experience that only full-body participation over time can develop. The following image (Figure 19.1) demonstrates this body knowledge as one can see the dancer on the bottom (aged 21) making the classical ballet pose *first arabesque*. What may be observed at a glance is that this dancer's range of motion is larger, and seemingly more effortless than the dancer (aged 32) on the top. While comparison isn't the entire point and visual observation limiting, a closer reading of the images may hint that the dancer on the top appears to be firing her stabiliser muscles in her abdomen, standing leg and spine, has weight more efficiently placed on her standing leg and, although is not achieving a comparable range of motion in the gesture leg to her counterpart, is relying on her decades of body knowledge to stabilise her body in this position. Accepting these limitations in range of motion while appreciating the nuanced way the dancer in the top image is holding this shape seems like a more common mindset in recent years and one that perhaps offers hope to dancers who can provide more qualitative nuance than ROM.

Appreciating the qualitative nuances that more seasoned dancers can bring seems more like a social movement making its way through dance; one that is long overdue, although still insufficient in its scope and reach. Alongside changing social thinking, perhaps the dance community at large is moving toward a wider and more unquestioning acceptance of the ageless ageing dancing body, or perhaps an acceptance of ageing in general. Is it then time to discuss the value of lived experience and how that relates to developing artistry? With lived experience comes a deeper understanding of artistry and an increased ability to bring emotional depth to a performance. Older dancers can enhance a performance with lived experience, bringing layers of compelling depth to a role that a dancer with less experience may not yet be able to offer.

FIGURE 19.1 Dancer aged 21 in first arabesque and dancer aged 32 in first arabesque. Copyright J. Cappello

Without a doubt the perception of ageing dancers varies from culture to culture., Rustad & Engelsrud state:

> One of our findings from the analysis of the literature is that young dancers from western European countries and the U.S. are concerned with age throughout their entire career, while in dance practices in Japan, being an older dancer is regarded as a value that gives flavor and energy to both to ageing and dance in a shared interaffective and mutual space.
>
> *(Rustad & Engelsrud, 2022, p.1)*

The authors describe themselves as being older, white, Norwegian dancing women and dance researchers—they state;

> and one of us a professional dancer—we (the authors) have personal experience with the ways people understand the relationship between dance and ageing. We frequently get questions and comments such as "Are you still dancing?" "But you don't look that old," and "Are your hips still functioning?"
>
> *(Rustad & Engelsrud, 2022, p. 2)*

The assumption of others seems to be that as age begins to limit their movement performance, professional dancers should retire. Further, that performance as a category implies a specific physical function apart from one's own feeling, kinaesthetic awareness and present energy. 'When exposed to the comments we often feel "stuck" within conventional categories and language which, in the situation, can be difficult to respond to' (Rustad & Engelsrud, 2022, p. 2).

Indeed, when the abilities of the physical body fall short of the heart's desire to move 'as one used to', perhaps dancers themselves could benefit from getting 'unstuck' in their own thinking about what is valuable and meaningful to them in a new stage of life and career. Eschewing the idea that one's only value lies in what one can bring to an audience with an expectation of a youthful performance, perhaps there is more value in creating performing spaces for the more seasoned ballet dancer who can bring their wealth of body knowledge and experience to new audiences.

Alessandra Ferri is an outstanding representative of a healthy ageing mindset in Classical ballet. Born in Milan in 1963, Alessandra Ferri was a principal with the Royal Ballet aged 19, and two years later was invited by Mikhail Baryshnikov to join the American Ballet Theatre. She retired in 2007, returning again in 2013. Ferri is now in the rare position of being a leading dancer performing internationally at the age of nearly 60. In an interview with *The Guardian*, Ferri shares:

> [T]his whole 10 years of afterlife has surprised me. I didn't plan it and I still don't know what I'm going to do even six months from now. I do class every day, but I don't know for how long. I have to for the next couple of months, I have no choice, because I am performing. And then I'll see. For the first time since I returned to dancing, I took five weeks off this summer. I was like: if I can't get back, I won't, but I need to have this break. It took me three months to get back into shape.
>
> *(Ferri cited in Crompton, 2023, para 2)*

Ferri continues and elaborates about her perspective on ageing:

> Even more now. It's really nice. I think there are phases in ageing, for a woman anyway. When you start getting to 45 or 50, usually that's the age where you think: I want to look younger. And then you get to a point where you're like: I don't care. This is who I am. I want to age well, because you want to look your best at any age and to feel good about yourself. But I'm turning 60, so leave me alone. I will look my best for me. You are who you are at 60, and you really embrace it.
>
> *(Ferri cited in Crompton, 2023, para 9)*

Ferri has given audiences the rare opportunity to witness her ageing, and to see the evolution of the body as it exists through the medium of dance. She also offers audiences over the age of 40 an opportunity to identify with her. Often, the young bodies on stage can reinforce the Western cultural mismatch between older people and dance. Ferri can provide a much-needed role model to younger dancers in Western European dance forms because these dancers have few who can outline long career paths in performance that point to the future (Rustad & Engelsrud, 2022). What this means for older but active dancers is a continued opportunity to practise or perform within the classical ballet canon beyond the imposed ceiling of 30 or 40 years of age, as well as an incentive to act as ambassadors against ageist readings of bodies.

Ferri's experience with her own process of rest, recovery and ramp-up to performance-ready standard, highlights the need for dancers to develop their own routines for self-care. How can dancers care for their bodies with career longevity and healthy ageing in mind? Extrinsic and intrinsic factors affect healthy ageing and hormone balance on a physiological and psychological level. Factors such as genetics, family history of diabetes, heart disease and high blood pressure are intrinsic, but can be modulated by nutrition and exercise (Menard, 1989).

Hormones, collagen and dancers' health

Extrinsic factors affecting career longevity are linked to behaviours like smoking, stress management, overtraining and insufficient caloric intake (Keay, 2022). Hormonally speaking, in her book *Hormones Health and Human Potential*, specifically in her chapter entitled 'Balancing Act', Dr Nicky Keay states;

> [B]alancing exercise, nutrition and recovery optimises hormonal health. Conversely, imbalances in these behaviours can compromise hormone health. Hormone dysfunction can arise as a result of mistiming between

external behaviours and internal biological clocks: circadian misalignment. This mistiming, together with a sedentary lifestyle, can lead to metabolic syndrome. Although exercise is beneficial for hormone health, too much of a good thing can be problematic. Exercise, with insufficient recovery time, can lead to maladaptation over different time scales from shorter-term non-functional overreaching (NFOR) to overtraining syndrome (OTS) in the longer term. Psychological dependence on exercise can have adverse health effects.

(Keay, 2022, p. 148)

Keay provides an excellent focus on the importance of balancing training load, recovery and nutrition. The nutrition piece for dancer-athletes is particularly important because, even when exercise and recovery are matched, inadequate nutrition can impact hormones and impair the positive adaptive responses to exercise in the long term. When food intake is insufficient to meet the demands of exercise and health, hormonal dysfunction can ensue. Often for dancers, trying to meet a specific aesthetic means insufficient daily caloric intake leading to disordered eating, which leads to hormonal dysfunction, therefore affecting ageing.

We can utilise studies on ageing collagen to learn more about joint health and ROM. No conversation about ageing collagen is complete without first addressing the concept of glycation. Collagen, the most abundant protein in mammals, is present in its different types throughout the body in both hard and soft tissues. The collagen superfamily comprises 28 members numbered with Roman numerals in vertebrates (I–XXVIII). The collagens most commonly associated with ROM are types I, II and III. Understanding how collagen glycates is important information in connecting lifestyle and nutrition with improvement in collagen health and therefore healthier ageing. This glycation leaves collagen 'cross-linked' or damaged and dysfunctional. In turn, this dysfunction presents as limited ROM, joint pain and overall stiffness (Zioupos, et al., 1999).

Glycation is the bonding of a sugar molecule to a protein or lipid. Advanced glycation end products (AGEs) can form both outside and inside the body and stem from this glycation reaction which can make cells stiffer, less pliable and more subject to damage (cross-linking) and premature ageing. Some extrinsic factors that can increase glycation are smoking and diet. For smokers, the manufacturing process of tobacco leaves as they are dried with sugar can leave behind AGEs that are inhaled. Dietary AGEs can form during cooking at very high temperatures and also from intake of simple carbohydrates and starches that turn to sugar in the body (Ramasamy et al., 2005).

AGEs increase in the brain during normal ageing. Interestingly, experimental evidence supports the premise that AGEs are further increased in the brain in the presence of vascular or Alzheimer's dementia (Ramasamy et al., 2005). Other intrinsic factors include family history, especially one of diabetes and the relationship between diabetes, cognitive decline and Alzheimer's disease is still under active investigation. In addition, inflammatory stimuli, physical injury, bouts of intermittent (or sustained) hyperglycemia, during which AGE formation is likely a key first step in a broad array of injury settings, can generate an inflammatory scaffold in AGEd tissues (Ramasamy et al., 2005).

Recent studies, such as the randomised double-blind study by Baye et al. (2017), which considered the beneficial effect of a low AGE diet on cardiovascular risk factors and inflammatory markers in overweight individuals have suggested that diets high in AGEs, such as those exposed to high temperatures like fried foods, may accelerate the consequences of natural ageing and diabetes (Baye et al., 2017). When tested in human subjects, the reduction of inflammatory mediators was observed in human diabetic subjects consuming low-AGE food (food cooked at lower temperatures for longer periods of time). Further, the restriction of glycotoxins (sugar) was found to reduce excess levels of AGEs in human subjects with renal failure. Taken together, these observations strongly suggest that lifestyle modification, including diet, may exert potent influences on inflammation, ageing and the consequences of diabetes (Ramasamy et.al., 2005).

How do dancers effectively interpret this information? In looking at both the intrinsic and extrinsic factors, dancers could benefit from learning about their family histories as well as taking a look at possible impacts from individual environments. Lifestyles that include plenty of rest, no smoking and nutritious food, including plenty of hydrating with water and quality lean protein, may also play an important role in healthy ageing (Koutedakis, 2004).

Why is the ageing dancer important to study? What wisdom do they have to offer? It is important to remember that no matter how old a dancer is, there is something to learn from them. Whether looking at studio practices learnt in youth that stand the test of time, such as periodisation, or analysing specific practices that were possibly contributory to accelerating the ageing process, like lack of rest and overtraining, the seasoned dancer has much to offer. Every individual dancer is like an island, having had similar experiences to their dancing colleagues, but just different enough to have a poignant and lasting effect on their physical, psychological and spiritual states of being. When these individuals share and speak of their experiences, they often do so with the same melody, but with slightly different harmonies. These body stories hold memory, pain, joy, choreographic recall, wear and tear, and vibrational energy each in ways worth exploring and passing down. They are often shared during master teaching sessions where younger dancers draw knowledge in the only way dancers know how—from dancer to dancer in class, person to person. No matter where one is on a dance family tree, what can be said is that experience is the teacher, the teacher learns and shares, and the cycle continues.

In some instances, however, the knowledge transfer includes bad habits. In his article entitled Conditional vs. absolute learning, the power of uncertainty', Richard Powers states;

> How you first presented a dance has tremendous impact on how you later dance it, as well as how much you enjoy it. Many dancers believe that the best first exposure to a dance form comes from the most highly specified, detailed, technically 'correct' teaching. The teachers tell us that they are experts, that there is only one correct way to do the dance.
>
> *(Powers & Enge, 2013, p. 35)*

This may create or perpetuate the idea that dancers are never to question a teacher's pedagogical methods and leaves a dancer ill-equipped to move forward in a way that could perhaps open new avenues of understanding and therefore improvement. The idea that a more inclusive and open-minded approach to teaching, learning and knowledge could help foster a more inclusive mindset, gives dancers an opportunity to continue growing safely into their own careers, whatever that looks like for them.

Offering a more inclusive approach to ageing dancers is not only important, but necessary. The conversation can be continued by looking at some of the benefits of ageing. Zara Abrams states:

> [F]or many, getting older is rewarding—adults tend to experience more wellbeing, life satisfaction and emotional stability as they age—and a growing body of research shows that a healthy lifestyle can slow and even reverse cognitive and physical decline. But most people still hold negative views of ageing.
>
> *(Abrams, 2020, para 1)*

Diehl et al. (2020) tackle the disconnection of ageing and positivity by refuting the major misconceptions about ageing and outlining how psychologists can help reframe the conversation. Perhaps the most pervasive misconception about ageing is that growing older mainly involves loss and decline. In fact, research suggests that for most mental abilities, statistically reliable age-related decline does not occur before the age of 60, and most adults do not experience noticeable ability declines until the late 60s or early 70s (Schaie, 2013). Moreover, emotional wellbeing and life satisfaction tend to improve as we get older (Carstensen et al., 2011). Another widely held belief is that changes associated with ageing are largely outside of our control.

The new narrative on ageing should reflect that diversity, say Diehl et al. (2020) and focus on challenges and opportunities rather than loss and decline.

The ageing dancing body is important. It always will be. The older dancer brings the wisdom of experience to pass on through generations, learning from battles fought, the possibility of alternative ways of being in and with dance, and hope in their belief. We need them. We are them. Let's continue, but more robustly, to appropriately appreciate and turn to them often for their knowledge, understanding and perspectives.

References

Abrams, Z. (2020). Older adults have more control over their ageing than they think. Retrieved January 14, 2025 from https://www.apa.org/monitor/2020/10/adults-control-aging

Baye, E., de Courten, M. P., Walker, K., Ranasinha, S., Earnest, A., Forbes, J. M. & de Courten, B. (2017). Effect of dietary advanced glycation end products on inflammation and cardiovascular risks in healthy overweight adults: A randomised crossover trial. *Scientific Reports, 7*(1), 4123. https://doi.org/10.1038/s41598-017-04214-6

Carstensen, L. L., Turan, B., Scheibe, S., Ram, N., Ersner-Hershfield, H., Samanez-Larkin, G. R., Brooks, K. P. & Nesselroade, J. R. (2011). Emotional experience improves with age: Evidence based on over 10 years of experience sampling. *Psychology and Ageing, 26*(1), 21–33. https://doi.org/10.1037/a0021285

Crompton, S.(2023). Alessandra Ferri: Dancing with Nureyev. I swear he had energetic aura around him. Theguardian.com. Retrieved January 14, 2024 from https://www.theguardian.com/stage/2023/feb/26/dancer-alessandra-ferri-baryshnikov-nureyev-woolf-works-royal-ballet

Diehl, M., Smyer, M. A. & Mehrotra, C. M. (2020). Optimizing ageing: A call for a new narrative. *American Psychologist, 75*(4), 577–589. https://doi.org/10.1037/amp0000598

Hamerman D. (1997). Ageing and the musculoskeletal system. *Annals of Rheumatic Diseases, 56*(10), 578–585. https://doi.org/10.1136/ard.56.10.578

Held, G. (2002). Research into the ageing process: A survey. *North American Actuarial Journal, 6*(3), 30. https://doi.org/10.1080/10920277.2002.10596054

Keay, N. (2022). *Hormones, health and human potential.* Sequoia.

Koutedakis, Y. (2004) The dancer as performing athlete, physiological considerations, *Sports Medicine, 34*(10), 651–661, https://doi.org/10.2165/00007256-200434100-00003

Menard, D., & Stanish, W. D. (1989). The ageing athlete. *The American Journal of Sports Medicine,17*(2), 187–196. https://doi.org/10.1177/036354658901700208

Powers, R., & Enge, N. (2013). *Waltzing: A manual for dancing and living.* Redowa.

Quin, E., Rafferty, S. & Tomlinson, C. (2015). *Safe dance practice.* Human Kinetics Press.

Ramasamy, R., Vannucci, S. J., Yan, S. S., Herold, K., Yan, S. F. & Schmidt, A. M. (2005). Advanced glycation end products and RAGE: A common thread in ageing, diabetes, neurodegeneration, and inflammation. *Glycobiology, 15*(7):16R–28R. https://doi.org/10.1093/glycob/cwi053

Rustad, H., & Engelsrud G. H. (2022). Everybody can dance-except ageing professional dancers! A discussion of the construction of the ageing dancing body in four dance texts. *Front Sports Act Living, 4,* 819572. https://doi.org/10.3389/fspor.2022.819572

Schaie, K. W. (2013). *Developmental influences on adult intelligence: The Seattle longitudinal study* (2nd ed.). Oxford University Press.

Wainwright, S., & Turner, B. (2006). Just crumbling to bits? An exploration of the body, ageing, injury and career in classical dancers. *Sociology, 40*(2), 237–255. https://doi.org/10.1177/0038038506062031

Zioupos, P., Currey, J. D. & Hamer, A. J. (1999). The role of collagen in the declining mechanical properties of ageing human and cortical bone. *Journal of Biomedical materials research, 45,* 108–116. https://doi.org/10.1002/(sici)1097-4636(199905)45:2<108::aid-jbm5>3.0.co;2-a

20

THE TREES, MY PELVIS AND DANCING THROUGH A LIFE

Celeste Nazeli Snowber

Introduction

What would it mean to embrace all the seasons of one's life through dance? To honour change within the body, through the soma and senses, dancing one's way through hormonal fluctuations, pregnancy, perimenopause, decay and loss and jubilation. There are no maps for such journeys nor are there criteria within academic and artistic institutions for these movements across time. As I reflect, as a dancer, poet, scholar, woman, mother, educator, I acknowledge I could never have gotten through without dancing through each phase of life. I danced through birthing my children, premenstrual shifts, divorce, teenagers, tenure, menopause and always in the natural world. The trees, sea, paths and trails beneath my feet became my living companions. My hands opened to a choreography of chance.

> Cradle of your yearning
> inner hospitality
> guests on the earth

I partnered myself with creation to find wellness—to sustain wellness. This poetic and autobiographical chapter explores the relationship between dancing in the natural world, site-specific performance and the life cycles of a woman's journey. My pelvis and hips are drawn to trees as a place to take refuge and expand my limbs. Just as their roots spread out in a wood-wide web beneath the soil, I too have roots that do not traverse in straight lines. I am drawn to the scars, marks and incongruencies in bark, the skin of the tree, and yet have not been as kind to my own decay and changes within

DOI: 10.4324/9781003382874-26

FIGURE 20.1   Celeste Snowber dancing with tree in UBC Botanical Garden. Photo by Rebecca Heyl

my bones, skin and cells. The tree beings are teachers to me—they are the lungs of the earth; my breath expands through my torso as I move in relation to their branches, leaves and trunks. I birth my being back to myself and honour all the parts of life. I am invited to honour, cherish and accept each transition. Dance is my invitation to connect physicality with spirituality. Bodyspirit soaring, even through letting go. Sensuous knowledge becomes my guide as I dance my way into wisdom. I invite you to reflect with me how a lifelong dance process honours embodied ways of inquiry and celebrates writing from the body.

This chapter is peppered with image, poetry, haikus, video links and poetic prose—performative ways of writing which honour the soles of my feet and the soul of my life. My body is a portal to listen to the marks of the bodysoul. I attend to the nuances of the rhythm of life; my feet respond to the earth's colours, textures and the edges between the land and sea. These are riparian zones, thin places between borders which call my full-bodied attention. I am a visitor here; the land tells many stories. I listen for the stories of the trees, and I come to honour my own. Dance has taught me to respect the complexity of my own storied life. Inner and outer landscapes transform into an artistic and somatic practice which is also a spiritual practice. I participate with creation in a reciprocal relationship where I listen and respond where time slows down in moving my limbs, hips, shoulders and pelvis with the rhythms of the land.

Making sense through the senses

> What if you stepped
> into your own life
> and began to love
> back all the pages
> in your own story?

I cannot make sense of the world unless I dance. I move, fall, contract and release through each season of my life, the internal tides, fluctuations and changes. The ebb and flow of tides, weather patterns, cycles of the trees, traces of soil, sea and sky are all part of the internal and external landscape that moves me. I rarely feel I belong in the places I reside—there is a longing to find a place to root. Like trees, my roots spread and reach to places in the soil that are not visible to the eye. The elaborate fungal network beneath the soil is necessary for sustenance to the entire root system of trees in the wood-wide web. The roots of trees are in a symbiotic community in the forest which has been so astutely articulated by Suzanne Simard (2021) in the book, *Finding the Mother Tree*. The interchange between the interior and exterior are central to the growth of the natural world, and the ground from which I create. Through this interconnection the trees talk and nourish one another in this communicative network.

My lifelong journey into dance, embodied ways of knowledge began in a child's response long ago. Long before I had any dance training, dancing and breathing were my natural responses to trees. When I was about three years old, we moved to a home overlooking the Atlantic Ocean in a little peninsula town called Nahant, outside Boston, Massachusetts. My earliest memory of this place was jumping out of the green Chevy Impala and letting the ocean and crabapple tree breathe me, and pulse into my little body. I recall dancing down my street, almost as if my limbs were finally free from the confines of the city of Cambridge where we lived previously. I have been dancing ever since in a call and response to creation. It is as if I have always felt the breathing of the ground beneath me; the eros of life flowing through me, and there has been a tangible energy from earth to flesh, sea to cells, and trees to body.

Life as incantation

I talk to myself, the world and unseen dimensions by stretching out my limbs—my branches, to find home. This home is always moving—in movement I find stillness. Breath and bone come to life and sustain life. Returning and turning to what matters, and how matter shifts. So many movement words are verbs of the heart and soul in a journey of kinetic trust.

I leap, bend, bounce, stretch, crawl, turn, saunter, arch and meander into transformation. I shift from one energy to the other and my whole body becomes incantation. The root word of incantation comes from the Latin, *incantare* which literally means to enchant. I am enchanted back to the reality that awe and magic are deeply woven into the journey. Even in the most difficult times, I allow my body to contract, tilt, sway and melt; one movement becomes another. And one emotion transposes to another. I dance my grief. I dance my loss. I dance through transitions. I dance to live.

> Textures tell it all
> branch holds illuminations
> let grief be our guide

Liana dance

You curl, fold, lean, climb
and announce your presence
root as you grow
around contours of trees
vigorous and vivacious
your trunks are limbs
holding water, living water
you are a living book
twining is your way
a path that is not straight
attaching by tendrils
kiwis and hemlocks
reaching for sky
dancing one, I fall into you.

To be a dancer, one must be an athlete of the body and an athlete of the heart. How is one trained for such a vocation? The emotional terrain of one's life is not always perceived as essential to creativity as technical skills in the pursuit of artistic excellence. However, it is our lived experience which forms, informs and transforms into the material and inspiration for creativity. My own scholarly background in phenomenology and arts-based research has provided an umbrella to develop embodied ways of inquiry within the academy, so I can honour the interconnection between my scholar, artist, dancer, poet, mother and human being (Snowber, 2002, 2012, 2016, 2017, 2020). It is ironic that I did not develop embodied ways of inquiry within a dance studies program or MFA programme, but within the field of education and curriculum theory. I now see the wisdom of how I was placed in an area of scholarship where I could live in an interdisciplinary, transdisciplinary and multi-disciplinary manner for the last 30 years and focus on integrating my art and scholarship.

I have written extensively about integrating embodied ways of inquiry and it is important to note that as a dancer, scholar, poet, mother, woman I do not separate the various areas of life (Snowber, 2018). Although the scope of this chapter does not go into detail about embodied inquiry; it is important to note that bodily knowledge in all forms are the ingredients for the artistic, spiritual and physical practice necessary for creation and research creation. Like the roots of a tree, our bodily experiences and perceptions are inextricably connected and necessary to feed the artistic process.

I did not have the privilege, as a single parent of three sons, to separate my own journey as a woman and mother from my research and performance. I have come to embrace my multiple roles and let them speak to one another. Here the mundane, messiness and holy all formed into one. Everything is material for learning, growth, writing, teaching and always creating and performance. Many of the dance pieces I created over the years in raising children became part of two different full-length shows—'Woman giving birth to a red pepper'[1] and 'Perfect imperfections: The art of a messy life'.[2] I want to emphasise that my own survival and what I call *surthrival* (the place to thrive) was in dancing through all the nuances of my life. I concur with poet Mary Oliver when she speaks of poems, 'I learned that the poem was made not to just to exist, but to speak—to be company' (2016, p. 16). The creative process whether it is dancemaking or wordmaking, both inextricably connected have been my companions.

My own time limits and constraint became a place to develop over the decades, somatic practices of walking, dancing and writing. I did not have the time to commute to studios or spend hours of time writing and dancing, so I combined them into one practice. Here I found that both were somatic practices where my walking led to writing and my dancing led to speaking and then all went into poems, essays and performances that eventually found home in, articles, chapters and books. After all, I am a scholar, and publication is central to the work that I have been tasked with as a researcher and artist. But more importantly, I found that too often we write from our heads, when it is our bodies which have the gems of fresh insight and inspiration. As I move, thoughts, words and poetry emerge from breath, and blood transforms to ink. I speak these words and then I write these words, and this is what I continue to do as a practice of writing from the body. If I dance and write for even 30 minutes a day, a book emerges in a year. It is the faithfulness to the practice; seeing the somatic practice is connected to all we are and do, whether it is cooking or researching, contracting and releasing or writing and mentoring. This process changes with age, but it is also what keeps one ageless. To move is to live. To dance is to live. To live is to write.

Years ago, I said, 'I will dance till I'm 40,' then it changed to 50, 60, and now as I move beyond 60, I am still dancing full out. In the next few weeks, I will perform four one-woman site-specific performance shows in a garden where I've been artist in residence. I will always dance, even if there are limitations. Movement is the pulse and heart of my life. I am disciplined in the practices of dancing, swimming, walking and kayaking because it is in movement where I find stillness and wellness, rhythm and inspiration, and most of all, the capacity to experience life with vitality, awe and astonishment. It is not an option to dance and create; this is a necessity as Rilke says—'a poem works when it springs from necessity' (Rilke, 1984, p. 49).

Call and response

> These trees are beings
> stop and let yourself be danced
> to earth's intelligence

I am in a call and response where dance has no boundaries—neither my failing knee, inadequate jumps, nor raging hormones. I dance through it all, and will continue to throughout my aging, ecstatic, beautiful, weeping body. I dance on chairs as in this performance, The Spirituality of the Knee[3] where the chair becomes both a place of limitation and a place of grace. Here there can be philosophical truths marinated in comedy. I also dance with the support of trees, with my weak knees. Dance teaches me to respect each season, to move through each season and to know that each phase has the artistic tools to create with. So, I listen. I dance. I move. I weep. I laugh. I come back and do this all over again, moment by moment, year after year, and thus—a life that has been well-lived. These may not all be dances for audiences. They have become my way of emptying, my invitation to be a tree in my own life. Rooted. Rising. Reciprocating and cooperating with my own nature. Here I celebrate cedar tree, my pelvis and dancing through a life. My pelvis has been the subject of many performances, whether it is through comedy, dance and spoken word exploring the roll in my belly, or the power of pelvic inquiry, or leaning my pelvis onto a tree.

If my pelvis could speak

If my pelvis could say anything
it asks to see itself as cedar
grounded and extended
where plaited branches grow
from invisible roots
knowing verticality
reaches from the centre

For too long my pelvis was unstable
causing misalignment, weak knees
bone on bone, cartilage decreasing
living on the outskirts of my body

I take my pelvis to the garden
where oak, maple, blue Spanish fir
crabapple and Western cedar dwell
their roots converse beneath my feet
letting my pelvis lead, hips sway
my metatarsals on the soil
limbs are fluid and strong
in the presence of trunks, branches, leaves
my body finds room to expand

Gravity and levity become partners here
return to the rehearsal
of being flesh with the earth's voice
hear the land and belly speak
where lifeforce breathes
rustles, echoes, rumbles, moves

and I am found.

The pelvis holds so much in our bodies. My pelvis holds my intestines, pelvic girdle, womb, sex organs and supports my trunk. The trunk of my flesh, the trunk of trees is interconnected. As a dancer who leans her hips into the natural world, I continue to feel the energy moving through my pelvis to what stands tall, rooted in the ground, opening to sky. I have come to see myself as a landscape dancer. Years of walking shoreline trails near my home resulted in dancing, writing poetry and site-specific performances in botanical gardens and marine parks. I always took my body as well as my notebook, in fact, my body *is* my notebook, recording the responses of changing creation, such as the different kinds of rain which is experienced in coastal British Columbia in Canada.

The soles of my feet become a portal to listen to the nuances of the earth's heart-beat as well as my own. I listen for the stories of the trees, and I come to honour my own. Dance has taught me to respect my own complexity. I participate with creation in a reciprocal relationship where I listen and respond where time slows down in moving my limbs, hips, shoulders and pelvis with the rhythms of the land (Snowber, 2022). I yearn to know the soil, sky and sea's textures intimately, by walking or dancing daily and knowing I am not separate from the earth but intimately connected to the land. Like Nan Shepherd, the writer, I resonate to returning to a place and feeling the aliveness through my body as she says, 'I have wanted to come to the living things through the forces that created them' (2014, p. 48). There is a language that echoes the earth's pulse, and all are vowels of the flesh of the earth and the flesh of the skin.

The changing weather is as much a companion in creating and responding as the winds which formed the shoreline. I am continually in a call and response to internal and external weather, whether it is my own hormones, or climate change shifting the landscape. I have always been influenced by the weather and am moved by how the wind places shells or broken branches on the path, revealing the wonder in remnants. A driftwood tree trunk changes its location from the ebb and flow of the tide.

Weather percussion

Symphony of sea and sky
weather as percussion
its beat changing, breathing
wind on its panoply

leaves, branches, pebbles
sticks, sea lettuce and bull kelp
move in soundscapes

we are created and recreated
in this living score
voices resonant with hums
saltspray songs

under the surface of you
a glaring holiness
vibrates

transfigured in your pitch

I too am a tidal creature and each time I come upon a windswept shore, the arc of my torso shifts its relationship to place. Creation's improvisation echoes my own improvisational heart and I keep cultivating my relationship to unpredictability—the essence of improvisation. Ageing is an improvisational process, as I do not know how my body will shift, change, respond or how my blood pressure or cholesterol level may rise or fall. There is an internal weather continually moving through the interiority of our bodies. Noticing one's own internal landscape is central to the creative process. All is performance material, the canvas on which I live, change and create. We are living artworks. When we expose ourselves to the elements, whether it is the inner or outer climatological patterns, there is an attunement to being alive. This is not for the faint hearted and involves risk and the act of bravery. Yet there is no other choice but to know that it is a privilege always to create, and here lies the place of hope in dangerous times.

Vowels of the body

I am more
of the earth
than I understand.

Made of fibres
air and water
fire and dust.
all possess capacity
for great life—
      great destruction.
floods of water
      ashes of fire
my task—
      honor them all.

Seasons of creation
enter my flesh
internal tides & external rhythms
rain, mist, flames and ice

The language of the moon
vowels of the body
hear the wind through sinews
feel the light in tissues
arc your back
to being recreated.

This poem is an example of my dancing turning into a poem, and then overlaying the poem on top of my dance. This process of interchange is one which allows for my own artistic and somatic practice to shift as I age and find new forms to play in.[4] The vowels of the body are portals to live, dance, pray and create.

I come back to my own Celtic roots and remember that the Celtic way of prayer encompassed 'no separation of praying and living; praying and working flow into each other', as writer Esther de Wall (1997, p. xi), articulates. As a woman with multiple demands, my limitations of time became a way to have hospitality to everything arising in my life and know deeply creating births from living artistically. In turn, this is what I offer all my graduate students in my Embodiment classes—to cultivate hospitality to all that is flowing in life, and let this be a guide to all research, artmaking and living. Intrinsic to arts-based research methods is the connection to the personal and universal; therefore, the autobiographical becomes a way to listen to one's own life and share with others. Living and being, creating and dancing spring from necessity but become life as incantation, art as incantation.

Limitations as riparian zones

The lesson I have learned over my lifetime of dancing is that what I perceive as a limitation can become an opening, a place of grace. My lack of access to a dance studio propelled me into a lifetime practice of dancing outside. Early on, when I was told by an orthopaedic surgeon that I would not dance again because of my knee, I began to dance on chairs. Thirty-five years later I am still dancing, and many dances and articles came forth exploring the chair as a place of possibility. Now with a knee replacement, I lean more often into trees and stones as places of support. The body is a riparian zone in and of itself, always changing and morphing into something else, cells dying and being reborn.

I have always been attracted to the beauty of a bark of a tree with all its irregularities and grooves—the literal skin of the tree being a place of deep beauty and resonance. This one tree in the University of British Columbia Botanical Garden, where I was artist in residence, is a spot I always dance with—it is a *stewardia senensis* with burnt umber and burnt sienna tones, I find myself moving in and with its bark as a space of home.

We do not often celebrate our own scars, irregularities, imperfections as we do the trees, or stones on the shoreline. We marvel in geological wonders or the rings on a tree, yet when there are wrinkles on our faces, there is not a celebration. I feel it is important to defy and disrupt notions of ageing and dance into my 90s, and let the wrinkles be there in all their glory. I worked hard for them and deserve each line crossing my face which meets the sky. My invitation to others as I dance in the botanical garden with certain trees, which have many marks on their bark, or fungus in their trunks is to open the place for the audience to shift their own relationship to their bodies.[5]

Everything in creation and the natural world is dying and birthing all at the same time. I am drawn to the fallen trees that have become nurse logs. Although they have ceased living, they are a habitat for many species of mosses, ferns, young trees, birds and creatures of the day and night. The leaves fall and turn to compost for the soil, new births arrive. One of the delights of doing site-specific work is being attentive to these cycles of birth and decay in the outer landscape as well as birth and decay in the inner landscape. This is beautifully articulated by Robin Wall Kimmerer, 'There is an ancient conversation going on between moss and rock' (2003, p. 5). Through dancing I am part of this ancient conversation.

Listening and responding to the rhythm of our seasons is central to letting our pelvis find the way to each somatic nuance as a fertile place for uncovering. One uncovers the intricacies of the pulse of the earth, the pulses within where our intuition can take flight. Here is the place to live poetically, as poet, scholar Carl Leggo speaks of (Irwin et al., 2019). Dancing the lifeworld, dancing our world, and poetising is our body's knowledge. I turn blood to ink, and blood to movement. Here bridges are created from the invisible to visible and crossing all borders. Dancemaking becomes our companion to the soul.

The process of ageing can be a riparian zone—the place between, a liminal space, that is fertile for growth. The value of inner growth, ageing and wisdom are the lessons not taught in art, dance, or music school, but can be what sustains a life of artmaking, a life of dancemaking. Too often there is a limit on the best years to dance. This is one more way dancers are bound by expectations put on bodies. We do not have bodies. We are bodies, and as women who shift, change, in a multiplicity of ways, it is dance which keeps us vibrant and wide-awake. Blooming, growing and transforming continues to happen in a life, just as embodied wisdom fosters a flourishing of life's journey.

This chapter is only a glimpse of some ways my own dancing practice has nurtured a fruitful life which has not only sustained me as a whole person, but provided the food for artmaking, scholarship and teaching. Blooming will keep happening. Dying will happen. Change will happen, but I know there will be dancing in some form. I return to ask this question, how do we know when the tree will bloom and how do we know when our bodysouls will bloom?

How do we know our own blooming?

How do we know our own blooming,
the beauty in each of us?
>   as much as you gaze
>   on the magnificence of magnolia
>   robust rhododendrons

passionate paperbark maple
dove-tree & lily of the valley bush
buds are growing within you
slowly, perceptively
asking to be watered.

The soul, the body thirsts
for air and water as do
the greening in the garden.
You are a garden
a hybrid paradox of beauty
fragile tendrils lie
in the soil of your heart.

Now is the time
to let the life you lead
be the mulch
of your own ripening.

Notes

1. See https://www.youtube.com/watch?v=ic-uof4EesQ.
2. See https://www.youtube.com/watch?v=_9b8wn6Ud7M.
3. See https://www.youtube.com/watch?v=NAA1EGmdmwI.
4. See https://www.youtube.com/watch?v=UpPfMikKLfs
5. For my work in the UBC Botanical garden see https://www.youtube.com/watch?v=QRWNRIFj06o and https://www.youtube.com/watch?v=JUCN-fceXjk.

References

De Wall, E. (1997). *The Celtic way of prayer*. Doubleday/Image.

Irwin, R. L., Hasebe-Ludt, E. & Sinner, A. (Eds.). (2019). *Storying the world: The contributions of Carl Leggo on language and poetry*. Routledge.

Kimmerer, R. (2003). *Gathering moss: A natural and cultural history of mosses*. Oregon State University Press.

Oliver, M. (2016). *Upstream: Selected essays*. Penguin.

Rilke, R. M. (1984) *Letters to a young poet* (S. Mitchell, Trans.). Vintage.

Shepherd, N. (2014). *The living mountain*. Canongate.

Simard, S. (2021). *Finding the mother tree: Discovering the wisdom of the forest*. Allen Lane/Penguin.

Snowber, C. (2002). Bodydance: Fleshing soulful inquiry through improvisation. In C. Bagley & M. B. Cancienne (Eds.), *Dancing the data* (pp. 20–33). Peter Lang.

Snowber, C. (2012), Dance as a way of knowing. *New Directions for Adult and Continuing Education, 134*, 53–60. https://doi.org/10.1002/ace.20017

Snowber, C. (2014). Dancing on the breath of limbs: Embodied inquiry as a place of opening. In A. Williamson, G. Batson, S. Whatley & R. Weber (Eds.), *Dance, somatics and spiritualities: Contemporary sacred narratives* (pp. 115–130). University of Chicago Press.

Snowber, C. (2016). *Embodied inquiry: Writing, living and being through the body.* Sense. Springer

Snowber, C. (2017). Living, moving and dancing: Embodied ways of inquiry. In P. Leavy (Ed.), *Handbook of arts based research* (pp. 247–266). Guilford.

Snowber, C. (2018). Embodied inquiry in holistic education. In J. Miller, M. Binder, S.Crowell, K. Nigh & B. Novak (Eds.), *The international handbook of holistic education*. Routledge.

Snowber, C. (2020). Mystery, magic and the mundane: A dancer's journey in the liturgy of life. In A. Williamson & B. Sellers-Young (Eds.), *Spiritual herstories: Call of the soul in dance research* (pp. 414–429). Intellect.

Snowber, C. (2022). *Dance, place and poetics: Site-specific performance as a portal to knowing.* Palgrave.

21

DANCING TO LIVE

Stella Eldon

Introduction

This chapter is part case study and part love letter to EncoreEast; in 'Dancing to live' I reflect on the vitalness of dancing as an older female, subverting the question of why we dance, to why don't we all dance?

EncoreEast is a dance company of predominately female dancers aged 55–82. Throughout this chapter I will refer to us as *older*, both as dancers and people.

As a company our focus is rooted in Western contemporary dance technique, but each of us has a different lived experience of dance. We have participated in dance to varying degrees throughout our lives; however, we are not professionals returning to practise. We are choosing to learn and develop as older dancers, not to extend a career, but to begin a journey. Ours is not a well-trodden path. We have no preconceived societal end-goal or capitalist career ambition driving us on and powering our motivation. On joining EncoreEast I was surprised by the passion and commitment I experienced. So, while dancing together I watched and listened, with growing wonder, respect and love for my fellow dancers. Now as EncoreEast's resident ethnographic researcher; I have spent many hours wondering, why. Why, do 16 older adults, spend so much emotional and physical energy learning, creating and performing dance?

Research in the field of dance and ageing predominantly reflects how sociocultural elements of dance affect us as we age. As a dancer and researcher in EncoreEast, I know there are no sociocultural agendas making us want to dance. We don't do it for our health, our sanity or social interactions (although all are secondary benefits). We dance to live. It is simple in the

DOI: 10.4324/9781003382874-27

FIGURE 21.1   Wonderland, a site-specific dance by EncoreEast © Stella Eldon

phenomenal doing of it; we feel it and somatically understand why we are there, but it gets complicated in the writing of it.

I will attempt to unpack what it means to 'Dance to live'. I communicate throughout this chapter with reference to visual and moving images, to help counter Western dance studies' overreliance on written representation, which can hinder our understanding of the impact of dance (Haseman, 2006). Please, take time to witness the movement of EncoreEast[1] and let the dance weave through my words to experience the phenomenal practice of dancing as an older adult, noting our somatic journey as we discover and value our moving, sensing bodies.

When EncoreEast come together, we do so to move, connecting somatically through our lived-in physiology. Dance is never easy, and the ageing body brings with it many challenges. It forces us to engage at a deeper level, recognising our pain and weaknesses, so we can work with them to find our strength and joy. Dance is a way of being in the world and feeling of the world.

Older dancers involved in our project *Home from Home*[2] were asked to articulate why they dance. They spoke about their experience from a somatic place that intersects emotion, intellect, physicality and spirituality:

> I feel a freedom I don't find doing anything else. When I see children walking down the street then suddenly skipping, jumping, sitting down or shouting spontaneously—not consciously thinking, just doing—dancing can give me that sort of freedom...

To be in my body. To be out of my body. To carve through space. To feel...

I dance because I don't know who I am when I am not. I feel like I have connected the dots and the world is as it should be.

(EncoreEast, 2023)

Our words come from a place of wholeness, an ineffable sense of knowing without knowing why we know. The words attempt to articulate a simply 'felt' explanation for a complex phenomenon. It is a space that fascinates me, contradicting the dominant perception of why older people dance which focuses on health and wellbeing.

I encounter dance and my experiences with EncoreEast as a phenomenologist. I experience the world through my lived (embodied) presence 'in the midst of it' and my understanding comes through my experience of it (Fraleigh, 1987). I position my understanding from my perspective as a woman and a dancer over 50. I stand within this experience and notice the external narrative placed upon older dancers. I feel the weight of it. The words it uses shape all conversations; this ageist narrative is socially constructed and has become all-encompassing, and like the magician's trick, leaves people unable to see the actual phenomenon of us.

By exploring motivations behind the Western sociocultural narrative of us, I hope to reclaim the power of our narrative. By freeing it from the decline versus successful ageing debate, I offer a space to truly see us. Only then can we begin to understand what motivates us to dance and the power that has.

The view from outside in

EncoreEast engage in an ever more intensive practice that deepens our understanding of what is possible physically and emotionally with our bodies. We learn new pathways that connect us internally and externally. Through these connections we are finding ways of being that stand outside the Western polarised decline versus successful ageing narrative (Sandberg, 2013).

Discussions in the UK on older people dancing are traditionally framed, measured and funded by this narrative. Research focuses on dance's benefits to our health, wellbeing, and societal relations. Extensive studies show dance has benefits for those with Parkinson's disease and dementia (Chappell et al., 2021). It is useful in the fight against cardiorespiratory disease and as a falls-prevention programme. Dance is used to tackle social isolation and enhance the wellbeing of older adults. (Hansen et al., 2021). These are all worthy goals but do not reflect the phenomenal lived or danced experience of older adults. Current research focuses on these secondary 'outcomes' of dance as they are easier to quantify and fit Western sociocultural narratives.

Linn Sandberg suggests a need for an alternative non-binary narrative to recognise the specifics of the ageing body without negation (Sandberg, 2013). The binary framing of age places responsibility and blame with the individual. We are forced into a no-win situation of 'succeeding' to fight the ageing process until we inevitably fail. If we are 'successfully ageing' we are permitted to remain in the dialogue of youth. Western media is full of references to older people who are 'beating' the ageing process, who through their efforts are remaining young and worthy of comment. The opposite decline narrative represents a 'failure' to stay young. An idea that not quite enough effort was made resisting the frailties of age with death as the final inevitable failure of life. A narrative that when internalised means we disable ourselves with inactivity, restricting our physical presence in the world and allowing society to reduce us.

This ageist separation inherent in the decline versus successful ageing narrative is particularly problematic as it is a separation of self. It denies half of our lived experience. It creates a position of othering, where the object of our prejudice is half of who we are, manifesting an internal fear and hatred which is externalised into societal gerontophobia. It allows people to regard old age as 'other' and once we have separated ourselves from older people, we don't need to acknowledge their needs as equal to our own, calling into question ideas of care and ethics (UN, 2019).

This decline narrative also facilitates framing the ageing body outside the accepted aesthetic norm (Cruikshank, 2009). Aesthetically, Western society presents youth as the ideal of both beauty and goodness. There is political power in creating an aesthetic that excludes and marginalises sections of society. It dictates what is valued, and who is allowed to be seen. The effect of this rhetoric is two-fold for older women; it stems both from the desire by society to limit and silence us as women and as older people. For centuries Western culture has sought to create an image of the female condition, which is so encompassing that women have internalised it, enacted it and reflected it back to society (Butler, 2006). We are then further hidden from view by Western society's endless negative representation of ageing.

In dance as in most Western artistic practices age has been marginalised. Here I draw parallels to Ann Cooper-Albright's research into dance and disability. She questions how the historical aesthetic of dance is disrupted by the disabled body. All dancers are connotated by 'the role of dancer…historically reserved for the glorification of an ideal body' (Cooper-Albright, 2017).

Art plays an important role in what is perceived as aesthetically and ethically relevant (Gadamer, 1960). Art and aesthetics help society change its relationship with itself. As dance is sited in the body, it offers the opportunity to challenge stereotypes. Bodies seen dancing can impact the experienced aesthetic. The aesthetic of the older body dancing expands the experience of dance, both as it is 'formed and performed' (Sheets-Johnstone, 2015).

It challenges stereotypes and through positive representation could affect society's relationship with its ageing-self.

There seem to be many good reasons to explore the motivations of older dancers to move and be moved by dance. How it could provide an insight into what Sandberg's 'alternative ageing' might look like and a blueprint to change the perception of what it means to be old. Yet there seems to be a form of societal blindness to us; a resistance to acknowledging the importance of this research. Sociocultural research limited to 'outcomes' ignores the complete phenomenal experience of dancing. This results in an over-simplification of our motivation to dance, as well as negating the aesthetic experience of witnessing older people dancing.

Looked at through the combined lens of ageism and feminism, we can begin to understand society's resistance to acknowledging the aesthetic value of older female dancers. Within this biopolitical framework, society needs to contain and curtail who can be seen and subsequently who can be valued (Foucault, 1978). I am referencing biopolitics not sited in an external, controlling authoritative power, but through 'the collective biopolitical power' we are all complicit in. Michael Hardt and Antonio Negri describe how we are all invested in maintaining the status quo to some degree. Through social constructionism, we establish an understanding of our world not based on our physical experience of it, but on our collective consensus (Hardt & Negri, 2000). So, first we 'other' half the population disempowering them for being female and then we 'other' half ourselves for getting old. The prejudice created establishes a power system that has been internalised over generations, a status quo that feels dangerous to disrupt. A power system which supports and is supported by Western capitalist society.

What difference can dance make, and why does it matter that a group of older women choose to meet collectively and push ourselves to be better dancers? It matters because it enables us to witness a chink in society's version of reality and this chink makes visible the possibilities in Hardt & Negri's collective biopolitical power. We are all participants in that collective and we all hold that power. By acknowledging our place and power in the collective whole, we begin to sense ourselves in the midst of Petra Kuppers' revolution,

> ...a creeping uncertain thing, there is neither decisiveness nor energetic push, but it is a limping thing, ducking under the hail of capital.
>
> *(Kuppers, 2017, p.107)*

Over recent years across all dance genres, there has been a slow trickle of interest in a small but growing number of older predominately female dancers, performing as either solo artists or as singularities within companies. Artists like Emilyn Claid, Liz Aggiss and Alessandra Ferriand[3] are often positioned as anti-establishment figures celebrating their unique talent and individualism. Within this positioning I sense a dichotic judgement occurring for other older female dancers. This divide seems to state that we can allow and appreciate this individual's performance precisely because they are 'different '. Their uniqueness places them on the outside, and this separation ceases to make them a threat. There is a sense they are exotic, non-representative, so there is a pleasure in witnessing their journey.

This rhetoric is often voiced when people encounter EncoreEast; they comment on our uniqueness and how we disrupt the established dialogue of age. This language of separation hinders research into the narrative of us. If we are a tiny minority, a non-representative group, then how can we be relevant to wider society. Conversely, my research of current practice means I encounter ever growing numbers of older dancers. Every area in the UK that has a Dancehouse,[4] also has a company of older dancers. My research led me to connect to companies from Australia to Canada, Chile to Singapore—a global phenomenon of predominately female, vital, dynamic, agentic dancers, all reclaiming their space and rewriting their story of ageing.

Society's lack of interest has a negative impact making it difficult to join up research both practical and theoretical. Without this coming together and furthering of ideas, we will all keep being 'unique' and 'not the norm', subsequently unworthy of attention. Paradoxically society's blindness to us also offers us a smokescreen, a space to play and develop, slipping under the pre-judging focus of society's male-gaze. If we don't matter to society, then we are free to discover our own way of moving and being seen. It gives us time to find out who we are, not in a thinking conclusive way, but in a developing, growing, shifting, dynamic, dancing way.

The view from inside out

Dance in Western culture is often regarded in two halves; the dancer (doing) and the dance (viewing/seeing) as if it is possible to have one without the other. By looking at the whole experience of dancing and framing it phenomenologically, I draw on Maxine Sheets-Johnstone's assertion;

> Dance is not only a kinetic phenomenon which appears, which gives itself to consciousness; it is also a living, vital human experience as both a formed and performed art.
>
> *(Sheets-Johnstone, 2015, pp. 22–23)*

Through this phenomenal perspective we begin to understand the vital experience of dancing and being seen to dance as older dancers. Like all things associated to dance we don't arrive at this understanding through thinking, reading and writing. We begin by doing, sensing, feeling, reflecting and doing again. Later we begin to see, recognise, mirror and develop. Everything is within the doing of dancing which brings me to the dichotomy of the question 'who is able to dance?' (Nakajima & Brandsetter, 2017). The key word in this question is *able* with its dual meaning of *permitted to* and *capable of*.

Through this chapter I have considered how society disables us as older dancers by its denial in recognising us phenomenally. Western society's internalisation of this suppression means, as we age, we begin to disengage with movement becoming steadily more sedentary. This process is cyclical; we restrict movement which in turn means we become incapable of moving. Dance becomes something we are only *able* to do (permitted and capable of doing) when we are young, fit and able-bodied. The journey then from non-dancer to dancer is also a journey of inhibition to self-permission. Granting ourselves permission to think of ourselves as dancers is crucial to the process. It allows us to engage fully in movement practice, through which we begin a learning journey. Somatically we start to understand the connections, strengths and weaknesses that trace through our bodies.

EncoreEast began our somatic journey during our research project *Focus*[5] with Russell Maliphant Dance Company (RMDC, 2021). Maliphant's somatic technique focuses on the whole experience of dance. As noted in our research 'he demonstrates the possibility of focusing attention and joining mind, body, emotion and spirit in the movement and moment of creativity' (Farmer et al., 2022). Maliphant's work is informed by Susan Klein's assertation that somatic practice is:

> a profoundly deep level of understanding the full use of the body as an integral whole to maximize full function of each individual's unique movement potential.
>
> *(Klein, n.d.)*

Through *Focus* we began an embodied, shared somatic practice to uncover a journey of awareness from inside to out. We learnt to locate each isolated action and reaction which enabled us to begin to connect to our full movement range. Through our somatic exploration we understand that although we share similarities in anatomy, each of us is unique; we are born unique and our journey through life leaves traces which affect our phenomenal whole. Through our practice we learn to trace our own movement flow and connections within ourselves. When we encounter blockages and resistance, we know they are remnants of the stories of our lives. Some blockages are externally imposed through our socio-political environment, and some internally created through our lived and learnt experiences.

Through this embodied practice we are exploring the possibilities of us. Ben Spatz states that 'embodied practice is structured by knowledge in the form of technique'. They approach embodiment not as an absolute but 'as

a field of variation' (Spatz, 2015, p. 43). These variations exist not only between us as differing individuals with distinctive anatomical structures and
genetic possibilities, but also within us; as time, experience and life transform
the bodies we live in. Through our exploration we acknowledge and respect
these variations finding pathways that suit the bodies we live in now. Each
stoop, each imbalance, each weakness reflects part of the uniqueness of the
life we live; all the joys and the tragedies are painted into our physical and
emotional being. It is possible the older we are the more intense this personal
internal somatic journey.

What of the other side of the Western dance divide 'viewing and seeing',
why does it matter that older female dancers are seen dancing? Historically
Western dance idealises the perfect human form as, young, fit, strong and
graceful. Its historical roots are embedded in the control of the female body;
how it moves, what is permitted to be seen and who is able to dance, are all
symptoms of patriarchal control and power. Control which is perpetuated as
women assimilate it into our internalised view and constructed projection of
ourselves (De Beauvoir, 2015).

Contemporary dance pushes against the boundaries of this 'perfect' expected aesthetic, but does it ever truly disrupt it. Like dancers with disability,
older dancers only become visible when we 'transcend' what is perceived
as possible for the ageing body in dance (Cooper-Albright, 2017). When
we dance, 'what is at stake... is not merely the definition of dance but the
larger (metaphysical) structure of dance as a meaningful representation'
(Cooper-Albright, 2017, p. 65).

It may seem paradoxical that I am arguing for the importance of dance
for older women, while understanding within the context of Western cultural dance, we work in a system that historically restricts and controls the
female form. The legacy of this control is still felt and witnessed within the
dance-world today. Many Western dance techniques teach us to embody an
aesthetic that best reflects the qualities of the given discipline and its sociocultural environment. Dancers work hard to master external aesthetics, which
are placed on malleable often passive bodies.

To understand this paradox, we need to return to our experience of dance,
the actual doing of it. While dancing, EncoreEast experience both an individual freedom and a sense of complete connection with ourselves, each other
and our environment. We catch glimpses of the humanising experience of this
full sense of completion. The experience inside the 'doing' doesn't reflect the
external socially constructed limits of dance.

Somatic practices offer us the possibility to negate the legacy of dance's
external systems of control. I acknowledge the complicated duplicity of
Doran Georges' assertation that Western contemporary dance's alignment
of somatic techniques with the natural body is focused through a Eurocentric specific white, able-bodied (*young*) lens of canonised art movements

(George & Foster, 2020) and consider the complexities of the relationship of EncoreEast with somatic techniques more broadly. EncoreEast developed our somatic journey through RMDC's practice. Maliphant's exploration of the somatic being driven by personal injury, led him to explore what is possible for each individual body as it exists physically in space and time.

Our journey began with slow focused inward attention; we found ways to recognise and engage with our phenomenal bodies, acknowledging their limitations and their possibilities. Within our practice we are not trying to negate weaknesses but find movement that negotiates and lives with our bodies' story. By striving to somatically trace our unique movement signature, we create an internal aesthetic strength. One that stands in opposition to external control and represents all of who we are, now in this lived moment.

For older dancers there is something important in the development of a practice that enhances life. A practice is not undertaken to reach a conclusion; it is repeated, adjusted and performed and then repeated again. Its eternal loop provides an antidote to Western society's expectation of age as a destination. It challenges the assumption that we are willing to settle, to live a life without aim or expectation. It creates a space for being in the here and now, fully present in the lives we are choosing to live.

Within EncoreEast I encounter our shared practice and open attitude which allow us to feel seen and noticed. We support each other to be both defiantly individual and joyously part of a shared collective conscience. The security this affords us establishes an arena where we feel able to take risks, both as dancers and women. Through risk-taking, we step outside ourselves and our experience and bring forth the possibility of being wholly with others (Gadamer, 1960). Through this idea of finding space to be 'wholly with someone else', we ethically understand how our actions affect the other. We learn to see and be seen, recognising our similarities and respecting our differences, which in turn lead us to a collective consciousness.

Collective conscious is a set of shared beliefs and moral attitudes that can enable unification in societies. It allows us to hold space for each other, sharing our strengths and supporting our weaknesses. Understanding doesn't mean EncoreEast always agree with each other, just that we know we are seen, recognised and understood. I align our collective conscious to anarchy and Colin Ward's belief in the power of 'a self-organising' society (Ward, 1996). Anarchy according to Ward is the shared social responsibility within society. It is not being ungoverned but to govern ourselves by the collective values we share. I see this reflected in EncoreEast. We live conceptually as anarchists, as it becomes increasingly harder to recognise ourselves within the capitalist ideals that frame Western societal rhetoric. So, we accept rules when they fit our needs, but our personal moral compass and collective conscience guide our values and actions.

The power within the possibility of EncoreEast's 'conscious collective' connects to ideals of freedom, care, kindness, cooperation, love, shared responsibility and commitment. Significantly these values are all traditionally positioned as female traits, to debate the worth of such traditional judgements is research further to this chapter. However, as a socially constructed society, we deal with the implications of these assumptions daily. As Western sociocultural, economic and political goals are driven by perceived superior male traits like independence, strength, aggression and assertiveness, Western society's labelling and positioning of these values as female, sets them in opposition to the norm. I would like to rejoice in this alignment and its effect on us as women and dancers. The values EncoreEast share are imperative, especially now in our world that seems politically to have lost its way, with its all-encompassing focus on capitalist profit, not to sustain community but as a free-floating ideology, adrift from any moral or communal values.

Where then are men in this female-centric world of older dancers I am narrating? They are not excluded; they dance with us finding their space in shared practice. Our phenomenal lived/danced experience negates the socially constructed view of us and society, and our physical experience shakes loose the collaborative consensus that holds us in the narrow confines of the societal status quo (Hardt & Negri, 2000). It is possible that dancing together gives us the opportunity to reimagine our collective social structures and who we are within them. Here is where we further catch a glimpse of Kuppers' revolution. Through collective biopolitical power, our seemingly insignificant actions of dancing together, brings into focus our lived experience, negating the accepted and expected external narrative. Again, we witness our revolution 'ducking under the hail of capital' (Kuppers, 2017, p.107).

Our positions outside the accepted aesthetic of Western dance culture creates an invisibility of us. This positioning means, in capitalist terms, our energy, motivation and drive are pointless as they can never be converted to a monetary value or capitalised on. Conversely this lack of acceptance, frees us from capitalist ambition. Anarchically, we dance anyway. Our drive and passion are focused on the phenomenal experiencing of dancing together as a collective—not what we might gain from that experience, but the moment at the nebulous of that experience.

Why don't we all dance?

Health and wellbeing are often the reason why older dance companies are created, which isn't surprising when the field is framed by research and funding from this perspective. Once established the focus quickly shifts to the phenomenal experience and what it means to dance. It is interesting to note how countries have different focuses; some working through the lens of the professional dancer and some firmly community based. While others, like

Australia are finding ways to develop, learn, create and perform combining both, Australia also proves there is no need to worry about what age is too old to dance. Eileen Kramer[6] a 108-year-old ex-professional dancer, is still choreographing work for her company of older dancers and Ripe Dance.[7] Members range from 60–101.

In Israel, Galit Liss[8] explores the aesthetic of older female dancers. Her research led her to develop a technique called *Gila* (meaning age, joy and discovery in Hebrew). Liss says, 'the work invites a search for personal and infinite movement, each in her own way and according to her abilities. The body becomes a "laboratory" – its own research site' (Liss, n.d.).

Connections created through dance mean I position EncoreEast not as unique but as the norm, ordinary people continuing to fully explore and experience the human condition. Through dance we learn to utilise equally all of who we are. In moments of moving together we catch glimpses of a sense of completion, being one with ourselves, each other and our environment. In these moments, we risk everything we know to be on the edge of what is possible. It is only in this space, slightly beyond what we think we know, can true creativity begin. It is not a safe space, but it is a space full of life.

Globally we are creating connections and through collaboration we are becoming more visible. Perhaps through this visibility everyone will find a space to dance and change the perception of who is *able* to dance. Any change to the accepted societal status quo takes a movement. Groups of individuals collectively choosing not to enact their expected roles. EncoreEast move, and in that movement we challenge society's expectations. Dance allows us to experience the absurdity of the decline narrative as we embody the counter argument, and the counter argument is simply life. We dance to live, life as a verb, all the doing that occurs between being born and dying and what a glorious 'doing' it is.

Notes

1. https://www.encoreeastdance.co.uk/portfolio/.
2. https://www.encoreeastdance.co.uk/portfolio/#cbp=https://www.encoreeast-dance.co.uk/portfolio/home-from-home/, Home from Home: EncoreEast's innovative project supported by the National Lottery through Arts Council England, co-commissioned by DanceEast, The Place and Norwich Theatre.
3. https://www.lizaggiss.com/current/english-channel/https://www.lizaggiss.com/, https://theplace.org.uk/events/autumn-2022-emilyn-claid-emilyn-claid-untitled, https://www.youtube.com/watch?v=W7Uk7RQu-1c.
4. Dancehouses are designed to provide space for dance participation, creation and performance. Artists and audiences can meet, dance, grow and develop https://www.ednetwork.eu/.
5. https://www.youtube.com/watch?app=desktop&v=xI8gXXpIOXE.
6. https://eileen-kramer.com/.
7. https://ripedance.com.au/.
8. https://en.galitliss.com/.

References

Butler J, (2006) *Gender trouble feminism and the subversion of identity*. Routledge

Chappell, K., Redding, E., Crickmay, U., Stancliffe, R., Jobbins, V. & Smith, S. (2021). The aesthetic, artistic and creative contributions of dance for health and wellbeing across the lifecourse: A systematic review. *International Journal of Qualitative Studies on Health and Well-being, 16*(1), 1950891. https://doi.org/10.1080/17482631.2021.1950891

Cooper-Albright, A. (2017). The perverse satisfaction of gravity. In N. Nakajima & G. Brandstetter (Eds.), *The aging body in dance: A cross-cultural perspective* (1st ed.). Routledge.

Cruikshank, M. (Ed.). (2013). *Learning to be old: Gender, culture, and aging*. Rowman & Littlefield.

De Beauvoir, S. (2015). *The second sex* (7th ed.). Vintage Classics. (Original work published in English 1952).

Farmer, C., Laws, H., Eldon, S. & Maliphant, R. (2022). Relationships between dance, health and aesthetic performance in a company of mature dancers: An exploratory study. *Journal of Dance and Somatic Practices, 14*(2), 197–216, https://doi.org/10.1386/jdsp_00084_1

Fraleigh, S. H. (1987). *Dance and the lived body: A descriptive aesthetics*. University of Pittsburgh Press.

Foucault, M. (1978). *The history of sexuality*. New York Pantheon Books.

Gadamer, H. (1960). *Truth and method* (2nd ed.). Sheed and Ward.

George, D., & Foster, S. (Ed.). (2020). *The natural body in somatic dance training* (Online ed.). Oxford Academic. https://doi.org/10.1093/oso/9780197538739.001.0001,

Hansen, P., Main, C. & Hartling, L. (2021). Dance intervention affects social connections and body appreciation among older adults in the long term despite COVID-19 social isolation: A mixed methods pilot study. *Frontiers in Psychology, 12* Retrieved January 14, 2024 from https://www.frontiersin.org/articles/10.3389/fpsyg.2021.635938

Hardt, M., & Negri, A. (2000). *Empire*. Harvard University Press.

Haseman, B. (2006). A manifesto for performative research. *Media International Australia Incorporating Culture and Policy, 118*(February), 98–106. Retrieved January 14, 2024 from https://eprints.qut.edu.au/3999/

Klein, S. (n.d.). *Klein technique TM*. Retrieved January 14, 2024 from https://www.kleintechnique.com/

Kuppers, P. (2017). Somatic politics: Community dance and aging dance In N. Nakajima & G. Brandstetter (Eds.), *The aging body in dance: A cross-cultural perspective* (1st ed.). Routledge.

Liss, G. (n.d.). *Galet Liss*. Retrieved January 14, 2024 from https://en.galitliss.com/

Nakajima, N., & Brandstetter, G. (Eds.) (2017). *The aging body in dance: A cross-cultural perspective* (1st ed.). Routledge.

Russell Maliphant Dance Company. (2021). Focus. Retrieved January 14, 2024 from https://www.russellmaliphantdancecompany.com/engage-blog/focus

Sandberg, L. (2013). Affirmative old age—the ageing body and feminist theories on difference [Special issue]. *International Journal of Ageing and Later Life, 8*(1). Ageing embodiment and the search for social change. https://doi.org/10.3384/ijal.1652-8670.12197

Sheets-Johnstone, M. (2015). *The phenomenology of dance* (5th anniversary ed.). Temple University Press.

Spatz, B. (2015). *What a body can do*. Routledge.

United Nations. (2019). We need to stand up now for the elderly. https://www.un.org/development/desa/en/news/social/international-day-of-older-persons-2019.html

Ward, C (1996). *Anarchy in action* (3rd ed.). Freedom Press.

United Nations. Retrieved February 13, 2024 from https://www.un.org/development/desa/en/news/social/international-day-of-older-persons-2019.html

22

BODY SCAPES

Celebrating seasonality of wellbeing in somatic dialoguing with the natural world

Anna Dako in collaboration with Martina Polleros

Introduction

Throughout the cycle of the year, there is a gentle shift happening in how our bodyminds operate and regulate. In my ongoing practice as an eco-somatic educator and therapist, I have been observing that the seasonality of wellbeing is naturally fostered by the changes happening in the natural world and the transformational energies that those changes are guided by (Dako, n.d., 2015, 2021, 2023a, 2023b). Every season, and every month, sends us its own inspirations and then guides the emergent clues to relate and respond to, in our inner experience of ongoing change.

In this paper, I will offer a reflective sharing of what will be a dialogical exchange built upon somatic movement sessions as inspired by cyclical changes in the natural world, as well as by the depths, rhythms and challenges of womanhood, as based on my personal practice.

Together with my collaborator, Martina Polleros, I have been offering monthly workshops called Body Scapes as an inquiry into the many essences of femininity. We have been running Body Scapes online, in the form of therapeutic sessions for women, as well as all others who identify as she/her. The sessions have been designed to inspire, explore and to support our individual journeys towards psycho-somatic wellbeing by attending to the natural rhythms as emergent somewhere between our inner bodies and the body of nature.

The sessions have been focused on voicing the reflexive thoughts on what nurtures us, what is the right pace of change and on how we can keep updating with our changing needs. The therapeutic outlook of Body Scapes was also meant to explore what seeks expression, what needs acceptance or what requires our conscious acknowledgement.

DOI: 10.4324/9781003382874-28

In gentle movement explorations, in guided dialogue with the body systems, we have been building and reflecting on our own body patterns that support the inner resilience and the sense of wellbeing inspired by the natural world. Whether it was about more rest, less emotional strain, more head space or less pressure to explore our individual body's makeup, this monthly occasion to widen our understanding on the many dimensions of eco-somatic psychology became the rhythm that Body Scapes was moving along with.

From autumn to winter, and from winter to spring, listening deeply into the essences of every month presented itself as an invitation, and the most precious inspiration to explore the cycles of 'the feminine'. Moving consciously through the year with the variety of weather spells pointed us at our individual levels of awareness about how we change. Whether it was about the cycle of a day, the monthly cycle or the season of life itself, we realised that the movement within us is ongoing, and that our health and wellbeing are strongly connected to our ability to flow with that awareness of change.

Helping our clients to grow skills in self-care and to increase their capacities for conscious change has become the essence of the monthly exchanges of Body Scapes. And for myself, as an eco-somatic facilitator, the mindful referring to the experiential intersections between seasonality and 'the feminine' has also become a reliable compass on this journey of continuous discovery while navigating between the inner and the outer worlds of experience.

In reference to my ongoing work within the field of eco-somatic therapy (Dako, 2023a, 2023b), I would here like to share the richness of our first-hand, personal experience, as female facilitators of Body Scapes. At the same time, our conversations have also grown alongside the themes that came from the experiences of the ever-changing group of participants who joined us within the first six months of the project. Building on relational connections between the seasonality of change in the natural world and the experiences of the feminine, the dialogues below will be offered in a reflective mode, covering the themes that emerged in the sessions between autumn 2022 and spring 2023.

Moving with the fallen leaves and the ever shorter days (November onto December)

Anna: We are sitting here with the colours of November. They are present in our thoughts as rich in inspiration, aren't they? At the same time, November has been the month that brought up a lot of associations with letting things go. Entering this autumn-like seasonality of seeing things go, looking at leaves departing from trees, came as a psychological challenge, I thought. And when I say it out loud here, I feel that the only way to find nourishment in letting things go, for me, corresponded to an inner agreement that

FIGURE 22.1   A mover (Anna Dako) stretched against the tree branches. Credit: Ronald Dako. Location: Kingswells, Aberdeen, 2021

FIGURE 22.2   A mover (Martina Polleros) stretched against a cairn. Credit: Delia Spatareanu. Location: Lecciore, Italy, 2019

the world was transitioning into something gentler, something of a slower, more accommodating way of being. Otherwise, the passing of the warmer months of the year, and a metaphor of letting them go, seemed to have been stirring up some anxieties.

Martina: Yes, yet to me, the essence of November time made itself known in movement full of commitment to cultivate ongoing transitions.

As movers, during our first Body Scapes session, we have been 'feeling into space' and transitioning towards the ground. And so, the diversity and richness of colours and the beauty around us felt like giving us an opportunity to feel into that rich space and to foster transitions of their energies onto the earth. Just like the leaves do, when they bring all this abundance of air-felt inspirations to the ground, November colours came then with a lot of nurturing qualities, felt in abundance of such transitional processes, from bearing fruit to bringing seeds onto the ground. And understood like that, it is not about losing anything, I felt, but about carrying on and following the earth's calling.

A: Indeed, feeling into the transitional qualities of air-to-earth dynamic has been so inspirational, and I felt it in movement as a dance of different levels of relations and a variety of spatial engagements. It could be compared to leaves swirling in the wind. Fostering acceptance in the autumn processes of transitioning can and did bring up a lot of emotion in me, when the inner self still hangs onto summer. And those emotions have also been shifting in volume, somewhere between being brought to surface and being caressed by the beauty of nature in full autumn, while heading towards the grey and the darker season.

M: That is exactly when we felt that we need to suck all this beauty in, before the winter comes, and before the darker months take over. Because we know that all this richness around is going to change.

A: In that way, embracing change and finding acceptance in letting things go came across as thinking forward. The days have been getting noticeably shorter. And just as the animals collect their food supplies for winter, we too needed to embrace what was offered before the cold set in. Feeling into those qualities in movement reminded me that it is important to find meaning in creating an immediate link between the present and the future, and to focus on embracing the creativity of change.

M: Both, trust in the future and the experience gained from the past come in, because we do not know what the winter will bring, or when the next year's spring bloom will come. For some, it may not come at all. November did remind me that celebrating death and dying is also part of the same cycle. It is another layer coming in. A layer embraced in fear and anxiety about dying. At the same time, we know, out of experience, out of the bigger life story, that nature will be reborn again, we have seen and danced with the seeds. This is what we trust.

A: The trust in stories bigger than our own does feel comforting. And, the natural world reminds us about those bigger stories. The stories, grounded in hope that life carries on, no matter what. And while we trust forward, we also experienced that time through remembering and cultivating the memories about the past.

M: The drawing that I made during our November session was also about collecting my own aliveness. It said: 'Radiating life, hello, so good to feel you'. And so, the empowerment of November came from the felt abundance of life and from remembering the power of the transitioning processes within me and around me.

A: Absolutely. We could then add that the strength of the memories became a helpful ally in transitioning forward.

M: True. I felt that heading towards lifelessness of winter is being helped by keeping the aliveness within, and I found a lot of empowerment in remembering the abundance of life when walking through a quieting landscape, and looking at the trees without leaves.

A: I also remember feeling something sensational while transitioning between November and December energies, and it was about finding nourishment in seemingly negative imagery, like bare trees and fallen leaves. I just needed to be open to appreciating different qualities of movement. After all, an activity of falling can be very joyous, and it helped me trust that whatever happens next is alright too. The journey of a leaf catching the wind and then landing gently on the ground did not feel sad to me. It was soothing in a way that its energies felt continuous, giving-in to the ground and in time, nourishing the roots. There is a lot of acceptance in the leaf's journey downwards, yielding softly towards the ground, and in trusting the earth.

M: That quality of readiness to let go was indeed in the month's offering.

A: What resonated with me was that the leaf catches both the cold and the warm blasts of late autumn winds, and I found a lot of inspiration, creativity and felt power of transitioning in its dancing *pirouettes* downwards. The leaf does not drop, really, but it dances while flying on the seasonal wind. That final flight feels inspired by its innate connectivity with the old and the new. And it has been so joyful and uplifting to be in that array of colours and movement engagements, as we felt in the movement session. At the same time, transitioning into wintertime when looking at the quality of movement of the leaves brought an image of the earth claiming all that it gave birth to back to itself, as if in an act of reclaiming or bringing it back home. To me, it was an image of leaves hugging the earth in search of warmth, and resting within the earth's embrace, while becoming the ancient earth again.

M: Finding warmth within and coming home to oneself were indeed very present in the sharing parts of our movement explorations. Movement reminded us that we create in constant relationship to others, but also ourselves. The silence of winter helped us appreciate the vibrancy of relationships instead.

A: Discovering the importance of offering ourselves a dose of self-love and feeling nurtured were indeed our follow up sensations, weren't they? I felt inclined to move backwards a lot, which reminded me about moving back to myself. At the same time, December helped us grow some additional skin layers, and thickening those layers of protection against the cold of the snow, while securing and nurturing the warmth within. Being ready to endure the cold builds on that layered-ness of relationships to self and other, while the darkness sinks slowly into that layered-ness too.

M: Sinking into that seasonal darkness and the shortness of the days, as I recall, was also brought into our movement as a relationship between moving against gravity and then letting go, giving in to the pull of the earth. So, again, nurturing awareness within relationships is what the energy of the ground revived.

A: And the nourishment from that has definitely been residing within the need for inner resting and allowing ourselves to rest and let go. Winter is the time of finding rest within the found warmth of self-care, while connecting to a bigger than our own cycles of life, the cycles of the earth, and finding nourishment in hopes for secure futures.

M: To me, being able to live that bigger cycle in our everyday life relates to looking after those transitional stages of wellbeing and to staying true to what the body really needs at different hours of the day. It is a huge lesson to learn from December, the lesson about the timeliness of different cycles in relation to our bodily needs for rest, for trust, and for remembering through belonging.

A: Minding the layered-ness of cyclical relationships is a wonderful reminder of the depths and the different rhythms of ongoing wellbeing, isn't it? In movement, wellbeing has been shaping itself as an ongoing relationship with the many living tissues of the world, that we all have to mind every single day. I came to realise that such heterogeneity of everyday experience feels very feminine.

Moving with the sun and the snow (January onto February)

A: January, and its New Year's inspirations for Body Scapes explorations. I think it was the time when we generally felt empowered by the energies of 'the new'. And it is such a cosmological event as well, isn't it? A new cycle of the earth begins and our cosmological connections, and patterns of those developing connections, felt a bit more alive too. The omni-directional capacities to breathe within and to breathe beyond our skin layers were the starting point to our movement session. In sensing, along with this new cycle, the transitional energies of moving at microlevels became more felt within their macrolevel contexts.

M: To embrace such breath, we really built from the previous months' sessions in being able to let go, to truly trust the unknown within the embodied self, flesh and bone, while being supported by the body of earth. The session you guided brought me in touch with this relational exchange of giving in and pulling away from the gravity. Legs, arms, pelvis, neck, moving into January has been full of letting go, while practicing openness to change. And that openness lets me focus on the workings of our circulatory system, letting the heart centre of the body expand onto the peripheries of the sensory experience. Thinking towards February, when the sap of the trees is already rising, January made me long for finding that lightness inside. The lightness that comes from the inner warmth of the feminine heart.

A: This dialogical movement between the gravitational pull and the push that we sank into during December helped January pick up on the importance of reaching out through the heart centre. Despite the cold, I felt that the strong sense of winter embrace as 'home-coming' grew from that rocking, and the pulsing activity of life sustained within. Feeling into the gentleness of snow through the fingertips became such a powerful experience for me. The ruthlessness of temperatures combined with the gentleness and the fragility of its textures, melting within seconds on the palm of my hand. The inspirational beauty of the snow and the sun together merged the qualitative array of being alive, in my experience.

M: Working with inspirations derived from the heart was so much about home-coming, and moving in connection to the circulatory system. It meant working with what I call an 'extended heart', while feeling the blood flow throughout the whole body. It is that warmth of the heart that resonates throughout the whole system of networks of veins and arteries, isn't it? Just like in the natural world, despite the winter cold, there is so much life going on underneath, which we normally do not see, but we can feel into, through its pulsing. All that aliveness is constantly there, just waiting for the right impulse to come to our attention.

A: Connecting the intricacies of the peripheral nervous system and the heart centre with 'sun and snow' inspirations felt very much alive in movement. The cold pushing us away towards the warm core reminded us about this inner rooting system, that in return empowers all the peripheries to be able to reach out and be curious about the cold. Sensing into the transitional energies between January and February resonated with that exchange between the warm and the cold that we constantly participate in. It reminded about regulating our body temperature, learning about our body preferences, but also about the role of movement in connecting those two extreme realities of being and living. The exchange between the circulatory system and the breathing, while the cold air, and then oxygen, is being distributed throughout the body felt very present in the ongoing complexity of that most basic, life-sustaining function of our bodies in movement. The omnipresent breath, that we tapped into in February, brought that dose of endless expansion within its own creativity, that felt awe-aspiring.

M: I remember you sharing the dimensionality of breath, and dimensionality of belonging through networks of relations alike, and feeling into the aliveness of breathing and pulsing fingertips.

A: The sensitivities of our hands and fingertips are often taken for granted. It felt important to realise that anything most minute, like a single snowflake, can provide tremendous inspirations for life and for feeling empowered just by admitting the complexity that we embody, especially us, women, always connected, under our skin, to the themes of ongoing flow, both nurturing and heart-opening.

M: February was also a lot about waiting for the right conditions to sprout. It raised a lot of questions about what wants to grow, what wants to evolve.

A: And in movement, we were working quite a bit with inbreath and outbreath as a playground for inner awareness about the depths of potential growth. Observing chaotic landscapes of inner potentiality through breath drew me a bit closer to the shadowed side of myself. Not knowing about what will sprout or how my inbreath will translate onto an outbreath resonated with that realm of unknown potentiality of change, coming or not coming. Discovering pathways of response to what the peripheries of the body picked up on added so much to this sensed melting pot of inner movement. Following the rhythms, temperature changes, sounds, heartbeat, and colours, I felt that through ongoing transformations, my body can keep evolving. It can continuously sustain this potential to shape its own identity. February reminded me about this very raw sense of self, rich in potential for change and development.

Very empowering. And every year that potential is different, which to me, speaks to the femininity itself, as the felt quality of time, full of potential for change.

M: The nonlinearity of that experience of self as ongoing creativity awaked in February did make me feel that I really needed it. I wrote about non-linearity as freeing myself from wearing any mask, as opposed to linearity that makes me brittle and stiff. During the February movement session, I also wondered about best ways to escape linearity and settle within the inner non-linearity, the playfulness and being beyond time. Femininity feels non-linear.

A: February did bring so much richness of coming into life, before the sprouting in the natural world actually happens. Creating new life felt grounded in creative chaos residing somewhere deep within.

Moving with the sounds of sprouting(March onto April)

A: March and April, such an intensive time for growth and new developments. Just after our March session, my mother's words came to me, the words about her fearing the spring as it comes with a lot of dying, and that only the strong enough can survive those months.

M: Coming into being does feel like a powerful act, like making a specific gesture. But to me, it is also simply always there. It is not about being strong or weak, feminine or masculine, but about being very simple, about being the basic quality of nature. It is just what nature does, a secret of life coming through, the very need of evolving dependent on the right conditions of light and water and the richness of soil. It is the time when the potentials of the waiting phases of our lives meet the phase of growth. In our lifetimes we all develop through stages of chaos and order. And March and April are those stages that sprout as a phase of ordering from the chaos of potentiality. And of course, all might feel vulnerable at first, but then, new sprouts gain resistance, the viral exchange of cycles, in nature and life. We all go through seasons, don't we? So again, the linearity and non-linearity continue to exchange in the creation of the inner and the outer landscapes, of our own bodies and the body of earth.

A: I think the biggest lesson learnt from our experiences of transitioning was realising that wellbeing runs in different phases, and that even in the phase of chaos there is always something to cling onto as safe, as inspiring, as nourishing and as empowering. The creative potentialities of January and February translated themselves onto visible reality in March and April, and those two months reminded us that going through phases of neglect, retreat or even deeply felt crisis were also parts of an ongoing journey of being well.

M: Development is indeed about asking yourself a question if we are strong enough to embrace the crisis, just as nature goes through the periods of non-living to be able to live again in spring.

A: To me, the most precious part of realising just that was in listening. Listening to the spring-born bird song. I felt that my spring-born movement came with a lot of new sounds that spoke directly for it, the sounds that went beyond any literal meaning of words. Listening and sharing presence in sound, takes over in spring, while life evolves ongoingly as movement. And we will continue with Body Scapes in months to come, open to discovering both the richness and the lightness of ongoing movement as inspired by the seasons in nature and life.

Conclusions and continuations

As an ongoing offering, Body Scapes has been both, a changeable and a change-loving space. The most prominent observation coming from our reflections on the work so far has been that the guidance in somatic experience of the feminine kept shaping as either inspiration, a form of nourishment or an opportunity for empowerment to change. As the project continues, our hopes are that the sessions will continue to expand on those three threads of relation to the natural world and that we will keep finding inner worth in the exchange of our experiences of womanhood in any life season.

It feels important to point out that Body Scapes sessions, guided in therapeutic movement, reminded that building, or working towards strengthening resilience has been happening through opening paths to inner awareness, and that there is this subconscious re-organisation of the body systems taking place, whenever that awareness is activated. Our somatic explorations within Body Scapes sessions underlined that body systems do seem to be learning from our conscious realisations of 'what is happening', both within and around us, and then they translate those changes onto our subconscious levels of functioning. And so, working with awareness of the many individual processes at play, and voicing those experiences means our living bodies are able to follow up on that awareness afterwards. They respond subconsciously, on physiological levels, to the conscious work done, so to speak, and the thematic relationships between conscious and subconscious processes of the feminine will continue being expanded on in our experiences of embodied seasonality.

Body Scapes has created many opportunities for learning about the patterns of inner re-organisation as inspired by what we observe in the natural world but also about how we translate those sub-conscious patterns onto continuous self-inquiry continuations. How do we learn to help ourselves, and seek nourishment in being open to processes of change, both gentle and abrupt? Becoming conscious of the subconscious processes of change, while observing how those subconscious processes of change translate themselves into our awareness and self-regulation is the ongoing motivation behind Body Scapes sessions.

In conclusion, the time in-between the sessions themselves becomes as precious as the time spent in conscious movement. Just like in the natural world, the versatile rhythms of nature never stop, even when we are in a 'pause mode', so to speak. Wellbeing does include modes of retreat, as transitioning onto autumn and winter months reminds. The inner intelligence of the body systems cannot be just invaded, when we mean 'building resilience', but it needs to be listened to and given time, even though, the inner shifts that follow our conscious realisations are not often validated or valued enough. That softer activity of the felt-body speaks for the feminine side of the experience of change.

To us, to guide the movement sessions through the processes of inspiration, nourishment and empowerment awakened by the natural world meant working on different levels of qualitative relating to self and other. How the natural world inspires us, but also how it is already present within our bodily systems becomes the living part of the many cycles of relation in being well. Our reflections coming from the Body Scapes sessions brought to light that it is through the dialoguing between the conscious awareness and the inner, subconscious functioning that creates those gentle shifts towards wellbeing.

As facilitators of such shifts, empowerment felt to be a conscious activity of finding tools to support resilience. Nourishment, felt like a bordering process, somewhere between the conscious and the subconscious exchange, semi-physical, somewhere between food for energy and food for thought. Finally, inspiration was the gentlest of these three processes, and it translated itself into our lives in many unaccountable ways, including this reflective paper.

To sum up, resonating with the inspirations driven from the changes in the landscapes around us did feel like a lively dynamic between nourishment and empowerment within the feminine aspects of being and relating, a journey full of never-ending inspirations.

References

Dako, A. (2015). Night(s) and day(s) on somatic adventures into the experience of inter-connectedness between 'knowing' and 'not knowing'. Retrieved January 14, 2024 from www.aberdeen.academia.edu/AnnaDako

Dako, A. (2021). On how to feel think in movement—a short introduction: Contemplating ecological belonging in somatic practice. *Journal of Dance & Somatic Practices, 13*,19–27. https://doi.org/10.1386/jdsp_00033_1

Dako, A. (2023a). *Walking to wellbeing—a guide to practising self-care in somatic felt thinking.* Author.

Dako, A. (2023b). Dances with sheep: On rePairing human-nature condition in felt thinking and moving towards wellbeing. Intellect Books, UK.

Dako, A. (n.d.). Forest Within: Reflections on the Felt Qualities of Living Entanglements, Retrieved January 14, 2024 from https://www.dunami-somatics.com/forest-within-reflections

FEMALE*TRACES*

Helen Kindred and Sandra Sok

...female journeys, waiting, bodily traces, patterns, dancing ground, spaciousness, body-space-environment, undulations, reflections, ritual, observation, boundaries, breath in our cells, softening, transformation, gathering, passion, place, wildness, re-wilding, dramatic felt, making connection, gathering, listening, possibility, flow, stability-instability, yielding-pushing, nurturing body, bodies of water, sensation, pulsation, belonging, shifting landscapes, inhale-exhale, inner connectivity-outer expressivity, events of the sea, waves, leaves (no) trace, human non-human, eco-feminism, feminist language, layering, female support, dancing goddess, speculative realism, visible-invisible, interconnectivity, trans-corporeality ...

Can we enter into the deeper pores in the skin?
Can we hear that voice of vastness from inside?
What lies beneath the surface?
Imagine you have no skin and you want to 'cover' yourself with the movement,
imagine you have no bones, your body is malleable, melting as a honey on the ground,
you are becoming your surroundings, your environment, camouflage and move with it...
your play full body as environment..
let a story grow inside you...
remember a moment...make a web of connections...
listen through your fingertips...

move from listening..
arrive again into the body...
into the world...
rub down...wash up old energies....land...time to be still...
delve deeply in to the vastness of the unknown...

RESOURCE LIST

Active Pregnancy Foundation https://www.activepregnancyfoundation.org/

Anna Dako https://www.dunami-somatics.com/body-scapes

Anatomy Trains https://www.anatomytrains.com/

Ausdance https://ausdance.org.au/

AWA DANCE www.awadance.org

BASEM Sponsored resources for dance performance www.health4performance.co.uk

BEAT https://www.beateatingdisorders.org.uk/

Birth Trauma Association www.birthtraumaassociation.org.uk

Dance Mamma www.dancemama.org/resources

Dance USA https://www.danceusa.org/

Doctors for Dancers https://doctorsfordancers.com/

Healthy Dancer Canada https://www.healthydancercanada.org/

International Association for Dance Medicine and Science - https://iadms.org/

International Continence Society https://www.ics.org/

Myofascial Release https://www.myofascialrelease.com/

National Institute of Dance Medicine and Science https://www.nidms.co.uk/

Nicky Keay Fitness https://nickykeayfitness.com/

One Dance UK National Body for Dance - https://www.onedanceuk.org/

Parents in Performing Arts https://pipacampaign.org/charter-programme

Pelvic Floor First/Continence Foundation of Australia https://www.pelvicfloorfirst.org.au/pages/the-pelvic-floor.html

Pelvic Guru/Pelvic Global https://pelvicguru.com/

Pelvic, Obstetric and Gynaecological Physiotherapy UK https://thepogp.co.uk/

Performing Arts Medicine Association https://artsmed.org/

Sport Ready Academy - https://www.sportreadyacademy.com/p/training-as-a-high-performing-female-dancer

Tamed Dance Medicine Germany https://www.tamed.eu/

The Adolescent Dancer https://theadolescentdancer.com/

The Fascia Hub https://thefasciahub.com/

The GuiDANCE Network https://www.onedanceuk.org/what-we-do/professional-bodies-and-partners/the-guidance-network

The Mummy MOT www.themummymot.com

Voices for Pelvic Floor Disorders https://www.voicesforpfd.org/

Your Pelvic Floor https://www.yourpelvicfloor.org/

INDEX

Western: Western aesthetics 69; Western canon 91, 209; Western dance 159, 210, 250, 255, 274–275, 281, 283; Western European 249–250, 253, 254; Western philosophy 67; Western society/culture 12, 81–82, 125, 167, 250, 255, 276–283; *see also* Europe and America

white (ethnicity) 57, 158, 226, 254, 281

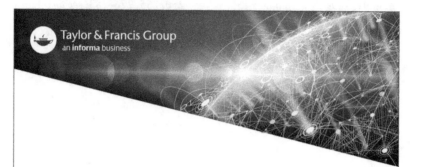

www.ingramcontent.com/pod-product-compliance
Lightning Source LLC
LaVergne TN
LVHW022208221224
799742LV00032B/799